Researched, written, printed and bound in
Canada.
First Printing.

Trade Distribution by:
Firefly Books Ltd.
3520 Pharmacy Ave., Unit 1-C
Scarborough, Ontario, Canada
M1W 2T8

Renewable Energy in Canada is a
registered non-profit organization
dedicated to the dissemination of
information about renewable energy
sources, technologies and related
environmental concerns.

ISBN 0-920456-40-5 (pbk)

Dedication:
To the people who gave us all that good
advice that we didn't use. Now's your
chance to say I told you so.

"The two big questions in solar greenhouse
design are: 'What did Nixon know?' and
'When did he know it?'"
— Tyeve Arkham

Canadian Cataloguing in Publication Data

Craft, Mark.
  Wintergreens

Includes index.
ISBN 0-920456-40-5

1. Solar greenhouses - Design and construction.
I. Renewable Energy in Canada (Firm). II. Title.

SB415.C72   635'.0483   C83-098438-0

WINTER GREENS

Solar Greenhouses for Cold Climates

Edited by Mark A. Craft

Illustrated by Terry Lyster

Contents

Introduction
Sheep's Clothing   1
Greenhouse Basics   5

Design
An Introduction to Design   17
Physical Fundamentals   25
Designing   44

Construction
Introduction to Construction   73
Foundations   77
Framing and Roofing   88
Glazing   99
Doors, Vents, and Jambs   107
Insulation and Sealing   114
Floors   117
Finishing   120
Inter-glazing Insulation   123
Soil Bed Construction   129

Management
Greenhouse Management   135
The Greenhouse Environment   140
Plants and Planting   151
Death and Destruction   166

Survey
Barrhead Greenhouse   183
Blackfalds Greenhouse   185
Detroit Lakes Greenhouse   188
Ecology House Greenhouse   191
Keswick Greenhouse   194
King Greenhouse   196
Pottageville Greenhouse   198
Millet Greenhouse   200
Mobile Home Greenhouse   203
Newfoundland Greenhouse   206
University of Saskatchewan   210
    Solar Greenhouse
West Vancouver Greenhouse   215
Ypsilanti Greenhouse   217

Appendix
Facts   221
Figures   231

Index   249

INTRODUCTION

A Wondrous Comparison

The difference between a biologically managed solar greenhouse, such as we recommend in this book, and the more common, climate-controlled greenhouse using supplemental lighting and heating is, in many respects, like the difference between a car and a bicycle:

1. Both accomplish the same task –– in one case to get us where we want to go, in the other to produce food. But one consumes fossil fuels while the other uses renewable fuels, in the form of direct solar radiation or, in the case of the bicycle, in the form of food fuel, which is an indirect form of solar energy.

2. Just as the transition from the car to the bicycle as the major mode of transportation will require a change in our existing structures and institutions (the design of cities, the distant suburban communities, etc.) so a shift from climate-controlled greenhouses and the current food processing, packaging and transportation systems to a system of regional solar greenhouses will require changes in diet, food quality and food distribution.

3. The bicycle was in use before the automobile was invented and early solar greenhouses were developed before the proliferation of climate-controlled greenhouses. But, in an era of cheap fossil fuels, neither of the simpler technologies was developed to any great extent. Why worry about making more sophisticated and useful human-powered vehicles when everyone could afford gasoline? Why improve greenhouse efficiency when cheap lighting and supplemental heating was available? Luckily, we are smarter nowadays. Aren't we?

4. If you are still in the bookstore and have read this far without making up your mind whether or not to buy this book, notice that it is easily carried, whether you're on a bicycle or on foot.

This book emphasizes the bicycle approach over the car approach. In other words, we always favour the more elegant technology and the simpler, low-energy method wherever it can fulfill the need. This preference does not mean that we are turning our backs on technology or rejecting moving parts. In many cases some sort of hybrid system may offer an attractive choice –– as in some heat storage systems. We are, rather, in favour of cleverness, of appropriateness, of simplicity, and of easy maintenance.

The Ecosystem Concept

We treat the greenhouse as an ecosystem and plan its use accordingly. The ecosystem concept comes from the insight that it is not the individual that is the biological entity, but the system. Hence we can best understand ourselves as beings if we look at ourselves in the proper context. A greenhouse may be viewed as an artifact designed to promote a part of the great cycle in which we participate.

Think of the human body as a living process. We require inputs of oxygen, water and food which are processed by metabolism into outputs of carbon dioxide, water vapour, urine, feces and ear wax.

Fig. 1 A solar powered vehicle

The natural ecosystem in which we evolved was configured to recycle our outputs into inputs. We cannot exist without a mechanism to convert our wastes back into food.

There are three jobs to be done in every ecosystem. In a greenhouse ecosystem the various participants function as:

Producers -- plants that convert sunshine into food.

Consumers -- the proprietor who converts food into human wastes.

Reducers -- various micro-organisms that convert human and plant wastes into compost.

There is a fourth participant whose job is not as obvious, but which makes the system interesting:

Parasites -- organisms that feed opportunistically anywhere in the system. The participants in an ecosystem each perform all these jobs at various times.

The more complex an ecosystem is, the more stable it is. The greenhouse should contain a wide variety of plants and other organisms.

Is This Book for You?

You'd better hope so if you've already bought it. Our goal throughout is to help you build a greenhouse in which you will grow food for your family. You may often also be able to vent excess heat from the greenhouse into your living area. Always keep in mind that there are usually better ways to provide solar heating to your house than with a greenhouse, and there are other ways to grow food. Outdoor gardens, plant shelters and cold frames, and pots on the windowsills come to mind. However, if you're looking for a greenhouse that can provide as much food as possible for as much of the year as possible, a pleasant living space, and a supply of heat to the house -- well, then you're in the right book.

Using This Book

We have attempted to simplify and demystify greenhouse design, construction, and management. There is a wider latitude in home greenhouse design than in commercial production greenhouses where light levels, construction and maintenance costs, and cash value of the crop are much more critical. This latitude has allowed us to develop and present a particular greenhouse design and to detail its step-by-step construction. We call this the Sundance Greenhouse.

Fig. 2 The Sundance Greenhouse

We feel that you should understand the design process for two reasons. The first is that, if technical or operational problems arise in your greenhouse, you will be familiar with the structure and function and be in a better position to develop solutions. Secondly, you may want to adapt our recommended design, or design your own greenhouse using our construction details. To this end we explain the physical principles, how these are applied in designing a greenhouse, and the development of the Sundance Greenhouse.

Although they are distinct sections in the book, design, construction and management must be considered simultaneously. You cannot design the greenhouse without management in mind, just as you cannot begin construction without first having developed working drawings. Before you begin designing or building your greenhouse, read the whole book thoroughly, then go back to consult specific sections as you need them.

Skills and Temperament

If you can read this book you can design and build your own greenhouse. We've included all you need to know about design, and the construction section takes you carefully and thoroughly through the building process.

We have assumed you know what nails are, what shingles look like and what a hammer is for.

You will have to be able to handle a pencil and paper and a few drawing tools such as a straight edge and protractor. This does not mean you have to become a draftsman or learn how to read blueprints, but you will have to produce clear, accurate working drawings before you begin buying materials or building the greenhouse. For beginning carpenters it is especially important that your working drawings cover all details and leave you with no uncertainties. If you want to use our recommended design but don't want to produce your own working drawings, we have indicated where you can purchase a complete set of plans for this greenhouse.

Take the time necessary to properly execute the carpentry details. Roofing, foundation, and glazing details must be properly done. Remember that, other than cost, the great advantage of doing it yourself rather than hiring someone else is that you can be sure it is done right.

It will require a certain amount of time daily or weekly to make proper use of a greenhouse (to water, plant, transplant, harvest and clean). Only with time will you become familiar with the workings of your greenhouse and have a feeling for its cycles and successions. Don't expect immediate results or push-button operation. It's much more exciting and satisfying than that.

You'll need to have patience. Don't get discouraged — when you pick that first tomato, you'll know it was worth it. Things will roll smoothly from there on.

This is a good place to discuss parameters. There are many ways to use a greenhouse and many ways to design it. To let you know what you're getting into, here are some of our biases, listed next to some of the alternatives which we may discuss more briefly:

Our Biases	Alternatives
family size	commercial or community size
owner-built or owner-designed	off-the-shelf/contractor built
used for food production for self-consumed food	sunspace or heat source selling surplus and seedlings
sun-powered (sun-heated and sun-lit)	supplemental heating and artificial lighting
use of inexpensive, new materials	recycled materials
vegetables grown in soil in deep soil beds	hydroponics or pots and other containers
greenhouse treated as ecosystem: using biological controls and composted soil	greenhouse as artificially maintained environment: purchased insecticides purchased fertilizers
attached greenhouse	freestanding
typical "solar" shape	quonset, A-frame, or dome
greenhouse used as a season extender where only that is possible	use of supplemental heating and lighting as above
manually operated vents and movable insulation	automated systems
northerly latitudes (three of the writers live between 52°N and 56°N latitude.)	North America from about 40°N to the arctic

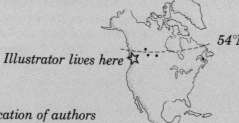

Illustrator lives here 54°N

Fig. 3 Northern location of authors indicated by small dots

Definitions

We've used a few terms already, and will introduce more later, which are sometimes controversial and can lead to confusion. To avoid any problems we have indicated here what we mean when we use certain terms.

biological management   The management system employed when the greenhouse is treated as an ecosystem in which all possible effects of a technique are considered before using it, and which emphasizes soil conditioning and plant health. Pesticides are rarely, if ever, used.

solar greenhouse   A greenhouse which is designed to make the best (i.e. most efficient) use of the light and heat from the sun to provide a proper environment for plant growth.

sun-powered   Using only the energy from the sun to accomplish the tasks in question.

climate-controlled greenhouse   One which uses supplemental lighting and heating to maintain a constant, year-round environment inside the greenhouse.

movable insulation   Insulation to cover glazing or windows, which is in place at night and removed during the day. Also referred to as shutters.

inter-glazing insulation   A movable insulation system in which blankets of insulation are used in between two layers of glazing.

cosmic importance   No small matter.

The Metric System

This system of measurement is in use throughout most of the world. It has been officially adopted in Canada and is used by science and industry in the United States. Consequently, most measurements will be given in metric units. To help those of us who are less adaptive than others, we have included the corresponding Imperial units in brackets where it is useful to do so. Temperatures are uniformly Celsius and so indicated (eg. 14°C). You will find a conversion chart in the appendix.

Due to our interest in preserving antiquities, we have continued to use some common terms derived under the olde system. For instance, a 2 x 4, which was not really two inches by four inches anyhow, is still called a 2 x 4 even though it is more properly a piece of dimensional lumber 38mm wide by 89mm deep. Similarly, since at this writing many common building materials are still available only in Imperial units, we have referred to them using these units, but indicating the metric equivalent (exact or approximate as the case warrants). You will find herein 2½ nails (60mm) and references to 2ft centres (610mm) to accommodate standard-size 4ft x 8ft plywood (1219 x 2438mm).

An Equivocation

Being only human at best, we will certainly have made mistakes and based some recommendations on out-of-date work or incorrect information. Although we strive for accuracy, such errors are inevitable. We welcome readers' comments on any of our recommendations and will incorporate such suggestions into subsequent editions.

Finally, it is worth remembering that, although we have carefully evaluated various designs and procedures, there can be no hard and fast recommendation for the perfect greenhouse design. Each greenhouse is site specific, use specific, and cost specific. While we have incorporated into our recommended greenhouse features which are among the most conserving of energy, money, and resources, you may decide to alter our design to make it more suitable to your situation.

We have used the SURVEY to present example greenhouses which differ in design from ours, and to report on other techniques and procedures. These examples either have great potential or demonstrate particular, unique features. While some of these greenhouses or techniques are conceptual, experimental, or outside our experience, we present them as interesting examples of other work.

Types and Uses of Greenhouses

We have been using the term "greenhouse" whenever we have talked about an enclosed area with enough glazing to admit a more than usual amount of sunlight. There are many ways to design and make use of such a space and we will examine some of them here. In doing so, we will also define the terms by which we will refer to these various configurations and functions.

The **stereotypical structure is one whose** main function is to grow plants. This general image is what we will mean when we say *greenhouse*. These houses can be used primarily for vegetable production, for ornamental plants, for starting seedlings or, as is most usually the case, for some mixture of these functions.

If a greenhouse is built as a separate structure, or attached to another structure by only a walkway, it is known, naturally enough, as a *freestanding greenhouse*. If a greenhouse shares one common wall (or, sometimes, two walls) with another

Fig. 4   Attached   Freestanding

structure we will call it an *attached greenhouse*. Most often, such a greenhouse is on the south wall of a house and has access doors both to the house and to the outside.

Greenhouses come in many different shapes as well. The common all-glass structure with a low, only slightly sloped roof we will refer to as a *glasshouse*. We have already referred to the typical *solar-shape* and by this we mean a greenhouse with a vertical or steeply tilted south wall, which most often has, in the case of an attached solar-shape, an insulated north wall shared with the house, in which vents, doors or windows are placed to allow air exchange. In the case of a freestanding solar greenhouse, the north wall is also tilted to a rather steep angle, insulated, and light-coloured to reflect the incoming sunlight.

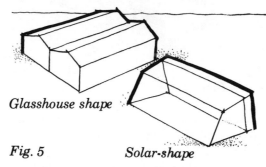

Glasshouse shape

Fig. 5   Solar-shape

In addition to these standard shapes there are *dome-greenhouses, quonset-greenhouses* and *A-frame greenhouses*. Respectively, these look like domes, quonsets, and A-frames.

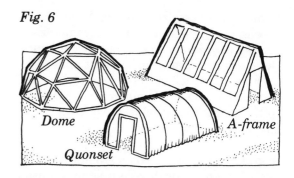

Fig. 6

Dome   *A-frame*

Quonset

A *pit greenhouse* makes use of the buffering effect of the earth by having its planting benches at ground level and the walkways below ground level. A close cousin is an *earth-sheltered greenhouse* which uses earth berms against the north wall and sometimes even on the roof.

Fig. 7 Pit greenhouse with berm

Freestanding greenhouses are used almost **exclusively for plant production. But in them,** and in attached greenhouses so used, **plants can be grown using a number of different** methods. The one we recommend **is the growing of plants in soil. Planting can** be done in deep soil beds, in pots and **containers, or in some combination of both** to make the best use of space. A method of greenhouse gardening which does not use soil is *hydroponics*. In hydroponic gardening the plants are grown in an inert material such as gravel which serves merely to hold the roots in place. All nutrients are carried to the plants in the solution with which the plants are watered.

A greenhouse (one used as a plant growing space) can most readily be used as a season extender, prolonging the growing season on both sides of summer without using supplemental lighting and heating. It can also be used for year-round production, although in some regions this will require the use of extra heat or light.

An attached greenhouse can be designed for purposes other than plant production. It can be designed for providing heat to the house during certain parts of the year (a *solarium*). It can also be designed to help cool the house in the summer. If it is designed as an extension of the living area, which the occupants can use as a sunroom for most of the year, we will call it a *sunspace*. While a strict sunspace will

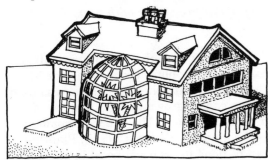

Fig. 8 Solarium

differ in design from a strict attached greenhouse, this is not to imply that you must have one or the other. Usually the structure will be planned as a greenhouse (for plant growth) but will also have designed into it a family area, where sitting, dining or reflection can take place.

In the next step, such a greenhouse/ sunspace may be designed as an integral part of the house itself, with no definite borders between the living area and the plant area. Such integrated designs are called *greenhomes* and usually make use of the glazed area as a greenhouse, a sunspace, and a solar collector for providing heat to the rest of the house.

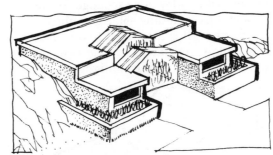

Fig. 9 Greenhome

A somewhat different type of integration is involved in planning the entire home around food production. For reasons of personal and regional self-reliance, and energy savings in the food system, this somewhat forgotten craft may be usefully revived. Too often, modern houses, even those with attached or integrated green-houses, tend to an urban uniformity of design in the use of interior space and do

not adequately allow for food processing, food storage, bread kneading, beer making, etc.

We will concentrate on an attached solar greenhouse, with plants grown in soil, used as a season extender, allowing for some living space and most often added on to an existing house.

Energy and Greenhouses

This is the important stuff. The stuff that is really the reason for this book. Even if some of us may not particularly care about energy as such, it is important that we be aware of energy sources and energy use. Ill-planned energy distribution and consumption can lead, and has led, to increasing regional dependence on other regions and increasing personal dependence on larger structures. Energy is the means by which we can improve our quality of life or destroy the ecosystems around us. Don't skip this section — we'll try to avoid energy preaching.

The concept of net energy is used when

Fig. 10 Net energy

examining the entire process of a particular means of energy production. Simply put, it is the energy output minus the energy input of a particular energy source. Remember that any production process requires energy from some source and, therefore, the materials used in the construction of an energy-producing device or structure have a certain energy "cost" to them. In addition, energy is required to operate and maintain the energy plant. It is analogous to investing a certain amount of money in hope of receiving a larger amount as a return. In some cases you may only break even and in other, even more unfortunate cases, you may receive less money in return than you originally invested.

We must apply the same analysis to our energy investments. Some are good investments and some are bad. Writers such as Amory Lovins have shown that energy sources such as nuclear power plants and tar sands plants are poor energy investments in that the amount of energy produced by such plants is only equal to, or even less than, the energy it takes to build and operate them. (And the conclusion was reached without taking into account the undesirable social and environmental consequences of these projects.) Many of the renewable energy sources, such as direct solar energy, and conservation programs are much better investments of our energy units.

Unfortunately, too often the economic balance (net dollars) takes precedence over

the energy balance, and such projects as the tar sands plants are built because the investors feel they can make a profit. This "profit" results because they are using cheap energy (low-priced oil and natural gas) to produce an equal or lesser amount of expensive energy (world-priced oil and gasoline). This manipulation of resources doesn't benefit the rest of us much, and seems even less advantageous when we take into account the negative social and environmental impacts that are always a part of such projects.

The net energy criteria should be applied to all energy producers — including solar greenhouses. This is not the place for a detailed energy evaluation of a greenhouse, but it is useful to consider a few points.

The energy output of an attached solar greenhouse usually takes the form of food and of heat supplied to the house. We are aware of the energy it takes to heat our homes, but less so of the energy involved in the food we eat. In the United States, the total food chain — including growing, distribution, packaging, processing and home preparation — uses 15% of all energy and costs in excess of 30 billion dollars annually. This use of energy has to be taken into account, in addition to whatever heat the greenhouse may supply to the house, when determining the energy value of an attached solar greenhouse.

The energy involved in making the material you use to build the greenhouse, the electricity used by your circular saw

and hand drill, the energy to print and distribute this book — all these, too, must be part of the energy equation.

Just think what this discussion would have been like if we hadn't said we were going to avoid preaching.

There is a group of writers and researchers who insist that solar greenhouses don't work, that they are too expensive, and that they use more energy than they produce. We feel they hold this opinion because they do not understand our concept of a solar greenhouse — one which makes the best use of the heat and light from the sun to extend the growing season as long as possible and, when possible, to supply excess heat to the house. Perhaps our concept is better called an energy-efficient or conserving greenhouse. We also think that they do not take into account the energy in the form of food the greenhouse may be producing. (We are speaking here of net food energy, which will already have subtracted from it any external energy costs involved in the growing of this food.) Solar greenhouse gardens can help us to save energy used in food processing and transportation since they can provide fresh produce directly to the region (or kitchen) when the food is needed.

A study in Ohio showed that field-grown produce, shipped fresh, used 7.91 MJ production energy per kilogram of food, and that yields were about 5.44kg per square meter (m²). A conserving green-house, on the other hand, was shown to have a potential yield of 174kg/m² while using only 0.70 MJ per kilogram of production energy. Even though this greenhouse was assumed to be heated in order to be used throughout the winter, when the total amount of fossil fuel was considered (including that used for packaging, transportation and greenhouse heating) a northern, conserving greenhouse in Ohio was shown to produce fresh winter vegetables for about the same amount of energy used to produce and transport imported fresh field vegetables. A solar greenhouse has the capacity under normal conditions to produce ten times the average field vegetable yields. On a residential scale, in today's economy an attached solar greenhouse owner can realize annual grocery bill savings of $52 to $70 (U.S.) for each square metre of greenhouse growing space.

Consideration of the food producing aspect of an attached greenhouse is important since the economic return for food produced can be from six to ten times greater than the fuel saved in the house. Even so, it is expected that (at least in the northern U.S.) an attached solar greenhouse can supply from 10% to 33% of home heating requirements. It is estimated, for instance, that an average dwelling in Minnesota will consume 93 to 112 GJ (82.5 to 99.0 MM BTU) annually and that an attached greenhouse could contribute 25 to 28 GJ (22.5 to 24.7 MM BTU).

A test of an experimental commercial greenhouse at the University of Saskatchewan demonstrated the viability of large, low-energy greenhouses. After testing their greenhouse, researchers concluded that most of the conservation features (the features in what we are calling a solar greenhouse) were worth while. Insulating the north and side walls of the greenhouse had immediate benefits in energy and cost savings. In conjunction with the use of a shutter system to insulate the glazing at night, heating needs were reduced by 60%. Even thermal storage proved to be beneficial, reducing energy consumption in the spring and fall and decreasing the risk of frost damage during a winter power failure. More importantly from a commercial standpoint, crop production in the solar greenhouse compared favourably to that in standard greenhouses.

Let's be clear that these examples are either estimates or data from specific cases. But the indications are obvious. Solar greenhouse do work and are worth while in terms of energy and dollar savings.

Three final points might be considered when trying to determine the value of a solar greenhouse. The first is what we might call the energy balance with the house. Let's assume an attached green-house is an integral part of the home heating system. For part of the year the greenhouse provides more heat daily than it needs for heating itself at night. At some point, a daily equilibrium is reached in which as much extra heat is provided to the home during the day as the greenhouse uses at night to keep from freezing. We may decide, as greenhouse users, to extend the growing season on either side of summer until this point is reached. In this

Total Fossil Energy Used in Winter Vegetable Production			
		Greenhouse Grown Produce	
Energy Input in MJ/kg	Field Grown Produce: Shipped Fresh	Conventional Greenhouse	Conserving Greenhouse
Production	7.91	0.93	0.70
Processing and Containers	2.79	2.33	2.33
Transportation	12.79	—	—
Heating and Cooling	—	162.82	20.35
Total Energy	23.49	166.08	23.38
Potential Yields in kg/m²	5.82	116.3	186.08

Adapted from Roller, 1977, "Energy and the Food Chain"

case, from a heating standpoint only, the greenhouse is a net energy producer.

We may, on the other hand, decide to extend the growing season even farther by considering the annual equilibrium. That is, to extend the growing season to the point that the annual amount of extra heat the greenhouse provides to the home equals the annual amount of heat the greenhouse needs to keep from freezing. In this case, considering only heat once again, the net energy of the greenhouse is zero -- but is not an energy consumer.

Just as important as energy considerations are the implications a series of northern solar greenhouses can have in helping us move towards regional self-reliance, at least in food. Greater geographical independence can be achieved by growing local produce for either personal use or the local market, and by the expansion of small business that would result. If we think for a moment how much our current food distribution depends upon a continuous supply of cheap fossil fuels, we will realize how important this regional self-reliance can become.

A final benefit gained from a system of northern solar greenhouses would be an improvement in food quality. Too often, vegetables are bred for their handling and transporting qualities and not for taste or nutrition. Processing is always detrimental to the food value, and usually detrimental to the taste as well.

We are not proposing to, nor suggest that you, do an exact, numerical analysis of your greenhouse. Rather, we advise you to keep these things in mind as you plan and use your greenhouse.

Regional Considerations

We had originally planned this book to include different design recommendations for the different bioregions or geographic regions of the continent. We soon found that the development of a "solaregional" map was not only nearly impossible, but also not very useful.

We were particularly sensitive to the design needs of the more northerly areas since we had heard so many times that in such cold climates solar greenhouses just don't make sense. New Mexico, the argument went, was one thing, but areas with cold climates, where you couldn't expect year-round use, could hardly justify solar greenhouses.

Peter Amerongen -- our carpenter whose greenhouses are designed for the area around Edmonton, about latitude 53°N -- works on the assumption that, in the extreme sections of Canada, if we take out the months of December, January and February, and somehow push November up against March, then we end up with a nine month "year" which has a winter similar to that of the less extreme portions of the continent.

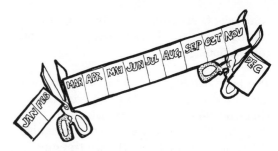

Fig. 11 The nine month year

Let's take the example of the highlands of northern New Mexico. The growing season there is approximately the same as that of northern Alberta. Yet, inside of an attached solar greenhouse in New Mexico, there is a year-round growing season -- even without the use of movable glazing insulation.

From this we think we can conclude that if it's worth it in New Mexico, it's worth it in the North. In the case above, comparing our abbreviated northern year to the complete southern year we have an extrapolated expectation for a good nine months' use from a northern solar greenhouse. Experience shows us that we can also expect use of a northern Alberta greenhouse well into December and starting in late February. For much of southern Canada and the northern United States, we would expect year-round use.

In most northerly regions, there will be a portion of the winter when a purely sun-powered greenhouse cannot be used for horticulture. Temperatures are not only low, but light is a limiting factor. As we shall see, there are some advantages to letting your greenhouse "rest" during these cold periods.

The fall (late September to late November) and the spring (March to May) are the times of the year when an attached greenhouse is most useful. These are also the times of year when the continental climate is most similar. (The most important variable from region to region is cloud cover --- the amount of direct sunlight you can expect.) These two seasons which bracket summer are when we can best use the greenhouse to extend the growing season. We also find that this is the time when the greenhouse can provide the most useful heat to the house.

We've come to agree with Peter, not only because he's probably right, but because it made writing this book a lot easier. Rather than detailing specific designs for specific regions, we have been able to concentrate on one useful standard greenhouse --- the Sundance Greenhouse, developed by Peter --- which can be adapted to most conditions --- including cloud cover. We have tried to indicate what some of these adaptations are and typical results of them.

AN ILLUSTRATED HISTORY OF GREENHOUSES

IN THE BEGINNING PLANTS WERE NAKED.

DURING THE ICE AGE THEY FROZE THEIR FRUITS OFF.

IN THE STONED AGE, THE NEANDERTHALS AND OTHER ROCK GROUPS BUILT PLANT SHELTERS. THE GLAZING MATERIALS WERE GRANITE. THESE SHELTERS WERE KNOWN AS GREYHOUSES.

...AND WERE VERY DARK.

AND COLD.

THEY HAD FOUND A WAY TO KEEP THE TEMPERATURE CONSTANT. BECAUSE IT WAS THE WRONG TEMPERATURE, THEY ALSO DISCOVERED EXTINCTION

ALONG CAME TECHNOLOGY

CROMAGNON PERSON FOUND THE FIRST CLEAR GLAZING MATERIAL ...AIR...

SUNSHINE WARMED INDOOR CROPS ALL DAY LONG.

UNFORTUNATELY AIR GLAZING HAD A VERY HIGH INFILTRATION RATE ON DARK AND STORMY NIGHTS

BAA.

ANCIENT HERDERS SEALED WINDOWS, STACKING THEIR FLOCKS BY NIGHT. THIS KEPT THE HEAT IN, ENRICHED CARBON DIOXIDE AND PROVIDED AUTOMATIC FERTILIZATION. FAMOUS FOR THEIR BALMY INDOOR CLIMATE, THE HERDERS BECAME KNOW AS SUMERIANS.

THE VIKINGS FOUND A MATERIAL GROWING ON WINTER LAKES WHICH COULD REPLACE AIR GLAZING. ICE FORMED A SOLID WALL, LETTING IN SUNSHINE AND KEEPING THE WIND OUT. IT HAD TO BE REPLACED EACH EVENING, BUT IT DID WATER PLANTS

THE CHINESE INVENTED **SOUTH**... AN INVENTION SO IMPORTANT THAT MANY CITIES, COUNTRIES AND EVEN CONTINENTS ARE NAMED AFTER IT.

TO THIS DAY, THE DIRECTION WHICH GREENHOUSES FACE IS KNOWN AS **ORIENTATION**.

ROMAN HORTI-CULTURALISTS TRIED COVERING GREEN HOUSES WITH THE MATERIAL USED IN EYEGLASSES. UNFORTUNATELY, THE ROMANS USED SEASHELLS FOR **SHADES**.

DRINK AGRIKOLA

SO ROMANS USED THE STRETCHED ENTRAILS OF GOATS, WHICH WERE OBTAINABLE CHEAPLY FROM CUT-RATE SOOTH-SAYERS, TO EVEN OUT GREENHOUSE TEMPERATURES

SIR VIVAL OF THE FITTEST

WHEN MEDIEVAL ARMOUR WAS HUNG TO DRY IN GREENHOUSE WINDOWS, IT WAS NOTICED THAT NOCTURNAL HEAT LOSS WAS REDUCED.

THIS PRACTICE BECAME KNOWN AS **KNIGHT INSULATION**

THE **CRYSTAL PALACE**...LARGEST & LEAST SOLAR GREENHOUSE EVER BUILT. THE CEILING LEAKED SO BADLY, THAT THEREAFTER ANY EFFORTS TO PLUG HOLES IN A GREENHOUSE WERE KNOWN AS **SEALING**. VICTORIANS WERE LOUSY SPELLERS.

THE MODERN AGE GRAPPLES WITH OVERHEATING. SCIENTISTS LOOK FOR THE UNIVERSAL **SOL-VENT**, A SOLUTION TO MAKING CONTROLLED HOLES IN GREENHOUSES OTHERWISE CALLED **VENTING**

VENTILATE

PREVENT

INVENT

ADVENT

event

VENTRICLE

VENTURE CAPITAL

MADE IN VENTURA CALIFORNIA

CIRCUMVENTION

SOLVENT

THERE ARE STILL UNKNOWNS.

IN THE SEARCH FOR THE PERFECT PLANTITARIUM, IT IS NOW UP TO YOU TO GET THE **BUGS OUT**.

DESIGN

Pep Talk

There is nothing mysterious or complicated about designing a greenhouse. While it is important that a proper environment for plants be provided and that certain conservation principles are followed, there is a certain latitude within these strictures. Greenhouse design is not an exact science and it will not be difficult for you to plan a greenhouse to suit your needs. This section tells you what you need to know to do it: how the sun supplies the necessary energy; the nature of heat and light; the requirements of plants; the characteristics of construction materials; and how this information is used to develop a greenhouse design.

The shortcoming of this book is that we cannot know all unique details concerning your situation. If you have a specific question, such as local foundation requirements, get expert advice. Your local

Fig. 12 Local foundation conditions

building inspector can often be helpful, and his advice is free. But don't rely completely on professionals or think that they are

necessary to get the job done. If you are using a contractor, for instance, be certain that you are able to supervise or inspect every aspect of the actual construction since the workers too often understand little about the design you have in mind and less about the concepts. If you're able, don't be afraid to do it yourself. Any greenhouse you build is going to be better than no greenhouse.

The "Two-step" Approach

You should approach the designing of a greenhouse in two steps. Step one, which we will cover in this section, is to decide on the use of the greenhouse, the shape, the features, and the approximate size. The second step, which we will detail in CONSTRUCTION, is to decide on the materials to be used, the exact size, and the construction procedures. These two steps are not totally separate; decisions made in one stage will affect things in the other, but it is a useful distinction.

At the end of step one you will have, for instance, rough drawings of the greenhouse shape and layout, and an approximate size of, say 2.5m by 5m. After you have completed step two you will have blueprints or working drawings which include exact dimensions that might end up being 2.44m by 5.06m to accommodate some feature of the existing house wall and conform to standard building material sizes.

Initial Considerations

There are certain questions you must be able to answer before you begin the actual designing of the greenhouse:
1. What will be the purpose of the greenhouse?
2. What features must be included in order for it to fulfill its purpose?
3. How much money is available for the project?
4. What materials are available?

Materials, such as standard-size construction materials or recycled glazings, can influence the exact dimensions and, to some extent, the shape and cost of the greenhouse. We'll examine materials in greater detail in construction.

The cost of the greenhouse will also be determined by the construction process you decide on. Don't forget, though, that this works the other way as well. That is, the amount of money you have to spend will determine the materials you use, as well as the size and function of the greenhouse. If, upon completing your materials lists, the cost of the greenhouse is greater than you are able to afford, then it's (literally) back to the drawing board.

The Purpose of the Greenhouse

The purpose is determined after the primary needs are established. In a greenhouse, the needs of both plants and people must be considered.

Graphs

It may be that in your training to become a top-notch auto mechanic or gardener you did not learn how to read graphs. Don't worry though; we're going to take care of that right here.

A graph can be thought of as a table of figures in a more . . . well, graphic form. Let's look at an example:

Table of the Weight of Oranges

Number of Oranges	Total Weight
1	150g
2	300g
3	450g
4	600g
5	750g

How can we put this on a graph? Start by making uniformly spaced marks along a horizontal line to indicate the number of oranges. The first mark is one orange, the second mark is two oranges, and so on. From the point which represents zero oranges, draw a vertical line upwards. Along this line make uniformly spaced marks to represent a certain number of grams. In this case each mark represents 150 although we could have just as well chosen each mark to represent 50 or 100.

Next we plot the points on the graph. Follow a vertical line up from the mark for one orange until it crosses a line coming horizontally from the mark for 150g and make a small dot at that point. This point

represents the fact that one orange weighs 150g. Next, make a point where a line from the "2" mark crosses a line from the "300g" mark and so on until you have five points (fig. 13).

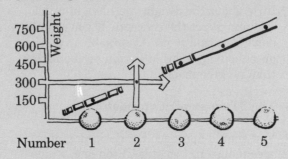

Fig. 13 The orange graph

Now we join these points together to give us a line called a curve (even though in this case it is a straight line). This curve can help us to predict what the weight of any number of oranges will be without having to refer to other tables. For instance, to find out what 6 oranges will weigh, follow a line upwards from the "6" mark until it crosses the curve. From this point, make a line horizontally to the left hand scale to find that we cross it at the "900g" mark. So, 6 oranges will weigh 900g.

We can even predict, using the same techniques, that 2½ oranges will weigh 375g, and so on.

The curve is not always a straight line. If the relationship between the figures in the table is not additive, as it is with oranges (this is called, for good reason, a linear

relationship) then the curve will, in fact, be curved. Here's an example.

Suppose you put $1000 in a savings account which earns 18% per year, computed annually, and that you allow the interest to be added to the principal each year. Here's how your nest egg will grow:

Table of Increase in Principal at 18% Annual Interest

Year	Total Amount
0	$1,000
1	1,180
2	1,392
3	1,643
4	1,938
5	2,287
6	2,699
7	3,185
8	3,759
9	4,435
10	5,234
11	6,176
12	7,288

Figure 14 shows the points plotted on a graph and the curve that results.

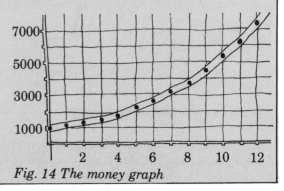

Fig. 14 The money graph

Plant Needs You must strive to create a complete and balanced environment for plants, and design the greenhouse to that end. In the controlled environment of a greenhouse, the welfare of the plants is in your hands to a much greater extent than in an outdoor garden. They depend on you not only for fertilizer and water, but for enough light, proper temperatures, and sufficient carbon dioxide and humidity levels.

More detailed information on plant requirements can be found later in this book, but here are the plant requirements to keep in mind while you are planning the greenhouse:
1. appropriate light levels –– both the strength of the light (intensity) and the number of hours of light per day (duration) are important.
2. appropriate temperatures
3. an appropriate atmosphere –– that is to say, proper amounts of carbon dioxide and water vapour.
4. a proper growing medium with access to nutrients in the soil.

Human Needs The greenhouse must also reflect the needs and constraints that arise from your particular situation. Some of the questions you might ask yourself are:
1. Who is going to use the greenhouse?
2. How much living space is desired within the greenhouse?
3. How much time is available for initial construction and long term maintenance and horticultural use?

4. What kind of plants do you want to grow?

Know yourself and plan realistically. We can't give you the answers to these questions, but we can point out one danger. The space in the greenhouse is very attractive, especially in regions with long, lingering winters. The sitting or living area of the greenhouse can easily expand to the point that it takes over the space originally intended for plants.

Designing and building a proper greenhouse is the easy part. Using it to the best advantage is a harder task. There are many examples of well-built greenhouses, but only a handful of well-used greenhouses.

Basic Design Formats

The three basic format options for greenhouses — freestanding, attached, or integrated (which we have called a greenhome) — are applicable in different situations.

In the case of a greenhome, there is no clear distinction between the living area and the plant area. The two spaces are thermally connected and depend heavily upon each other for temperature and other conditions. Because of this connection, designing a greenhome is only possible in the case of new construction or under conditions of a major retrofitting of an existing house. A greenhome is usually the most difficult of the three formats to design properly.

An Armchair Visit

One of the best introductions to the benefits and features of attached and freestanding greenhouses is to visit working examples of these types of structures. Such a trip will provide you with an impression of how things can look and work.

In case you cannot arrange a tour of a local solar greenhouse, we are providing a paper tour to both a freestanding and an attached greenhouse. Please wipe your feet at the door. Thank you.

Freestanding Greenhouse Tour As we approach the greenhouse from the east, on the path leading from the owners' home, we first notice the distinctive shape. Instead of the low-roofed, all-glass greenhouse we may have been expecting, we see that this structure has a much steeper roof, and further, that the slope on the south side of the roof, to our left, is much steeper than that on the north side. This lopsidedness is accentuated by the fact that the south face slopes down almost to the ground until it reaches a vertical kneewall about one metre high.

A very distinctive feature is a square, chimney-like box which rises from the centre of the north slope at the peak. We discover that it is, in fact, a solar chimney and that it is basically a tall, hollow box which is closed in on the north side and fitted with fibreglass glazing on the south side, facing the sun. The solar chimney acts as part of the greenhouse ventilation system. As the sun heats the air inside the chimney, this warmer air rises up and out the top, drawing fresh air from the greenhouse in at the bottom and, thereby, sucking fresh outside air in through the greenhouse vents.

We can also see that there is glazing on only the tilted portion of the south wall and on the southern third of the east wall. The other surfaces are opaque and look just like the walls or roof we would expect to find on a house or shed.

There is not much else to notice about the south wall since, other than the kneewall, it consists exclusively of rigid fiberglass glazing material. We quickly tire of looking at this face because the fibreglass is translucent and looking through it is somewhat like trying to look through a frosted bathroom window. (Although some of us may have had more experience in this practice than others.) We can't see very well what's inside the greenhouse.

Walking back around towards the northeast corner, we notice a large, screened vent low on the east wall. Continuing on we come to the east end of the north wall where there is a small porch attached to the structure. This serves, we learn, as an air-lock to protect the plants from direct blasts of cold air. It also doubles as a storage shed and potting room.

Upon entering, we find one of the owners

at the workbench preparing soil for seedling plants. He is an older gentleman whose crotchety veneer hides a heart of gold. As we wait for him to finish his task, he describes some of the less visible aspects of the building. We discover that the north wall and the north roof are not hollow frames. They have been insulated with fibreglass batts, which are protected on the greenhouse side, behind the wall panelling, by a carefully sealed polyethylene vapour barrier. The foundation is insulated too, with a rigid, waterproof insulation, to prevent heat from leaking out into the ground.

Fig. 15 A freestanding solar greenhouse

He takes us on a tour of the crowded interior. It is mid-March, which means that in this part of the world we cannot expect to see buds on the trees for a couple of weeks, yet the greenhouse is warm and already filled with plants. A soil bed, a little under one metre wide, **runs across the** south wall of the greenhouse and is occupied by salad greens. Soon, we are told, these vegetables will be replaced with tomatoes and long English cucumbers. Our attention is drawn to the fact that this bed of soil is 450mm deep and that it is built on top of a layer of rocks.

The centre area of the greenhouse is taken up by two large benches which leave just enough space for 600mm wide aisles on all sides. The benches have slatted surfaces and one is filled with a collection of trays and pots of various sizes and shapes, making use of all available space. Flats of newly germinated bedding plants are parked everywhere they can receive adequate light and heat.

Beneath the benches we find what is at first an indefinable jumble of things. The owner explains that this space is used for bins which hold compost with earthworms working in it, and for general storage of extra pots and soil. We also learn that much of the space beneath the benches was originally intended to hold rocks.

The owner explains that he had designed the greenhouse to avoid overheating (and to store some spring and autumn heat) by making use of the thermal mass of the gravel floor and the rocks beneath the benches. However, there had been occasional heating problems anyway, probably because the floor and the rocks could not absorb heat fast enough, so the family decided to try adding more thermal mass in the form of water. He points to the collection of black 5-gallon pails arranged against the north wall. These metal pails, which he has acquired during the last year, are filled with water, and certainly reduced daytime overheating and made a noticeable difference in the night-time temperature of the greenhouse. He adjusts the amount of water storage with the seasons by adding or removing buckets and, in the winter when he does not use the greenhouse, he removes all of the water.

We see that the west wall is glazed to the same extent as the east wall and that the unglazed portions of all interior walls are painted white. This design, in conjunction with the angle of the north roof, reflects light and provides better lighting for the plants.

We notice for the first time that there is a layer of the common thin plastic, polyethylene, on the inside of all the glazed areas. Even though this is a type of poly-ethylene which is treated to prevent rapid deterioration in the sunlight, the owner tells us that he expects to replace it every three or four years.

Above our heads is the vent which opens into the solar chimney. The other parts of

the ventilation system consist of a low screened vent on the west wall, which matches the one we had noticed on the east wall, and a triangular vent high on the east wall. This vent opens from the outside and is now closed and locked since it is needed only during the warmest days of summer.

The family has used the greenhouse for three years. They discovered the first year that none of them liked tending the greenhouse during the very cold weather, especially since there was very little that survived and the greenhouse would have required supplemental heat in December and January. This coming winter, though, they are going to try some of the Chinese greens they have been reading about and hope to harvest these crops into December. As a group they are quite pleased with the greenhouse, although they feel it would work better in the winter if they could figure out a good method of insulating the south wall glazing at night.

Attached Greenhouse Tour At first we think we're in the wrong neighborhood. Instead of the detached houses on spacious lots we had expected, we find ourselves in the middle of a townhouse development. But as we approach the address indicated we find that we are not lost. There, clearly, on the south side of one of the town-house units, is what we might mistake for a lean-to shed, were it not for the large area of glass.

Our guide, who also built the greenhouse, responds to our surprise by pointing out that the existing wall of her house was perfect for an attached greenhouse. It had a clear southern exposure, the outside water tap was there, and so was an electrical outlet. The existing porch light was rewired to light the greenhouse sitting area. There were operable windows into the living room as well as a door.

We enter the greenhouse from the living room to find that it was planned to include space for both plants and people. The north and south walls are lined with benches with an aisle between them the length of the greenhouse. On these benches sit large pots and boxes of soil. The plants we can recognize include tomatoes, peppers, lettuce, some radishes, and sundry greens. The observations are confirmed when our guide tells us that mostly salad vegetables are grown in this greenhouse from late February until early December.

The sitting area in the greenhouse consists of a small, nicely tiled section immediately in front of the door to the house. It contains a very small table and a couple of chairs to allow the occupants to enjoy the late winter sun.

During the first fall of use, our guide informs us, a hydroponics system had been installed against the north wall. However, it was found that the temperature swings inside the greenhouse affected the hydroponically grown plants adversely while the soil-based plants were not bothered. For this reason it was decided to remove the hydroponics.

Because the greenhouse is less than 2^{1}/$_{2}$m wide, we walk single file down the aisle to the other end of the greenhouse, where a door opens outside to the east. This door, and the triangular-shaped portions of the east wall to the south of it, are double glazed with glass. Above the door is a large triangular vent which is screened to prevent insects from entering.

Our guide briefly draws our attention to the west wall which has an area of glazing roughly equivalent to that of the east wall, but which has a large vent down at ground level.

It strikes us that this greenhouse doesn't seem nearly as small as we might expect because the south wall is completely glazed with glass. This provides a view and a sense of openness which is lacking in fibreglass greenhouses.

The south face of the greenhouse is at a

steep angle of about 75°. The roof slopes down from the house to meet the south face and is completely opaque and insulated. The portions of the east and west walls which are not glazed are also insulated.

The south wall is constructed of 2 x 6s on about 900mm (3ft) centres. Due to what at first appears to be a curious construction technique, the two layers of glass are spaced about 110 or 120mm apart (about 4^{1}/$_{2}$in). When we ask our guide about this, she walks back inside and turns a crank located on the east wall, next to the door. To our surprise, this lowers a batt of fibreglass insulation *in between* the two

Fig. 16 An attached solar greenhouse

layers of glazing. She tells us that this is the movable insulation system which is used at night during the heating season to prevent large amounts of heat from escaping through the glazing. There are also detachable shutters made of rigid insulation which perform a similar function when installed on the inside of the endwall glazing. These are stored behind the door in the living room during the day and are pressed in place against the glass at night.

The greenhouse had originally been designed so that the fibreglass movable insulation would store in a bin beneath the plant bench along the south face. But the owner found that the insulation did not fall freely into the storage box and that the tops of the bench ended up having to be too high. So, she changed her plan so that the movable insulation now stores up above a false ceiling and below the roof vapour barrier.

There is no visible heat storage other than the concrete floor, which is protected from heat loss by perimeter insulation. Our guide tells us that excess heat is vented to the house during the heating season and to the outdoors during the summer. On cold fall nights the windows or door to the house are opened to prevent the greenhouse from freezing. A few times, on particularly hot, late-September days, with the fall sun flooding the greenhouse, the ventilation has been less than adequate and temperatures in the greenhouse have risen to 40°C.

Comparison of Attached and Freestanding Greenhouses

An attached greenhouse has several advantages over its freestanding counterpart. It allows for more convenient access in cold and inclement weather. Fresh herbs and vegetables are more readily available to the kitchen and the daily management routine is more easily taken care of. It provides added living space and a pleasant spot for sitting in the February sun.

The connection with the house is also beneficial in that heat can be exchanged with the house. The greenhouse will be able to provide excess heat to the house on sunny spring and fall days while the house can supply any necessary heat to the greenhouse during the night. The buffering effect of the house is beneficial, as is the heat lost through the south wall of the house, which would otherwise be wasted. Often the basement or another existing room can be fitted for use as a potting and storage room. The greenhouse also benefits from carbon dioxide exchange with the house.

From a construction standpoint, an attached greenhouse might be cheaper than a freestanding one because you need to build only three walls. Greenhouses need not be attached only to a house. They can also be found attached to garages, saunas and other buildings such as apartments, hospitals and restaurants.

Sounds great so far. But don't forget that the foundation of an attached greenhouse will have to be more substantial, to match that of the house, than that of a freestanding greenhouse. Also, the construction and the finishing must generally be better in order for an attached greenhouse to fit in with the existing house. These factors tend to increase the cost of an attached compared to a freestanding greenhouse.

A working greenhouse results in a certain inevitable clutter of pots, plants and soils. A freestanding greenhouse can help you to avoid having this clutter spill into your living area. And, of course, if your house is situated so that there is no good southern exposure and there is no good way to attach a greenhouse to it, then you are limited to a freestanding greenhouse.

Considering all the benefits, we think that an attached greenhouse makes so much sense that we wouldn't build a freestanding one unless there were simply no other option.

Design Objectives

Glasshouses, or all-glass greenhouses, provide generous amounts of light to plants but they make very poor use of that light. Such structures overheat dramatically on sunny days and cool quickly at night. Wise design can go a long way towards correcting these problems while still providing enough light for plant growth. We are placing our design emphasis on greenhouses which are both energy efficient and suitable for horticulture. Such greenhouses must be designed by integrating and balancing four main objectives:

1. maximization of heat gain during the heating season
2. minimization of heat loss during the heating season
3. maximization of the quantity and quality of sunlight available to the plants
4. maintenance of internal air temperature at levels that allow vigorous plant growth

Fig. 17 A four way balance

Of course, the design must also make allowances for budget; for site restrictions; for other plant considerations such as maintaining carbon dioxide and humidity levels and accommodating soil beds, pots or other plant containers; and for the dimensions of available building materials.

The Great Canadian Way

The four main objectives will not be perfectly met in any greenhouse design. Optimizing one will have a negative effect on one or more of the other. You will have to compromise.

A good example of compromise is in the number of layers of glazing to be used in the greenhouse. To lower the amount of heat loss through the glazing, it may seem that the sensible thing to do is to increase the number of layers of glazing to provide more air spaces. However, glazing materials absorb and reflect a certain amount of light. Therefore, each additional layer will mean that less light is available to plants inside the greenhouse. More on this later.

The Anatomy of a Solar Greenhouse

Here are some features typically found in solar greenhouses, along with the effect they have on greenhouse performance.

Factors Maximizing Heat Gain During the Heating Season

1. orientation of the greenhouse — the closer to the south the better
2. the south wall glazing angle — to pass the most and reflect the least amount of sunlight during the heating season

Factors Minimizing Heat Loss During the Heating Season

3. common or insulated north wall
4. perimeter insulation
5. movable insulation for glazed areas
6. insulated roof
7. tight construction
8. double glazing

Factors Enhancing Natural Light

9. reflective north wall surface
10. minimizing shading by structural members
11. transmission qualities of glazing material
2. south wall glazing angle

Factors Controlling Temperature Swings

12. vents to exterior
13. vents to house
14. heat storage — concrete floor and gravel
15. heat storage — water in containers
16. heat storage — deep soil beds built on rocks
5. movable insulation
6. insulated, opaque roof — to shade the back of the greenhouse from the summer sun

Physical Fundamentals

Understanding the Source

The sun is the main source of heat and light in a solar greenhouse and, in fact, it provides the primary energy for all life on Earth. Understanding some basic facts about the sun and its relationship with Earth is a fundamental part of the greenhouse design process. So let's begin with some information about old Sol . . . .

A Noteworthy Star Our sun is a star. If you could view it from somewhere else in the galaxy, it would appear to be rather ordinary. The sun is what astronomers refer to as a "main sequence" star, which means that its activities are fairly respectable and predictable. It has none of the science-fiction allure of the rarer star types — the exploding nebula, expanding giants, or dying white dwarves (which was one of the original Disney characters). However, from the Earth's perspective, the sun is rather special. Moreover, the very fact that our sun's nature is fairly constant is of great importance to the maintenance of life on Earth.

The sun is a very hot place — its surface temperature is about 6000°C. This great heat is generated by nuclear fusion reactions. Fusion reactions involve the union of atomic particles to create new, larger atoms; during the process some of the matter is converted to heat. Obviously, a process of this sort cannot go on forever, but the sun is expected to continue its present pattern for billions of years to come, so there will still be plenty of time to

enjoy your greenhouse once it's finished. The sun's great heat causes it to radiate energy out into space. These emissions are various forms of light — 49% infrared light, 46% visible light and 5% ultraviolet light.

Besides being very hot, the sun is quite large. This size, or mass, is the source of the gravitational attraction which causes the smaller bodies we call planets to move in orbital paths around the sun. In addition to defining the Earth's orbital path, the sun's influence is expressed in the tidal patterns of our seas and oceans.

While pursuing their orbital paths, the planets intercept small amounts of the radiant energy emitted by the sun. Because the sun emits in all directions,

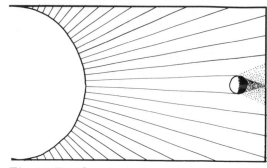

Fig. 18 Earth intercepts

and the Earth is only a tiny speck millions of kilometres away, the Earth's outer atmosphere collects only an extremely small fraction of the original emissions. Even so, this small fraction, known as the solar constant, represents tens of thousands of times the total energy used

by all people on Earth in one year. Only about one-half of this energy reaches the Earth's surface directly. The clouds and dust in the atmosphere reflect or scatter one-third of the incoming light. Water vapour, carbon dioxide and ozone absorb an additional 15% — an action which removes most of the destructive ultraviolet component.

Almost all of the activities taking place on the Earth's surface or within its atmosphere are caused directly or indirectly by the sun's radiation. Weather patterns (temperature, precipitation and wind) and plant growth are examples of solar power at work. In fact most of the fuels used by humans are merely sunlight that was collected by plants and stored in

Fig. 19 Stored energy

their body tissues. Direct use of solar energy to provide light and heat in a greenhouse is only an attempt to develop a small scale system patterned on the planetary one.

Earth-Sun Orbital Relationship At any given place on the Earth's surface, the hours of sunlight in a day and the path the sun makes across the sky vary according to a predictable, yearly pattern. Near the equator, these seasonal differences in day length and sun position are very subtle. As we move towards either the north or south poles, however, the differences become increasingly pronounced. Because such variations influence greenhouse design, determine how much solar light and heat the greenhouse can expect, and indicate the amount of shading by nearby objects, it is important to understand why these seasonal changes occur and the specifics of the solar pattern that exists at your location. This understanding can be gained by studying the Earth's orbital relationship with the sun.

The View from Space   The Earth moves in an almost circular orbit around the sun. The sun sits slightly to one side of the centre of the orbital path causing the distance between the sun and Earth to vary throughout the year. The Earth is closest to the sun on December 21 (144.5 million kilometres) and farthest away on June 21 (154.3 million kilometres). Living in the cold parts of the northern hemisphere, we know only too well that December 21 is not the warmest, sunniest day of the year — there must be a factor other than mere distance that determines the seasonal pattern. This critical factor is the 23.5° tilt of the Earth's north-south axis which affects the way the sun's light shines on the Earth's surface. We can understand the ramifications of this tilt by following the Earth through one annual cycle, beginning on September 21.

September 21 is called the fall or autumnal equinox. As its name implies (equi — equal + nox, night) it is one of two days in the year when the day and the night are the same length. This is because the sun is shining directly on the equator at this time so that a specific spot on the globe spends half the day in sunshine and the other half in darkness.

By December 21, the day called the winter solstice, the earth has moved in its orbit, retaining its tilt, so that the sun shines most directly on a band 23.5° south of the equator (known as the Tropic of

Figures

There are certain shorthand ways to indicate very small or very large units which we can use to make talking about them easier. We know that one hundred is 10 x 10, or the product of two tens. Similarly, one thousand is the product of three tens, 10 x 10 x 10. Another way of writing these figures is 10^2 (one hundred) and 10^3 (one thousand). An easy way to remember this short form is that the superscript number indicates a one followed by that many zeros. For instance, 10^6 would indicate one followed by six zeros — 1,000,000 — or one million. If we know the distance from the Earth to the sun is 150,000,000 kilometres, we can also write this as 1.5 x 100,000,000km or 1.5 x 10^8km.

Numbers less than one are indicated by a negative superscript. An easy way to think of these figures is to start with a one and, instead of moving the decimal place to the right (by adding zeros as above), move the decimal point to the left, creating increasingly smaller numbers. Therefore, 10^{-3} would indicate a one with the decimal point moved three places to the left (.001) or one-one thousandths (1/1000). Therefore, a wavelength of 10^{-6} metres is only 0.000001m long, one-millionth of a metre. One-billionth of a metre (10^{-9}) is called a nanometre or a millimicron. Wavelengths of visible light range from about 390 to 760 millimicrons.

Another use for superscripts is to indicate area or volume. For instance, instead of writing "square metres" or "m x m," we can write "m^2" (or ft^2). Similarly, volume (m x m x m) can be indicated by "m^3."

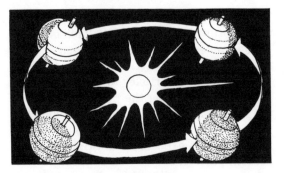

Fig. 20 Seasons and dates

Capricorn). As the Earth turns, spots in the northern hemisphere spend more of the day in darkness than in the sunlight. In addition, the sunlight has to pass through more of the Earth's atmosphere to reach the surface. This results in the typical short northern day, with a weak sun low in the southern sky.

By March 21, the spring or vernal equinox, the sun is again shining most directly on the equator. During the period between December and March, northern days have gradually been lengthening and the sun has been getting higher in the sky.

The summer solstice, June 21, finds the sun directed at the Tropic of Cancer, 23.5° north of the equator. This is when northern locations experience the most hours of sunlight and the sun is at its highest point above the horizon. By September 21, the sun is directed at the equator again, with the predictable effect on day length and solar position.

Thus we see that the tilt of the planet's axis causes the incoming sunlight to be directed at different parts of the globe throughout the year, resulting in cyclical variations in temperature, day length and position of the sun for any earthly location.

There is another important pattern that affects life on Earth, just as much as the seasons. The Earth completes a rotation about its own axis every 24 hours (a fortunate figure for clockmakers who otherwise would have either a surplus or

shortage of numbers) which means that the section of the globe receiving incoming sunlight is constantly changing. This rotation is what gives us day and night and creates the earthly illusion that the sun moves across the sky from east to west each day.

The View from Earth   As we sit here on Earth watching the sun, the cause of the changing solar patterns is not very clear (which is why it took humankind a couple of thousand years to figure things out) but

Latitude

Latitude refers to the distance north or south of the equator, which is at 0° latitude. If you picture a cross-section of the Earth, it becomes readily apparent that there are 90° between the equator and either of the poles. Hence, the north pole is at 90°N latitude, the south pole is at 90°S, and all other points on Earth are in between. These imaginary latitudinal lines run parallel to each other, each degree being separated on the Earth's surface by a distance of 111 km.

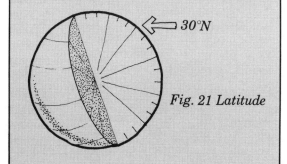

Fig. 21 Latitude

the effects, especially to those living far north or south of the equator, are obvious. North of the equator, in winter, we have short days. The sun moves from south of east to south of west in a shallow arc across the southern horizon. As we have seen, this effect is at its extreme in late December, the time of the winter solstice. In summer, on the other hand, the sun rises north of east and moves across the southern sky in a high wide arc to set, late in the day, north of west. (The higher the latitude, the farther north the sun rises and sets until, in the far north at high summer, the sun never sets.) These daily solar patterns are always symmetrical — the afternoon pattern is a mirror-image of the morning pattern. The sun reaches its highest point at midday — noon, solar time (called, not surprisingly, solar noon). All places on the Earth's surface that are at the same latitude experience the same solar pattern.

Solar altitude and solar azimuth are the ways of describing the sun's position in the

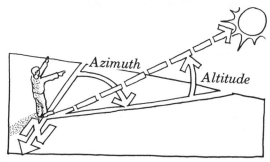

Fig. 22 Azimuth and altitude

sky. *Solar altitude* is a numerical way of indicating how high in the sky the sun is, or to put it more formally, it is an expression of the sun's position relative to the horizon. Altitude is expressed as an angle, the number of degrees above the horizon. (The horizon is 0°.) During the day, the sun's altitude increases until it reaches its highest point at solar noon. The highest solar altitude of the year, for any given northern latitude, occurs in late June, at the time of the summer solstice.

The *solar azimuth* describes the sun's position relative to true south. It too is expressed as an angle, true south being 0°. Except at noon, when the azimuth is 0°, the position of the sun will be either so many degrees east or west of south and must be so indicated. (For instance, at equinox the sun rises at 90°E and sets at 90° W.)

Graphic representations of the yearly sun pattern that occurs at a particular latitude are called *sun-path charts* and are a useful design tool. These charts, which plot altitude against azimuth, allow you to see at a glance the annual variation in the solar arc. Sun-path charts indicate day length, position of the sun at any given time, the angle of the incoming sunlight and, we will see, can be used to analyze the solar potential of a building site.

Understanding Heat and Light

Light

Incoming sunlight exerts great power over our surroundings and it behooves us to investigate the nature of that light. An exhaustive study is not necessary, but it is helpful to understand the major energy input of a solar greenhouse.

Light is as peculiar as it is powerful and it has fascinated man for centuries. It is still not clearly understood, probably because there is little else in the human experience with which to compare it. The Greeks thought that light was a stream of tiny particles. This idea remained the accepted one until the late seventeenth century when a Dutch scientist formally proposed an explanation of light as wave motion. Today, after much study and debate, both these concepts are considered valid and the accepted hypothesis, the wave-particle theory, assumes that light has a dual nature. For the sake of simplicity we will speak in terms of light waves.

Visible light is a small part of the electromagnetic spectrum, a large array of wave forms. Many of the other forms of wave energy in the spectrum are not as readily perceived as visible light, which is itself comprised of a range of wavelengths. We can see these components neatly arranged when we look at a rainbow or observe a prism separate a beam of sunlight into bands of color. That pretty striped pattern is called the *light spectrum*.

The components of the light spectrum differ in their *wavelength* and their *frequency*.

Electromagnetic waves are generated by the movement of electrical charges within atoms and molecules — the higher the energy level, the shorter the wavelength. As we have seen, the sun radiates energy in three main categories: ultraviolet, visible and infrared. Let's look at the way these three energy types affect our earthly environment and our greenhouse design.

Ultraviolet (UV) is the high-powered component of incoming sunlight. Only the longer UV wavelengths (those closest to violet on the spectrum) reach the Earth's surface. They account for about 4% of incoming sunlight on a clear day. This is the portion of sunlight which causes sunburn and bleaches colour out of materials. The shorter UV wavelengths are absorbed in a layer of the upper atmosphere where their energy is used to create ozone. Life on Earth is dependent on this screening process because exposure to a high level of UV is damaging to living organisms. In greenhouse design, our major concern with the UV component of sunlight is its effect on plastic glazing and insulation materials, which tend to degrade quickly if they are not protected in some way from direct sunlight.

Visible wavelengths account for 45% to 50% of the sunlight reaching ground level on a clear day. Our eyes are sensitive to this type of energy and green plants use selected wavelengths for photosynthesis. Of the three components of sunlight, visible light is the least affected by its passage through the atmosphere, although the blue wavelengths tend to be scattered by atmospheric dust and water vapour (which is why the sky appears blue). Visible light is important to the greenhouse for both plant growth and heat.

Infrared wavelengths (IR) make up the remaining half (46% to 51%) of the sunlight reaching the earth. It is the shorter-wave infrared (called near-infrared since they are near the red portion of visible light) which predominates because much of the longer wave IR is absorbed by the atmosphere. The infrared component is also important as a heat input in a greenhouse.

Light Meets Matter Light moves easily through the relative vacuum of space but that is not the case when it hits the gases of the Earth's atmosphere and the solids and liquids on the planet's surface. Light interacts with matter in three ways: transmission, reflection and absorption.

If a beam of light encounters matter and can pass through it, relatively unchanged, the material is said to be transparent; it allows *transmission*. Frequently, matter is

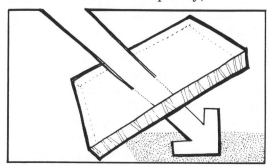

Fig. 24 Transmission

only transparent to certain wavelengths. The atmosphere, for instance, is more transparent to some waves than others. Glass is another example — it is transparent to the visible and near-infrared wavelengths present in sunlight, but not to the ultraviolet ones. A surface which does not allow transmission of light is said to be opaque.

If incoming radiation penetrates the surface of matter it meets, but is not transmitted, it is *absorbed*. The energy in a light beam excites the molecules of the absorbing matter causing its temperature to rise, at least at the collecting surface.

Wavelength and Frequency

Think of light moving through space, oscillating as it moves so that it resembles a wave. Depending on their place in the light spectrum, the different colours of light exhibit different wave patterns. The waves from colours at the infrared end of the spectrum oscillate up and down relatively infrequently and have a relatively long distance between the peaks of the wave. This distance is called the wavelength and the number of oscillations per time period is called the frequency. Waves at the ultraviolet end of the light spectrum have a higher frequency (more rapid oscillation) and shorter wavelengths.

Despite their differences, these waves all travel at the same speed through a vacuum, a phenomenon rather like that of an adult and a small child walking together. The adult takes long, lazy, infrequent steps. In order to keep pace, the child must take shorter, more frequent steps. The adult represents the long-wave, low-frequency end of the spectrum; the hurried youngster, the short-wave, high-frequency end.

This analogy can also help you to remember that the high-frequency waves (the young child) contain more energy than the low-frequency part of the spectrum (the older adult).

Fig. 23 Wavelength and frequency

Fig. 25 Absorption

Reflection occurs when light striking a surface is redirected. If the surface is very rough, then the light is scattered or diffused. A smooth, highly-polished surface, such as a mirror, reflects light in a more predictable manner: the angle at which incoming rays strike a smooth, reflecting surface (*the angle of incidence)* will be equal to the angle of the reflected rays (*the angle of reflection*).

Fig. 26 Reflection

These three types of interaction are not mutually exclusive. In fact, it is more likely that at least two will occur together. The colour of an object indicates that certain wavelengths are being absorbed and others

reflected. A yellow colour, for example, results when all of the visible wavelengths other than yellow are absorbed. Yellow is reflected and seen by our eyes. True black and white are exceptions to this — black suggests total absorption of visible light while white results from total reflection.

Collecting Light Insolation is a short way of saying "*in*coming *sol*ar radi*ation*"; it should not be confused with insulation. The insolation level for a given place and time depends on the distance the sunlight must travel through the atmosphere to reach the ground, and on the cloud coverage. Higher solar altitudes and clear atmospheric conditions result in greater insolation levels. Thus on a clear day, the insolation levels will be highest at noon. (Never would have guessed it, would you?) Insolation is measured in kilojoules per square metre (KJ/m^2) (or BTU/ft^2). Insolation rates, the amount of energy received in a given time (for example, $KJ/m^2/day$) are used to predict heat gain when doing design calculations.

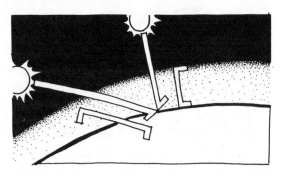

Fig. 27 Distance sunlight passes through atmosphere

Fig. 28 Radiation

In the northern hemisphere solar radiation tends to come from the southern half of the sky. When the sky is clear, the majority of insolation comes directly from the sun. When the sky is heavily overcast, the incoming light is scattered, and diffuse radiation of a lower intensity is received from all parts of the sky.

A greenhouse needs to collect sunlight for plant growth and heat, so its design must promote light transmission through the transparent covering — the glazing material. Light is most completely transmitted if it strikes the glazing materials at an angle 90° from the material's surface. That is, transmission is optimized if the incoming (or incident) light is perpendicular to the glazing. (This is defined as an angle of incidence of 0°.) The more the angle of incidence varies from this perpendicular position, the greater the proportion of light is reflected instead of being transmitted. It would be relatively simple to achieve optimum transmission and thus collection if the sun always shone from one point in the sky and clouds never interfered with the incoming radiation.

However, the sun's position changes constantly throughout the day and the daily pattern varies from season to season. How can we collect light from this moving source when the greenhouse glazing surface is stationary?

One way is to orient the glazing so that it is most directly exposed to the sun for the greatest part of the day. In other words, face the glazing south. This also usually means that the long axis of the greenhouse should run from east to west, again to expose the greatest amount of glazing to the sun. In practice, the actual orientation can vary somewhat without significantly affecting the amount of sunlight collected, but the main glazing surface should be within 30° east or west of true south. An east of south orientation is considered preferable to one that is west of south because it allows the early morning sun to come in. Plants make efficient use of morning sunlight while afternoon and evening light from the west often tends to cause overheating.

The angle of the south glazing also has an important influence on the percentage of light entering the greenhouse. Since the solar altitude changes throughout the year, the glazing will be perfectly perpendicular to the incident radiation only twice a year at most. The optimum angle for solar transmission at any particular time of year increases (becomes steeper) as you go farther north, since the sun is lower in the sky at high latitudes. When deciding on the angle of the south face a compromise

must be made between optimizing collection for a particular time of year (for, instance, late February and late October) and considerations such as construction ease and characteristics of building materials.

Even when incoming light is perpendicular to a glazing surface, transmission is not complete. Glazing materials absorb a small percentage of light, the exact amount varying from one material to another. A single pane of window glass transmits about 89% of the incoming perpendicular radiation. Cold climate greenhouses are usually double glazed; that is, they have two layers of glazing material. This is done to reduce heat loss, which is very rapid through a single glazing layer in cold weather. However, the extra layer of glazing reduces the amount of light transmitted since it too absorbs and reflects some of the incoming light. For comparison, if one layer of glass allows 89% transmission, two layers of glass will allow only about 79% transmission (0.89 x 0.89 = 0.79) (The actual measured figure for double glass is 80%).

When sunlight strikes surfaces inside the greenhouse, it is either reflected or absorbed. The upper portion of the north wall is usually painted white or covered with a reflective material so that light striking it will be reflected onto the plants. A white painted surface is usually considered superior since it results in diffuse reflection of almost all light that strikes it (remember that the colour white

indicates total reflection). Light so diffused appears to be the most useful to plants. The plants in the greenhouse absorb certain wavelengths, from both diffuse and direct sunlight, for photosynthesis. Many other surfaces inside a greenhouse absorb light energy and so increase the internal heat. Certain types of materials, such as water or rocks, are placed in a greenhouse solely to collect this light and store it as heat.

Heat

When light is absorbed by a material, it is transformed to heat. The word heat, at least in a scientific sense, refers to the energy contained in the vibrations of the molecules in a material (or in a defined space). The vibrations are in the form of random movement of the molecules so that adding more heat to an object increases this random movement but does not cause the object to move physically, or change location. Added heat can change the physical state of matter; it will eventually change a solid to a liquid, or a liquid to a gas.

The activities of heat are studied in the science of thermodynamics. Certain thermodynamic principles or laws can help us predict how incoming energy will affect an object or system. The first law of thermodynamics, which is the law of conservation of energy, states that energy can be converted from one form to another but cannot be created or destroyed. When energy in the form of light, for instance, strikes and is absorbed by the dark-coloured soil in a greenhouse, the light energy is transformed into heat energy (increasing the vibration of molecules in the soil) thus raising the temperature of the soil.

The second law of thermodynamics tells us that heat cannot flow spontaneously from a material at a lower temperature to a material at a higher temperature. It, rather, will always move from heat-rich areas to heat-poor areas. The greater the

Fig. 29 Second law of thermodynamics

difference in temperature between the two areas, the faster the heat will move. Heat is moved, or transferred, in three ways: by conduction, by convection, or by radiation. Since all of these types of heat transfer occur in a greenhouse, they deserve attention.

Conduction   Thermal conduction is the process of heat transfer through a material by vibration of molecular particles. Since, as we have seen, the vibration of molecules involves no material movement, heat can

be conducted through solids. In fact solids, such as iron and steel, are usually the best conductors of heat. Materials which are poor conductors, such as fibreglass batts, are called insulators.

Fig. 30 Conduction

Convection   Convection is heat transfer by the movement of materials from warmer areas to cooler areas. This can occur only in liquids and gases (the fluids — things which flow). When part of a fluid is warmed, it expands and becomes less dense than the surrounding material. This part then rises, while cooler, denser fluid falls to take its place. Such motion is often called a convection current and is the way a gravity furnace heats your house. It is

Fig. 31 Convection

also happening in the air around you as you sit reading this book.

Radiation   To understand radiant heat transfer, think back to the discussion about the electromagnetic spectrum. Hot objects (objects with their little molecules vibrating like crazy) radiate or emit a certain level of infrared radiation. The amount of radiation produced depends on the temperature of the object and the ability of its surface to emit. Flat, black surfaces are good emitters, while shiny, metallic ones are poor emitters. A wood stove with nickel-plated knobs exhibits both qualities. The flat, black sides of the stove radiate well, you can feel the heat from some distance away. The shiny knobs, on the other hand, are poor emitters, the heat just sits on the surface waiting for the unwary to touch it. Radiation is increased with an increased temperature difference between the hot object and a cooler object which it can "see." Remember that the waves themselves are not "hot," they are only transformed to heat when they are absorbed by an object.

Heat Transfer at Work in the Greenhouse   Let's assume that it is now winter and take a look at what's happening to the heat in a typical greenhouse.

Energy enters the greenhouse in the form of sunlight (short wave radiation) after transmission through the glazing material. This light energy is absorbed as heat by some of the materials in the greenhouse which it strikes including the soil and any heat storage material which has been provided.

Via conduction, the heat moves into the body of the collecting object if the collecting surface of the object is at a higher temperature than its interior volume (which is usually the case). The air layer immediately next to the collecting surface is also heated by conduction. This causes convection currents — warmed air rising and cooler air moving in to take its place. Although the air itself moves in a circular pattern (from the bottom to the top to the bottom of greenhouse) convection currents result in temperature stratification so that the temperature at the ceiling will be much higher than the temperature at the floor.

An object which has absorbed heat will radiate long wave infrared to cooler objects that are within its sight. At night, green-house objects such as the soil and water storage will radiate to heat plant leaves and the glazing.

Heat Loss The air heated by conduction and moved by convection is confined by the shell of the building. If there are cracks and gaps in the construction joints or around doors and vents, then some of the warm air will move directly outdoors. Cold air will be sucked in through other cracks to maintain the air pressure in the building. This direct air exchange with the outdoors is termed *infiltration* and is considered a type of convective movement.

Wind blowing against the exterior surface accelerates the rate at which infiltration occurs.

Convective air currents and radiation transfer heat energy to structural parts of the greenhouse, both opaque and transparent. Heat from warmed air moves by conduction into cooler walls. Temperature stratification intensifies this activity in upper parts of the greenhouse since heat from the higher temperature air will move even more rapidly into the walls. Thermal radiation generated by warm

interior objects flows to cooler walls where it is absorbed. The heat absorbed by the walls, whether by conduction from the nearby air or from radiation from warm bodies, moves by conduction through the walls toward the cooler temperatures of the outdoors. Once there, either small convection currents generated by the heat of the building or wind (which is a large scale convective movement) carries the heat away to the Great Beyond.

Heat also leaves the building by conduction through the floor and footings

Greenhouse Heat Movement

1. solar radiation into greenhouse
2. convection currents within water heat storage
3. conduction into the soil
4. conduction through the house wall
5. radiation from water storage to shaded rock bed
6. conduction into the depth of the rocks
7. conduction through the glazing
8. convection air currents due to heated elements within greenhouse
9. convection air exchange with the house
10. convection through the upper vent to the outdoors.
11. conduction through the floor and perimeter
12. outdoor convection carrying heat away from glazing
13. conduction through the roof
14. conduction through the kneewall
15. convective infiltration losses

Fig. 32 Movements of heat in an attached greenhouse

of the greenhouse, into the surrounding earth. Conduction and infiltration are the main sources of heat loss, convection air currents and radiation are the "delivery systems" moving heat to cold exterior walls.

Methods of Controlling Heat Loss in the Winter Greenhouse:

1. Reduce the ability of the building's shell to conduct heat:
   — Insulate all opaque walls.
   — Use more than one layer of glazing. The air spaces between the glazing retard conduction and the establishment of convection currents.
   — Insulate the foundation and/or the floor.
   — Provide an insulating cover for the glazing at night.
   — Use seasonal insulation to cover areas of glazing which do not receive significant direct sunlight during the winter.

2. Reduce infiltration:
   — Be careful during construction.
   — Install a continuous vapour barrier.
   — Caulk the joint between the framing and the foundation as well as the joints in the vapour barrier.
   — Use weatherstripping on doors and vents.

3. Reduce air stratification:
   — Stratified hot air may be circulated through either the lower regions of the greenhouse, the attached building, or a separate heat-storage facility.
   — Movement of this hot air makes the greenhouse more uniform in temperature. Thus, the lower areas are prevented from becoming cold enough to seriously retard plant growth, and the upper parts of long vines or hanging plants are protected from becoming too hot.
   — Interrupting the heat stratification pattern also reduces the conductive losses through the glazing layers adjacent to the warmer air. This air circulation can be accomplished through the use of a small, low-power fan placed high in the greenhouse, which will also serve to reduce glazing condensation.

4. Retain heat in storage until required:
   — Heat held by thermal storage materials will not warm the greenhouse air as rapidly and will thus reduce stratification and the related heat loss problems. These materials will then radiate heat as greenhouse temperatures cool at night.

Methods of Controlling Overheating in the Summer Greenhouse

1. Disallow the summer sun:
   — Increase the glazing angle.
   — Provide shading.
2. Increase ventilation to the outdoors.
3. Increase amount of thermal storage.

Understanding Plants

A complete analysis of the physiology and the needs of plants is beyond the scope of this book; indeed it is beyond the scope of any single book. However, you do need to have some idea of how plants grow and what they need to grow so you can provide for these things in your greenhouse design.

Photosynthesis Photosynthesis is a process in which plants use carbon dioxide and water to produce some simple plant sugars, which are in turn used to construct more complex molecules such as proteins, vitamins, and nucleic acids. This process is powered by light. Chlorophyll, a photo-sensitive pigment in plant leaves absorbs energy when sunlight falls on them. However, certain wavelengths of light are absorbed much more strongly by the cholorophyll than others. (Green, for instance, is reflected, resulting in the colour of the leaves.) Generally speaking, the blue and red regions of the light

Fig. 33 Photosynthesis: Carbon dioxide and water in the presence of sunlight are converted by chlorophyll into sugar, oxygen and water.

spectrum are the most important for photosynthesis.

The hours of daylight, the light intensity, the amount of carbon dioxide available, and the temperature all affect the rate of photosynthesis. These factors are also interrelated. For example, increasing the temperature in the greenhouse will have little effect on photosynthesis under conditions of low light, yet will have a great effect at high light intensities. The length of time each day that light is available to the plants in a greenhouse is at least as important as the intensity of light, since photosynthesis will still occur in levels of light much lower than the optimum.

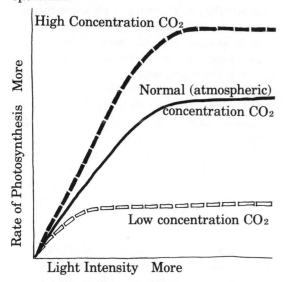

Fig. 34 Schematic example of how rate of photosynthesis is affected by varying CO_2 concentration. Adapted from Biology.

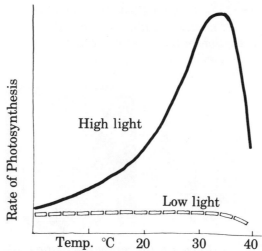

Fig. 35 Schematic example of the effect of temperature on photosynthesis at low and high light intensities. Adapted from Biology.

Artificial Lighting Using artificial lighting to supplement the sun is an energy-intensive practice. However, it may be appropriate in the late winter to help to make seedlings ready for transplanting into the spring greenhouse garden. A few extra hours of light each day can be beneficial to seedlings during February and can, in fact, make the difference in having seedlings ready for transplanting when the greenhouse warms up.

Different types of lighting give off light from various parts of the spectrum and the ideal source is one which provides exactly the type of light which the plants need (such as the reds and blues important to photosynthesis). Ordinary incandescent bulbs are strong at the red end, but weak in the blue light spectrum. Fluorescent

Fig. 36 The direct approach — natural light

Fig. 37 The indirect approach — artificial light
Energy is lost every step of the way:
 • The sun lifts water from the ocean
 • Clouds deposit it behind a dam
 • Falling water generates electricity
 • Transmission losses
 • Low efficiency electric light

tubes are somewhat better in the blue range and particularly strong in the yellow. A combination of fluorescent and incandescent lighting makes a good mixture, although the use of cool white fluorescent tubes by themselves is probably satisfactory for most applications. Fluorescent tube manufacturers make a variety of different types of lights which attempt to provide exactly what plants need. However, as these are relatively expensive and decline in efficiency with age, they are probably not necessary for the short periods during which you may wish to use supplemental lighting.

Temperature While different greenhouse plants respond most favourably to different temperatures, most plants grow best between 12°C and 30°C. Extreme low temperatures result in the freezing and death of greenhouse crops. Many of the non-fruiting, leafy green vegetables do fairly well at temperatures below 13°C and some will, in fact, survive the occasional frosting. But, as we have seen, the rate of

Fig. 38 Plants and temperature

photosynthesis is heavily dependent upon temperature, so temperatures much above or below this range are not conducive to satisfactory plant growth. Too high temperatures will stress plants, cause soil to dry out rapidly, and make the plants more susceptible to disease and insect infestation.

Even more important to plants than air temperature is soil temperature. While the

tops of plants can withstand a certain amount of day-to-night (or diurnal) fluctuation in temperature (which is fortunate since a solar greenhouse is inevitably going to experience such

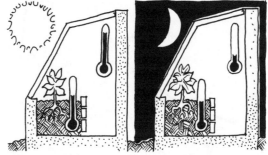

Fig. 39 Diurnal temperature fluctuation — greater in the air than in the earth

inconstancy) the roots are much more sensitive to change. Deep soil beds in the greenhouse will store a certain amount of heat and will protect the roots from temperature fluctuations similar to those in the greenhouse air temperature.

Don't panic if your greenhouse drops below 13°C or goes above 30°C. In a northern greenhouse in February, the air temperature may rise to 27°C during the day and drop to 5°C at night. Such swings have to be expected, but if you do your best to minimize them and make sure that the roots are protected, your plants — and you — will survive.

Means of temperature control include proper ventilation, thermal mass in the greenhouse, heat exchange with the home, the use of movable glazing insulation, and deep soil beds to protect the roots.

Humidity Just as greenhouse crops will do best within a certain temperature range, so they will do best under conditions of proper humidity. The ideal relative humidity in a greenhouse is around 60%, which means that the air is holding 60% of the total amount of moisture that it could possibly contain at that temperature. When the relative humidity is too low, plants transpire faster, the soil dries out quickly and requires frequent watering, and conditions are ripe for pests such as spider mites. In a greenhouse, the relative humidity will vary throughout the day as the air temperature changes.

Carbon Dioxide Carbon dioxide, as previously noted, is used by plants during photosynthesis. The rate of photosynthesis is proportional to the amount of carbon dioxide available. It has been the practice in some commercial greenhouses to increase the atmospheric concentration of carbon dioxide (normally about 0.04%) in the greenhouse air to increase the rate of photosynthesis. An important means of making carbon dioxide available to the plants is to keep the greenhouse air moving so that the plant leaves always have access to fresh sources as they use up the carbon dioxide in the air immediately around them. There is little here to concern the home greenhouse user — there is usually enough air movement due to ventilation and heat exchange with the house that the carbon dioxide levels in an attached greenhouse will be as good as or better than outdoors.

Soil Most of the complex molecules in plants are comprised mainly of six elements: oxygen, hydrogen, carbon, nitrogen, phosphorus and sulfur. We've already seen that plants use carbon dioxide (CO_2) and water vapour (H_2O) to supply oxygen, hydrogen and carbon. The other three nutrients must be supplied by the soil. Besides these basic nutrients there are others, called trace elements, which are also essential to plant growth. These trace elements include copper, zinc, manganese, boron, sodium and molybdenum.

To be usable by plants, all these nutrients have to be present in a soluble form so that the plant roots can take them up. The Big Three, then — nitrogen, phosphorous and sulfur — must be in the soil in the form of nitrates, phosphates and sulfates.

Soil also contains numerous organisms which maintain soil fertility and are beneficial to plant growth. It is important that oxygen be present, both for these organisms, and for plant roots.

To ensure proper plant growth, the soil must have a structure which the roots can penetrate, it must be able to contain oxygen and let carbon dioxide (a waste product in the soil system) escape, and it must provide adequate drainage while retaining sufficient water for plant growth.

Understanding Building Materials

Most of the building materials used in the construction of a greenhouse are common ones: nails, caulking, weatherstripping, shingles for the roof, concrete or treated lumber for the foundation. Although aluminum or even plastic tubing can be used for framing, we recommend the use of dimensional lumber (the standard 2 x 4s or 2 x 6s you find in any lumber yard). Wood is durable, easy to work with, readily available, and still relatively inexpensive. Aluminum framework can be narrower to support the same amount of weight, thus casting fewer shadows into the greenhouse, and it lasts forever, but aluminum is a poor insulator and it is expensive.

Insulation Air is the only insulation available to us and the various insulating products differ only in the number and type of air spaces they form. Because a greenhouse has a relatively small insulated surface area compared to the glazed area, the type and even the level of insulation is not as important as in a

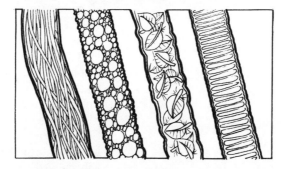

Fig. 40 Insulation is packaged air

house where there is proportionally much less window area. Although the insulating of the roof and, in the case of a freestanding greenhouse, the north wall, are important, wall insulation assumes a secondary position to such things as controlling infiltration and using movable insulation on the glazed areas.

We can distinguish four types of insulation, which are perhaps best described by their methods of installation.

Batt or *roll-insulation* is installed into hollow spaces in walls and ceilings before they are closed in.

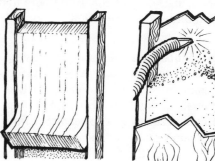

Fig. 41 Batt insulation   Blown insulation

Blown or *poured insulation* acts as a loose fill and is blown or poured into cavities, as you might have guessed.

Foam insulation comes in liquid form (sometimes in two separate components) and special equipment is used to spray it into cavities or onto the outside of walls (particularly masonry walls).

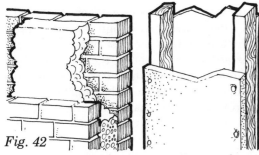

Fig. 42

Foam between bricks   Rigid insulation

Rigid insulation or *board* insulation comes in flat sheets of various thicknesses and insulating values, and is the best material for insulating beneath concrete floors and around foundation perimeters.

Glazing Materials   We are strongly biased towards glass as a glazing material and recommend its use in most attached greenhouse applications. But, if for some inexplicable reason you've read this far and still don't trust our judgement, we'll introduce you to the most important factors which influence the glazing choice. In doing so, we will perhaps also be able to make you more clearly understand our glass bias. No other single glazing material yet produced combines all the beneficial qualities of glass.

Initial Considerations   Glazing choice will influence other design and construction decisions. If the glazing material comes in three-foot (914mm) widths you cannot put framing members on two-foot or four-foot centres (610mm or 1219mm). A heavy

glazing material such as glass will require a stronger structure. A greenhouse using polyethylene is fundamentally different from one using glass. You will not likely, for instance, want a polyethylene greenhouse to be an extension of your living area, as it is not going to last as long, etc. (Although, in some cases, polyethylene may act as a temporary glazing until a more permanent material can be used.) Different materials will also require different construction and glazing details, as we will see in CONSTRUCTION.

The other side of this coin is that design

may influence or determine a glazing choice. Non-tempered glass, for instance, cannot be used as a roof glazing material. If you have located a cheap source of non-tempered glass (which we'll get to presently) your design should be inclined toward a higher, steeply sloped south wall to eliminate the need for roof glazing, which would require you to use a more expensive plastic or tempered glass.

Insulation			
	MATERIAL	RSI/mm	R/in
Batt or roll-type:	Fibreglass Batt	0.022	3.17
	Rock wool batt	0.023	3.32
Blown or poured:	Fibreglass loose (blown)	0.015	2.16
	Fibreglass loose (poured)	0.021	3.03
	Rock wool loose (blown)	0.019	2.74
	Rock wool loose (poured)	0.021	3.03
	Cellulose (blown)	0.025	3.61
	Cellulose (poured)	0.024	3.46
	Vermiculite	0.016	2.31
	Polystyrene (loose)	0.020	2.88
	Wood shavings	0.017	2.45
Foam:	Polyurethane	0.042	6.06
Rigid:	Expanded Polystyrene (white)	0.027	3.89
	Extruded Polystyrene (blue)	0.032	4.62
	Polyurethane	0.042	6.06
	Fibreglass sheathing	0.031	4.47
	Glass fibre board	0.028	4.04
	Mineral aggregate baord	0.018	2.60
	Fibreboard	0.019	2.74

Maximizing Heat and Light   The glazing in a greenhouse has an effect on three of the four greenhouse design objectives, to wit:

- maximizing heat gain
- minimizing heat loss
- maximizing light levels

As with all aspects of greenhouse design, the effect of glazing on each of these objectives is related to its effect on the other two.

All glazings either reflect, absorb, or transmit the various parts of the light spectrum. To help maximize both heat gain and light levels inside the greenhouse, as much sunlight as possible should be admitted into the greenhouse space. To accomplish this, a glazing material should have a low reflectivity and a high transmissibility.

Some reflection occurs when light strikes the surface of the glazing as a result both of the properties of the material and of the angle of incidence. The amount of light reflected at the surface of the common

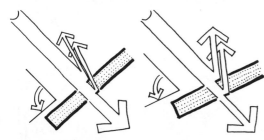

Fig. 43 Angle of incidence affects transmissibility.

glazing materials is relatively small, in the order of 4%. Since the light must pass through two surfaces (the front and the back) to get through one layer of glazing, the total reflection for each layer of glazing is double this percentage, or in the range of 7% to 10%. This proportion increases, however, as the angle of incidence increases. That is, the farther away from a perpendicular angle the light strikes the surface, the greater the reflection. A light source parallel to the glazing will experience 100% reflection.

As figure 44 shows, most common glazing materials are grouped around the 90% transmissivity level when the angle of incidence is 0°. This figure remains surprisingly consistent until the angle of incidence reaches about 50°.

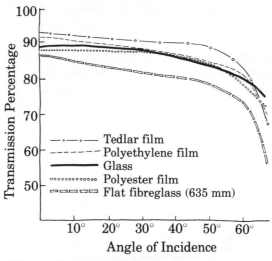

Fig. 44 Percent of light transmission as a function of angle of incidence for various glazing materials.

That the common greenhouse glazing materials have a high level of transmittance, also means that they absorb very little of the incoming light. In fact, the amount absorbed is so slight that we don't think it's worth worrying about. What is more important in this regard is that some plastics deteriorate in sunlight so that, with time, they absorb greater amounts of the sunlight. While most rigid-plastic materials are now made resistant to this kind of decay, one of the beauties of glass is that it does not undergo such deterioration.

While it usually doesn't make critical differences in home greenhouse use, the transmission of light is also important. Plants are very sensitive to light levels, particularly the fruiting plants. It has been shown in commercial tomato greenhouses that a decrease in light levels results in a corresponding decrease in production. For example, 10% less light results in 10% lower yields.

Any decrease in light levels is compounded by the use of multiple glazings. Previously, we explained that if one layer of glass transmits 89% of the incident light, then two layers will transmit about 80%. Such factors are critical in commercial tomato greenhouses, where every pound of produce is important. Where double glazing is used in such commercial operations, greater consideration is given to the choice of glazing. If we assume, for instance, that Tedlar (a brand of transparent film sometimes used as a glazing material) has

93% transmissibility, (see chart on p. 244) then two layers (.93 x .93) result in about 86%. (The actual figure is 88%.) When we compare this possibility to glass' total of about 80% we can see that this may make an important difference in yields.

But transmission of the light striking the glazing surface is not the whole story. Much more important to the amount of light which actually gets into the greenhouse is the angle of incidence. As the angle of incidence increases, the amount of solar energy falling on each square metre of the glazing decreases. For instance, the amount of solar energy per square metre when the angle of incidence is 45° is only about two-thirds of the solar energy when the angle of incidence is zero. See below (fig. 45).

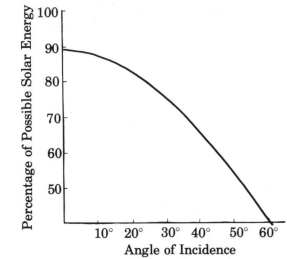

Fig. 45 Percentage of possible insolation transmitted through glass at various angles of incidence

The ideal glazing has low reflectivity, low absorption, high transmissibility, and maintains its level of transmittance for a long period. So that means reflection and absorption are bad, right?

Well, not exactly. To minimize heat loss, we want a glazing which will prevent the heat from the sun, which we have allowed into the greenhouse, from getting out. How does it do this? Well, first we have to look at how the heat got there, and what form it is in.

When the sunlight passes through the glazing and strikes an object in the greenhouse — plants, thermal storage, or other materials — part of it is absorbed and used either to power photosynthesis (in the case of plants) or to heat up the object (in the case of almost all materials). But some of the energy from the light is re-radiated from these objects in the form of long wave infrared radiation. We will call this thermal radiation to distinguish it from the infrared component of sunlight. It is not visible but acts to heat up our bodies or whatever objects it may strike.

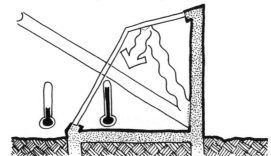

Fig. 46 The greenhouse effect

Since we want to stop this thermal radiation from escaping (to minimize heat loss) we want a glazing which will reflect it. The result of allowing the sunlight into a space, but stopping the thermal radiation from escaping is referred to as the "greenhouse effect". Alright, you say, so

Transmission and Angle of Incidence

Figure A is meant to represent the amount of solar energy striking a surface of one unit area which is perpendicular to the sun's rays. Figure B shows what happens if we pivot the surface so that it approximates a steep greenhouse glazing angle. Less solar energy will be falling on the original unit area at this angle. The fractional amount of solar energy striking the surface in Figure B compared to Figure A can be indicated by the ratio b/a.

The graph uses the example of glass and combines the transmissibility of glass with the amount of solar energy per unit area at various angles of incidence.

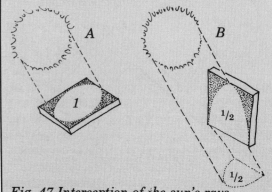

Fig. 47 Interception of the sun's rays

just tell us what glazing material transmits sunlight in one direction and reflects thermal radiation in the other.

Here's the bad news: there isn't one. Or, more accurately, there isn't one which is much beyond the experimental stage, or which you could afford to use in a greenhouse.

It turns out that all available materials which transmit the visible part of the light spectrum either transmit or absorb infrared. If a glazing absorbs all or part of the thermal radiation, it will re-radiate from both of its surfaces so that some of the absorbed infrared is re-radiated back into, in this case, the greenhouse.

So, for the function of minimizing heat loss by trapping thermal radiation, our best glazing would seem to be one which absorbs the most thermal radiation. Glass provides the solution once again, as it absorbs almost 100% of this radiation. In fairness, many of the plastics are also good in this respect. The best of the thin-plastic glazing materials can absorb in the area of 90% of thermal radiation while most of the heavier plastics are even higher. Polyethylene, at the other extreme, absorbs in the area of only one-fifth of thermal radiation.

We've set you up. Now you're waiting for us to tell you that glass is the best and polyethylene hardly works at all in minimizing heat loss.

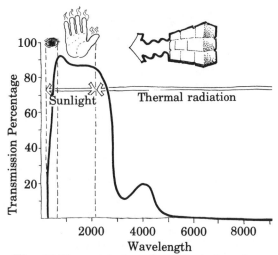

Fig. 48 Transmission characteristics of glass
Most sunlight is transmitted.
Most thermal radiation is absorbed.

We have to come clean here and tell you that what actually happens inside of a greenhouse — what really keeps it warm — is that the glazing prevents convection heat loss between the objects inside the greenhouse and the external air. This is a much more important factor than the radiation greenhouse effect we've been worrying about for, lo, these many pages. For the most part, glazing materials are similarly effective in minimizing heat loss. Sorry.

Constructive Thinking   Other glazing material considerations include strength and stability, ability to withstand the elements and longevity, transparency, ease of installation, availability and cost.

Strength and stability refer to such

physical characteristics as how much buffeting, bumping, or pressure the material will stand before it will crack, warp, or tear. Glass, for example, won't warp, but it will crack under pressure or if it receives a sharp blow, much more easily than will the rigid plastics.

The thin, flexible plastics vary in their resistance to tearing. Some of them, while not very likely to tear, can permanently stretch and deform when buffetted in heavy winds or be otherwise misshapen. In most cases, these roll plastics, as we will call them (since they almost always come on a roll, like wrapping paper) are usually used as inner glazing behind glass or a more rigid plastic. (Although they can also be used for outer glazings — especially the polyvinyl fluoride, Tedlar.)

Resistance to cracking and stretching is one of the factors that determines the *longevity* of a glazing material. Another factor is the ability to resist ultraviolet degradation. A glazing with strong resistance to the elements of nature is one which does not suffer significant deterioration in thickness, in transmissibility or in strength. Glass is the best example although it is susceptible to hail damage. Though thicker plastics are better than thin ones in this regard, most unprotected plastic glazings, such as fibreglass, weaken over time and transmit decreasing amounts of light when exposed to the sun. This degradation is caused by the ultraviolet component of the incoming sunlight, so to prevent it, the glazings must be fortified against radiation. If you use a plastic glazing, make certain to use the "greenhouse" or "solar" version of it. These include an ultraviolet inhibitor as part of the material or as a separate coating. The difference in longevity is definitely worth the slightly greater cost.

On the other hand, it is not prudent to automatically trust a product just because the manufacturer claims that it has been so protected, and provides a warranty. Find out exactly what the warranty means. (A 20 year warranty from a company which has been in business for two years doesn't mean much.) Also, remember that there are inevitably mistakes made when producing a new product. Glass is an old product.

Some glazing materials are *transparent.* Others are *translucent;* they transmit light, but you cannot readily see through them. Although it might seem contrary to common sense, the transmittance characteristics of the translucent glazings are about the same as those of the transparent materials. The biggest difference is that light passing through the translucent glazings is more diffuse. There

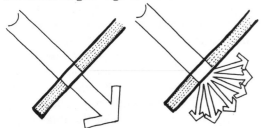

Fig. 49   Transparent   Translucent

are indications that diffuse light in the greenhouse is better for plant growth (perhaps because the glazing then better emulates the sky) and for transferring heat into passive thermal storage materials. Of course, if one of the purposes of the greenhouse is to give you a place to sit and enjoy the view, then translucence is not desirable.

The *ease of installation* involves such things as handling, cutting, and the actual process of installing the glazing material. Plastics are definitely lighter than glass, usually a lot lighter. A 900mm x 1800mm (3ft x 6ft) piece of 5mm glass can weigh 23kg (50 lbs) and must be handled carefully since it is much more susceptible to cracking.

Other than the roll plastics (which are extremely easy) there is really not much difference in the difficulty of cutting plastics or glass once you have learned the technique.

Due to its weight and fragility, glass requires a stronger and more carefully built structure than plastics, and the details can be trickier. However, plastics have a much greater expansion coefficient (greater expansion and contraction with temperature changes) which must be allowed for. While expansion tolerances must be built into a plan using glass as glazing, they are much smaller and much easier to deal with than those needed for plastics, which can buckle if not properly installed.

There are a couple of other factors you might run across in connection with glazing materials. The insulating value of a single layer of any glazing material is so low that it is not worth mentioning — especially when you remember that the main function of glazing is to create a barrier to convection heat loss. So we won't mention it.

Another factor is the degradation of the glazing material under heat. This is taken into account only when selecting a material as a cover for a solar collector. It is safe to assume that the temperatures experienced in a greenhouse will not adversely affect the material.

Choosing a Glazing   In spite of the numerous and sometimes contradictory considerations involved in a glazing choice, it turns out that the usual determining factors, and probably the most important from an owner-builder's point of view, are:

- availability
- cost
- longevity
- ease of installation

This is where we feel glass really shines. Glass is a universal product, available everywhere, and you are much more likely to be able to find inexpensive sources for glass than for any of the plastic glazings. You can usually locate cheap glass at major glass distributors — which are often branches of glass manufacturers. Just look in the yellow pages under "Glass Manufacturers." They often have sheets with slight imperfections or other manufacturing errors (such as a stained or slightly off-size batch) which are available at reasonable prices. In addition, there is an increasing tendency for glass manufacturers to produce large sheets of glass (perhaps 2.5m by 3.5m) and to cut whatever pieces are needed from them. This process results in a lot of scraps, or off-cuts, which can also be purchased cheaply.

Therefore, although glass is usually cited as being more expensive than most of the plastic glazing, because of the availability of this bargain-basement glass, it often turns out to be the best among the rigid glazing materials.

Tempered Glass   You are just as likely to find surplus or off-size tempered glass as you are surplus non-tempered glass since it is commonly used as patio-door glass and for many other applications. We recommend the use of tempered glass whenever possible. Because non-tempered glass can splinter into dangerous shards if it breaks, you should never use it as overhead glazing.

Page 245 lists the major types of glazing materials available in each of three categories (glass, rigid plastic, roll plastic) and includes a comparison of their characteristics.

Glorious Glass or "Why We Like Rigid Silicon Glazing."

1. The common greenhouse glazing materials are similarly effective in allowing light into the greenhouse and minimizing heat loss.
2. Glass does not deteriorate under ultraviolet radiation.
3. Glass can be indefinitely exposed to rain, wind and snow and maintains the same strength, thickness and shape.
4. Glass has a small expansion coefficient.
5. Glass is available everywhere.
6. Cheap sources of glass can be located in almost every populated region.
7. Cutting glass is exciting.

Designing

Site Analysis

It is important to develop a sense of where you are before you begin to build your greenhouse. By where you are we mean your latitude, the regional climate, and the climate of your immediate surroundings — the *microclimate.*

The *latitude,* as we've seen, will dictate maximum solar potential through the various seasons. Northern latitudes have relatively short winter days with the sun low in the southern sky. The height of the sun in any particular season will determine the glazing angle for optimum solar collection in that season.

The *climate* is another important factor which influences the amount of sunlight you actually receive. A greenhouse in a

Fig. 51 Climate

region which experiences frequent cloudy conditions will receive significantly less direct sunlight than one in a region of clear skies. The standard Sundance Greenhouse, for instance, is designed for northern regions with relatively clear

conditions, such as most of the Canadian Prairies. This greenhouse is visually "open" to the south, the direction of incident light most of the time. When the sky is overcast, light comes more uniformly from all areas of the sky and it may be necessary to have more of the greenhouse able to collect this light. This could mean a roof glazing or a higher south wall glazing. (In commercial tomato greenhouses it can lead to the necessity of north wall glazing.) The figures for hours of bright sunshine (pp 254-255) can help you to determine how your region compares to others in hours of bright sunshine.

Another climatic condition that will affect greenhouse design and performance is temperature, as in colder weather a greenhouse requires more heat (solar or supplemental). *Degree days* is a measure of the extent of cold temperature in a specific region. It refers to the number of degrees per day that the average temperature falls below a level of about 18°C. If the outside average temperature is 17°C for a 24-hour period, that is one degree day. If it is 16°C it is two degree days, and so on. Degree days are usually given in monthly or yearly totals and can give you an idea how much energy is required over a season or a year to keep the greenhouse at acceptable temperatures. The *design temperature* will indicate the coldest temperature that can be expected in the region for 99% of the time. The Sundance Greenhouse performs satisfactorily in northern areas with total annual degree days of over 6000C° and design temperatures of about -40°C, which

covers virtually all of the inhabited areas of the north.

If you were building a new house, although you would have no control over the regional climate, you would have some influence on the microclimate. But if you are adding a greenhouse onto an existing house, your ability to influence even the microclimate is limited.

The ideal site for an attached greenhouse has a clear southern exposure through a 180° arc, with trees and building far enough away so as never to cast a shadow on the greenhouse. In most situations,

Fig. 52   180° south sweep

particularly in an urban setting, there will be nearby buildings or trees which will shade the greenhouse for portions of the day, or even for whole seasons. There is little you can do about moving your house or other existing buildings, although you can cut or trim trees.

Other things which can be lumped into microclimate include proximity to property lines, local by-laws, site drainage, snow loads, the condition of the existing house, and local wind patterns and the sheltering effect of nearby shrubs, trees or buildings.

Southern orientation Since the sun is predominantly in the southern sky, a greenhouse must be allowed an un-shadowed view of the south throughout most of the year. To guarantee this position you will first have to know which direction is south.

There are some fairly exact methods for determining south but there are two factors which temper the necessity for absolute accuracy. One is that a deviation of up to 30° in either direction (east or west) from true south will not significantly affect greenhouse performance. If a choice is possible, an orientation to the east of south is preferable to one west of south since this will favour collection of morning sunlight, lessen afternoon overheating from the low western sun, and make use of

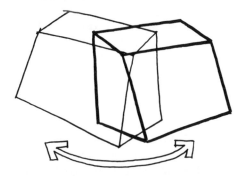

Fig. 53 A 30° deviation in either direction from true south is satisfactory

the house to shelter the greenhouse from the north, northwest, and west winds which are predominant in many regions.

The second thing that alleviates the need for exact accuracy in orientation is that, in most cases, the house is already in place. It is an easy enough process to locate the most southerly-facing wall of your house, which is where the greenhouse should go. If, in the most extreme case, a corner of your house points south, then try to place the greenhouse on the southeast face, as close to the edge as possible.

Fig. 54

You can determine south in a number of ways. If you know when solar noon is (and don't forget that your clock can be almost two hours off solar time during daylight savings periods) remember that the sun is then due south in the sky. Either make note of an object that is south of the house or, better yet, drive a stake into the ground, note where its shadow falls (in a north-south line) and drive in another stake at the end of the shadow. If you live close to the centre of a time zone (one not corrected along geographical or political boundaries) you can fairly safely assume

that noon, standard time, is close to solar noon.

Fig. 55 Finding North and South with the noon sun

Another way to determine south is to note where the sun rises and sets on a particular day. South is exactly halfway between these two points.

Fig. 56 Bisect sunrise/sunset

Most areas have a grid of major roads running either east-west or north-south. It should be easy to determine which are the north-south roads and from that to get an accurate enough idea of which direction is south. And finally, you can use a compass.

To be accurate, allow for the magnetic deviation in your area. This can be quite great in areas of northern Canada.

Shadow Analysis Most greenhouse sites experience some shading. In urban areas it is usually from nearby buildings. In rural locations, from nearby buildings, trees or hills. If you live near a dirigibledrome you may experience occasional shading from blimps in a holding pattern. Remember that the length of a shadow cast by an object varies directly with the solar altitude. At the time of year when we need every bit of light, for both photosynthesis and heat, shadows are at their longest so that objects at some distance may shade the greenhouse.

You can predict the shadows that will be cast by existing objects by using sun-path charts. Charts for various latitudes can be found on pp 240-243. Choose the one which is nearest to you in latitude and plot the silhouettes of nearby objects onto it. Wherever the silhouettes extend into the arches marking the solar path, shading

Fig. 57 Obstruction siting

will occur. You can use a compass and protractor to determine the height and location of nearby obstructions and to plot them on your chart. This procedure is explained in the Appendix.

A silhouetted sun-path chart is a useful design tool and can help you to determine how much sunlight you can expect over the year, or even on a particular day. In the case of a freestanding greenhouse it will help you decide where best to locate the greenhouse. If the silhouetted chart shows you that one location will result in extensive shading from an object to the east, for instance, then try to move the greenhouse farther west (to Vancouver perhaps). In the case of an attached greenhouse, the completed chart may encourage you to slide the greenhouse farther east or west along the house wall, if this is possible, or to cut down or trim nearby trees. (Unfortunately, it might also encourage the torching of a neighbor's garage — which can result in hard feelings, especially if his car is parked inside.)

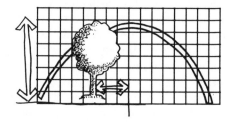

Fig. 58 Sunpath chart

One micro-climatic condition which affects the solar potential and may affect the

accuracy of your sun-path silhouettes is the slope of the site. If you are located on a south slope, for instance, you are not only sheltered from the north winds, but are more likely to have a clear southern exposure. If you are on a north slope, however, you will be more often in shadows. Also in the case of a north slope, be careful not to assume that the top of the hill, to the south, is the horizon. In other words, the hill itself has height, and hence altitude, and can not be considered to be 0°.

Heat Management

Heat management in a solar greenhouse involves temperature control and the intentional transfer of heat from one area to another. On a seasonal basis, you can think of it as being concerned with keeping temperatures up in the winter and down in the summer. On a daily basis, it involves keeping temperatures up at night and down during the day. In a freestanding greenhouse you can transfer heat to or from thermal storage, or to the outside. An attached greenhouse gives you the further option of heat exchange with the house. Other aspects of heat management include shading, ventilation, heat storage and the use of movable insulation.

Control of Heat Loss A major source of heat loss is *infiltration*. Unwanted air leaking in through cracks in structural members, around the glazing, or through door and vent seals, can be minimized by attention to tight construction during the

Fig. 59 Infiltration

building process. A vapour barrier — a polyethylene sheet installed on the inside of insulated walls or roofs — not only prevents cold outside air from getting in, but also prevents moisture from the greenhouse from seeping into the insulation and framing members. It is important that the vapour barrier be continuous; it must be free of holes and gaps, and over all the insulated areas of the greenhouse.

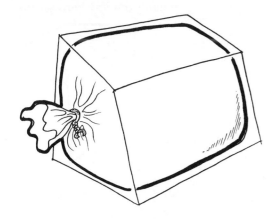

Fig. 60 Continuous vapour barrier

Proper weatherstripping on exterior doors and vents is also very important to controlling infiltration. Such openings should be built to seal properly and weatherstripping should be checked and adjusted (or replaced) seasonally. Attention to details of sealing the glazing and the unrestrained use of caulking are additional methods used to reduce infiltration.

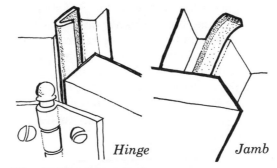

Hinge   *Jamb*

Fig. 61 Weatherstripping

Insulating all opaque surfaces to reduce the rate of conduction through the walls and roof is another means of controlling heat loss.

Shading Shading is useful for keeping summer temperatures (and daytime temperatures) down to appropriate levels. The most common way of providing shading is by designing parts of the structure itself to shade the inside of the greenhouse. Overheating can most readily occur in the hot months, when the sun is high in the sky; yet during the cold months, when the sun is low, we want as much sunlight as possible in the greenhouse. Therefore, if we install an opaque

roof which just barely shades the greenhouse from the high summer sun, it will be high enough not to interfere with the low winter sun.

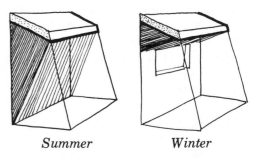

Summer   *Winter*

Fig. 62 Shading

A common approach is to try to design a roof overhang which will completely shade the south wall of the house on June 21. This helps to keep the house cool, excludes a large portion of that day's sunlight from the greenhouse to lessen overheating problems, yet allows sunlight to fall on greenhouse plants. As the winter solstice approaches, more of the house wall and more of the greenhouse are flooded with sunlight until, on December 21, the sunlight is high up on the house wall (the north wall of the greenhouse). This effect is more pronounced at northerly latitudes since the sun is quite low in the sky.

While this is a good approach to design, there are drawbacks to it. Remember that the sun does not swiftly change from a high altitude to a low one, but does so slowly, day by day, over half of the year. This means that if your greenhouse is shaded only for June 21, you will have some hot September days with sunlight pouring into the back of the greenhouse, which may result in some overheating. On the other hand, a roof or overhang which provides shading on August 30 will also provide shading on April 12. August 30 occurs at a warm time of year, when shading will be welcome in the greenhouse while on April 12 sunlight will be needed to provide heat.

Deciduous trees are sometimes recommended as a useful means of shading a greenhouse. A tree to the south of a greenhouse will retain its leaves in the summer and early fall to provide shade, and shed them for the winter and early spring, to allow sunlight to strike the greenhouse. But we don't like this idea for two reasons. In the first place, northern areas will often receive a frost in August or early September, which will cause the trees to begin to lose their leaves, even though there are some pretty warm and sunny days ahead. Secondly, even without its leaves, a deciduous tree can cause an undesirable amount of shading during the winter. For similar reasons we don't like

Fig. 63 Deciduous trees have shadows even without their leaves.

the use of vines growing on the glazing of the greenhouse or the use of whitewash on the glazing (which lowers light levels too drastically). It's also a mistake to assume that because the greenhouse is in shade, it will be cool. Heat can build up even in a shaded area if the air is not moving.

There are a couple of ways to provide seasonal or temporary shading. One is the use of adjustable overhangs on the roof, but a better option is to use exterior blinds made of wood or bamboo slats. These allow a certain amount of direct sunlight into the greenhouse (through the gaps between the slats) and can be rolled when not in use. It's a good idea to remove them during the winter months.

Fig. 64 Roll blind

Ventilation Ventilation is important not only for keeping the temperature down, but for a number of other purposes as well. Ventilation helps to control humidity, brings in fresh air (and consequently carbon dioxide) for the plants, and helps to keep the air moving in the greenhouse which, again, provides the plants with

access to fresh sources of carbon dioxide and sometimes assisting in pollination.

There are numerous configurations of vents to the outside. In every case there should be at least one low vent and one high vent. They may be placed in the kneewall, along the ridge, in the glazing itself, in the roof, or in the endwalls. Vents in the endwalls are the easiest type from a construction point of view. Since this configuration has performed satisfactorily, it is the one we recommend. We also like the idea of providing a couple of big vents rather than numerous small ones since there is that much less weatherstripping and sealing to worry about. The exterior door can be used to supplement ventilation during hot, fall days.

If the wind in your region is predominantly from one direction (from the west in most regions) you can use this fact to assist in ventilation by placing the low vent on the

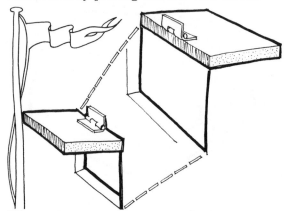

Fig. 65 Low vent down wind, high vent 25% larger

side facing the wind, and the high vent on the other end of the greenhouse. The high vent should be somewhat larger — at least 25% larger if possible.

Sizing the Vents The amount of air moving through the greenhouse vents depends on the difference in height between the vents, the difference in air temperature between the top and bottom of the greenhouse, and the size of the vents. The amount of ventilation you need for cooling will be influenced by the glazing angle, the glazing area, and the amount of thermal storage included in the greenhouse. Given the variables involved, we've found that it's difficult to recommend an exact vent size. A greater difference in height, for instance, will mean that the vents can be smaller.

We suggest that the total vent area be at least 1/6 of the total south-facing glazing area, including any roof glazing. Green-

houses with glazing angles of less than 60° may require more than this amount. If you have any doubts, it is better to err on the side of larger vents.

Exterior louvers (used to protect the vents from rain) and screens will interfere with the air flow and lessen the amount of air which can pass through the vents. Keep this in mind as you plan your vents, but, whatever the case, the vents must be screened to keep out unwanted pests.

Vent Management You must make certain to place and use your vents so that cold air does not flow directly across the plants. This is a concern particularly in the case of kneewall vents or glazing vents placed at plant level. If you do have to open an exterior vent during freezing weather, open just the top vent so that cold air coming in will have a chance to warm up a bit before it reaches the plants. During most of the cold weather, extra

heat from the greenhouse will probably be vented into the house and little exterior venting will be needed, so this problem can be avoided altogether.

Fig. 67 Use high vent in cold weather to give air a chance to warm

It is important that you be on hand to open and close the greenhouse vents as necessary. Neglecting to provide ventilation for even one sunny day can result in a temperature so high that the plants will die. There are some types of vents and vent mechanisms which are operated by heat from the sun and open the vents if you forget.

Automatic Vent Openers These contrivances consist of a liquid-filled cylinder with a piston at one end. As the air temperature increases, the liquid expands and forces the piston outward. A rod attached to the piston is connected to the vent itself and, as the piston moves, the vent opens. When the air temperature drops, the liquid contracts and the weight of the vent pushes the piston back in place, closing the vent.

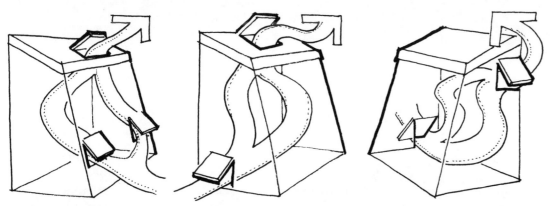

Fig. 66 Various venting vectors

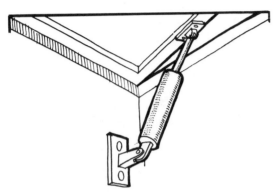

Fig. 68 A heat motor vent opener

Because these automatic openers depend on a vertical force (the weight of the vent) to close the vent, they will not completely seal a vertical endwall vent unless it is weighted to change its centre of gravity. Also, because they are powered by the hottest air, which is at the top of the greenhouse, they cannot be used directly to open a bottom vent.

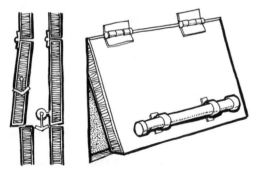

Fig. 69 Weighted vent closer

Recent tests indicate that there are a number of qualities, prices, and characteristics among the available automatic vent openers. If you are interested in one

of these devices there are factors you should consider when comparing brands:

1. How much weight will the opener lift? The vent has to be heavy enough so that it will not be blown open by gusts of wind.
2. At what temperature will it begin to open the vent?
3. How quickly does it open the vent and to what distance?
4. Is it adjustable for temperature?
5. Does it have overload springs?
6. Is it corrosion resistant? (A greenhouse is humid.)
7. If it will be in direct sunlight, is it protected from or resistant to deterioration?
8. What is the manufacturer's warranty?

Factors Influencing Ventilation

Factors Determining Air Movement Through Vents

1. difference in height between the vents (A − B)
2. difference in air temperature between vent levels ($T_A - T_B$)
3. size of the vents

Factors Influencing Air Temperature in the Greenhouse

1. glazing angle
2. glazing area
3. amount of thermal storage

Fig. 70

*lower sloped glazing *increased glazing area *reduced thermal storage	>	higher air temperatures	>	increased need for ventilation	>	*larger vents *greater difference in height (A − B)

Solar Chimneys Another innovation in greenhouse ventilation is solar chimneys. These devices are tall, narrow, chimney-like boxes with glazing on one or two sides, which use solar heat to induce greenhouse ventilation. Sunlight striking the box warms up the air inside it. Since warming makes the air more buoyant, it rises to escape out the top of the chimney, drawing air through the greenhouse. An automatic vent opener is usually used on a vent at the top of the chimney to open it at a certain temperature. However, a manual vent would work just as well since the value of the solar chimney is not so much automation of the ventilation as governing the ventilation. The neat trick is that the brighter the sunlight, the hotter the air in the solar chimney gets and the faster it rises, thereby increasing ventilation. More sun equals more heat equals more ventilation.

Fig. 71 Solar chimney — more sun, more draw!

In cases where you have not provided sufficient ventilation and the greenhouse is

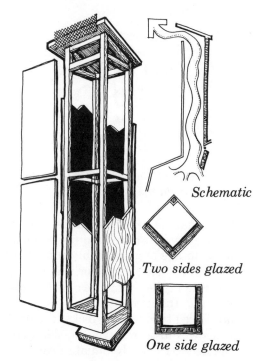

Schematic

Two sides glazed

One side glazed

Fig. 72 Solar chimney — Exploded view

overheating, you may want to consider installing a small electric fan, which can be fitted with a thermostatic control, to increase air flow through the greenhouse.

Air Exchange with the House As we have noted, during the winter months it is most likely that any venting from the greenhouse will be into the house. In addition, warm air can be provided from the house at night to maintain greenhouse temperatures. In addition to heat, the greenhouse can provide fresh, oxygen-rich air and extra humidity which, in most areas, will be welcome in the house during the winter months.

The vents between the house and the greenhouse do not have to be very large — no more than 1/10 of the greenhouse floor area. The best option is to use existing vents or windows in the house wall and you should, in fact, try to place your greenhouse so that it will include such features. A couple of small windows or even a single door are usually satisfactory. If there are no existing openings in the wall, put in a couple of small vents, one high and one low. Make sure that they are insulated and fitted with good seals, especially if you let the greenhouse freeze for a period in the winter.

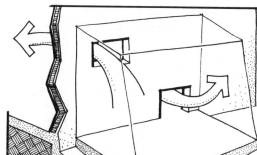

Fig. 73 High and low vents to house

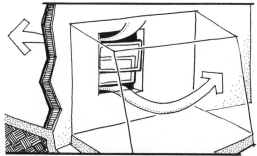

Fig. 74 Casement windows as vents

Fig. 75 Door vent to house

We recommended three methods of heat exchange with the house, the choice of which depends on the size of your greenhouse:
- Less than 15 m² of floor area: The great majority of attached home greenhouses fall into this category. Existing doors or windows or a couple of vents are generally satisfactory for this size of greenhouse.

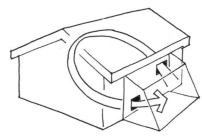

Fig. 76 Less than 15m² — natural ventilation

- 15 m² to 35 m² of floor area: For this size, a return air duct should connect the greenhouse to the house furnace so that excess heat from the greenhouse can be more uniformly distributed to all areas of the house. The installation of a damper control in the duct will be necessary as well.

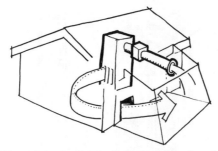

Fig. 77 15m²-35m² — distribution by furnace and damper

- More than 35 m² of floor area: Such a large greenhouse will require a separate heat storage area, probably consisting of a rock bed beneath a floor slab of concrete in the living area of the house. Air from the greenhouse will be fan-forced through the rocks; the heated rocks will in turn warm the slab floor; the floor will slowly radiate heat into the living area during the night.

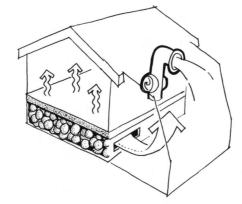

Fig. 78 Over 35m² — forced air into rock storage

Heat Storage

Materials Most materials will absorb some sunlight in the form of heat. Those which can absorb and store a significant amount of heat can be used for thermal storage in the greenhouse which is important for two reasons:
1. Thermal storage keeps the greenhouse warmer at night.
2. Thermal storage keeps the greenhouse cooler during the day.

Materials used for thermal storage will absorb heat when the sun is shining — while the greenhouse is heating — and release heat at night or during cloudy periods. Because they can absorb a great deal of heat, they can also prevent the greenhouse air from overheating during the day. The function of thermal storage, therefore, is to reduce the daily temperature swings in the greenhouse.

The materials usually used for heat storage in greenhouses are water, stones or rocks, concrete, and bricks. Water can hold more heat per volume than any other of the common materials, and is in fact the standard by which they are measured.

Sizing For a solar greenhouse we feel that the more thermal storage the better. Of course, this has to be compromised with the need for space in which to grow plants. We recommend that the heat storage in a greenhouse be equivalent to 75*l* to 125*l* of water for every square metre of south-facing glazing area, including any roof glazing. (This amount equals 1.5 - 2.5

Fig. 79 Comparative heat storage volumes

Imperial gallons per square foot or 1.8 - 3.0 U.S. gallons per square foot). 75l/m² is a minimum figure. Greenhouses with reflective roof flaps should tend toward the higher end of this recommendation.

To take a simple example, if the greenhouse has 10m² of glazing area (about 100ft²) you must provide heat storage equal to that of 750l to 1250l of water (about 200-325 U.S. gallons). The lower figure will result in greater temperature swings, and the higher figure, in decreased temperature swings. The heat storage can be in the form of water, masonry, or some combination of both. For instance, 1250l of water represents ten boxes 0.5m on a side (about 20in).

Fig. 80 1250 l of H₂O

No matter what form the heat storage takes, it is more useful if it has a large surface area for its volume. To understand why, let's distinguish a couple of different levels of heat storage. *Primary* heat storage consists of materials within the greenhouse itself which act to minimize diurnal temperature swings. That is, they absorb heat during the day and release it at night. *Secondary* heat storage reserves the heat for longer periods in order to be able to provide it when needed, perhaps five to ten days later.

In a home greenhouse, there is limited space available for heat storage materials. We feel that what room there is should be devoted to levelling the daily temperature swings and providing heat during cool spring and fall nights especially in northern locations. In the case of an attached greenhouse, long term heat storage can, in a sense, be provided by the house.

To moderate day-to-day temperature fluctuations, the heat storage must be able to absorb and radiate heat rapidly. A larger surface area for a given volume will provide more space for absorption and radiation. 200-litre oil drums (the ubiquitous 50-gallon drum) have been commonly used in solar greenhouse applications, but they provide only a relatively small surface area for their volume and would be better used, if space allows, for secondary storage. Much better for primary storage are tall, narrow, metal containers. 5-gallon metal buckets stacked and painted a dark colour make good water containers. Buckets or other containers made of thick plastics are not as good as metal at transferring heat. Long term

Fig. 81 Stacking buckets

storage of water in a metal container will require the addition of a rust inhibitor.

Whatever type of container you use, it will be more effective as a heat absorber if it is black, because black, as we have seen, indicates the total absorption of light. However, the use of black containers means that no light will be reflected off them, back onto the plant canopy. The greater the extent that storage containers cover the north wall, the more pronounced this effect will be. To ensure that the plants receive some light reflection from the north wall, we suggest that you paint your heat storage containers a colour other than black. A flat red would be a good choice as the colour indicates that the surfaces are reflecting red light back onto the plant canopy, and we have seen that plants make good use of the red portion of the visible light spectrum. Whatever you do, don't use green. You'll understand why if you stop to think about it.

One of the best solutions for a home greenhouse, and one which provides lots of surface area and avoids the problems of poor heat transfer in plastic containers and rusting in metal containers, is to use tall, narrow metal cylinders. You can buy galvanized air-conditioning ducts, which are sold by the foot or metre, or you can have a local sheet metal shop make up some stovepipe-like cylinders. The cylinders or ducts should be of 26-gauge metal and about 250mm (10in) in diameter. Set them upright in the greenhouse in forms of concrete to make bottoms and paint them flat red or blue. Inside of the ducts, place 6-mil polyethylene tubes, made for the packaging industry. The polyethylene bags hold the water and the round metal cylinders provide the support and surface area.

Surface Area and Volume

A given volume of water has the capacity to hold a certain amount of heat, no matter what shape the container. One litre of water in the shape of a cube will hold as much heat as one litre of water in the shape of a tall, narrow cylinder. However, the container which holds the water in a shape that exposes more surface area to the surrounding air (the tall cylinder in this example) will provide a greater opportunity for heat collection from the surrounding air during the day and for radiation at night. This results in more rapid heat transfer which will be more useful in preventing overheating in the daytime and freezing at night.

Here is a comparison of the surface area of a 200-litre metal oil drum and two tall cylinders. The volume of water in one oil drum equals the combined volume of water

Fig. 82   220 litres of water stored in two modes

in the two cylinders. However, the surface area of the drum (the top and sides) is only about half that of the combined cylinders, 1.85m² for the drum and 3.60m² for the cylinders.

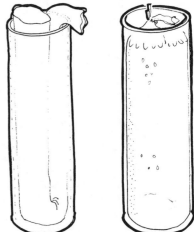

Fig. 83 Bag doubled over in duct as water storage

Northern Options   So much for our recommendations. Now let's look at the realities of heat storage in a northern greenhouse. As the chart on p. 249 of the Appendix shows, it is unlikely that you will have the space or the money to provide the recommended amount of storage materials in the form of masonry. You are going to have to use significant quantities of water. If you live in an area where the greenhouse is not going to freeze, or if you are going to keep the greenhouse heated during the winter months, then your worries are over — simply supply water storage as we have recommended. However, if the greenhouse is not going to be in use during the coldest

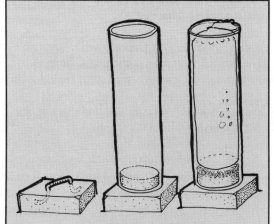

Fig. 84 Method for permanent installation of a stabilized water heat storage (especially advisable in seismic areas)

1. Cast rebar loop into floor slab.
2. Pour concrete plug at bottom of duct tube. (Make sure rebar is buried and surface is smooth. Use flashlight and tamper pole.)
3. Pad bottom with a soft, non-decomposing substance and fill double water bag.

months and is going to be allowed to freeze, the water storage inside of it is also going to freeze, But, not to worry. Here are the options for this case:

Option 1. Use only masonry storage materials and use as much as you can afford or fit in. This alternative will result in a lower heat-storage capacity than if you had used water. But, contrary to our recommendations, experience tells us that you will still end up with a reasonably good greenhouse. You may want to provide larger vents to avoid daytime overheating, which means you are more likely to have to dump heat that will be required to get the greenhouse through the cold night.

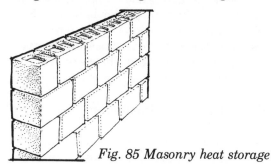

Fig. 85 Masonry heat storage

Option 2. Use water in the greenhouse as we recommend, but empty or drain the containers in the winter. Before you elect this option, stop to think about how much work this can be. The metal cylinders we have recommended have no provision for drainage and providing a tap at the bottom would be a very difficult task. The only way to remove water from them is to siphon it. It may seem easier to unstack 5-gallon buckets, dump them, then stack

and fill them again in the spring, but remember that to meet our recommendations 45-50 buckets will be required. That's a lot of buckets to move. If you have a floor drain in the greenhouse connected to a storm sewer (an unlikely occurrence in a greenhouse — see CONSTRUCTION p. 117), then you can drain or siphon the water right into it. If not, you will have to haul the water outdoors or into the house.

Fig. 86 Empty water containers to avoid freezing

Option 3. Store the water in flexible containers which will expand as the water freezes, without bursting. You might be able to use recycled or purchased 4-litre (1-gallon) plastic jugs such as those that bleach, windshield-washer fluid, or engine-block antifreeze come in. In a scientific test under carefully controlled conditions we were able to determine that such containers, when filled with water just short of maximum capacity, were able to withstand freezing and thawing without leaking and without apparent damage. (We filled a couple of jugs with water and put them outside, next to the house, during the winter). Since they do tend to bulge when frozen, they will have to be held in place by some sort of rack so that a stack of them will not fall over. (The rack will also have to be built to cause minimal shading). We have no idea how long these containers will last under greenhouse conditions.

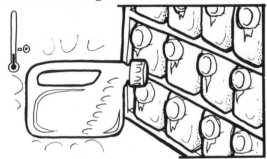

Fig. 87 Frozen plastic containers in a rack

Option 4 Use water in the greenhouse as we recommend and protect it from freezing by the addition of antifreeze. Three common substances which are added to water to prevent it from freezing are calcium chloride, methanol (methyl alcohol), and ethylene glycol. Calcium chloride is used in liquid-filled tractor tires

Antifreeze Solutions

The number of degrees the common antifreeze solutions will depress the freezing point of water are listed in the Appendix (p. 249). Assuming a greenhouse is in an extreme climate (where we want to protect the water down to −35°C) which will require 1000 *l* of water to meet our heat storage recommendation, we have indicated a typical quantity and cost of the antifreeze material.

Fig. 88 Add antifreeze

to prevent the water used in the tires from freezing. Methanol is used as gas-line antifreeze and as fondue fuel. Ethylene glycol is one of the common engine-block antifreeze solutions. Calcium chloride will corrode metal and it should not be used in a container where the water is in direct contact with metal. However, in our system the polyethylene tubes will protect the metal cylinders from the corrosive effects of water and calcium chloride.

Movable Glazing Insulation

In a well constructed greenhouse, the greatest single area of heat loss is through the glazing. Most of this loss occurs at night or whenever there is little or no sunlight. During these periods, when the plants cannot benefit from the heat and light from the sun, a significant amount of heat loss can be prevented by using some sort of a movable insulating shutter to cover the glazed areas of the greenhouse.

For all but the most casual use, we feel that a movable insulation system is a must for cold-climate greenhouse. It can help to

reduce temperature swings, relieving the strain on plants; extend the growing season at each end of summer; and, if the greenhouse uses supplemental heat, reduce fuel bills significantly. Numerous studies at various institutions and in commercial greenhouse have shown that fuel savings of up to 60% can be expected from the use

An example of the effect of movable insulation on the heat gain through south-facing glazing

To demonstrate the importance of movable insulation in northern climates, here is a comparison of the net heat gain (solar gain minus heat losses) which can be expected through a south-facing window during an average winter in Saskatoon.

Net Heat Gain Through Vertical South Window (MJ/m²)
Saskatoon
Average Year
November 1 to February 28

double glazed (12mm air space)	−42
triple glazed (12mm air space)	+277
quadruple glazed (12mm air space)	+321
double glazed + night insulation (RSI-1.8) (R-10)	+687

Notes: a) 1 Mj/m² = 88.2 BTU/ft²
b) Saskatoon: latitude 52°N, 6077 C degree days, 2403 hours bright sunshine

of night-time glazing insulation. Of course, when deciding on a movable insulation system, you have to be aware of the energy and dollar costs of the system and make sure that the expected fuel savings, or increased production, more than offsets them. Careful design and choice of materials can make certain that it does.

Unfortunately, all of the common movable insulation systems that we have considered have drawbacks in cost, in use, or both. We have developed a system which we feel is the most useful and we report on it in detail. But first, let's look at the types of shutter systems and examine their advantages and disadvantages.

Exterior Insulation Exterior insulations, as the name implies, are all located outside of the greenhouse. The main advantage of them is that the shutters do not get in the way of the plants and do not take up valuable greenhouse space. A disadvantage is that the insulation is exposed to wind, rain, snow, and sunlight, which will definitely limit its life. Another problem, which occurs in cold climates, is snow and ice build-up either on the shutters or along the edges of the glazing. This eliminates the possibility of a tight seal.

We've seen that heat is lost from a greenhouse when warm air rises next to the glazing and heat energy is transferred through the glazing to the outside air. No matter what type of shutters are used, it is important that they be arranged so that,

when closed, convection currents are not able to carry greenhouse heat away. Even shutters with a high insulating value will not be very effective if they do not seal. For shutters, a good edge-seal or a tight fit against the glass is important to eliminate the possibility of convection currents. A further problem with exterior shutters is a human one. Greenhouse users are often reluctant to go outside in cold weather to put shutters in place at night and remove them in the morning.

Fig. 89 Exterior insulation must be well sealed

Types of exterior shutters Exterior shutters are most often made from rigid insulation, and usually have at least one reflecting surface to redirect radiation back

Fig. 90 Detachable exterior shutters

into the greenhouse when they are closed. They can be as simple as detachable units which are pushed in place at night, fitting snugly against the glazing materials, and which are physically removed during the day.

Another broad category is hinged exterior shutters. These can be hinged either at the top, bottom, or sides. A bottom pivot allows the shutter to drop down to be used as a reflector during the day, to direct extra sunlight into the greenhouse. However, in

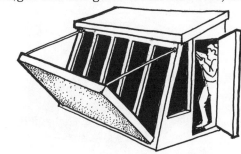

Fig. 91 Bottom hinge exterior shutter

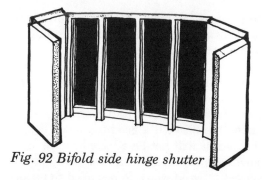

Fig. 92 Bifold side hinge shutter

cold climates this is disadvantageous since snow not only provides an excellent reflecting surface, but tends to get in the way of shutters which swing down. A better option is a top hinge, which folds up onto an insulated roof, or side hinges which allow the shutters to swing completely out of the way during daylight hours.

A hinged roof flap, developed by Solar Applications and Research in Vancouver, serves a dual purpose, as an insulating shutter for night-time use and as a reflector during the day. We think this is a wonderful option for mild, cloudy climates.

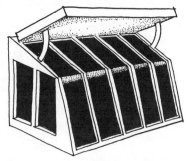

Fig. 93 Hinged roof reflector/insulation flap

A final, less common, exterior option is the use of insulating blankets, which roll up or down when not in use.

Interior Insulation Interior shutters are out of the weather and are shielded from destructive ultraviolet radiation by the glazing material. If a good edge-seal is achieved, it will not be affected by ice or snow. Because interior shutters are not exposed to wind, they do not need to be as durable as exterior shutters, but they must be protected from, or resistant to, the high humidity levels found in a greenhouse. An insulating material which gets saturated loses its insulating value.

Movable interior insulation can be awkward and cumbersome and take up space better used by growing plants. Where to store shutters or curtains during the day is a dilemma. It is also, more often than not, difficult to maintain a good edge-seal with movable interior insulation — particularly true in the case of an angled south wall — and it is very difficult to apply to roof glazing.

Another problem associated with interior insulation is glazing condensation. When even a tight-fitting interior shutter is removed in the morning, the warm, humid greenhouse air strikes the glazing, which is colder, since it has been insulated from the greenhouse during the night, and condensation occurs. In cold-climate greenhouses this condensation can result in a significant amount of ice forming on the interior glazing surface, This ice takes some time to melt off. This problem can be somewhat alleviated by waiting until the sun has warmed the glazing before the shutters are removed, but interior shutters should not be left in place on glass glazing in hot sunny weather since heat can build up unevenly across the glazing and result in thermal stress which may cause the glass to break.

Types of interior shutters Interior shutters can be made using rigid insulation. However, if they are hinged at the top or sides, they get in the way of the plants.

The two best ways we've seen to use rigid insulation for interior shutters are, first, as pop-in shutters (particularly for vertical and endwall glazing) which are removed to the house during the day for storage and, second, as a bifold shutter, hinged at the top, which stores against the ceiling.

Fig. 94 Pop-in shutter (interior)

Fig. 95 Horizontal bifold interior shutter

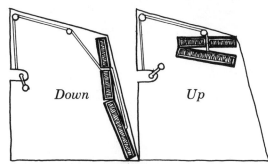

Fig. 96 Horizontal bifold interior shutter

Another type of interior shutter made from rigid insulation is similar to the hinged exterior roof flap described previously. Developed by Reed Maes in Michigan, it consists of a pivoted insulating flap which is above head level but still inside the glazing. This shutter eliminates the problems associated with exposure to weather and allows the flap to be used as a reflector as well. It seems most suited to freestanding greenhouses.

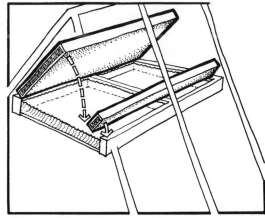

Fig. 97 Reed Maes flap (interior, overhead water storage)

Various types of pull-down shades are commercially available. The most promising of these systems consists of stiff yet flexible shutters that slide up for storage on runners which also provide a good seal. The major drawback is cost.

Insulating curtains and blankets are also used in greenhouses to inhibit night-time heat loss. These covers either pull up or off to the side for storage. We think they are awkward and we worry about the edge seal. In commercial greenhouses, overhead blankets are also used.

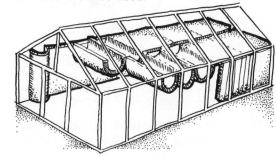

Fig. 98 Interior insulating curtains

Inter-glazing Insulation By now you realize that we are not satisfied with any of the common shuttering systems we've described. To eliminate many of the problems, we recommend that you use an in-between-the-glazing, movable insulation, which we call inter-glazing insulation. Here are the advantages of this system as we see it:

- The insulation does not get in the way of the plants.
- It stores out of the way and out of sight.
- It is not exposed to the weather.

- It is protected from the moisture in the greenhouse so that fibreglass insulation, which is much cheaper than rigid insulation or special insulating blankets, can be used.
- Convection heat loss problems are avoided since the insulation lays against the inner layer of glazing.
- Because the inner layer of glazing is on the inside of the insulation, the glazing stays warm so that morning condensation problems are eliminated.

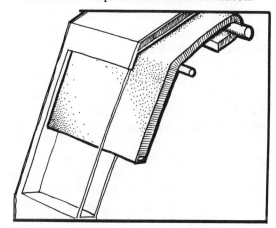

Fig. 99 Batt insulation between glazing

Because this system allows you to use fibreglass insulation, the material costs for inter-glazing shutters are about the cheapest of any type of movable insulation. Materials other than fibreglass can be used as the insulation and we have experimented with dacron sewn into woven polyethylene so that it looks like a very long sleeping bag.

The drawbacks to this system are that the construction details are a bit more complicated (although we give you the easy-to-follow instructions) and we are not certain what the lifetime of fibreglass insulation so used will be.

The use of fibreglass inter-glazing insulation for greenhouses was developed at the University of Saskatchewan and we report on their work in the SURVEY section. It was adapted for use in attached greenhouses by Peter Amerongen, our carpenter. The system is very simple in the telling: The two layers of glazing on the south wall are spaced about 125mm (5in.) apart and at night a fibreglass batt about 65mm (2.5in.) thick is raised or lowered into this space. The fibreglass can be stored at the bottom (as in the University of Saskatchewan examples) or at the top, above a false ceiling (as in our basic recommendation). It is very important that the glazing be at an angle of at least 10° from vertical. In our example we use an angle of 75°, which is 15° from vertical. This allows the fibreglass to lay against the inner layer of glazing when it is in use, and prevents convection heat loss. For this reason it cannot be used in conjunction with vertical glazing, and we therefore recommend the use of pop-in shutters made of rigid insulation for any endwall glazing.

Whichever option you choose, we feel that it is important to use some kind of movable insulation in your greenhouse. Even a simple curtain with one or two reflective layers is surprisingly effective. Although we think that inter-glazing shutters are the best overall choice, perhaps the simplest system, and one that can be easily used in existing greenhouses, is to use pop-in shutters which fit snugly against the inside of the glazing, and store somewhere in the house when not in use.

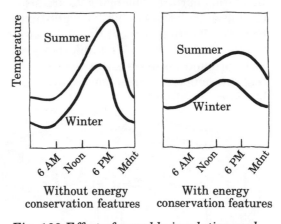

Fig. 100 Effect of movable insulation and thermal storage on greenhouse temperature

Daily Greenhouse Performance

The performance table and the graph in this section are the result of a computer model of a Sundance greenhouse. The greenhouse was assumed to be located in Edmonton, Alberta in the clear, cold prairie climate. It has a south wall angle of 60°, 8.3m² (89 ft²) of south-facing glazing, and 830 litres of water for thermal storage (equivalent to 100l/m² or 2 gal/ft² of glazing). The greenhouse is double-glazed with glass and uses movable glazing insulation at night.

The table shows the results we would obtain on a clear and moderate January day with outside air temperatures ranging from −18°C to −3°C. We can see how much heat will flow to the house for each hour of the day, as well as the hourly fluctuation in temperature in the outside air, in the greenhouse air, and in the water storage. The particular day detailed in the table is

the second of a three day period.

The hourly fluctuations in the greenhouse air temperature and the water storage temperature are plotted on the Day #2 graph. During the daylight hours, the temperatures of both the air and the water rise, but the air temperature rises more rapidly. As the sun sets, the greenhouse air cools more rapidly than the water. However, we can see the value of heat storage as, at about the 16 hour mark, the drop in the air temperature is halted and the air temperature curve becomes parallel to the water temperature as the water gives up some of its heat to the greenhouse air.

The combined graph below shows the three days in succession and further illustrates the moderating effect of heat storage.

Fig. 101 1 = Without Heat Storage
    2 = With Heat Storage

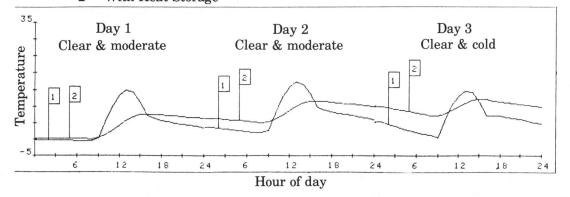

Hour of day

Hourly Greenhouse Energy Summary - Day #2: Clear & Moderate

Hour of Day	Heat Flow Greenhouse to House KJ	Temperature in °C		
		Outside Air	Green-house Air	Water Storage
1 (Midnight to 1:00am)	1199	−15.0	3.5	6.3
2	1188	−15.0	3.3	6.1
3	1236	−16.0	3.1	6.0
4	1224	−16.0	2.9	5.8
5	1272	−17.0	2.6	5.6
6	1259	−17.0	2.4	5.4
7	1306	−18.0	2.2	5.2
8	1293	−18.0	2.0	5.0
9	1079	−14.0	2.7	5.2
10	1140	−10.0	7.6	6.0
11	1179	−6.0	12.2	7.1
12	1267	−4.0	15.6	8.5
13 (Noon to 1:00pm)	1308	−3.0	17.2	9.9
14	1327	−4.0	16.5	11.0
15	1148	−4.0	13.7	11.5
16	1007	−6.0	9.5	11.5
17	1090	−8.0	8.8	11.4
18	1122	−9.0	8.3	11.2
19	1160	−10.0	7.9	11.0
20	1201	−11.0	7.5	10.8
21	1242	−12.0	7.2	10.6
22	1283	−13.0	6.8	10.3
23	1324	−14.0	6.4	10.1
24	1365	−15.0	6.1	9.9

EFFECT OF GLAZING OPTIONS
Edmonton, Alberta; January;
60° South Wall Tilt; 8.3 m² Glazing Area;

Double Glazed, No Movable Insulation

Day	Average Greenhouse Air Temperature in °C	Heat Flow (MJ/day) House to Greenhouse	Heat Flow (MJ/day) Greenhouse to House	Net Heat Gain (MJ/day)
#1-Cloudy & Moderate (-11.5°C)	-0.6	40.8	16.9	-23.9
#2-Clear & Moderate (-11.5°C)	3.6	25.0	23.5	- 1.5
#3-Clear & Moderate (-11.5°C)	5.2	3.2	25.9	22.7
#4-Clear & Cold (-19.2°C)	3.4	15.1	35.1	20.0
#5-Cloudy & Cold (-19.2°C)	-0.9	53.0	28.4	-24.6
#6-Cloudy & Moderate (-11.5°C)	-0.5	37.0	17.0	-20.0
Total Six Day Net Heat Gain				**-27.3 MJ**

Triple Glazed, No Movable Insulation

Day	Average Greenhouse Air Temperature in °C	Heat Flow (MJ/day) House to Greenhouse	Heat Flow (MJ/day) Greenhouse to House	Net Heat Gain (MJ/day)
#1-Cloudy & Moderate (-11.5°C)	-0.5	28.9	17.2	-11.7
#2-Clear & Moderate (-11.5°C)	3.6	18.8	23.4	4.6
#3-Clear & Moderate (-11.5°C)	6.0	0.7	25.9	25.2
#4-Clear & Cold (-19.2°C)	3.6	9.0	35.3	26.3
#5-Cloudy & Cold (-19.2°C)	-1.2	36.4	28.9	- 7.5
#6-Cloudy & Moderate (-11.5°C)	-0.3	25.3	17.4	- 7.9
Total Six Day Net Heat Gain				**29.0 MJ**

Double Glazed, Movable Insulation

Day	Average Greenhouse Air Temperature in °C	Heat Flow (MJ/day) House to Greenhouse	Heat Flow (MJ/day) Greenhouse to House	Net Heat Gain (MJ/day)
#1-Cloudy & Moderate (-11.5°C)	0.0	13.7	17.8	4.1
#2-Clear & Moderate (-11.5°C)	4.9	8.6	25.1	16.5
#3-Clear & Moderate (-11.5°C)	7.3	0.0	29.2	29.2
#4-Clear & Cold (-19.2°C)	7.9	0.0	39.4	39.4
#5-Cloudy & Cold (-19.2°C)	1.1	7.1	31.5	24.4
#6-Cloudy & Moderate (-11.5°C)	0.5	4.3	18.7	14.4
Total Six Day Net Heat Gain				**128.0 MJ**

Effect of Glazing Options

These three tables show the net heat gain in a Sundance greenhouse if it is (1) double glazed and no movable insulation is used at night, (2) triple glazed and no movable insulation is used, or (3) double glazed and movable insulation is used. The example greenhouse, located in Edmonton, Alberta, has a 60° south-wall angle, 8.3m² (89ft²) of south-facing glazing, and 100l of water thermal storage per square metre of glazing (2 gal/ft²).

The tables show the total net heat gain for six consecutive days in January. Double glazing used with the movable night time insulation again proves to be the best option, registering a significant net heat gain even on winter days.

Heat Storage Capacity

We recommend that you provide heat storage in your greenhouse equivalent to the heat storage capability of 75*l* to 125*l* of water for every square metre of south-facing glazing area, including roof glazing. Since 1 litre = 0.001 m³, this recommended amount is equivalent to 0.075m³ to 0.125m³ of water for every square metre of glazing. Our medium recommendation of 100*l* can be thought of as one cubic metre of water for every ten square metres of glazing.

These recommendations assume that the sun is shining directly on the storage materials. If the materials are in a shaded area of the greenhouse, they can provide only about 25% of the intended effectiveness and your figures must be adjusted accordingly.

The heat storage can be in the form of water or masonry. Thick masonry elements can usefully store heat in only their first 100mm (4in) of thickness. Therefore, in order to determine the useful heat storage volume of a masonry wall in cubic metres, for instance, compute its surface area (height x width) and divide by 10. (Since 100mm equals one tenth of a metre, h x w/10 will give you the useful heat storage volume in cubic metres. To determine cubic feet of heat storage, divide the surface area [in square feet] by 3.)

Stones, concrete, and brick can hold less heat per volume than can water. To obtain the water equivalent of a given volume of masonry, use the following figures:

To Determine Equivalent Water Volume:

Multiply	by
Stone volume	0.385
Concrete volume	0.515
Mortared brick volume	0.430
Loose brick volume	0.385

Example Let's assume we're working on a greenhouse with a large concrete-filled, cement-block north wall which has 10m² of south-facing glazing. From our recommendations it is clear that this greenhouse will require .75m³ to 1.25m³ of water equivalent heat storage. Since more is better, we will choose the latter figure. Let's determine how much of this heat storage the concrete wall will provide and how much extra water will be needed to reach the recommended amount.

This is a big wall, 3.7m x 2.4m with a surface area of 8.88m². Since we can count on only the first 100mm of depth for heat storage, the total useful heat storage volume is

$$8.88/10 = 0.89 \text{ m}^3$$

To determine the water equivalent of this volume of concrete:

$$0.89\text{m}^3 \times 0.515 = 0.46\text{m}^3 \text{ of water equivalent}$$

Therefore:

   1.25m³ recommended water equivalent heat storage
 − 0.46m³ water equivalent in concrete
   0.79m³ extra water storage to be provided

Since one cubic metre equals 1000*l*, this means about 800*l* of water must be stored in the greenhouse, in addition to the concrete wall. (Remember that if the containers which hold the water are placed in front of the concrete wall so that they shade it, the concrete will only be 25% as effective as heat storage.) The cylindrical ducts previously described hold about 50*l* per metre of height. If these are used you would need about 16m of total height, or, for instance, seven cylinders each about 2.3m tall. (If we had chosen the lower end of our recommendation, 75*l*/m², we would need only about three such cylinders.)

What this example shows us is that, even with a modest glazing size, a large amount of masonry can supply only a relatively small part of the required heat storage (in this case 35% to 50%). Smaller amounts of masonry will supply even less. In fact, it is not worth doing the water equivalent calculations unless your greenhouse contains a large masonry element, such as the concrete wall described above.

Another rule of thumb If the greenhouse contains some areas of masonry such as rocks beneath a deep soil bed, an exposed concrete floor, or concrete planters,

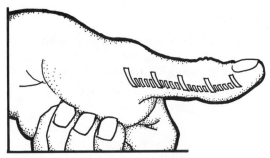

Fig. 102 A rule of thumb

provide at least 75*l* to 100*l* of water per square metre of glazing area. If the greenhouse contains no such elements, or if it makes use of a reflective flap, provide 100*l*/m² to 125 *l*/m².

Developing A Shape

A Quick Revision We are now at the stage of actually designing the greenhouse. Let's take a moment to review all the considerations. We will have to take into account in our design the things we have learned about:
- *Heat Management:*
  — maximizing heat gain during the heating season
  — minimizing heat loss during the heating season
  — maintaining sufficiently cool temperatures during the summer
- *Light Management:*
  — maximizing sunlight in the greenhouse, which is used for heating purposes and by the plants for photosynthesis

- *Plant Needs:*
  — temperature
  — carbon dioxide
  — humidity
  — water
  — nutrients
- *Human Needs:*
  — intended use of the greenhouse
- *The Sun Path:*
  — the exposure to the sun
- *The Regional Climate:*
  — cloud cover
  — temperature
- *The Micro-Climate:*
  — wind patterns, etc.
- *The Existing House:*
  — size, orientation, shape, features

We considered all these points when we were developing the design for the Sundance Greenhouse and here are some of the things we knew we wanted:
- suitability for high latitude, and cold climates (Edmonton is at latitude 53°N, has about 56000 C degree days, a design temperature of -34°C, and relatively sunny conditions
- attachment to the house for easy access, maintenance and heat transfer
- a plant growing area using deep soil beds
- a small sitting area
- double-glass glazing
- movable inter-glazing insulation
- as much heat storage as possible
With these basic requirements in mind, we began to develop a shape.

The South Wall The long wall of the greenhouse, which contains the most glazing and is the main collection surface, should face as close to south as possible. As we've seen, the position is already determined in the case of a greenhouse to be attached to an existing house, but the angle of the glazing in the south wall is a factor over which we do have control. The optimum transmission of available solar energy is achieved in clear weather if the glazing is perpendicular to the incoming sunlight. This can be determined for any particular time of the year by consulting the sun-path chart for your latitude to determine the solar altitude at that time. Subtracting the solar altitude from 90° will yield the optimum glazing angle (90° — solar altitude = optimum glazing angle). However, keep in mind that the drop off in transmission due to the angle of incidence is relatively small (just over 3%) up to an angle of incidence of 15° (below). This

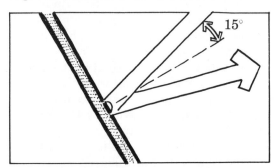

Fig. 103 Angle of incidence =15°

fact provides some latitude in the glazing angle. We considered a number of possibilities:

Vertical glazing
- Heavy glazing, such as glass, can be accommodated without having to use extremely heavy lumber as glazing members, which would more greatly shade the greenhouse.
- Collecting low-altitude sunlight and sunlight reflected off snow can be done reasonably well.
- Lots of head room is provided, behind the glazing, in the greenhouse interior.
- Much of the higher-altitude sunlight is reflected, meaning that, if used in combination with a solid roof, there will be limited light in the greenhouse interior from late spring until early fall. But this circumstance will also tend to minimize overheating.
- Fibreglass inter-glazing insulation cannot be accommodated.
- This shape is easy to build.

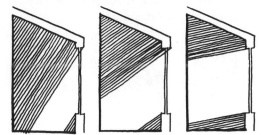

   June 21   March/Sept. 21   Dec. 21
Fig. 104 Vertical glazing and shading

Low-angle glazing — aimed at the summer sun
- Heavier framing members and tempered glass or plastic glazing materials are required.
- The summer sun is readily admitted which can lead to overheating.
- Head room is limited behind the glazing.
- The amount of winter sunlight collected is limited, particularly at higher latitudes, and benefits from snow reflection cannot be taken advantage of.

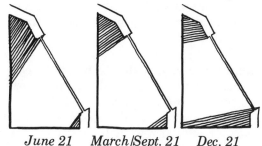

   June 21   March/Sept. 21   Dec. 21
Fig. 105 Low angle glazing

Steep-angle glazing — aimed at the winter sun
- Collection of winter sunlight is good.
- Benefits from snow reflection can be received.
- Some summer sunlight is allowed to penetrate toward the back of the greenhouse, yet overheating tends to be minimized.
- Inter-glazing insulation.
- Lots of headroom is provided.

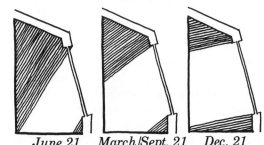

   June 21   March/Sept. 21   Dec. 21
Fig. 106 High angle glazing

On the basis of the above comparison, we decided to adopt a steep angle, approximately perpendicular to the December 21st sun. (While noon on December 21 is not a particularly good time for growing plants, you can see by consulting the sun-path chart that most of the winter sun is within 15° of being perpendicular to such a south-wall angle.) This turns out to be the latitude plus twenty degrees: (Latitude° + 20° = recommended south wall angle). In Edmonton, for example, this angle is 53° + 20°, or 73°. We, in fact, chose 75° and we recommend that, no matter what your latitude, the south-wall angle be no greater than 75°, since a certain amount of tilt is needed to make the inter-glazing insulation lay against the interior glazing layer to prevent convection heat loss. Because of this need and because we have shown that 15° variation in the south-wall angle will not significantly affect performance, a greenhouse anywhere in the regions we are addressing ourselves to (latitude 40°N to about 65°N) should have a south-wall angle of between 60° and 75°.
Recommended south wall angle: 60° to 75°

Kneewall   Another possible south-wall feature we had to consider was a kneewall, for which there are four options:
1. a vertical frame kneewall built on top of a concrete foundation wall
2. a high concrete-block foundation wall built on top of footing
3. angled, glazed south wall running up from a foundation wall.

4. an angled south wall with a bottom portion opaque and insulated

Fig. 107

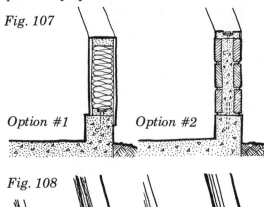

Option #1   Option #2

Fig. 108

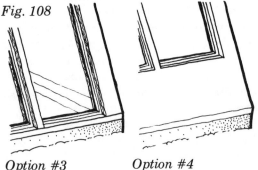

Option #3   Option #4

We were concerned about the structural instability of a vertical kneewall built on top of the foundation wall — unless the roof and south wall were to be one piece. (This is a good configuration only if you wish to install glazed kneewall vents). However, since we wanted to use a waist-high, deep soil bed along the south wall, there was no sense running the angled glazing right down to the foundation wall. Since we were not planning on working with concrete blocks, we elected to use option 4: to run our south wall angled studs from the short

foundation wall up to the roof, and to insulate the bottom portion of them to the height of the soil bed.

By protecting the structural and opaque members, this method also allows us to use the foundation wall and the lower portion of the south wall to form one side of the deep soil bed.

Height of South Wall As we shall see, the height of the south wall, the roof slope, the depth of the greenhouse, and the greenhouse area are all interdependent. An opaque roof (which we will shortly recommend) in conjunction with steep south-wall glazing will shade part of the greenhouse for all of the year, or all of the greenhouse for part of the year, but we didn't want it to shade all of the greenhouse for all of the year. We decided to start with the assumption that we would design the greenhouse so that:

1. on June 21 no sunlight would strike the house wall at solar noon, and
2. on December 21 the sunlight would fully strike the window(s) on the existing house wall to allow natural light into the living area of the house.

There is nothing special about the selection of these shading criteria — they are merely what we decided to start with. Obviously, these criteria will not apply to every house, but here is an example of a typical house at latitude 53°N (December 21 sun at 13°, June 21 sun at 60°).

We draw a 13° angle to indicate the position of the winter sun in relation to the top of the window.

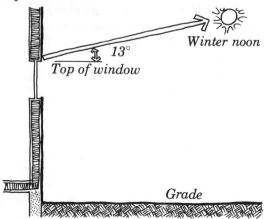

Fig. 109 Aim winter sun at top of window or door

An angle of 60° from the bottom of the house wall will indicate how far we want the June sun to extend into the

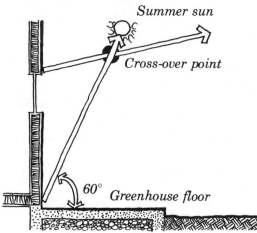

Fig. 110

greenhouse. From the intersection of these two lines, we extend a roof slope to the house wall, and the selected glazing of 75° down to the ground to indicate where the foundation wall should be.

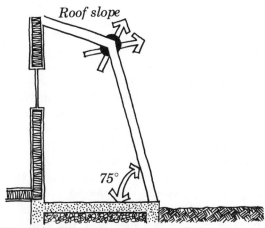

Fig. 111 Fit roof slope and wallslope to cross-over point

We're not done yet. We have to decide if the greenhouse depth this south wall/roof configuration provides is adequate. In the case shown in figure 111, the greenhouse house depth is about 2.2m (7¼ft). If all we want to include in the greenhouse is a south wall soil bed, a walkway, and room for heat storage along the north wall, then this is a satisfactory depth. However, if (as we usually choose) we also want a soil bed or bench along the north wall, the greenhouse will have to be deeper. Let's say we want to deepen the example greenhouse interior to 2.6m (8½ft). We will have to move the foundation out by 0.4m. Here are the south wall/roof options:

1. Move the south wall out farther and make the roof higher to retain the original glazing angle and roof slope. The sunlight will be only slightly farther up (above the window) on December 21 and slightly out from the house wall on June 21. Quite satisfactory, what?

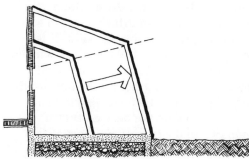

Fig. 112 Option #1

2. Move the south wall out farther to retain the original angle, but use a lower roof slope so that the roof joins the house wall at the same position as in the original example.

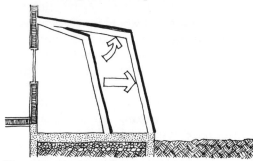

Fig. 113 Option #2

3. Leave the roof where it is, but decrease the south-wall angle so that the south wall will join the roof and the new foundation position. This will yield exactly the same shading characteristics as the original configuration.

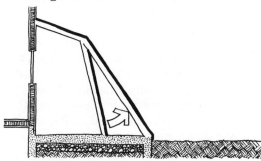

Fig. 114 Option #3

4. Move the south wall out, retaining the original angle, and extend the original roof slope out to meet it. This will result in a bit more year-round shading.

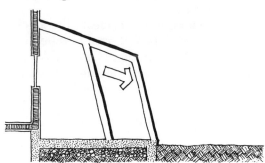

Fig. 115 Option #4

Any of these options is satisfactory. We'd tend to choose the first one if the existing house allows for it.

The shading criteria that we began with are rather arbitrary, but the point of this exercise is to demonstrate the relationship between height, depth, roof slope, and glazing angle in the greenhouse, and what kind of juggling you can do.

Even though this is just one example, at one latitude, on one house, we think that the procedure is clear and that you should be able to use it in any situation. There are handy trigonometric methods to determine the ratios involved in the south wall/roof/depth configuration, but we have to admit that we usually use a protractor, straight edge and graph paper and jockey things around until we're satisfied. (It is important that when planning on paper you draw to scale.)

What's Left: *The Roof*   We decided on an insulated, completely closed roof for a number of reasons:
1. In the high latitude, clear climate of the Prairies, roof glazing to collect diffuse sky radiation is unnecessary.
2. A solid roof greatly simplifies construction and makes it less expensive.
3. We want to minimize winter heat loss through the roof.
4. A false ceiling below the roof can provide a place for storage of the inter-glazing insulating shutter.
5. It is simpler to install vents in the endwalls than in the roof.

We remembered to take into account the snow load in areas of heavy snowfall and to carefully specify vapour-barrier details

for the insulated roof. Whenever possible, we try to match the roof slope to that of the house roof.

The North Wall   In the case of a freestanding greenhouse, or an attached greenhouse built off an east or west wall, the north wall can be built at an angle to optimize reflection and divert the north wind. In our case, an attached south-side greenhouse, the existing house wall is insulated and vertical. We wanted windows and doors not only for access and heat exchange with the greenhouse, but also for a visual connection which opaque vents could not provide. We decided that if windows and doors were not part of the existing wall, we would install them.

To bounce light back onto the plants, the north wall should have a reflective surface. We try to paint the house wall white, but this is sometimes tempered by taste or a desire to retain the original finish.

East and West Walls   For construction reasons, these walls would be vertical. Because we were interested in a plant producing greenhouse, we decided to maximize light levels by including as much glazing as possible in the endwalls. Virtually the entire east and west ends were marked for glazing, including the exterior door. We also decided to use removable push-in shutters, made from pieces of rigid insulation, for the endwall glazing. This choice adds to the flexibility of the design since we have the option of leaving the shutters in place during the

winter months, thereby turning the glazed surface into an insulated wall. In cases where the greenhouse would be constantly shaded by nearby objects, we would be more likely to build an insulated wall on that end.

We also elected to use the endwalls as locations for the vents. We already mentioned that construction of endwall vents is easier than that of roof vents and that sealing problems are minimized. We designed a large, screened vent low on the west wall (the prevailing wind direction) and another high on the east wall to provide for cross-ventilation and to allow as large a distance as possible between the heights of the vents. The placement of the vents helped to determine the location of the door, on the east end, with the vent above it. The door would be screened and suitable for summer ventilation.

The Floor   We decided, whenever possible, to use a concrete floor. This is permanent, easy to maintain, provides a bit of thermal mass, and (gulp) consumes a lot of energy in its manufacture. The extent to which the concrete would cover the floor of the greenhouse would determine the structure of our soil beds, or vice-versa. If the concrete pad was to cover the entire greenhouse floor, we would build the deep soil bed on top of about 450mm of rock, to provide adequate soil drainage. However, we recommend that the pad not extend beneath the soil bed, so that the soil in the bed can connect to the earth. (See MANAGEMENT for more on this).

Fig. 116

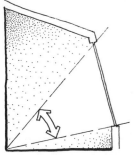
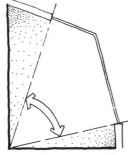

Opaque roof
Cloudy conditions

Glazed roof
Cloudy conditions

Roof Glazing A process similar to the one we have followed may be used to develop a greenhouse shape for any set of circumstances. By adjusting the height, depth and width, the Sundance Greenhouse can be usefully adapted to any climate in the northern part of this continent.

The only major change we would recommend would be for regions with extensive cloud cover. These regions will need to collect solar radiation from a larger area of the sky. One way of allowing more diffuse sky radiation into the greenhouse is by providing some roof glazing. We have supplied construction details for a south wall/roof glazing configuration which makes use of our inter-glazing insulation system. A problem with roof glazing in northern climates is that the roof will not be able to shade the greenhouse from the sun on clear summer days. In certain situations, roof glazing used in conjunction with the reflective roof flap developed by Solar Applications in Vancouver provides

an excellent solution. In other situations you will have to provide movable shading from the summer sun.

Fig. 117 Peter Amerongen's favorite greenhouse

My Favourite Greenhouse
by P. Amerongen

If the existing house (or design for a new house) permits, you might consider a two-storey greenhouse. The higher south glazing increases the light levels and heat gain substantially, which eliminates the need for east and west glazing. Such a design allows for more insulation and easier vent location in the endwalls. By confining the glazing to one surface, the installation of an inter-glazing insulation system solves the night insulation problem by itself. Another advantage is the physical and visual access from the house to the greenhouse on two levels.

CONSTRUCTION

If you've read what we said in DESIGN you'll have an understanding of how we developed the Sundance Greenhouse, and a feeling for any adaptations required to suit your climate and needs. If you haven't read DESIGN you should feel guilty (the work we put into it for you!), but you can still start right here and, by flipping back to look over the decision-making parts of DESIGN, learn how to build a greenhouse that will perform satisfactorily in most regions across the northern part of this continent. We'll remind you once again that, before you settle on the exact shape and size, read MANAGEMENT so you will know how you are going to use the greenhouse and what this will mean in terms of layout, access, and so forth.

Choice of Details

There is a multitude of possible details for greenhouse construction. The suitability of each alternative varies from one situation to another. Rather than attempt to present them all, we have instead described at length the details most suitable for one particular greenhouse, and briefly examined some alternatives. The procedures described should be adaptable to almost any situation. To assist you in choosing the most apt approach, we have outlined briefly the problems facing you at each stage of construction. By keeping in mind what is required at each stage, and generalizing from the step-by-step instructions, you should be able to handle any situation. Don't be afraid to improvise,

but check your ideas out with someone experienced before going too far.

Building Codes and Permits

Municipalities in most parts of North America require that you have a building permit to make an addition to your house. Before giving you a permit the authorities will usually want drawings of your proposed greenhouse to satisfy themselves that what you are building will stand up and not present a hazard to anyone. Apply for your permit as far ahead as possible because the approval time (or time needed for changes) can result in a delay in construction. Remember that you will also have to comply with local zoning regulations concerning such things as lot lines. The building inspector can be a source of useful information regarding standard practices in your area for such things as foundation design and snow-load requirements.

Cost

Generally, we specify materials and procedures that will result in the cheapest greenhouse possible without jeopardizing its efficiency. We cannot offer much specific information on cost because of regional variations and the problem of inflation. To a large extent, costs will depend on the standards you adopt and the intentions you have for the space. If the greenhouse is primarily to be a food-producing and heat-conserving structure,

you will probably find good quality construction-grade lumber adequate for the finish work. On the other hand, if the greenhouse is also an extension of the living area in an expensive house, you may require things like factory-built window units, stock mouldings and clear lumber. The cost difference can be substantial. If you are not concerned about appearances or longevity, you can build a greenhouse using 2 x 2 lumber and polyethylene glazing, which would still be better than nothing and still provide heat and food. This simple approach is perhaps more suitable as a freestanding greenhouse than as something that will be part of your house.

Recycling glass and other materials can lead to considerable savings. Glazing material can be the single biggest item in your budget, especially if you must order odd sizes or make cuts that result in waste. Get your glazing material first, then design the frame to accommodate it.

Construction Sequence

In general, following the order of presentation in this section will result in the most efficient construction. In some areas we have made specific recommendations; for example, you can save a lot of masking or scraping by painting the stop and frames before installing the glass. There are often reasons for proceeding differently such as wanting to close the greenhouse in as quickly as possible, or not having the paint when you need it. The order we are suggesting has evolved partly from doing things the hard way and wishing we had proceeded differently.

Safety

Presumably one of your reasons for building a greenhouse is a commitment to your own health and the health of the planet. It would be counter-productive to break your neck, lose an eye or poison yourself with a wood preservative.

Fig. 118 Safety equipment

* Wear ear and eye protection when operating power tools.
* .Hand-held circular saws can jump back out of a cut if the blade becomes jammed. Table and radial arm saws can turn pieces of wood into dangerous projectiles. Familiarize yourself with these hazards before proceeding.
* Some wood preservatives contain deadly poisons. Pentachlorophenol, the active ingredient in many preservatives, contains traces of dioxin. Avoid the use of pentachlorophenol based preservatives, and use the others with caution.

* Wear a dust mask when handling fibreglass insulation.
* Wear gloves when handling and cutting glass.
* Keep the work site tidy so that if you do fall from a roof or ladder your landing will be no worse than necessary.

Freestanding vs Attached

We confine our discussion to the construction of an attached greenhouse. The attached greenhouse makes so much sense in terms of energy conservation and convenience we think it's the reasonable choice if your site allows for it. If you have to, or want to build a freestanding greenhouse, it should be very simple to follow the step-by-step instructions for an attached greenhouse, making the necessary modifications. A freestanding greenhouse is in some ways easier to build since there are no problems with frost heaving in relation to the house and no problems with tying into the existing wall or roof.

Rot

Rot is the most serious threat to the longevity of any wood-framed greenhouse. It occurs on unprotected wood surfaces which are repeatedly exposed to water and air. Condensation on the inside and rain on the outside are unavoidable. Surfaces particularly prone to rotting, such as sills and window trim, should be protected in several ways; they should be sloped to encourage drainage and protected with paint or preservatives. The best solution is

to use woods with natural rot-resistance, such as cedar or redwood. Also, avoid using sapwood. Heartwood in any given species tends to be more rot-resistant. In cedar, fir, and hemlock, the heartwood is usually reddish while the sapwood is white. In pine, the heartwood is usually yellower than the sapwood. With spruce it is very difficult to tell the two apart.

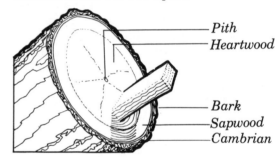

Fig. 119 Tree cross-section

Try to construct your greenhouse so the parts most prone to rotting are replaceable without major renovation. Be very careful to protect the load-bearing members and the planks which sit on the foundation — replacing them would be a major undertaking.

Another series of problems results from warm, moist air escaping the greenhouse through cracks between framing members and gaps in the vapour barrier. As this warm air cools, the moisture condenses and freezes. When it thaws, in warmer weather, the wood in the walls will get wet. Being inside the wall, it may take a long time to dry. This situation can be avoided by careful attention to vapour barrier details, and by sealing around the glazing and trim pieces.

Sizing It Up

The design section will have helped you determine the approximate size and shape of your greenhouse. Now let's examine the existing building to see what limitations there might be on the greenhouse.

• Will the greenhouse obstruct windows or doors that are important to you? Can these be used for access to the greenhouse or for providing air exchange with the house? You may have to adjust the greenhouse size either to avoid, or to include these openings.

Fig. 120 Items to look for when siting attached greenhouse

• Is there sufficient vertical space between the house overhang and the ground to allow the greenhouse roof to butt against the house wall? Is it possible to build the greenhouse roof as an extension of the house roof? If so, can you tie either or

both of the greenhouse end rafters to rafters on the house roof? (This is not critical, but makes the tie-in easier.)

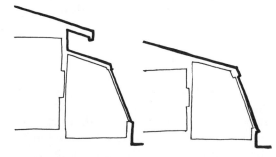

Fig. 121 May fit to roof

• Will the foundation be high enough above the surrounding ground? The siding should be a minimum of 200mm (8in) above the ground, and the ground should slope away from the house and greenhouse to provide positive drainage.

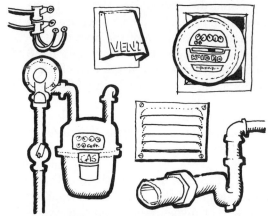

Fig. 122 Items to avoid when placing attached greenhouse

• Are there any utility lines in the way? (gas, power, water, sewer or telephone)

Can you work around these or must they be moved?

Another factor which will determine the exact greenhouse size will be the size of the glazing. We recommend the use of tempered glass, which cannot be cut. If we assume that you have located a quantity of reasonably-priced tempered glass, your only choice in the width of the south wall, for instance, will be how many panels wide to make it. (For example, if the glass size indicates that the glazing framing member will have to be on one-metre centres, you will probably decide to make the greenhouse either 5 or 6 metres wide.) Even if you are using non-tempered glass or a plastic glazing, it makes sense to let the width of the glazing material determine the stud spacing and, hence, the width of the greenhouse.

The height of tempered glass may have some influence on the height of the south wall, but this is less critical since we show you a way to splice a piece of non-tempered glass to a piece of tempered glass to increase the glazing height.

The next step is to determine the exact dimensions of the greenhouse. Pay particular attention to the south wall. Because you want to maximize light and heat gain there should be no solid framing. The size of the glazing material and the thickness of the east and west walls will determine the length of the south wall, and therefore of the foundation and excavation. We recommend laying out the top and bottom plates for the south wall before doing anything else. These plates can be useful measuring sticks for the excavation, for forming, and for placing the anchor bolts. Read the sections on framing, glazing, and insulation to help you make the necessary decisions.

The endwall dimensions will be determined by the space available on the house wall, the roof angle, and the glazing angle. The dimensions are not affected as much by glazing material sizes because there is usually some non-glazed portion in the walls, the size of which is variable. Because of the shape of the endwalls, you will have to use at least some non-tempered glass, cut to fit.

Laying Out the South Wall Plate

The south wall should contain as much glass as possible. The most effective way to maximize the glazing on the south wall is to let the glazing material determine its dimensions.

Example: Assume that 5m (16 ft) is the approximate greenhouse length you want and one which will fit on the space available. Assume also that you have a source of 34 in x 76 in (864mm x 1930mm) tempered patio-door glass. Since you are planning to use inter-glazing insulation, you have chosen detail A in fig. 187. Because you have an unobstructed site, and food production is your major concern, you have decided that the endwalls are going to be mostly glazed. This choice

means that, since the area left to be insulated will be small and the use of 2 x 6 framing for its extra insulation capacity is not warranted, the endwalls will be of 2 x 4 construction.

Having made these decisions you can either proceed to lay out the bottom plate on the piece of lumber (preferably treated) which will serve that purpose, or do it on paper. We'll do it on the board. Start at the west end, measure across 1¹/₂ in (38mm) for the first stud, another 3¹/₂ in (89mm) for blocking for the endwall construction (make this distance 5¹/₂ in (140mm) if you are using 2 x 6 endwall framing) and then another 1¹/₂ in (38mm) for the next stud. The first piece of glass butts against this latter stud, but remember to allow ¹/₄ in (6mm) for expansion and to ensure an easy, loose fit. The glass is 34 in (864mm) wide and there should be ¹/₄ in (6.4mm) clearance on each side, so measure 34¹/₂ in (876mm) to the edge of the next stud. Continue along until you get close to 16 ft (4.88m). We notice that after the fifth panel space we are at 185 in. (4.7m).

It's time to draw the last stud and allowance for the east wall. The total length of the plate comes to 191¹/₂ in (4.864m) 195¹/₂ in (4.966m) if the endwalls are 2 x 6s. This measure, then, is the exact length of the greenhouse. Double check your measurements on this one — if you discover a space that is an inch (25.4005mm) too narrow when you go to put the glass in, you might be rather upset. Cut the plate to length. It can serve

as a pattern for the other plates and a measuring stick for the excavation and form work.

Choice of Foundation

In general, whatever foundation works for your house will work for your greenhouse. The building inspector is going to consider an attached greenhouse a part of your house, and will require a foundation having similar frost resistance and bearing capacity. Because some soils require wider footings or deeper piles than others and because frost depth varies from practically nothing in coastal areas to 2.5 metres or more in cold areas, it is impossible for us to make a recommendation which will suit all situations. Do whatever is common practice in your area. If you want to deviate from that type of foundation do so only after checking with a local building inspector, engineer, or experienced contractor.

Frost heaving is probably going to be the major determining factor in foundation choice. The greenhouse should not be able to move in relation to the house. The general consensus is that the foundation should start below the frost line. In some cases that would mean a 2.4m (8 ft) basement wall, which would be very expensive. A grade beam on piles will accomplish the same thing. Another option which may work in some areas is a shallow foundation with a skirt of insulation around it to deter frost penetration. We recommend this type of insulation anyway to control heat loss. However, its benefits in preventing frost heaving could be negated if you allow the greenhouse to freeze in December and January.

If the greenhouse is an addition to your living space, you will have no trouble justifying a "Cadillac" foundation. If it's primarily a food and heat producer, you may want to consider the post or railroad tie foundation. A freestanding greenhouse will work on almost any foundation since frost heaving will have very little effect.

Following is a description of 4 foundation options:
1. grade beam on piles
2. foundation wall on strip footing
3. slab on grade
4. pier foundation using railroad ties

Fig. 123 Grade beam on piles

Grade Beam on Piles   Properly designed, this foundation will work for any situation. The greenhouse rests on the piles, which transfer the load to the ground at the bottom and through friction at the sides. The grade beam itself should not sit firmly on the ground or it will still be susceptible to frost heaving. 50mm to 100mm (2 in to 4 in) of straw or hay, placed on the ground between the pilings before pouring the concrete, will eventually rot out leaving a void under the grade

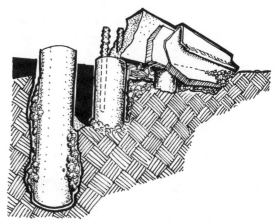

Fig. 124 Grade beam on concrete piles

beam. Check with a local expert on the required diameter, depth, and spacing of the piles, and the depth and width of the grade beam. Because of the light weight of a greenhouse you may be able to get away with a 150mm (6 in) grade beam instead of the usual 200mm (8 in).

Foundation Wall on Footing   This foundation is the most common type in many regions. The strip footing should be below the frost depth and sit on undisturbed earth. The foundation wall can be poured concrete or concrete blocks. Pour the strip footing by adapting the method outlined in detail for a grade beam. Gouge a keyway (required for bonding the foundation wall) in the strip footing immediately after levelling the wet cement. Concrete blocks using standard mortar or surface bonding might be easier than forming the wall on top of the strip footing unless you have access to grade beam forms. Because of the small loads

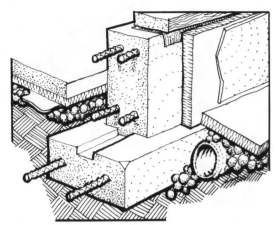

Fig. 125 Standard footing

involved in a greenhouse, a foundation wall may be adequate without the strip footing, depending on local soil conditions.

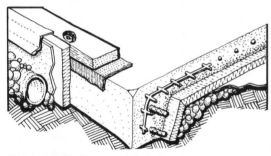

Fig. 126 Slab on grade

Slab on Grade   This foundation is the cheapest and easiest kind because it requires the least form work and provides the floor at the same time. The slab on grade option is ideal in regions such as the west coast, where frost heaving is not a problem. A floor drain is advised.

Dig out the top soil and replace it with compacted sand. Be sure that the top of the slab will be high enough above the surrounding ground to allow proper drainage. The lip around the edge should sit on undisturbed ground. If you dig too deep in some spots, pour more concrete. Do not fill in unless you are prepared to tamp that area thoroughly. Follow the directions for forming a grade beam to get your forms square, level, and straight. Read the section on floors for some instructions on pouring the slab. Put four pieces of #8 ($^1/_2$″) (#15 metric) reinforcing steel bars around the perimeter.

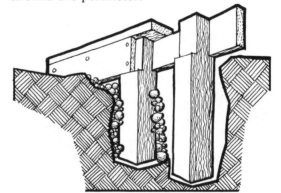

Fig. 127 Rail tie or treated post with treated wood beam

Railroad Ties or Pressure-Treated Post Foundations   This option is for those not anxious to use concrete. Local conditions will determine the required depth and spacing. Used railroad ties can often be obtained economically but because their maximum length is usually 8 ft. (2.4m) you may need to use more of them spaced closer together than you would of longer,

pressure-treated posts. Before deciding to use any kind of pressure-treated or preserved wood in greenhouse construction, be sure to read our warnings regarding wood preservatives (page 121).

Lay out the location for each post and drill the holes. Using a long board or pole, tamp the bottoms of the holes until they are rock hard. Place the pilings and drive them with the heaviest maul or sledge you can find so they are firmly seated. Align the piles as you backfill with sand or gravel. Tamp often with a long thin bar. Remember that piles rely partially on friction from the sides for their bearing and resistance to frost heaving.

When the piles are set, use a level in order to determine level marks on the corners; then use a chalk line to mark the remaining piles so they can all be cut to the same height. Marking them inside and out will make it easier to make a level cut. Notch in the sill members and fasten them with at least $3^1/_2$″ (89mm) hot galvanized nails (Galvanized lag screws would be better.) These members must be of pressure-treated lumber. All cuts should be painted with preservative. Choose and use preservatives with extreme caution (see "Paints and Preservatives" in "Exterior Finish" section).

Caution: Before doing any digging or boring locate any water, sewer, power to telephone lines that might be buried in your way.

Measuring Tricks

Building a greenhouse requires a lot of measuring. For a professional-looking job, the following tips might be useful and time-saving.

1. First, for accurate work, we recommend a very sharp 2H or harder pencil or knife to give a thin clear line.

2. The ends of many standard measuring tapes are inaccurate. The problem is that, because of excessive play in the tape end, an inside measurement will become inaccurate when the tape is hooked on the end of the stock to mark the length. Check your tape as in fig. 128. Hook it onto the end of a board with a clean square end; measure 1 ft or 500mm, marking it very precisely. Now hold a block on the end of the board and measure 1 ft (or 500mm) with the tape end pushed against the block. If there is no difference between the two marks, your tape is one of the few good ones. If there is a difference, allow for it when transferring an inside measurement to the stock you are cutting. In some situations you can overcome the problem by measuring from the 1 in or 10mm mark or some other even number. This adjustment must be done carefully to avoid serious errors.

3. In some cases, it can become difficult or impossible to get the tape end or body into corners to obtain a measurement. Very carefully cut a block which is precisely one foot or 500mm or some other even number in length and which has one square end and one end that will fit into the tightest corner you have. The ends must be square because you are going to use it to make a mark the length of the block from the corner. Now measure to the mark and add the length of the block.

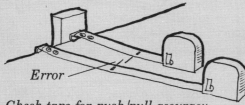

Error

Check tape for push/pull accuracy.

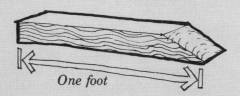

One foot

Fig. 128 Tape check and measuring stick. For accurate measurement in those hard-to-reach places, add length of stick to tape reading.

Laying Out Angles

Translating the angles (60° — 75° tilt) you arrived at in the DESIGN section can be a bit of a problem. A knowledge of trigonometry might be useful, but don't worry about it. The numbers in the following table will give you a ratio between the length of the side opposite the angle and the length of the side adjacent to the angle. For example, if you want to lay out a 75° triangle with the short side (BC)

.50m long, multiply .50m by 3.7321 to get 1.866m. Measure this amount off at a right angle to make line BA and join A to C using a chalk line or straight edge. You can now use this triangle to set a sliding T-bevel to draw cutting angles. Now that wasn't so bad, was it? We didn't mention the word hypotenuse even once. You can also lay out angles with a framing square using the same ratios.

Angle	Ratio (Tangent)
80°	5.6713
75°	3.7321
70°	2.7475
65°	2.1445
60°	1.7321
55°	1.4280

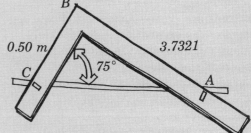

Fig. 129 Using a framing square to generate angles by ratios

Foundation Layout and Form Work

The following method is suitable for a strip footing, a grade beam, a grade beam on piles, or a slab on grade. The actual case we will deal with will be a grade beam on piles. Variations required for other foundation options should be quite obvious.

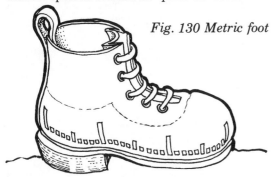

Fig. 130 Metric foot

Excavation   Place stakes to indicate the extent of the excavation approximately 300mm (1 ft) beyond the anticipated corners of the outside forms for the footing or grade beam. If the excavation is to be more than 600mm (2 ft) deep, locate the stakes somewhat farther out — about 600mm for an excavation of 1200mm or more. This will mean a bit more digging, but if you are planning to lay insulation along the perimeter (as we recommend) any extra digging to widen the trench to give you more room to work will not be wasted.

Make the bottom of the excavation as even as possible, taking care not to dig too deep. Footings or grade beams not on piles must rest on undisturbed earth to avoid settling. If you do accidentally dig a spot too deep,

plan to fill it in with extra cement as you pour rather than trying to fill it in with earth.

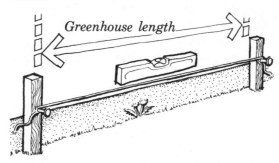

Fig. 131 Locate greenhouse ends along the south wall of house. Make allowances for insulation on foundation.

Layout and Forming   1. Locate the ends of the greenhouse foundation on the house and add an allowance for the thickness of the endwall forms and the thickness of the insulation. (We recommend that you place the rigid grade beam insulation inside the forms so the concrete will bond to it, but if you prefer you can glue it on afterwards.) Make end marks on the house at what will be the top of the greenhouse foundation, and make them level with each other. Measuring from the bottom trim or the house soffit at both ends will probably be close enough, but it wouldn't hurt to check with a water level, a site level (often erroneously called a transit) or a carpenter's level with a perfectly straight board. (Very few levels are accurate enough for this. Take one reading, then without moving the level in relation to the board, turn the whole assembly end-for-end and take another reading. If the two don't

agree average them.)

2. Prepare some stakes for your form work. For a grade beam 600mm (2 ft) high stakes can be made from 2 x 4s or unplaned 1 x 4s. The stakes should be long enough so that they can be driven into the ground 150mm to 300mm (6 in to 12 in) and still extend above the tops of the forms above ground. (A 600mm high grade beam requires stakes about 900mm to 1000mm long.) For the edge of a slab or a strip footing, planed 1 x 4s will suffice since there is much less weight of concrete to hold in place. Stakes sharpened with a circular saw (skill saw) will tend to go into the ground with less twisting than those sharpened with an axe. Try to use scrap lumber for stakes rather than cutting up new boards.

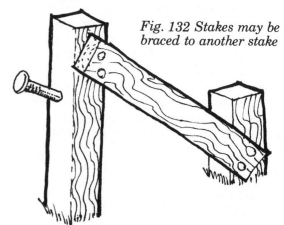

Fig. 132 Stakes may be braced to another stake

3. Drive a stake outside each end mark made above. If it is possible nail these stakes to the house at the top; if not, secure them plumb with a brace out to **another (short) stake as in fig. 132. Place**

Fig. 133 Use the south wall sill as a template, prepare site and lay out basic dimensions.

other stakes at a distance from the house (opposite A & B) equal to the north-south dimension of the foundation plus an allowance for the thickness of the forms and insulation (if you are putting it in the forms). Use a framing square lying on the ground to get these stakes just outside of "eyeball" square in relation to A & B. Take care to drive the stakes plumb and brace them back to shorter stakes behind them.

"Wait a minute" you say, "eyeball square is not close enough". Right. What we want you to do is build the outside forms for the south wall about a foot too long on each end, then we'll square it up accurately. In spite of seeming complicated and round-about, this method (used routinely by thousands of carpenters) will help you to get the foundation square, level and true without resorting to trial and error. Hang in there and read to the end -- it's worth it.

4. Locate the foundation height (using the marks on the house) on the stakes using one of the following methods:

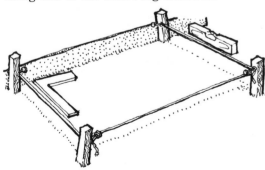

Fig. 134 Square up outline of greenhouse

- Use a perfectly straight board and a carpenter's level. Remember to turn the level and board end-for-end to check your first reading, and average if necessary.
- Use a water level. This tool is just a hose with clear ends so you can see the water level. Avoid getting large air bubbles mixed in with the water as they can throw your reading out.
- Borrow a builder's level or transit if you can.

5. Now is the time to drill the piling holes if they are needed. (See box, p. 83.)

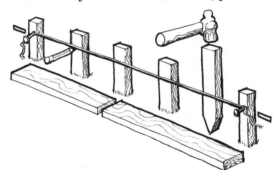

Fig. 135 Stretch a string along stakes

6. Stretch a line along the inside faces of the outer stakes at the heights just marked. The string should be so tight it almost breaks. Site down it to see if there is any sag. Drive a stake about every 600mm (2 ft) (750mm for a strip footing) along the string, taking care to keep them plumb. Lay the first, top row of forming boards beside the stakes so you can drive a **stake to support any joints** (fig. 135). The forms should extend about a foot beyond the end stakes to allow for any error you

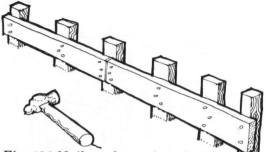

Fig. 136 Nail up the top board of form

might have made in estimating a right angle. Mark where the string crosses the stakes, making allowance for any sag, and remove the string. Nail the forms to the stakes (fig. 136) using $2^1/2$ to $3^1/2$ in (65 mm to 90mm) nails, taking care not to knock them out of plumb. Think about how the weight of the wet concrete will want to distort the forms and plan on dismantling them as soon as it is dry. The concrete will push the forms against the stakes so they don't need to be nailed heavily. On the other hand, the concrete will try to spread the corners, so they must be secure.

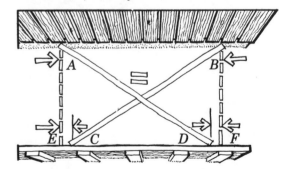

Fig. 137 Squaring side walls

7. Measure the distance AD where D is a point which you guess is square with B (fig. 137). Measure this same distance from B

Drilling Piling Holes

In order not to break the continuity of the instructions for forming the grade beam, we here describe the drilling of the piles separately. This step should be done just after driving the corner stakes and before placing the remaining stakes for the south wall, since additional stakes would get in the way.

The corner piles should be drilled in from the corner somewhat to ensure that they aren't outside of the endwalls. Remember we haven't located the intersections of the endwalls with the south wall yet. You can eyeball a straight line between the two corner stakes to locate any other pilings you may need along the south wall since it doesn't matter if the piles are an inch (25.40005mm) or so off.

One piling should be drilled for each endwall. Use the framing square to locate a point perpendicular to the house wall and about two feet out from the marks you have made there. Drill a hole at this point at each endwall.

Depending on the soil, you may have several ways to get the pilings drilled. You can hire someone with drilling equipment — a well driller or someone with a tractor mounted posthole auger. There is also a variety of power equipment you can rent; this option may not work if you run into rocks. If 200mm (8 in) pilings will suffice, you may be able to use a hand-powered

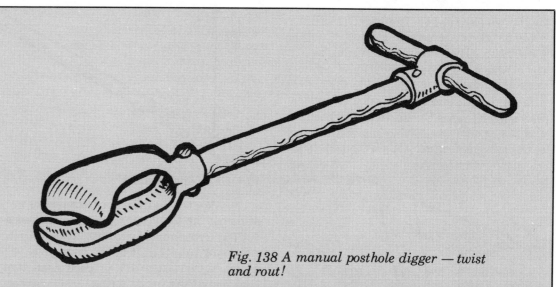

Fig. 138 A manual posthole digger — twist and rout!

posthole auger set at its maximum diameter. Start by drilling all the holes as deep as the auger will go, then take the auger apart and add a 1200mm (4 ft) extension. A piece of 19mm (3/4 in) iron pipe (black or galvanized) with standard pipe thread and a 19mm (3/4 in) coupling will extend most augers. (This pipe is the kind used in bar clamps.) Drill all the holes as deep as this combination will go and repeat, adding another extension if necessary. The work will go faster and easier if you keep the auger sharp. With any auger, always sharpen the cutting edges on the inside.

In some soils, it will be necessary to pour the pilings and grade beam separately because of the danger of the piling caving in while forming the grade beam. Even in

good solid ground, don't drive stakes too close to the holes, and keep them covered to prevent dirt and debris from falling in before you fill them. The bottoms should be clean and solid. Two pieces of #8 (1/2 in) (#15 metric) rebar should extend from the bottom of the hole to within a few inches of the top of the grade beam. Vibrate the concrete in the holes vigorously with a 2 x 2 or a pipe.

The weight of the greenhouse and grade beam should be on the piles and not on the ground. To accomplish this balance, place a void form in the bottom of the forms between the pilings before pouring. The void form, usually 50mm to 100mm of straw or hay, will rot, leaving a void so that when frost action causes the ground to heave, it will not disrupt the grade beam.

to give you a point C. The line CD will probably be the wrong length but it will be parallel to AB and its centre square to the centre of AB. Measure CD and subtract it from the length of AB. Divide the difference by 2 and add (or subtract if CD was longer than AB) this figure to each end of CD, and you have a line EF which is the same length as AB and square to it.

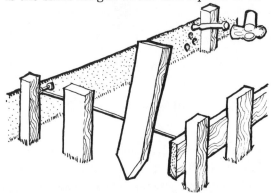

Fig. 139 Drive stakes for side forms and drill out foundations of existing house

8. The rest is easy. String a line from A to E and B to F and drive stakes for the side walls as in step #6. Nail the endwall form boards in place and to the south wall forms. Reinforce the corners with cleats.

9. Engineers will probably tell you to tie the new foundation into the house foundation. They're right. If you are using piles, locate one as close as possible to the house wall (2 ft — 600mm — is fine). Use a star drill or a hammer drill to bore two holes for reinforcing steel. Grout the steel into these holes before pouring the concrete.

Fig. 140 "Star hammer"

10. Measure in from each corner the width of the foundation plus an allowance for the form lumber and insulation (if you are going to install it at the time you pour). Place strings and proceed as in step 6 to install the inside forms.

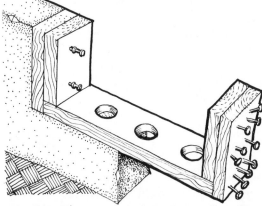

Fig. 141 Cut-out in foundation walls with porcupine board

11. Exterior doorways should be framed **directly into the forms, if necessary.** The distance between the treated 2 x 4 nailers should be the rough opening width; that is, the width of the door plus the

framing material plus an allowance of 20mm (³/₄ in.) Nail the bulkheads and the bottom piece solidly and drill 1-in (25mm) holes in the bottom piece so you will be able to tell when the concrete has entirely filled the cavity. You will have to pay careful attention when pouring the concrete to make it run under here. Pour from both sides, push it under and vibrate the forms with a hammer.

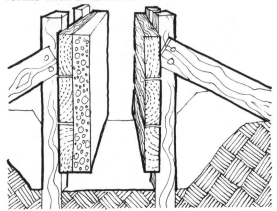

Fig. 142 Insulation on inside of outside form

12. Install the rigid insulation inside the forms now (if you have decided to follow our recommendation).

13. Install the reinforcing steel, and wire it in place (fig. 145). The rebar ends should overlap each other by 16 diameters (15mm bar = 240mm). Secure the forms together with 1 x 2 strips or wire between the stakes. Tamp earth against the bottom of the forms to prevent concrete from leaking out between any gaps that might exist.

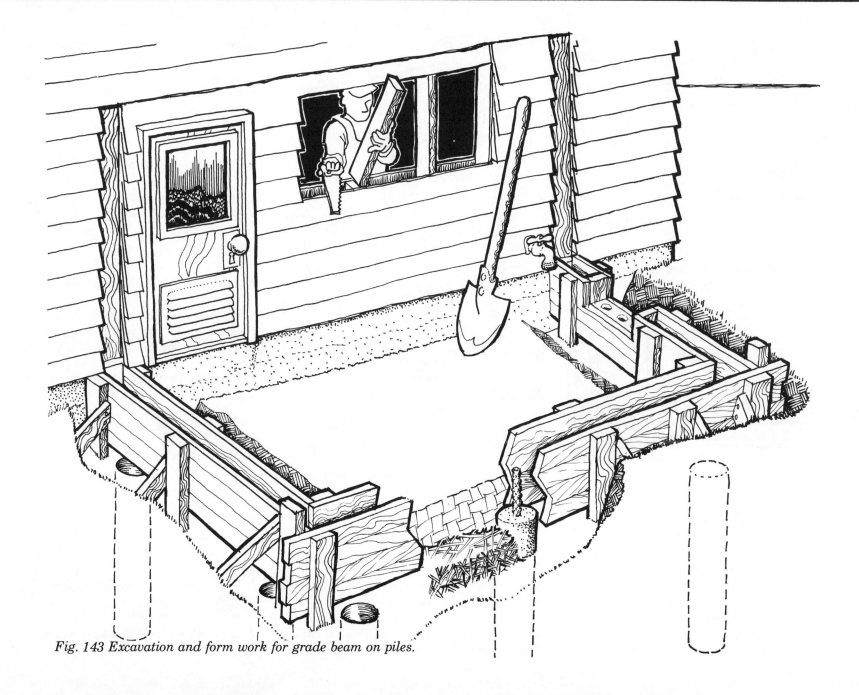

Fig. 143 Excavation and form work for grade beam on piles.

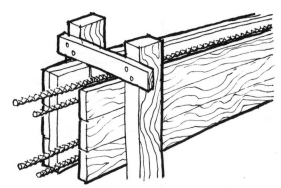

Fig. 144 Install rebar in formwork and tie tops of stakes together

14. Check the forms and, if necessary, straighten them with braces.

Fig. 145

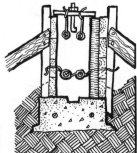

Standard footing form

Foundation wall with insulation on outside of form

Concrete is very heavy and will move or even break weak forms.

15. Pour the forms full of concrete. Resist the temptation to make the concrete soupy for a better flow because too much water weakens the finished product, causes cracking and reduces resistance to frost damage. Vibrate the concrete by working a 2 x 2 through it. Tap the forms with a

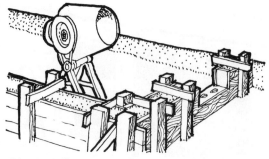

Fig. 146 Pour concrete

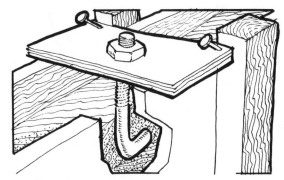

Fig. 147 Anchor bolts set

hammer to give smoother sides. Too much vibration will cause the forms to spread.

16. Smooth the top of the concrete and install the anchor bolts, vibrating them gently with a hammer so the concrete will flow right around them. Take care not to damage the threads when placing the anchor bolts. Keep them about 100mm (4 in) away from doorways and avoid locations where vertical framing members contact the plate. The bottom plate we've suggested you make will show you where the studs are located so you can avoid them. Make sure the ends of each segment of the

plate will be bolted down. An economical way of making anchor bolts is to cut and bend an unthreaded mild steel rod and use a die to thread it after the concrete has set.

Fig. 148 Pull up a chair and wait...

17. Pull up a chair and wait for the concrete to set, you've finished your foundation. The concrete will take a few weeks to get really strong but you can proceed the next day as long as you're gentle with it.

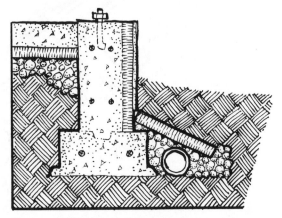

Fig. 149 Completed standard footing

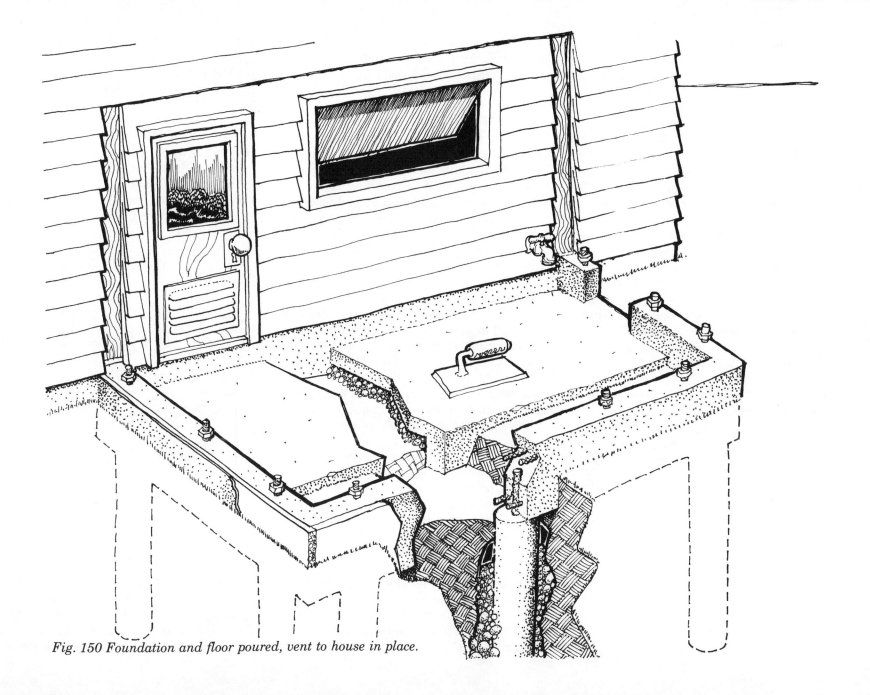

Fig. 150 Foundation and floor poured, vent to house in place.

Framing Materials

Use only good quality, straight-grained lumber, free from major knots and defects. Avoid any traces of rot. Fir and pine lumbers are preferable to spruce because they are somewhat more rot-resistant. If your budget can stand it, pressure-treated lumber is worth while for the sill plates. Use only hot dipped, galvanized nails. The small extra price is well worth the rust-resistance. Dry wall screws often come in handy for a variety of situations and are usually cheaper than ordinary screws. They come in lengths from 1¼ in to 3 in (32mm to 76mm) and can be driven with a ³/₈ in drill fitted with a Phillips screwdriver bit. The longer ones are sometimes handy for awkward nailing situations.

Framing Strength

Let's examine the strength requirements of various components of the framing.

Fig. 151 Use a double header if rafters don't sit directly over wall studs

South Wall   While we've always used 2 x 6s, 2 x 4 studs on 3 ft (914mm) centres will handle almost any situation (and cause less shading). The top plate should be doubled unless all the roof rafters sit directly on wall studs.

East & West Walls   If you build the roof as we suggest, its load is carried on the south wall and the house wall. This means that the east and west walls carry only their own weight. As a result we can omit the double 2 x 4 headers commonly used over most openings. Note that we've used a header over the vent opening in the west wall because of the weight of the glazing above it.

The Roof   The rafters are really the only members in the greenhouse whose strength we need to worry about. We must consider two components when determining the load-carrying capacity of a roof member: the weight of the snow likely to accumulate (snow load) and the weight of the roof itself (dead load). Page 248 has an allowance for the dead load of a roof.

Let's go through an example. Assume that the maximum ground snow load in your area is 1800 newtons/m² (37 lbs/ft²) (You can get this figure from your local building inspector.) 60% of this figure is 1080 newtons/m² (22.2 lbs/ft²). Each rafter carries the load from half way to its neighbor on one side to half way to its neighbor on the other side. If our rafters are spaced 400mm (16 in) apart, each rafter carries 200mm (8 in) on either side for a total of 400mm (16 in) of roof. Each linear metre of rafter carries 400mm/1000

or 0.40m² of roof. Each linear foot of rafter carries 16 in/12 or 1.33 ft² of roof. 0.40m² x 1080 newtons/m² = 432 newtons per linear metre of rafter (1.33ft² x 22.2 lb/ft² = 29.5 lbs per linear foot of rafter). We go to the next highest value in the table on p. 89, which is 600 newtons/m (40 lbs/ft). Reading down we can see that a 2 x 6 will span up to 2930 mm , (9'7"), a 2 x 10 will span up to 4940 mm (16'2½") and so on for this type of snow load.

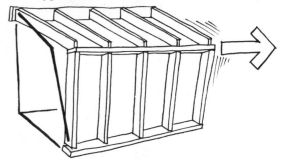

Fig. 152 Racking — unbraced

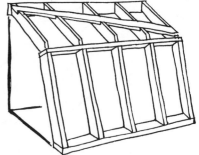

Fig. 153 Racking stopped by brace

We should also be concerned about *racking* strength. Racking is the way an unbraced building would distort in a strong wind. This malformation can be prevented in an attached greenhouse by using plywood or

Rafter Spans

These notes apply to a variety of rafters carrying ceiling and roof dead weight plus snow load. Roof joists are made from No. 2 grade spruce/pine/fir planed lumber.

Notes:

1. A *newton* is the exact metric equivalent of a pound in that it includes the pull of gravity as well as the mass (in kilograms) of an object. In everyday use, however, we simply assume that the pull of gravity is equal on all objects on Earth and so we uniformly ignore this factor. The only reason we mention newtons here is because Canadian snow load figures will be in newtons per square metre rather than kilograms per square metre. If you like, you can think of a kilogram as equivalent to about 10 newtons, but don't worry about it. Simply take your local snow load figure in newtons and plug it into the example we have done and it will all work out. We promise never to mention it again.

2. Do not design a roof for less than 950 newtons/m² (20 lbs/ft²) snow load, no matter what.

3. Design the roof for 60% of the heaviest ground snow load in your region, unless the roof is sheltered by an adjoining wall or roof. Sheltered roofs should be designed for about twice the ground snow load because snow drifts will collect on them.

4. Gypsum board or plaster ceilings require stiffer joists than indicated on the chart.

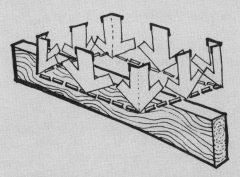

Fig. 154 Force on a rafter per unit area (lb/ft²) (Newtons/m²) etc.

Snow load in pounds per foot length

Rafter Size	20 lb/ft (300 n/m)	40 lb/ft (600 n/m)	60 lb/ft (900 n/m)	80 lb/ft (1200 n/m)	100 lb/ft 1500 n/m
			(Newtons per metre length)		
2 x 4 (38mm x 89mm)	8'-10" 2710mm	6'-7½" 2020mm	5'-9" 1750mm	5'-2" 1570mm	4'-8" 1430mm
2 x 6 (38 x 140mm)	13'-7" 4150mm	9'-7" 2930mm	8'-4" 2540mm	7'-5" 2270mm	6'-9½" 2070mm
2 x 8 (38 x 184mm)	17'-11" 5470mm	12'-8" 3870mm	11'-0" 3350mm	9'-10" 3000mm	8"-11" 2730mm
2 x 10 (38 x 235mm)	22'-11" 6990mm	16'-2½" 4940mm	14'-0" 4280mm	12'-6" 3820mm	11'-5" 3490mm
2 x 12 (38 x 286mm)	27'-10" 8500mm	19'-8" 6010mm	17'-0" 5200mm	15'-3" 4650mm	13'-11" 4250mm

Includes 20 lb/ft (300 n/m) for dead weight
Includes 40 lb/ft (60 n/m) for dead weight of roof, joists and ceilings

diagonally applied 19mm (1 in nominal) boards for roof sheathing.

Framing Construction

Framing a greenhouse is somewhat different from framing a house or garage. Many of the framing members are either window frames themselves or have window-frame material attached directly to them. It's worth taking extra care to cut and nail accurately because it will allow you to mass-produce the jamb, stops, and trim pieces when you install the glazing.

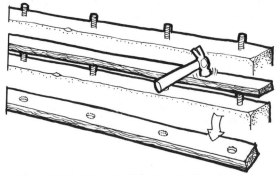

Fig. 155 Setting bolt holes in the plate

South Wall Cut the sill (bottom) plates to length if you haven't already done so. (If you can afford to, this is a worth while place to use pressure-treated wood.) Mark the anchor bolt locations as in fig. 155. taking care that the plate is directly over its intended position end to end and front to back. Drill the holes 6mm (¼ in) larger than the bolts to allow some adjustment. If the top of the bolts are at different heights you may have to mark the top ones, drill these holes, then repeat the process for the

lower ones. Then, put the plate back in position to check the hole locations. Use a round file or a small chisel to adjust if necessary. If you don't do this checking and adjusting now, you will wish you had when the sill is nailed to an entire wall and you can't get it to drop over the bolts.

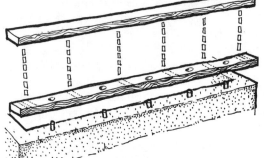

Fig. 156 Lay out stud locations on sill plate and top plate and make sure anchor bolts fit sill holes.

If you haven't already done so, lay out the front wall stud locations on both the sill plate (with the holes) and the top plate. They should be the same length and quite straight.

Lay out and cut the first stud for the south wall. Its length will be determined by several factors: the size of the glazing; how you install it; the heights of the top and bottom of the glazing as determined by things like the sun-angle and how high you want your plant beds; and accommodations of an inter-glazing insulating system. The bottom angle of the stud is the same as the glazing angle and the top cut is square. It must be notched at the top to hold the lintel. Use the first stud as a

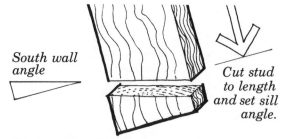

Fig. 157 South wall stud may be cut to length with sill angle set at the same time

pattern for marking the rest. They should be straight-grained with no major knots or defects. Few pieces of lumber are perfectly straight; most have a slight bend or crown to them. Always place and cut lumber so the crown is up so that the load will tend to straighten the crown.

Determining South Wall Stud Length Start with a scale drawing of a cross-section of the greenhouse similar to the one you drew in "Developing a Shape", p. 64. If you are adopting our recommended inter-glazing insulation system, use the top plate and lintel detail on p. 100. If you are not using the inter-glazing insulation, use the double top plate detail as in fig. 151 on p. 88. Here's how to determine the south wall stud length when using our standard movable insulation detail:

1. Draw in the south wall plant bench to scale at the desired height.

2. Draw in the opaque, insulated part of the south wall. This section will be the lower portion of the stud to the height of the plant bench.

3. Measure from the top of the opaque part to the bottom of the lintel.

4. Compare (3) to the length of your glazing material.

At this point there are three possibilities:

1. The glazing length, plus an expansion allowance, is exactly the same as distance (3 above). If this is the case give us a call right away so we can enter your name in the Greenhouse Hall of Fame.

2. The glazing (we're assuming you are using glass) is too long. If you are using non-tempered glass the procedure is clear — simply cut it to length. If you are using tempered glass (as we recommend) you have two choices:

    (a) Raise the roof
    (b) Lower the opaque portion of the wall. This process will mean lowering the level of the plant bench as well, and you may even decide to lower the level of the greenhouse floor.

3. The glass is too short. This, the most likely possibility by far, leaves you with three choices:

    (a) Raise the plant bed and the opaque portion of the south wall (and the greenhouse floor if necessary).
    (b) Lower the roof either by using a steeper slope or maintaining the original slope and dropping the whole thing down. (You could, of course, use some combination of (a) and (b)).
    (c) Glue a shorter piece of non-tempered glass to the tempered glass to stretch it.

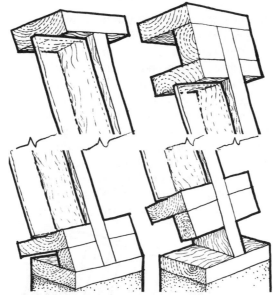

Fig. 158 Raise the opaque portion or lower the roof

Our Recommendation If the glass length is within 150mm (6 in) of distance (3) above we would use (a) (raising the opaque portion) or (b) (lowering the roof) or some combination of the two. If the glass is more than 300mm (12 in) short, we would glue another piece to it (see p. 104).

Remember that there is a lot of latitude in your decisions in this area except for such constraints as matching the greenhouse roof to the existing roof.

Stud Length Once the above decisions have been made, and your scale drawing is adjusted and completed, measure the stud length in the drawing. For an inter-glazing insulation greenhouse, this length will be

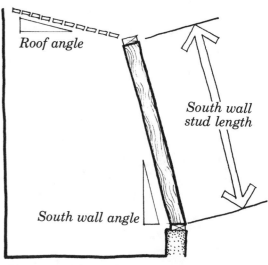

Fig. 159 Make scale drawing to determine south wall stud angle and exact length. Be sure to account for bottom sill and top plate.

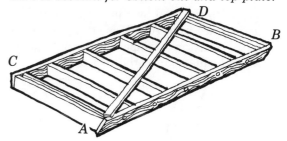

Fig. 160 South wall assembled with temporary brace

from the top of the sill plate to the bottom of the top plate (not the bottom of the lintel). When the studs are all cut, nail the south wall together using three 3½ in (90mm) hot galvanized box nails in each end of each stud. Use the straightest studs on the corners. Since the top plate carries the rafters, it will be easier if you mark out the rafter locations on this piece before you nail it to the wall which you are about to stand up. At the same time, you might well mark out the rafter locations on the 2 x 6 ledger which will carry the rafters at the house wall.

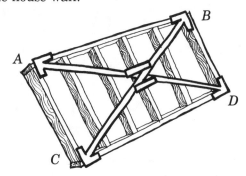

Fig. 161 Square up wall by making distance from A to D equal to B to C

Square up the wall by adjusting it until the distance from A to D is equal to C to B (fig 161). Fasten a temporary brace to keep the wall square until the roof is on.

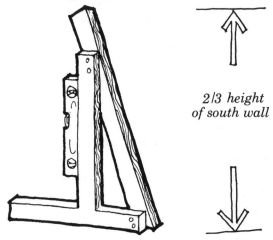

2/3 height of south wall

Fig. 162 Jig for setting south wall angle

An easy way to orient the front wall is to nail together the jig shown in fig. 162. Lay out the required angle (your glazing angle) on a sheet of plywood or similar surface and build the jig on top of it. The two longer 2 x 4s should be very straight. Get some 2 x 4 braces ready. Bolt down the bottom plates on the east and west walls so you will have some place to nail the braces. Cultivate a couple of strong friends quickly. Get them to help you erect the wall and drop it over the anchor bolts. Use the jig to tilt each end to the proper angle.

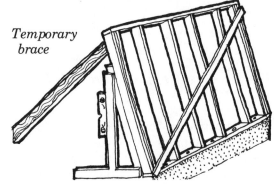

Temporary brace

Fig. 163 Use jig to set up south wall

Tack the braces on to hold the wall in position. The inside top corners of the wall should each be the same distance horizontally from the house wall and vertically from the bottom endwall plates. Make any necessary adjustments and nail the braces securely. Fasten the bottom plate down with nuts and washers. Cut off the tops of the anchor bolts flush with the nuts.

Roof Now we start on the roof. Roof slopes are usually expressed as a ratio of

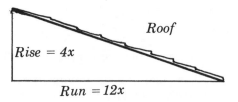

Roof

Rise = 4x

Run = 12x

Fig. 164 A 4-12 roof

the rise to the run. A 4-12 roof is one having a vertical rise of 4mm for every 12mm of horizontal run. If we know the total horizontal run we can easily calculate the total vertical rise. The greenhouse roof pitch will likely match the roof on your house or work into available space. Let's assume it is 4-12 (a very common roof pitch). Project a level line from A to B (fig. 165) and measure this distance. Repeat at the other end and check that both marks on the house are at the same height. Calculate the rise that corresponds to a run of AB (in the case of our 4-12 roof it will be $4/12$ x AB or $1/3$AB) and measure perpendicularly up this amount from B at each end. Snap a chalk line between these

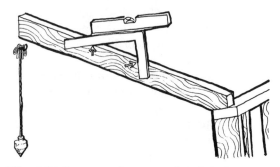

Fig. 165 Set up rafter, use plumb bob to locate end rafter end over side wall edge

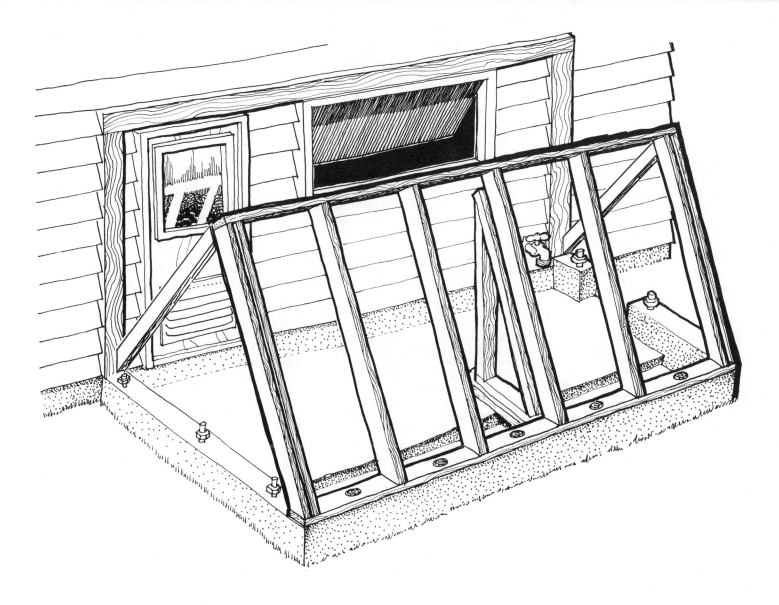

Fig. 166 South wall in place

points. Use a plumb bob or level and straight edge to project plumb lines up from the outside edges of the east and west wall bottom plates.

Laying Out the Ledger Plate If you haven't already laid out the rafter locations on the ledger and the top of the south wall, do it now. Use a spacing that will accommodate standard insulation and sheathing sizes: i.e. 16 in or 24 in centres (406mm or 610mm). If your design has roof vents which require more than one rafter space, allow for them now. Try to locate the studs in the house wall where the ledger will be nailed. Nail the ledger in place above the chalk line with 4-in (100mm) box nails, trying to get 3 in each house wall stud.

Fig. 167 Ledger plate

Attaching the Ledger Plate to a Masonry House Whereas with frame housing the ledger plate can be simply affixed directly to the existing studs of the building, attaching the plate to a solid brick, concrete block, or even stone wall will demand a bit more time. Initially ³/₈ in (10mm) holes should be pre-drilled in the

ledger plate, then the location of the holes should be marked onto the masonry while the plate is held temporarily in place. Once the holes have been marked, a concrete bit or a hammer drill can create the necessary opening for the shields. Drill into the brick directly, not the mortar. If you are using a ³/₈ in (10mm) lag bolt, the hole should be drilled with a ⁵/₈ in (16mm) bit to the depth of the shield. A lead shield is usually the cheapest and easiest means of encasing the lag bolt, but other expanding plugs can be equally effective.

Fig. 168 Use a carbide drill to set lead plugs into bricks if you are setting your ledger plate against a brick wall

Once the shields have been hammered into the hole, the plate can be put up into its location. The lag bolts, usually 3in (25mm) long, should be fitted with a washer and lagged through the wood into the lead shields, using either a socket set or a pair of vice grips. As a rule, a bolt every 36 in (900mm) should suffice unless extra-ordinary loading is expected.

Rafters Cut the roof angle on a piece of 2 x 6 longer than your rafters need to be. Tack a scrap on top of this piece so it will stay on the ledger plate while you

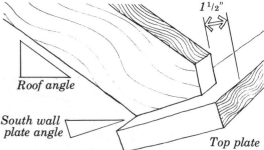

Fig. 169 End of rafter is set by angle of top plate and trimmed to nose into a 2 x ___ piece of wood on the outside edge of the top plate

trace the angle where it intersects the top wall plate and the plane of the front wall. Project the plane of the front wall across the board and shorten by the thickness of the front roof plate. Cut this rafter carefully and use it as a pattern for the rest. Nail the rafters, using the straightest ones on the ends, to the plate on the house wall using one of the methods below.

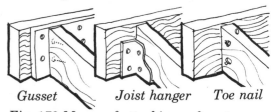

Fig. 170 Means of attaching rafters to ledger plate

Our preference is for the criss-crossed toe nails (3¹/₂ in) but care must be taken not to make hamburger out of the end of the rafter. (Vegetarian carpenters must be careful not to make tofu out of the rafter.) If you use the plywood gusset, be sure to take it into account when making the rafter pattern.

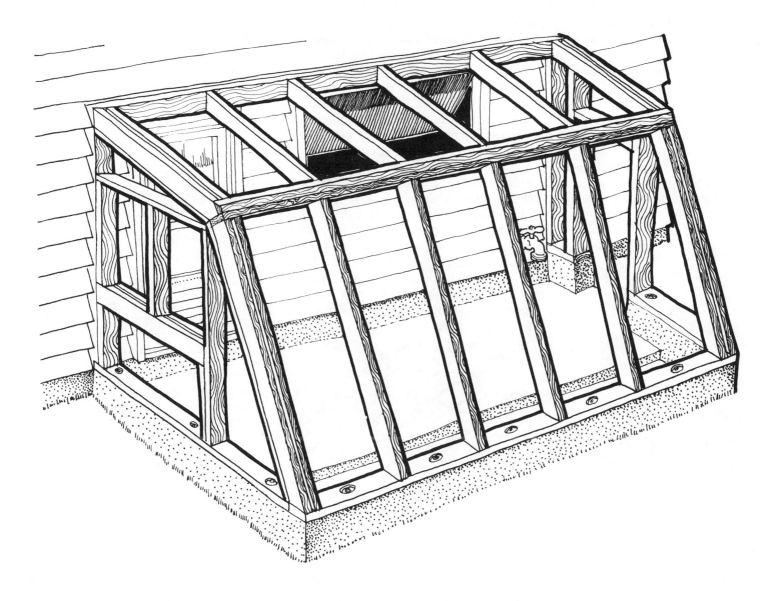

Fig. 171 Rafters and end wall in place

For now, simply tack the rafters in place on the front wall. Fig. 173 shows how to cut the front roof plate with the funny angle that goes on the end of the rafters. Use a sliding T-bevel to determine the angle, and transfer it to the circular saw. Use a table saw or radial arm saw if you have access to one. Nail this plate solidly to the rafter and toe nail it to the top wall plate. Check to make sure that the front face stays flush. Now nail the rafters down securely to the top wall plate.

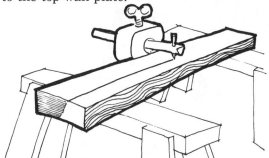

Fig. 172 Scribe a line along stock

Fig. 173 Ripping stock — set the desired angle on the saw

Attaching Rafters to an Existing Overhang If your greenhouse roof is to be an extension of the existing house roof,

proceed as follows (see fig. 174). Remove the soffit and lookouts out to a foot or so (300mm) on either side of the greenhouse. Cut the fascia and the rough fascia on the house as shown. Nail the greenhouse rafters solidly to the side of the house rafters. The house rafters are very likely spaced to accommodate standard sheathing and insulation sizes. The greenhouse rafters should be long enough to rest on the top plate of the house wall. Trying the greenhouse end rafters and wall plates can be a bit tricky. Nail the end rafter into the end of the house rough fascia where you cut it off and pry back the shingles far enough to nail through the sheathing. Try to put in some blocking in order to provide something to secure the greenhouse top wall plate to.

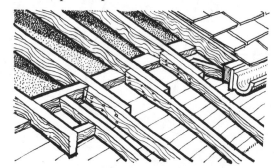

Fig. 174 Attaching greenhouse rafters directly to house roof rafters

Endwalls Start the endwalls by nailing 2 x 4s (or 2 x 6s if that is your choice) to the end rafter, the front wall and the house wall. Attach the 2 x 4s to a masonry house wall the same way you attached the ledger plate (see p. 94).

If your house has vinyl or aluminum siding it is advisable to cut out strips of siding where the greenhouse walls connect to the house. Otherwise the endwall studs will crush the siding when nailed to the house wall.

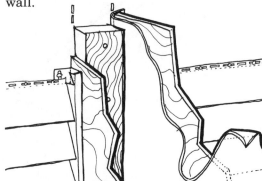

Fig. 175 Attaching J-strip and end wall joist to existing house through siding. Note that vapour barrier is attached to inside of inside wall sheathing.

To cut out a strip of siding, snap vertical (plumb) lines to indicate a space which allows for the thickness of the framing, the sheathing, the inside finish, plus 6mm ($1/4$ in) on each side for the new "J" trim required to finish the cut ends of the siding (see fig. 175). The siding can be cut with a circular saw with a plywood blade installed backwards and set to the required depth. Wear ear and eye protection and be careful. This is a noisy and potentially dangerous job. The saw blade can bind and propel the saw backwards out of the cut. Cut from the top down whenever possible. Finish the ends with tin snips.

You can figure out the exact configuration of endwall framing by taking into account

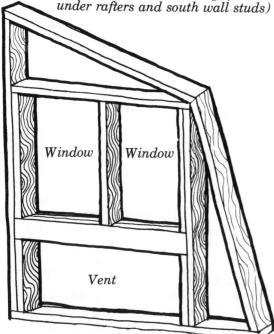

Fig. 176 Typical west wall framing (fits under rafters and south wall studs)

Window Window

Vent

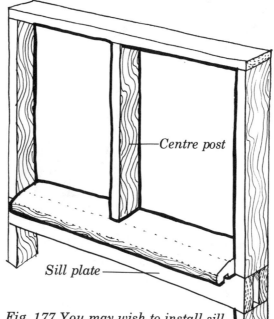

Centre post

Sill plate

Fig. 177 You may wish to install sill plate before centre post of window to ensure better water tightness.

what we have said about your site, vent requirements, glazing sizes, and the lackadaisical attitude of the telephone company. Fig. 176 shows an example you might find useful. Remember that the tops of the glazing must be low enough to accommodate the false ceiling in our standard, top-storing inter-glazing insulation system. Normal framing practice requires a header and cripples to transfer vertical loads around wall openings. In most cases, you can omit these items as long as the rafters run parallel to the endwalls as we have recommended, because there is a negligible amount of roof load transmitted to the endwalls. There is a header over the vent in fig. 176

because it is beneath glass glazing, which is itself fairly heavy. Note that the vertical member separating the glazed sections on the west end is part of the finished installation and should be a choice board: straight-grained, small knots, etc. You can save some cutting and get a more water-resistant job by putting this piece in after the finished sill and head (fig. 177). In general, it is easier to cut and install the longest pieces first. Take care to maintain a 6mm to 12mm (¼ in. to ½ in.) tolerance plus an allowance from the jamb and sill material. Make the openings too big rather than too small; glass doesn't respond well to planing.

If you're not using a false ceiling, add 2 x 4 backing for your ceiling now — it is a lot easier before the roof is sheeted. Use any suitable scraps.

Sheeting the Roof Use plywood or 19mm (1 in nominal) lumber. 8mm (³/₈ in) plywood is adequate for rafters spaced about 400mm (16 in) apart and theoretically, even for 600mm (24 in) spacing, but in the case of 600mm spacing we recommend 11mm plywood sheathing. If you use 1 in lumber you should probably apply it diagonally to provide racking strength, although we rarely do.

There is an easy way to get the sides straight. Let the sheathing hang over the ends slightly and omit nailing into the end rafters. When all the sheeting is in place, snap a chalk line along the edges. Trim the sheeting along these lines. Now you can pull the end rafters in or out so they can be nailed flush with the now straight sheeting. Use 2 in to 2½ in (50-60mm) coated nails spaced every 200mm (8 in).

Sheeting the Endwalls Use 8mm plywood. You can use the sheathing to take bends out of framing members adjacent to openings. Start a nail, bend the offending member straight, then drive the nail the rest of the way.

Finishing the South Wall Now is the time to close in the opaque section of the south wall. Snap a chalk line across the south wall at the height of the bottom of the 2 x 6 rough sills to indicate the top of the cripples. Use 2 x 6s as cripples and nail in place. Now nail in the 2 x 6 rough sills. Next put in the 2 x 4 blocking for the opaque portion sheathing. Sheet the opaque section of the south wall leaving room for the drip cap.

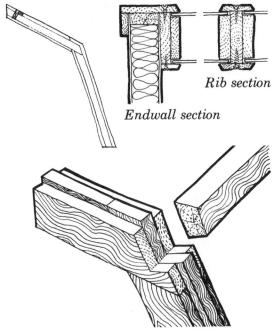

Rib section

Endwall section

Fig. 178 Rib construction — laminated boards

Framing for Roof Glazing You don't need to read this if you are planning an opaque roof. If, in a cloudy climate, you have decided to add some roof glazing, fig 178 demonstrates a method we've used successfully to facilitate the use of both roof glazing and inter-glazing insulation. Start by laying out a pattern on a clean flat surface (the sub-floor of a house under

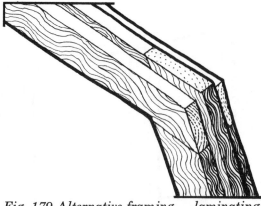

Fig. 179 Alternative framing — laminating roof joists and south wall studs.

construction, or a garage floor.) Build the first frame, tacking it together so you can do a trial fitting. If it fits, use screws or spiral nails and a waterproof glue to fasten it together, and proceed to make the rest of the frames using this one as a pattern. Fill the nail or screw holes and paint with at least two coats of top quality exterior enamel.

Fig. 180 Flashing inserted under horizontal siding to protect roof of greenhouse

Roofing and Flashing Shingle the roof according to the shingle manufacturer's recommendations. The shingles should extend at least 25mm (1 in) beyond the greenhouse fascia. The joint between the

greenhouse roof and the house wall needs flashing on top of the shingles; it should be sealed carefully to the house wall to prevent water from running in behind it. In the case of wood siding it is often possible to slip the flashing up under a piece of siding.

Fig. 181 Fashioning flashing with boards and clamps

The installation of the flashing over the roof is often complicated when attaching the greenhouse to a masonry building. Standard practice in this case involves cutting a slit into the mortar located between courses of brick or block, and inserting a flange of the flashing into the cut line. This will ensure that any water running down the facade of the building runs over the flashing. Once the flashing has been installed into the cut, either caulking or additional mortar should be used to fill the hole.

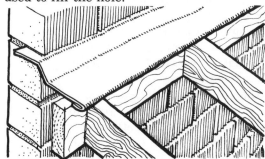

Fig. 182 Insert flashing in masonry over wall/roof junction

Most of the details in this section reflect our bias toward glass. Since the various plastics are generally easier to install than glass, we will confine the treatment of them to the details discussed on pages 103 and 104.

The glass or other glazing you have decided on will already have determined the overall size of your greenhouse. The sizes available determine the spacing of the framing members and the overall height. It is worth noting, however, that there is some leeway. Pages 105 and 106 give you some hints on the thrills and excitement of cutting glass. We show you how to glue two pieces of glass together with silicon sealant and/or joining bars.

Tempered glass cannot be cut but we have successfully extended its length by gluing a piece of non-tempered glass to it. Overhead glass must be tempered for safety reasons. Wired glass may be specified in some building codes, but we don't like it. Doors that are mostly glazed should use tempered glass.

Fig. 183 A.B.C. — *Always Be Careful with glass*

Preparing the Openings

Stock Decision   Normally, in residential construction, the jamb (door, window, or vent frames) is made of clear kiln-dried fir or finger-jointed pine. Such lumber now costs $2.00 to $3.00 per board foot, or more. A reasonable alternative is carefully picked construction grade fir, cedar, or pine. Bevelled cedar siding is particularly useful for window sills because the bevel provides the necessary drainage, and cedar's natural oils tend to resist rot — a must for this particularly sensitive area. While cedar is becoming scarce, it is much more justifiable to use it in this critical application, and so avoid the use of toxic wood preservatives, than to use it as decorative interior wall panelling. Since most of the jamb and trim material will have to be ripped on a table or radial arm saw to give you the right size, you will be able to cut out or around some defects. What you should seek is almost clear, straight-grained lumber that is as dry as possible. Try to avoid using sapwood. Using a 'planer' type saw blade to rip your

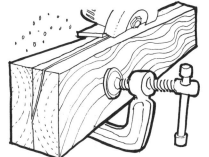

Fig. 184 *Ripping a shallow angle (window sill, door jamb, etc.)*

stock will result in cuts that are smoother and require less sanding (or none at all depending on how fussy you are).

Cutting the Stock   When you have decided which of the various glazing details (p. 100) suits you best, determine how much of each jamb, sill, window trim, and window stop you will need and what their widths and shapes are. In each case set the saw, make a sample piece from a scrap, and check its width by holding it in position before proceeding to cut all you need of that size. Cut a little extra to allow for errors. Keep the stock as uniform as possible. In some cases, the sizing can be fairly critical.

Although it is not crucial, you will get a better seal if you put in the insulation and apply the vapour barrier prior to installing the jamb. It will be worth your while at this point to make yourself a mitre box with all the angles you will need in it. That would include 90°, the glazing angle, the angle you use for sill drainage, and the angle of intersection of the front wall and the roof. It should have the capacity to handle your widest piece of jamb.

Fig. 185 A mitre box — *x = width of widest jamb being used in greenhouse*

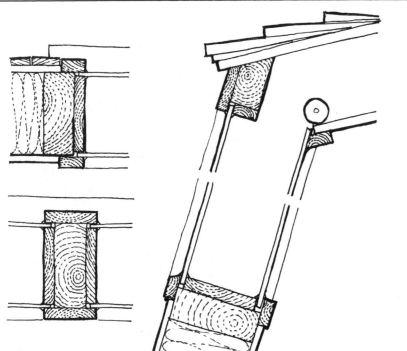

Fig. 186 A simple glazing detail

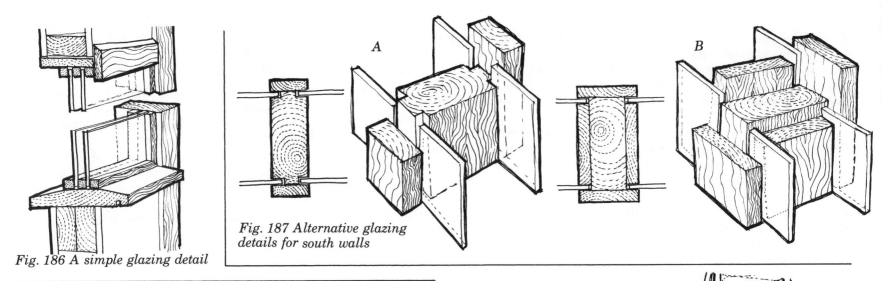

A

B

Fig. 187 Alternative glazing
details for south walls

Fig. 188 Front wall glazing (section)

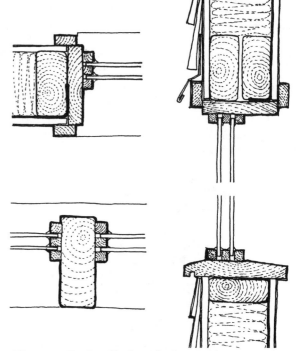

Fig. 189 Endwall glazing (section)

Installing the Jamb Cut and install the sills first to prevent any water running down the jamb from getting into the framing. It is very important that the sills be sloped to ensure drainage. They should also have a drip cut to prevent water from running along their bottoms and into the framing. Note the way the sills are cut to run under the outside trim.

in (50mm to 60mm) hot galvanized casing nails about every 400mm. Most of the nails can be located where they will be hidden by the glazing and the stops. Cut and fit the stops and trim pieces. Here is where you will find out if your framing was accurate or not, and wish that it were if it isn't. Now, you may have to measure and cut each piece separately. Cut the

stops to fit snugly; if you bow out the centre while you tuck the ends in place, the piece will snap into place. Unless you are using stops with a fancy profile, simple butt joints will do. Butt joints make the stops easier to remove in case of glass breakage. Note that the bottom stops should be bevelled and the side pieces which butt them will have to be cut accordingly.

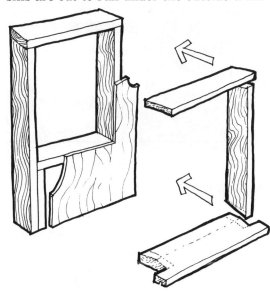

Fig. 190 Head, jamb and sill for endwall opening and vents

Look at the end of each piece before cutting it to determine which side is the heart side; keeping the heart side out will ensure that any cupping caused by drying will not curl the edges away from the framing. Lay a healthy bead of caulking (acoustical sealant is best) on the vapour barrier and push the sill or jamb into it. Nail these pieces in place using 2 in to 2¹/₂

Fig. 191 End window/vent with head, jamb and sill fitted

Fig. 192 Side window with glazing stops installed

Now is the time to paint everything: jamb, trim and stops. The advantages of painting now are that you can just slop it on without trying to keep the glass clean and that you can paint all four sides and the ends of the stops and trim.

Since the endwalls will not contain inter-glazing insulation, the middle stops are narrower than similar spacers used in the south wall. Nail the middle stops in place using either hot galvanized casing nails or fluted flooring nails.

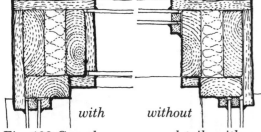

with   *without*

Fig. 193 Greenhouse corner details with and without inter-glazing insulation

Venting the Glazing Space   Skip this paragraph if you are using sealed units. If you are using two single sheets of glass, as we recommend, you will have to provide ventilation holes to allow moisture which may accumulate between the two layers to escape to the outside. Moisture can get into this space in several ways: during construction, through small leaks from the inside, or via migration through the wood. Venting inter-glazing insulation space is crucial. There is bound to be some air leakage from the greenhouse through the operating cord tubes, and the resultant moisture must be allowed to escape.

Drill 10mm ($^3/_8$ in) holes parallel to the glazing first and put a straw or splinter in the holes to give you something to aim at when drilling the holes from the outside. The holes from the outside should be sloped up to prevent water from running in. Push a little piece of screen or loose fibreglass into the front holes to keep out insects and dust. Next, give everything a second coat of paint, getting some into those holes you just drilled.

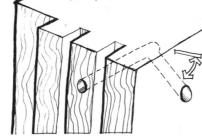

Fig. 194 Drill $^3/_8$ inch vent hole to inter-glazing space. Slope up from outside to prevent rain running in and plug with fibreglass insulation to keep the bugs out.

Installing the Glass

Now you can start putting in the glass. Countersink any nails in the sill which the glass could possibly sit on. The glass should rest evenly on the sill and not be supported on only one corner. Remedy any problem with softwood shims or neoprene setting blocks. If you are using our interglazing insulation system, do not install the inner glazing at this time.

Caulking   Secure the glass with the stops you previously cut and painted. Seal around the edges with silicone sealant.

(See p. 116 for comparison of caulking compounds.) Besides having the advantages outlined, silicone is the easiest caulking to apply neatly. Cut a small hole (5mm) in the tip of the tube and start in the least conspicuous place you can find. You might even want to lay a few practice beads on some scrap wood. Keep your body in a comfortable position so you can maintain a steady hand. Squeeze the gun.

Fig. 195 Caulking technique — tip should lead slightly

Move along smoothly and stop when you have to click the gun to avoid ripples at those points. The tip should press the bead into the corner slightly. Keep the tip clean

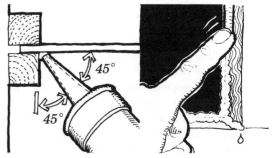

Fig. 196 Hold caulking gun at 45° to corner bead; smooth bead with finger

or it will smear the edges of the bead. With practice you'll be an expert. Probably the first few beads will need to be smoothed out; a finger is the best tool for this piece of handiwork. Spit on your finger so the caulking won't stick to it. Seal anything on the outside that looks like it might admit water and anything on the inside that might leak air (see "Sealing and Insulation").

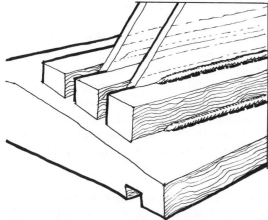

Fig. 197 Window details: beveled stops; drip cut; caulking — silicon sealant

Sealed Units

Double-glazed, factory-sealed units can occasionally be obtained at reasonable prices due to overstock, unclaimed special orders, or slight imperfections. Sealed units are composed of two sheets of glass held apart at the edges by a square tube usually filled with a moisture absorbing material (silica gel or a molecular sieve) which keeps the air dry enough to prevent any condensation. The units must be handled

carefully because they are heavy and even a small chip can break the seal. The openings should be lined with a strip of glazing tape (fig. 198.) The glazing tape will allow an even pressure all around the units. Use setting blocks under the unit so

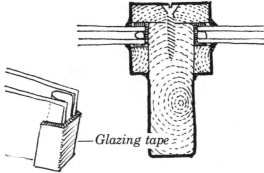

— Glazing tape —

Fig. 198 Line openings with glazing tape

that the weight of the two sheets of glass is born evenly. The setting blocks should be softwood or neoprene 3mm ($^1/_8$ in) high, as wide as the unit is thick, and 100mm (4 in) long. They should be centred $^1/_4$ of the

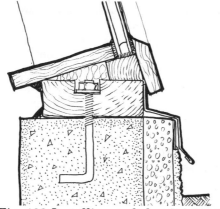

Fig. 199 Installing sealed unit in south wall section glazed to foundation

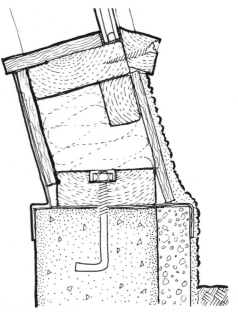

Fig. 200 Installing sealed units into opaque section of south wall

width of the unit in from each corner. The tape around the edge of the sealed unit should be removed just prior to installation.

Plastic Glazing Materials

We have not devoted much space to glazing details for plastic glazing materials partly because of our bias towards glass and partly because the details we've shown for glass can easily be adapted for plastics.

There is a large variety of plastic glazing materials available. We will briefly discuss two of the more common types: fibreglass reinforced polyester and acrylics. You would be well advised to obtain the manufacturer's instructions if you intend to use a particular plastic.

Fibreglass Reinforced Polyester or FRP is usually sold in rolls 4 ft wide, 50 ft long (1.2m x 15.2m). Installation of fibreglass is a relatively simple matter although care must be taken to avoid bulges, which as well as being unsightly, can be difficult to seal. Begin by cutting the plastic to size using metal shears (tin snips) or a circular saw with a plywood blade, installed with the teeth backwards. Check the plastic against the framing. If it fits, apply a bead of caulking (silicone or "Mono") to the frame. Locate the plastic over the opening and tack it to the frame using one nail (1 in roofing nail) in the centre at the top. Pull down firmly and nail the bottom, again with one nail in the centre. Do the same with the sides, then work out toward the corners, nailing every 200mm (8 in). Finish applying the first layer, install the spacers, and continue with the second layer. Alternatively, the second layer could be applied to the inside, creating a space for inter-glazing insulation.

Rigid Acrylic Glazings   These glazing materials have a higher coefficient of expansion than any other. A 1.2m (4 ft) panel should have at least a 6mm (1/4 in) allowance for expansion. Use neoprene gaskets as they allow for expansion and contraction more readily than nails and caulking. Acrylics are easily scratched and should be handled carefully.

Splicing Glass

Often the glass you are able to find at a reasonable cost (see Appendix) will not be long enough to glaze the desired south wall height. For example, patio-door glass, an excellent source of tempered glass, comes in 76 in (1930mm) or 68 in (1727mm) lengths, but your design may call for glazing that is 90 in (2300mm) long. There are several ways of handling this problem, all of which involve the joining of a shorter piece of non-tempered glass to the tempered glass.

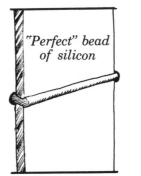

"Perfect" bead of silicon   *"H" clip*

Fig. 201 Splicing glass

You can make an "H"-shaped bar out of fir, which joins the two pieces (above). If you are installing an inter-glazing insulation system, be sure to bevel the corners of the bar so they will not catch the insulation. You can also frame horizontal divisions similar to the vertical ones, although this will increase shading and eliminate the use of inter-glazing insulation.

A third alternative is simply to glue two pieces of glass together with silicone sealant. Every engineer and architect we talked to advised against this technique, but we've had good luck with it. (We've used it successfully on three greenhouses to date and in each case the joint has been subjected to year-round temperature extremes, including -35°C in the winter.) The dangers are that it can leak if not properly done and that it might cause the glass to break. With this warning, we include instructions below.

Start by installing the lower piece, holding it in place with a couple of small blocks. Check the fit of the top piece. If it fits, apply a small bead of silicon to the top of the top of the lower piece as neatly as possible. A small notch (1mm to 2mm) cut in the end of the caulking tube will help to steady the gun as you lay down the caulking bead.

Install the upper piece by bringing it straight down from above so as not to push the silicon inward. Don't force the two pieces of glass together; try to maintain a cushion of silicon between them. Some silicon will squish out; allow it to dry, then trim it with a razor blade. For double glazing you won't be able to trim the inside of the second joint, but by then you'll be an expert and you will have done a tidy job of applying the silicon. Be sure to leave enough room for thermal expansion.

It is difficult to recommend firm guide lines for this technique. We've used it to glue 3 ft x 2 ft (900mm x 600mm) pieces of float glass to the top of 3 ft x 6 ft (900mm x 1800mm) tempered glass, with good results. If the top piece were to be any larger than that, we would recommend using the "H" channels, a technique we've used successfully to join two large pieces of tempered glass.

Because of the sloped front glazing, it is possible that in some situations the top of the south wall will be directly over the walkway. In such cases, the tempered glass should be moved to the top, and the joint between it and the non-tempered glass should be built with an "H" channel.

We do not recommend splicing glass for roof glazing.

Glass Cleaning Tips

Any dirt that gets left on the inside of double glazing is there forever. It may well be that the outsides will be too dirty for anyone to notice but if you want the option of clean glass, here's a formula for your own low cost glass cleaner.

Metric	Imperial
125 ml sudsy ammonia	1/2 cup sudsy ammonia
500 ml isopropyl alcohol	1 pint isopropyl alcohol
5 ml dish detergent	1 teaspoon dish detergent
enough water to fill a 4 litre (1 gallon) jug.	

Apply with a spritzer (spray bottle) and use a car windshield squeegee to wipe off the excess. Wipe with newspaper to remove streaks.

Cutting Glass

Glass cutting is fun. The best part is the suspense of wondering if you'll get a clean break, then the crrrack as you find out. You'll need a few things. The essentials are: a good glass cutter (the German ones with the green handles are our favorite —

Fig. 202 Basic glass cutting tool

they are available from most glass shops), some kerosene or other light oil, a straight edge (a strip of plywood or 1 in lumber will do but it should have a smooth, splinter-free edge), a friend or some clamps, and a flat place to work (a piece of thick plywood on a couple of saw-horses will do). A pair of

Fig. 203 Running pliers for snapping off small bits of glass along a scored line

running or tile cutting pliers is very handy if you have to cut off any thin strips. These pliers are available in most large hardware outlets for about $12.00 but nobody seems to know what you're talking about so take a picture along if you go to get some.

Measure out the size you need, marking it with a felt pen and keeping in mind that you want the glass to be 9mm to 12mm (3/8 to 1/2 in) smaller than the opening in both directions. For wierd shapes, you might want to make a cardboard template, check it against the opening, and trace it onto the glass. Clamp, or have your friend hold the straight edge along the line you want to cut, allowing for the offset of the cutting wheel from the edge which will ride along the straight edge. Now paint some kerosene along the proposed cut. You must run the cutter along the straight edge in one continuous pass, going over it only once. Any overlaps or skips in the scoring will usually cause the break to veer off to one side or the other. You might want to practice on some scraps to get the feel of it. (The problem with this is you might not have any scraps til you try it and make a mistake.) When making long cuts it is important to position yourself so you can comfortably reach all the way from one end to the other. Be sure to score the glass all the way to both ends.

Slide the scored line so it is directly over the edge of the work surface. Keep the work surface clean so as not to scratch the glass while sliding it. Support the piece that you will be breaking off because it may now break under its own weight.

Now comes the exciting part. Push down sharply, putting as even pressure as possible along the length of the piece you are breaking off. Crrrrrrrack! Whew! It broke clean. If you must cut off a long narrow strip — 100mm (4 in) or less — running pliers will make the job easier. Snap the score line as in fig. 204. This is fun, too. It is quite fascinating to watch the break start at the pliers and run to the other end. Occasionally, with or without the running pliers the glass will break leaving a little corner stuck on one end. Use the widest pliers you have to break this piece off. Sometimes you have to chew away at it, with pretty crude results, but that's all right because the stops will cover it. It's important not to leave the score line too long before breaking because, glass being a fluid, the score line tends to flow back together.

Fig. 204 Snapping off a long length of glass by bending along a scored line over a straight edge. Wear gloves!

Doors

Exterior Door   It is best to have a glazed door. You can buy a manufactured, pre-hung door, (which will consist of the assembled door mounted on hinges inside the jamb) and forget about the following instructions. Or you can buy a new or recycled door, build the jamb, and hang it yourself. Or you can build the door yourself using our easy-to-follow recipe for glazed doors.

Building the Jamb   The door jamb should be constructed using good quality straight-grained fir or pine with a minimum of knots. If you are building the door yourself, you have a chicken and egg situation. On one hand, the rough opening in your framing determines the jamb dimensions, which also determines the door size, which in turn determines the glass size to a large extent. On the other hand, the glass for the door, especially if you are using tempered glass, influences the door size, which determines the jamb dimensions, which in turn determines the rough opening in the framing — which you have already completed. The best approach is to choose the door glazing *before* you frame the rough opening. The jamb should allow 6mm (¼ in) tolerance all the way around the door so it will swing freely. The outside of the jamb should be 20mm (¾ in) narrower (10mm on either side) and 13mm (½ in) shorter than the rough opening.

Cut the jamb, sill, and trim, keeping in mind that you want it a hair too wide (a metric hair) rather than too narrow. Fig. 184 shows how to mill this material with a circular saw if there is no table or radial arm saw available. (You can also buy door jamb material milled from clear fir or finger-jointed pine, but it costs an arm and a leg. Or, you can assemble a jamb without milling as in figure. 205. It is almost

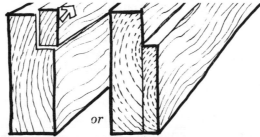

Fig. 205 Manufacture of a door jamb: 1. saw out (rabet) door stop or 2. build up stop. (Seal and glue!)

impossible to cut the bevel for the sill completely with a power saw. Lay out the bevelled face using an adjustable tri-square (combination square). Cut as much as you can and then break the wedge off, or finish the cut with a hand saw. Trim the remaining material with a plane, trying to leave the line.

Cut the joints as on page 108. We find it easier to mark and cut the hinge mortises before assembling the jamb. Nail and glue the jamb together using 3½" (90mm) box nails.

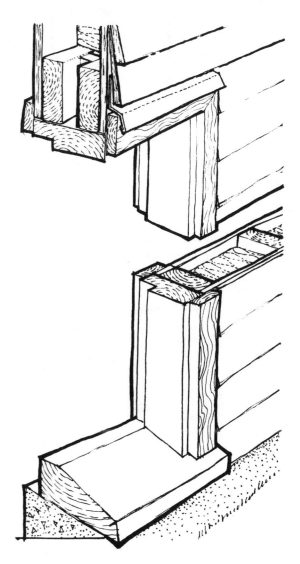

Fig. 206 Door jamb — over-all view

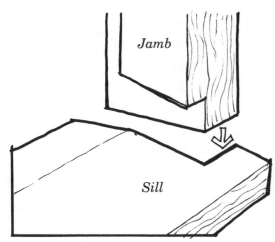

Fig. 207 The jamb is sawn out to fit over sill. Sill is notched to wrap around the jamb. (Seal and glue!)

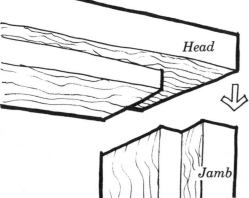

Fig. 208 Notch out door stop in jamb head to fit over door jamb. (Seal and glue in assembly to keep water out.)

Building the Door   Standard entrance doors are 3'0" x 6'8" (914 x 2032mm). That is as good a size as any, but anything narrower than 2'6" (762mm) becomes difficult to negotiate with a wheelbarrow.

It is best to use tempered glass in the door if you can. If you cannot, the bottom two feet (600mm) should not be glazed because of the potential for breakage.

Let us assume you are using tempered glass. The glass size will largely determine the door dimensions. The sides and top of the door should be at least 125mm (5 in) wide and the bottom at least 190mm (7¹/₂ in). This material should be very dry, straight-grained fir or pine with a minimum of knots. The rabbets can be cut with a table saw, a radial arm saw, a router, or even a circular saw. Note that the rabbet on the sides run the entire length and are deepened to form the tenons for the top and bottom joints. The mortises are best cut on a table saw but they can be done with a hand saw and a chisel. Clamp the door together without glue first to check it for squareness. You can adjust it by trimming the ends of the top and bottom with a block plane. Glue the joints, clamp it together, and drill the dowel hole 12mm to 19mm (¹/₂ to ³/₄ in wide). Squeeze

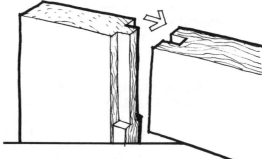

Fig. 209 Rabet and notch side and top of door. Note: glazing may be rabetted in as well (glue and clamp)

glue into the dowel holes and flute or groove the dowel so excess glue can escape. If you don't provide an escape route for the extra glue, the pressure can split the wood. Drill the vent holes as shown below and give the whole door two coats of paint.

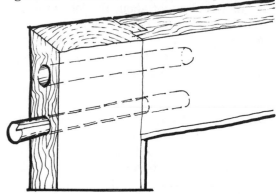

Fig. 210 Drill holes for dowels and add glue. Notch dowel to allow excess glue to escape.

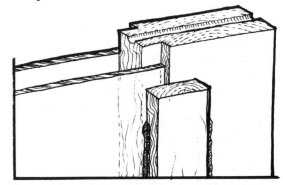

*Fig. 211 Mounting double glazing on door. Note: **Use only tempered glass!** Place sticker or ornament on glazing to prevent people from taking a short cut through the glass. Drill vent holes to inter-glazing space using silicon sealant around battens. Vent hole.*

Install the glass, securing it with the trim using 1¹/₂ in (38mm) casing nails or fluted flooring nails.

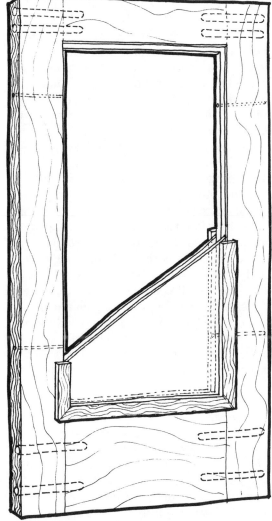

Fig. 212 Making a glass door — overall view

Hanging the Door   An exterior door requires three 4 in (100mm) hinges. Install the hinges on the door first. They should be located 150mm (6in) from the top, 150mm (6in) from the bottom, and in the centre. Cut the hinge mortises with a chisel or router. Separate one of the hinges and use it to check the depth of the mortise. It should be as perfect as possible. The side away from the pin should be a hair too deep rather than too shallow as in fig. 213 or it will prevent the door from closing properly. Screw the hinges down so that the pins go in from the top.

Fig. 213 Mortise outside leaves a hair deep into frame and jamb to avoid levering screws out of both when closing door!

Align the hinge side of the door with the corresponding jamb and mark the hinge locations on the jamb very carefully. Cut the hinge mortise as in fig. 213. Screw down the appropriate half of the top hinge only. Install the jamb in the rough opening using shims in order to get it plumb. Secure the jamb at the top and bottom on both sides using two 3¹/₂ in (90mm) casing nails at each location. Hang the door on

Fig. 214 Pre-hang door — install hinges on door; mark hinge mortises on jamb and mount

the top hinge, and screw in the lower hinges after mating the halves and inserting the pins. Use shims and casing nails every 400mm (16 in). Align and secure the centres of the jamb. Apply the exterior trim. Install the lock set using the manufacturer's instructions.

Vents

The sizing and general location of the vents is covered in DESIGN. If at all possible, we think it is easier to build and operate vents in the endwalls. Roof vents are harder to seal around and vents in the south wall interfere with inter-glazing insulation. In general, it is wise to make the vents too big rather than too small. You can easily open them only partially but it is very difficult to enlarge vents once the greenhouse is finished. Remember when framing the upper vent opening to allow for the inter-glazing option's false ceiling.

The jamb, trim, flashing and sealing details are quite similar to those for endwall glazing. Note that the screen is on the *inside* of the vent. The problem with this detail is that the screen will interfere with direct operation of the vent from the inside. The alternative, with the screen on the outside, will allow rain to come

through the screen and become trapped at the bottom of the vent jamb, creating a potential rotting problem. The vents can be made to open inward by using a louvre to keep water from getting behind the screen, but you must increase the vent size because louvres can cut the effective area of the vent by 50% or more.

All the vents shown in our details are insulated to at least RSI-1.76 (R-10) using 2 in (51mm) extruded polystyrene rigid insulation (blue styrofoam). Other types of rigid insulation can be substituted. In some cases it may be desirable to use glazed vents. These can be built using the instructions for building a glass door (see p. 108).

Building the Vents Because of the thickness of the vents, it is necessary to bevel the edge opposite the hinge in order for them to clear the jamb when swinging open or closed. Fig. 216 shows how to determine the required bevel. It's a toss-up

whether it's easier to bevel the end piece and then construct the vent, or build the vent square, keeping the nails holding the plywood out of the way, and then cut the whole thing to shape. The vent should be 6mm (1/4 in) smaller in both height and width than the finished opening. Nail the frame together, cover one side with plywood, fasten with finishing nails and glue, fit the insulation inside the frame, and cover the other side. Pieces of piano hinge 50mm (2 in) or more in width and at least three screw holes long work quite well on vents. They save a bit of time because they can be applied without a hinge mortise. Piano hinge is a bit more susceptible to rust and should be given a light coat of grease occasionally. Secure the vent in the closed position, then install the inside stops, pressing them snug against the vent with a piece of weatherstripping between. Apply the weatherstripping after all the stops are installed in such a way that the joints in the weatherstripping do not line up with the joints in the stops. Caulk the inside of the stops (or set them in a bed of caulk in the first place), staple the screen in place and put in the other set of stops.

Fig. 217 shows a very simple operator mechanism. The vent is hung in such a way that its centre of gravity is inside the hinge and causes the vent to begin opening once the cord releases the latch. The cord then pulls the vent to the desired height. There is also a variety of operators available commercially for awning and casement windows. However, except for the scissor type, they can be tricky to install.

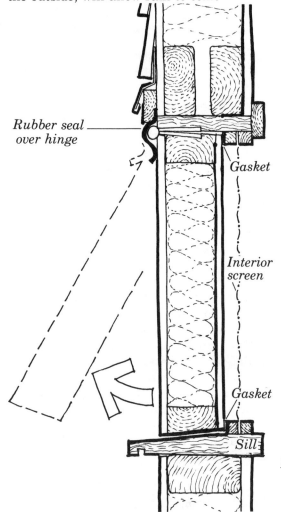

Rubber seal over hinge

Gasket

Interior screen

Gasket

Sill

Fig. 215 Vent for endwalls and insulated shutter

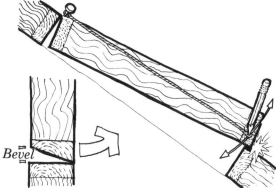

Bevel

Fig. 216 Draw a radius from the hinge with string and pencil which will allow leading edge of vent to pass into opening

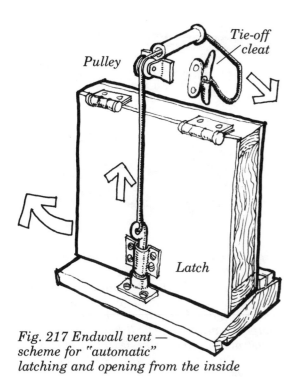

Fig. 217 Endwall vent —
scheme for "automatic"
latching and opening from the inside

Roof Vents If you cannot supply ample ventilation through endwall vents, you will have to put vents in the roof. The main problems with roof vents are keeping water from leaking in around the vent, and the possibility of weakening the roof if the vents must extend through more than one joist space. The solution to the water problem is proper flashing (see fig. 218). When forming and installing the flashing, think about how water behaves — it always runs downhill. It will be necessary to do a little caulking on the corners. Fig. 219 shows a roof vent which solves the problem of weakening the roof, by sitting the entire vent above the rafters. Note the

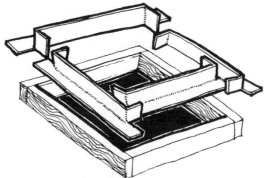

Fig. 218 Flashing for a raised vent — caulk
or tar corners and edges

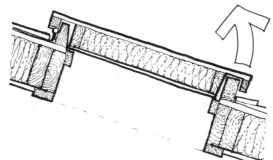

Fig. 219 Raised roof vent — note how edges
are beveled to avoid binding in the swing

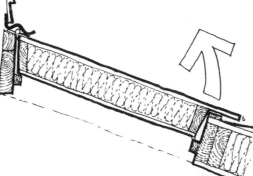

Fig. 220 Flush roof vent — note that flap
laps roof to shed water and edges are
beveled

caulking required to maintain the integrity of the vapour barrier. The 1 x 2 in stop should hide and seal the joint where the curb, roof sheathing, and blocking come together. The curb should be carefully toe nailed to the rafters and blocking. The same effect can be achieved by using 2 x 10s around the inside of the vent opening and notching it over the rafters that run through. In general, you will save some effort by making the east-west dimension of roof vents small enough to fit between two rafters rather than having to install extra rafters.

Fig. 221 shows a detail which simplifies the flashing and curb somewhat but requires reinforcing the roof to compensate for cutting a rafter.

Fig. 221 Framing a roof vent opening —
double adjacent rafters and cripples

Power Vents and Fans In early spring and late summer there are days which start out with very cold mornings but have bright sunshine most of the day. To maximize heat gain on such days, you may want the vents closed in the morning but open to distribute heat to the house or outside by noon. If you can't be there at noon, you might resort to some kind of automatic venting system. The most benign choice is the use of heat motors. They act similar to hydraulic cylinders, but are fairly expensive and have limited strength and strokes.

Another possibility is the use of thermostatically operated electric fans. These devices can replace the top vent, but you still have the problem of either getting the bottom vent open, or leaving it open when you leave in the morning. You can buy the fans and thermostats separately and connect them together. An economical alternative is the use of an attic venting fan which is already wired to a thermostat. These high-capacity, relatively low-priced units have one potential problem (besides the fact that they use electricity and contribute to the rationale for nuclear power plants): they switch on at about 38°C which, even allowing for some heat stratification, could be a bit too high to avoid overheating problems.

Cutting Holes through the Existing House Wall

Frame Wall It may be necessary to cut an opening or openings in the wall of the building to which you are attaching the greenhouse. The following procedure can be used for any opening — door, vent or window. Let's assume we are working on a vent. Start by drawing a diagram which includes the vent size, the size of the finished opening and the rough opening, and the outside dimensions of the exterior trim. Cut a small hole about 300mm square in the interior drywall in the approximate centre of the vent location. Note where the studs are and try to locate the vent so that one side of the rough opening will be the thickness of a framing member (38mm, 1$\frac{1}{2}$ in) from a stud. If you are not committed to a particular shape, it would be good to design the vent so that the rough opening is two stud thicknesses (76mm, 3 in) less than the space between two studs. You will need a hole big enough to give you access to cut off the stud(s) far enough back so you can get a header in at the top and a rough sill at the bottom. On the sides you need only to be able to get the cripples in, but you might as well cut the drywall back to the centre of the nearest stud. Lay out and draw the lines for cutting the drywall.

Using your diagram, lay out and draw the lines which describe the outside of the exterior trim. Do this marking on the inside and extend the lines outside of the drywall you are about to cut. Cut the drywall away using a utility knife. This labour may seem difficult and tedious but you can save a bit of trouble later on if you can avoid cutting the vapour barrier. Slit the vapour barrier from corner to corner and fold it out of the way. Cut out the insulation. Using a straight 2 x 4 and a combination square, develop the outside trim lines on the inside of the sheathing. Drill small holes through to transfer the

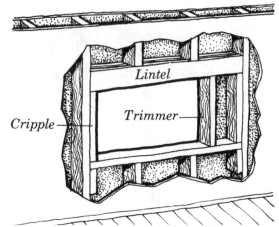

Fig. 222 Cutting a hole in an existing wood stud wall. Note: Brace and reinforce all bearing walls during this process!! Install cripples on existing studs to hold up lintel and sill plate. Use a trimmer to define rough opening size. Don't hack gyproc as illustrated, rather, trim neatly on centre line of stud to make a neat patch job possible.

lines to the outside. Snap the outside lines with a chalk line. Set a circular saw to cut the depth of the siding thickness and cut out the siding only. If the exterior is stucco, use an abrasive disc in the circular saw. Be careful, because the line you cut is going to be the joint between the exterior finish and trim. Now lay out the rough opening on the sheathing and cut it out. Cut out any studs flush with the inside drywall. You may need a chisel to finish the cut. Install the cripples with the blocks to support the sill already fastened. The cripples must be nailed very securely to the studs in order to carry the load of the cutoff stud(s). Nail blocking to the header and sill to support the drywall seam at top and bottom. Put in the header and sill; 3 in (75mm) drywall screws (or any long screws) might make the connections a bit easier. Finish framing the opening if it doesn't fill the entire space and proceed as described previously for any vent, door, or window. Re-insulate and repair the vapour barrier using acoustical sealant to connect the old and the new.

Masonry Wall Many consider dynamite the only solution to installing a new opening in a solid brick house. But hold the fuse for a bit – opening a large hole in a solid brick or concrete block wall is not all that hard, and may provide some real satisfaction. Initially, determine the size of the door opening. Once you have marked out the height and the width of the opening you will need (making sure to account for the additional rough framing which will be needed), slight alterations may prove to make the task easier. Remove the course of bricks or blocks directly above the opening. Getting the first couple of blocks out is usually slow work. Break the mortar around the brick with a cold chisel and loosen it until it can be removed. You would be wise to start from the middle of the course to keep the edges clean.

Once the first brick is removed, progress to each side until you are at the end of the desired opening. For the top course, you will want to extend the opening another foot on each side to provide a seat for the new lintel. Temporary bracing of the wall

above can be provided with wood shims until you are able to install the new lintel.

Fig. 223 Carefully remove course of bricks where lintel is to go

Once the opening has been made you can put the new supporting lintel in place. In some cases the load may demand the installation of a very strong lintel. Steel "I"-beams can be purchased from local scrap metal dealers. Alternatively, the chart on p. 248 outlines the required dimensions of wooden lintels.

Once the new lintel has been installed, the fun begins. The bricks or blocks located below the lintel can be banged away with a sledge hammer or any convenient tool. Care should be taken not to disturb the bricks which are at the edge of the

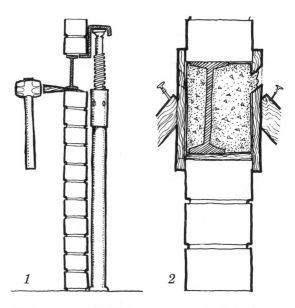

Fig. 224 1. Install L-jacks along opening to replace temporary bracing then install I-beam and wedge tight against upper bricks.
2. If necessary, you can finish lintel in concrete as shown by forcing concrete into form. Use bottom plate cut to size carefully fitted around wedges. Note: **Don't under jack or over jack** as either strategy will bring the house down. Establish firm bearing every second or third brick!

opening. Any cutting can be done with a rented cement saw. You will be more likely to end up with straight lines if the opening is marked with a chalk line. Once the lintel is in place and the edges of the opening have been squared, the rough framing of the door can be installed.

Insulation and Sealing

Insulating Materials

Insulating materials are rated according to their ability to resist the flow of heat. The higher the numerical value of the rating, the better the resistance. Metric units are referred to as the "RSI-Rating" and the imperial as "R-Value." For a given thickness of an insulating material, the R-value figure will be about 5.67 times the RSI figure.

Fibreglass insulation has the highest heat resistance per unit cost. It is also the easiest to install in most wall and roof situations. It can be cut easily with a serrated bread knife, although any knife will do. It will, however, wreak havoc with the cutting edge. Wear a particle mask to avoid inhaling the fibres.

Rigid insulation, while considerably more expensive, usually has a higher insulating value per unit thickness. It is useful for insulating the foundation and the earth beyond, vents, under floors, and in some movable insulation systems. The table on p. 250 compares the common insulations.

It is difficult to present hard and fast rules governing how much insulation to use in various parts of the greenhouse. We can only offer suggestions and discuss a few general considerations. If you are planning to keep your greenhouse heated and in use all winter, higher levels of insulation are warranted, especially if the greenhouse is designed to maximize heat gain and minimize heat loss on the short winter days (no roof glazing and minimal endwall glazing). If on the other hand your main concern is building a season extender which may freeze during the worst part of the winter, higher insulation levels will have little value. In a greenhome, it is advisable to insulate the greenhouse area to the same levels as the rest of the house.

Where to Insulate

Floors   There is some controversy about whether or not to insulate beneath a greenhouse floor. One school of thought says that most of the heat is lost around the perimeter anyway and that the earth can be used as thermal storage. Another school says that since the temperature of the soil is only 39°F to 45°F (4°C to 7°C), much of the heat stored is not recoverable and there is a steady drain from the greenhouse the rest of the time. We feel that it is not reasonable to try to use the earth beneath the greenhouse as thermal storage since it can prevent the greenhouse from freezing only in marginal cases. We recommend installing about 2 in (50mm) of rigid insulation beneath the floor with an insulating value of R8-R10 (RSI 1.4-1.8). Use white styrofoam board since it is cheaper per unit than the blue styrofoam. To increase the insulating level, simply increase the thickness.

Foundation   It is definitely worth insulating the outside of the foundation and laying a skirt around the perimeter (see fig. 225). Use rigid insulation with an R value of about 10 (RSI 1.8).

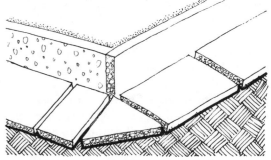

Fig. 225 Laying a skirt of insulation around the foundation

Roof and Walls   In greenhouses the glazing accounts for more than half of the heat loss. The foundation losses and infiltration together account for more than one-third (assuming a very tightly sealed building). This leaves the walls and roof responsible for less than one-sixth and probably in fact, for less than 10% of all heat lost. It is evident that even large changes in the insulation levels in the roof and endwalls will not have a great effect on the overall thermal performance.

The roof is usually a fairly large expanse framed with 2 x 6 rafters and should use R20 (RSI 3.53) insulation. We recommend 2 x 4 framing with R12 (RSI 2.12) insulation for the endwalls rather than 2 x 6 framing with R20, for these reasons: it is slightly cheaper and easier to work with 2 x 4 lumber; you can use 1 x 6s for jamb material only if the framing members are 2 x 4s. The use of 2 x 6 framing would require the use of 1 x 8 jamb material and it is becoming increasingly harder to find good 1 x 8 lumber.

In general, the less glazing there is in the endwalls, the more sense it makes to use more insulation and, hence, 2 x 6 instead of 2 x 4 framing.

Sealing

There are two major reasons for sealing a greenhouse as tightly as possible. Cold air leaking in and warm air escaping account for 30% to 35% of the heat loss in most frame buildings. Greenhouses, with all their windows, vents, and relatively small expanse of insulated walls, have enormous potential for heat loss by infiltration. Sealing the vapour barrier joints and edges with acoustical sealant, and weather-stripping the vents, doors and operable windows will keep this loss to a minimum. On the other hand, you might argue, plants need carbon dioxide for photosynthesis, so why bother with the tedious job of sealing when you need to bring in fresh air anyway? Well, for one thing, in the winter months plant growth is usually quite slow due to the low light and temperatures. Also, adequate carbon dioxide can usually be obtained from air exchange with the house.

The second reason for a tight seal is perhaps the most important. Air leaving any warm building carries moisture, a phenomenon especially true of a green-house. As this air moves through the wall, either via gaps in the vapour barrier or spaces around windows and vents, it cools off as it nears the cooler exterior wall (see fig. 226). Because cold air cannot hold as

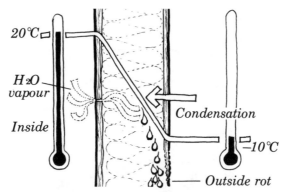

Fig. 226 Why sealing is necessary — thermal gradient thru a wall

much moisture as warm air, the vapour condenses at some point inside the wall, thus raising the ugly spectre of rot. Because it is inside the wall you probably won't know about it until it's too late. It is much better to seal the greenhouse completely and control the air change with a vent if necessary.

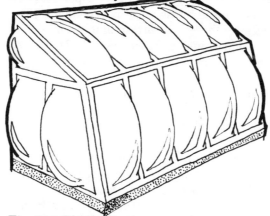

Fig. 227 Think of using a continuous membrane to make your greenhouse totally air-tight then vapour barrier, gasket and caulk to that end

Vapour Barrier

A vapour barrier is an impermeable material which is placed on the warm side of the insulation to prevent the warm, moist greenhouse air from filtering into the wall. Although the normal practice has been to put all the insulation on the outside of the vapour barrier, it is not necessary. In fact, a vapour barrier that is immediately behind the wall covering in a house wall stands a good chance of being punctured during electrical work, interior finishing, etc. It turns out that the vapour barrier is just as effective if it is some-where in the first third of the insulating value of the wall. That is to say, at least two-thirds of the insulation must be on the outside of the vapour barrier and no more than one-third on the inside. In that location, the moist interior air cannot reach the point at which it cools enough to condense (called the *dew point*) and the vapour barrier is protected from damage during further construction or finishing.

Use 6 mil (0.15mm) polyethylene for the vapour barrier. Align any joints in the vapour barrier along a stud or another solid surface so the two pieces can be pinched together by the wall covering or trim. Be sure to apply a generous bead of caulking between the two layers. Acoustical sealant is best for this purpose and for sealing the vapour barrier to the window, door, and vent frames, because it never hardens and does not shrink and crack. It is also quite inexpensive.

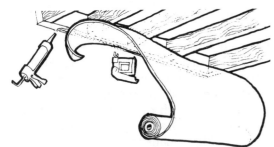

Fig. 228 Applying vapour barrier to greenhouse roof — staple through a continuous bead of caulking to effect air-tight seal

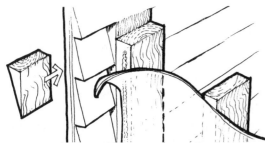

Fig. 229 Use shims or foam or caulking to effect tight seal between house and greenhouse and apply vapour barrier continuously to greenhouse walls

The inner glazing and the frames and trim that hold it act as the vapour barrier in the window areas. It is important to maintain a complete seal on the warm side of the wall to prevent condensation. You will notice that in sealing around the windows (fig. 230) the vapour barrier is folded around the corner. The sealing must be done in the inner third of the wall. Pay particular attention to the corners as they are the most difficult places to seal both with the polyethylene and the frame and trim details. Remember the old saying: "Caulk is cheap." Don't rely entirely on the details we have shown. Try to imagine at every stage where leaks might occur and what you can do about them. Care and attention to detail here will certainly pay off.

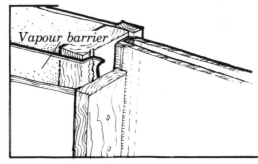

Fig. 230 Wrap vapour barrier around window framing and apply caulking about ¹/₃ of the way toward the exterior

It is almost impossible to get a perfect seal between the house and the greenhouse, because there is a certain amount of air movement inside the house wall. Do the best you can.

Sealants and Caulking

Silicone   Silicone is wonderful stuff. It is long-lasting (up to 20 years) and inconspicuous. While it is very expensive, its superior workability results in less waste and better coverage than most other caulkings. It is very strong, remains elastic and stands up well to ultraviolet radiation.

Acrylics ("Mono")   These sealants are cheaper than silicone and have about the same strength, flexibility and life span. They must be warm for easy application. Acrylics tend to degrade in ultraviolet radiation more than silicone.

Most cheap architectural grade, oil-based caulkings are not worth bothering with. They dry out, harden and crack in a relatively short time.

Glazing tape   This tape is a durable commercial glazing compound used for installing sealed units in wood or metal frames. It comes in rolls with a paper backing. Although it is more expensive than silicone or "Mono" it is easy to use and remains flexible indefinitely. It should be used when installing sealed units in any position and when installing glass as a roof glazing, because it provides a uniform bearing surface, eliminating the possibility of uneven pressures on the glass. It is available from most glass shops.

Neoprene   Neoprene is a good gasket material for installing rigid plastic glazings because it allows a large degree of expansion and contraction. It is also useful for flashing over vent hinges.

Acoustical sealant   An excellent, cheap caulking for sealing the vapour barrier, this great goop will not harden, dry out or crack. All edges and joints in the vapour barrier should be given a generous bead of acoustical sealant and held in place by the inside finish or trim. Joints should always occur on a stud or other framing member so that they are firmly clamped together.

A greenhouse floor can be anything from gravel walkways to poured concrete with ceramic tile. Here are a few considerations.

1. Any excess moisture must be able to drain away either through the floor drain or through cracks between bricks or stones.

2. The floor must be rot-proof.

3. It is advantageous to be able to clean the floor to avoid tracking mud into the house and to prevent mould problems.

4. For most northern regions we recommend insulation under the floor. It is not necessary for the floor to extend under the plant bench but it is worth while to insulate under it.

Floor Construction

Concrete Floor We will describe how to prepare for and pour a concrete floor. It is easiest to do it before the framing, if you can arrange it. The preparation for a brick or formed stone floor is similar. For a slab on grade, the procedure will be the same as we describe here except that the edges are thickened and the finished level will be determined by the height of the forms you build. The edge of a concrete floor will also have to be thickened if you are planning to build a masonry soil bed wall on top of it.

First, determine the level of the top of the floor. The factors affecting this level are the height of the glazing, the soil depth you want, the height of the existing ground (you can make the floor any height you want if you are willing to move enough dirt in or out). A concrete floor should be

100mm (4 in) thick, on top of 50mm (2 in) of insulation and 100mm (4 in) compacted gravel or sand. The base beneath the sand or gravel should be undisturbed earth. If after removing the top soil the floor level is going to be too low, add more than the 100mm of sand or gravel to get the height you want.

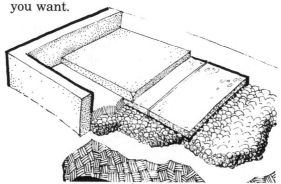

Fig. 231 Insulation under the concrete slab (but not under deep bed planter if applicable)

Mark the height you have decided on for the finished floor in each corner and snap chalk lines connecting them. If the slab is not going to extend under the front plant bench, and we recommend that it doesn't, build a form where you want the concrete to stop.

Floor Drain Install the floor drain so the top of the pipe is a few inches above the finished floor level, and close off the end to keep debris from falling into it. The best solution to the drainage problem would be to tie into the house drain line, but it is seldom practical because the amount of water in question is small (unless someone leaves the hose running).

There are several simpler solutions. If the house has weeping tile, drill down with a posthole auger until you hit the gravel that the weeping tile is buried in and install a piece of drain pipe. Back fill around the pipe with gravel.

For houses having no weeping tile, a hole filled with gravel will allow the water to percolate into the soil. Run the pipe to within a few inches of the bottom of the hole so that if the hole fills with water you can pump it out. Another solution that will work if the floor is above the outside ground is to place a horizontal pipe into the grade beam at floor level and slope the floor to that point. Plug the pipe in cold weather and screen it to keep out rodents. A slope of at least 1:100 is required.

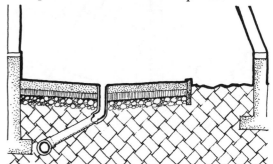

Fig. 232 Suggested drainage scheme — grade floor to drain and lead to perimeter drain tile

We will assume that you are using a floor drain. Wrap a ring of a tape around the floor drain pipe at a level approximately 25mm (1 in) below the floor level as marked on the foundation walls.

Base Preparation   Place and compact the gravel or sand so that you have a smooth and even surface 150mm or 6 in (50mm for insulation plus 100mm for concrete) below the finished floor line sloping to 150mm below the tape on the floor drain. A rented jumping jack tamper is best for tamping sand, but for the area in most greenhouses a couple of 2 x 4s nailed together with a hole drilled at a comfortable height for a handle will do. Whew! Wetting the sand down will make the compaction easier. Use a board as a straight edge to check the level of the sand or gravel. The top side of a rake is best for moving the sand or gravel around.

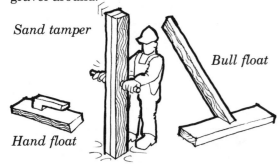

Sand tamper

Bull float

Hand float

Fig. 233 Simple tools

Now place the insulation. We recommend 51mm (2 in) of the cheap white styrofoam board; it will give an RSI value of 1.37 (R8).

Strictly speaking, the floor should probably be reinforced with 6 in x 6 in (150mm x 150mm) #10 gauge welded wire mesh, but on a slab this size you can probably get away without it. Put it in place now if you are going to use it. You are ready to pour.

Pouring and Finishing   Try to place the wet concrete as close to its final position as possible; you will save yourself a lot of work. You have probably seen people levelling concrete by pulling a board (a very straight board please) across it with a sawing motion along the top of some forms (a process called *screeding*). In the case of our greenhouse, the forms will be missing on one (if you are not pouring under the plant bench) or both sides and you want the floor, not level, but sloped towards the drain. You can use a strip of wet concrete (called a wet screed) instead of forms as a guide for screeding.

Make one wet screed by placing a line of concrete about a foot wide along the grade beam, using a hand float to level it up to the chalk line. Now level a gob of concrete around the floor drain, even with the tape, forming a second wet screed. Next, fill in between these two surfaces and level it off with your straight board, using the concrete surfaces as a guide. Keep the board sawing back and forth and watch that ends neither dig into nor rise above the wet screeds. As you are placing the concrete it is very important to vibrate it with a rake to work the voids out of it. If using wire mesh, pull it up into the concrete as you go.

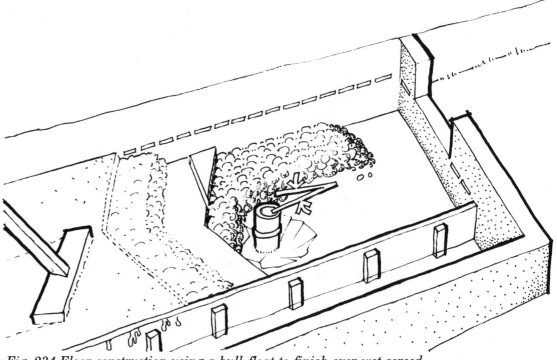

Fig. 234 Floor construction using a bull float to finish over wet screed

After the concrete is screeded, it should be floated to bring up the finer material for finishing and to work the larger rocks down. Floating should leave a smoother surface than screeding and may for some tastes be smooth enough. Fig. 233 shows a wooden hand float which will suffice if you don't screed further than you can reach back with the hand float before going on. For large areas, use a bull float. It may be desirable to float a second time after the concrete has begun to sit if you are not planning a trowelled finish.

At this point, place the anchor bolts that you will need for the north wall of the soil bed. Steel trowelling should be done when the water sheen disappears from the surface of the concrete and it will sustain foot pressure with only 5mm indentation, although the edges, which usually give the most trouble, may be started before then. A pair of knee boards, about one foot by two feet, will enable you to work the areas that can't be reached otherwise. By 'walking' them you can get everywhere. A stick nailed to the topside of the walking boards will make them easier to move.

Timing is critical. If you trowel too early the surface lacks durability, and if you start too late or work too slowly it becomes impossible to get a smooth finish. A broom finish is a lot easier to achieve but a bit more difficult to clean.

Brick Floor   Prepare the base as you would for concrete. However, you need only

75mm of sand under the insulation and you don't need a floor drain. Leave small gaps in between the pieces of insulation to allow water to run through. Level another 75mm of sand on top of the insulation and lay the bricks. Sweep sand into the cracks.

Alternative floors:

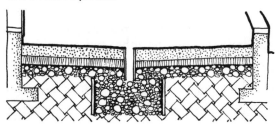

Fig. 235 Gravel sump

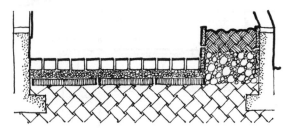

Fig. 236 Brick (note gaps in sub-floor to drain water)

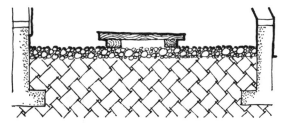

Fig. 237 Minimal floor (gravel with wooden trestle)

Exterior

There is a wide variety of exterior finishes to choose from. The bevel, drop, and channel wood siding patterns are all fairly easy to apply. Batten-and-board or board-and-board patterns using lumber will do fine. Stucco can be applied in a variety of textures and colors and is a durable, low-priced finish. Aluminum or vinyl siding also require little or no maintenance but they can be tedious to apply on small areas with lots of windows. (To some extent that's true of wood siding as well.) Choose a finish that will match or complement the finish on the existing house. You might also want to look at the house for guidance on exterior trim details.

You should probably apply an exterior finish to the perimeter insulation first. Stucco, pressure-treated plywood, and asbestos cement board are all suitable. We have successfully applied stucco (in two coats) by fastening mesh to the bottom plate and letting it hang over the insulation. The stucco adheres quite well to

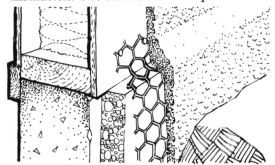

Fig. 238 Chicken wire and stucco rendered over foundation insulation

the white styrofoam. Flashing is required to cover the top of whatever you apply to the insulation (unless of course you simply use flashing all the way to the ground). If you use stucco, nail the flashing in place before applying the stucco so the flashing can provide an edge for the stucco.

We will describe briefly the procedures for applying horizontal wood siding. The preliminary steps for other types of

1. outside wall intersection (greenhouse)

2. house wall/greenhouse wall

3. wall/roof intersection

4. wall/window head

5. sill/shutter detail

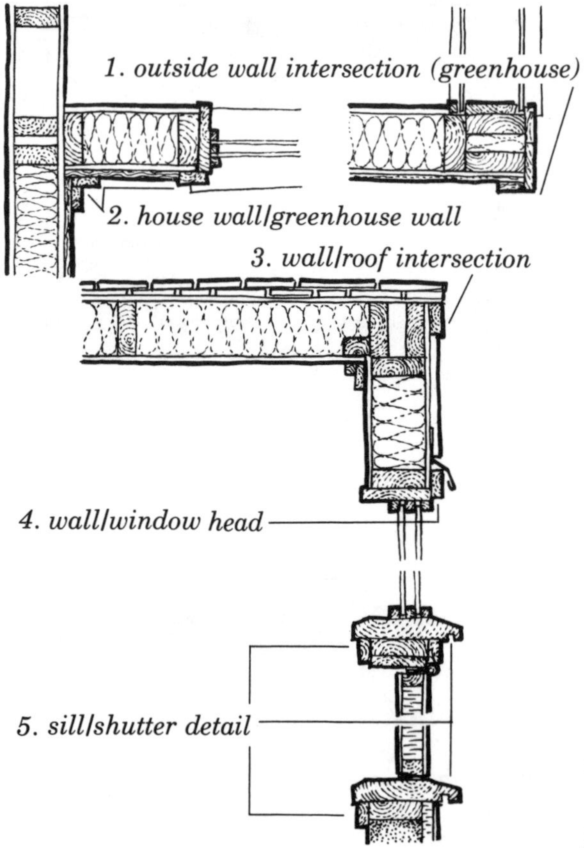

Fig. 239 Typical construction/trim details

exterior finish will be similar up to the application of the siding itself.

With the flashing in place, cover the area to be sided with building paper, starting from the bottom so that the laps will shed any water which manages to penetrate the siding. Next, apply the exterior trim to the corners, and around the window, door, and vent openings using galvanized nails. Copy the details used on your house or refer to

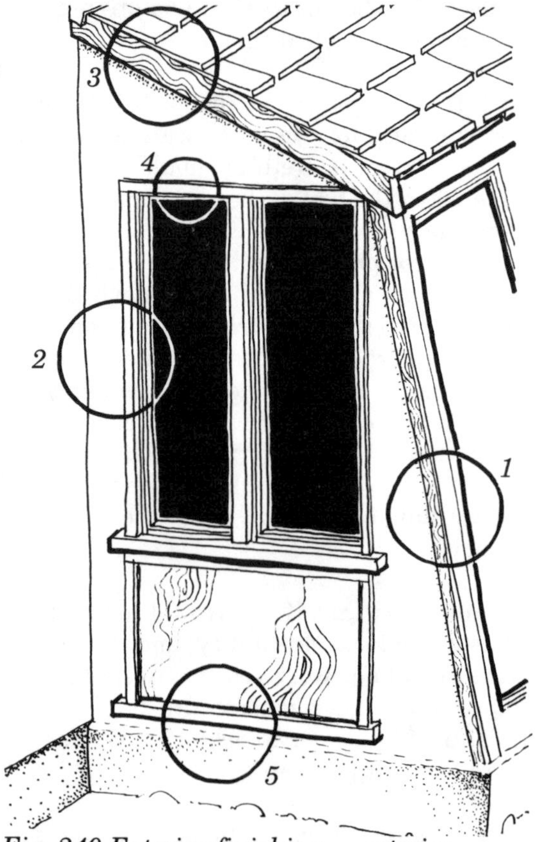

Fig. 240 Exterior finishing — exterior location of the five details

the glazing and ventilation chapters in this section. Apply flashing over the trim above those openings.

The siding should be applied level with uniform spacing. If it is the same as the house siding, the horizontal lines should meet at the corners even if it means ripping the bottom piece. With bevel siding it will be necessary to start with a strip under the bottom piece so that it will have the same tilt as the rest of the siding. This strip should be 10mm (³/₈ in) up from the butt edge of the bottom piece.

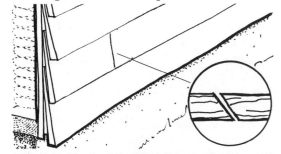

Fig. 241 Typical bevel siding including 45° splice and bottom strip

If possible, always keep the heart side of the wood out. The siding should be nailed with galvanized siding nails; one nail in each stud, just above the hidden top edge of the board below. Any joints required between two pieces of siding in the same row should be mitred at 45° (see fig. 241). Examine the finished job for places water could get in and caulk with a matching colour of "Mono" caulking.

The fascia (the trim around the roof) should be good quality cedar, fir, or pine.

Any joints should be mitred. Aluminum fascia is maintenance free and readily available.

It is good practice to stain the siding, trim, and fascia before putting it up because doing so allows you to protect the area hidden by the overlap and the back side. We recommend stain instead of paint because it penetrates deeper and will not blister due to moisture migration from the inside.

Interior

The inside finishing materials should be able to stand high humidity levels. Some suggestions are plywood, rough lumber, pre-finished panelling, water resistant (green) gypsum board, or exterior siding — perhaps the same as is on the north wall already. To maximize light levels and minimize heat loss, the finish on the endwalls and ceiling should be as reflective as your taste will allow. Flat white paint is the most common choice.

Apply the interior trim as shown in the details in the glazing and ventilation sections. Be sure to bevel window trim to allow for drainage of any condensation running off the glazing. Examine the trim around the windows, keeping in mind that the inside glazing must form a continuous seal with the vapour barrier. Caulk as necessary.

If you are using stain, be sure that it is not one containing pentachlorophenol, as this

material is toxic to plants and humans as well as fungi and insects.

Preservatives

The humidity levels in greenhouses create ideal conditions for wood rot and tempt us to reach for a handy preservative. Wood preservatives are long-lasting, potent chemicals which are designed to combat bacteria, fungi, and insects for many years. The properties which make them effective in preventing decay also make them dangerous to plants and humans. In a 1978 study, the Environment Protection Agency (EPA) in the United States warned that exposure to *pentachlorophenol, creosote,* and *arsenical* compounds can cause cancer, tumours and birth defects. The EPA, unless Ronald Reagan dismantles it first, intends to bring in regulations governing the use of these wood preservatives. Among the precautions being considered are:

- Treated wood must not be used indoors or where it might contaminate "animals, food, feed, or water."
- People applying preservatives must wear gloves and other protective clothing.
- Treated lumber must be labelled with a warning that users wear gloves, disposable coveralls, and dust masks. Scraps must be buried rather than burnt.

Clearly, you should avoid using wood treated with these materials where it will be exposed to the air and soil in a greenhouse. Let's take a closer look at these and some other wood preservatives.

Pentachlorophenal Stay away from products (including some stains) containing this chemical. While it is very effective and economical, it contains a dioxin, and wood treated with it will emit vapours for up to seven years which are toxic to plants and humans. These vapours are absorbed into the body through the skin as well as through inhalation.

Creosote Creosote is used in the treatment of railroad ties, telephone poles, and fence posts. You are most likely to encounter it in recycled railroad ties. While the toxicity of creosote diminishes with time, the hazards are difficult to assess. Handle the railroad ties with care and be sure that they are isolated from the air and growing medium in the greenhouse. We advise against using new railroad ties since both the toxicity and the expense tend to be high.

Chromated Copper Arsenate (CCA) and Ammoniacal Copper Arsenate (ACA) These preservatives are commonly used to pressure-treat plywood and dimensional lumber for wood foundations. The EPA estimates that a carpenter spending a lifetime working with CCA- or ACA-treated lumber would have a 1 in 10 chance of developing cancer.

The effectiveness of the arsenates and the fact that the pressure-treating causes much deeper penetration than can be achieved with brushing or dipping, makes the use of pressure-treated lumber very attractive in the parts of the greenhouse most

susceptible to decay. If you do use it, wear gloves and a particle mask to avoid inhaling the sawdust. Isolate it from the greenhouse air and soil by completely covering it with 6-mil polyethylene and a protective layer of wood.

Less toxic preservatives include:

Copper Napthenate (green) and Zinc Napthenate (clear) These preservatives are much less toxic than those mentioned above, but should still be used with caution. They are the active ingredients in "Cuprinol" and some stains. Commercial greenhouse operators use copper or zinc napthenate to treat flats and the wood around soil beds.

Copper Sulphate (bluestone) Copper sulphate has long been used by farmers to treat fence posts. The material to be treated must be soaked so the copper sulphate can work its way into the wood from the ends by capillary action. Copper sulphate is used to control algae growth in dugouts.

"Cunilate" (soluble copper 8 — Quinolinolate) This preservative, while relatively difficult to find, has a low toxicity to humans. It is permitted by the U.S. Food and Drug Administration for treatment of wood used in food handling — such as fruit and vegetable harvest baskets, wood parts in commercial refrigerators and refrigerated trucks.

A recipe for a homemade wood preservative can be found on p. 129 ("Soil Bed Construction").

Paint Versus Stain

There is some question about whether paints or stains provide better protection for the wood in a greenhouse. Paints applied to clean, dry wood protect the surface by sealing it and making it impervious to water vapour. If, however, the seal is not complete and moisture can enter the wood, this moisture can cause the paint to blister and peel. Repainting then involves a lot of tedious scraping and sanding. Paints do have the advantage of being more reflective than stains.

Stains protect by soaking an oil and sometimes a preservative into the surface; the penetration is deeper than it is for paint. The surface can still breathe, allowing moisture to enter and escape without blistering or peeling. Restaining is easier than repainting. The drawbacks of stain are that the centre of the wood is not protected from moisture and that the preservatives used in some stains can be toxic.

Our conversations with some experts resulted in a bias toward paint for the interior and stain on the exterior. There are paints manufactured specifically for use in greenhouses. They are highly reflective and formulated for high humidity conditions. If you cannot obtain greenhouse paint, a good quality, high gloss, exterior grade latex will serve the purpose. Apply a primer and two coats of paint. If you choose stain for the inside, be sure that it is not one containing pentachlorophenal.

Top-storing Inter-glazing Insulation

The simplest and best inter-glazing insulation system involves storing the blankets in a false ceiling. Fig. 242 shows the blankets in the daytime (up) position. The blankets are drawn into the night position by pulling on the cord.

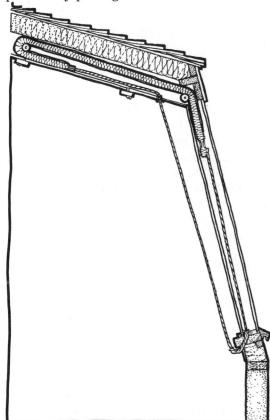

Fig. 242 Section thru greenhouse showing typical rigging of batt insulation

We suggest that you install the rollers and guide tubes in only one section initially

and try the system out with a blanket to make sure there are no bugs before mass-producing the whole thing.
The roof insulation should be installed and held in place with a 6 mil polyethylene vapour barrier which is held up with lath or with staples through fibreglass tape.

Fig. 243 Inter-glazing insulation slides up and down between the glazing on the south wall and under the roof

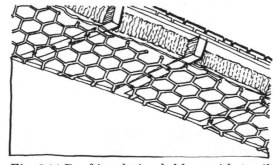

Fig. 244 Roof insulation held up with 6 mil poly supported by chicken wire, lath or stapled through fibreglass tape

Installing a False Ceiling

Install the 2 x 4 ledger strip on the back wall of the greenhouse. This strip must be low enough to allow room for the blanket to fold around the roller. A space of 200mm (8 in) is adequate for blankets up to 5mm (2 in) thick. Next, cut the ceiling joists to length with the appropriate angles.

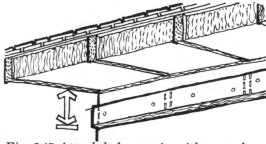

Fig. 245 Attach ledger strip with enough room for insulation blanket to pass over roller

Determine the exact length and angles by cutting the first joist a few inches too long, with one end cut the approximate roof angle (see roof trimming). Hold this joist in place with its south end running past the stud. Correct the top angle by tracing

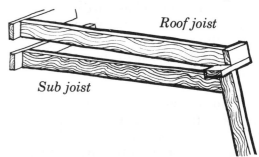

Fig. 246 Ceiling joist in place (runs from ledger to south wall stud)

along a straight edge. Hold the joist in position again and scribe the south end. Check this joist in the other locations and use it as a pattern for making the rest. Install the bushings for the top rollers on the joists before fastening the joists in position.

The bushings are 38mm (1¹/₂ in) lengths of 6mm (¹/₄ in) copper tubing with both ends flared. With a chisel, cut a small notch across the top of the joist, 100mm (4 in) from the top (north) end. Set the tube in the notch and secure it with a short piece of plumbing strap (see fig. 247).

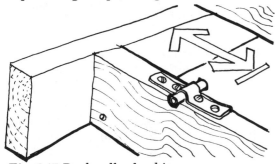

Fig. 247 Back roller bushing

Now fasten the joists in place using toe nails or long (3 in, 75mm) drywall screws. The nails or screws on the sides of the joist at the bottom end should be countersunk to avoid snagging the blankets.

Next, install the bushings for the rollers at the top of the glazing. The rollers should be located so their tops are just above the plane of the bottom of the false ceiling joists, and 9mm (³/₈ in) from the top glazing support. The bushings should be

sections of 6mm (¹/₄) copper tubing, slightly shorter than the width of the stud plus the jamb.

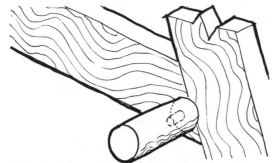

Fig. 248 Installation of front roller with pins and drilled dowels

These pieces of tubing should be cut with a fine-tooth hack saw rather than a tubing cutter to minimize the burr on the inside of the tube. Use a small, round file or knife to remove any burr that is left after cutting. Drill the hole perpendicular to the frame because the bushings serve the rollers on both sides.

Cut the rollers (1¹/₂ in — 38mm — fir dowelling) to length. They should be about 1mm to 2mm (¹/₁₆ in) shorter than the space. Drill 25mm (1 in) deep holes in the centres of the dowels and insert 6mm (¹/₄ in) copper tubing bushings. The holes should be carefully centred and parallel to the length of the dowel.

Install the rollers using pieces of 3mm (¹/₈ in) diameter brass welding rod for pins. The pins should be dipped in hot paraffin or bees'wax to provide lubrication. Start at one end of the greenhouse. Insert a pin in

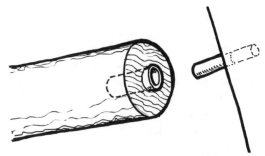

Fig. 249 Use an expanded copper bushing set into hole centred and aligned with length of dowel and metal pin set into lower rafter/ceiling joist

the bushing in the jamb at the outside wall and push a roller onto it. Then, install the other pin by pushing it in from the next section. Repeat the same procedure until you reach the last section. Assemble the last roller in two pieces, using a piece of 38mm (1¹/₂ in) ABS plastic pipe to join them. Countersink the screws which hold the assembly together.

Install the vapour barrier on the bottom of the ceiling joists (see "Vapour Barrier and Sealing"). This section of the vapour barrier should tie into that on the endwalls, and be sealed to the north wall.

Now it's time to install the ceiling. It should consist of 25mm (1 in) nominal lumber, shiplap, or channel siding. Start at the south end. The first board should be cut on an angle and then have 38mm (1¹/₂ in) wide, 6mm (¹/₄ in) plywood strips nailed to it to support the top of the glazing. Note that the strip cut off the first ceiling board can be used to hold the glazing in place. The 2 x 6 stud must be notched to the depth of the jamb to accept the first ceiling board.

Install tubes for the operator cords using the threaded, brass tubes sold for household lamps. For the top tubes, use a washer and a small block of 6mm (1/4 in) plywood to pinch the vapour barrier to the ceiling. Tighten the tubes in place using another nut and washer. The bottom tubes can alternatively be copper tubing with flared ends. Leave a 600mm (2 ft) gap approximately in the centre of the ceiling for access to the blankets and the rollers. Cut the vapour barrier and fold it around the edges of the access hole. Reinforce this edge with fibreglass tape and staple it to the ceiling. Attach a strip of sticky-backed neoprene weatherstripping to the tape. Construct the cover for the access hatch .

Thread the cords through the tubes and install the blankets. Check to ensure easy operation and proceed to install the inner glazing.

With the curtain in the down position, tie a loop in the upper cord that will act as a stop preventing the blanket from falling into the cavity. Run the lower cord through that loop, tighten the cord (and the blanket), and tie off the lower cord.

There are several minor improvements that can be made if you have control over the length of the south wall glazing material — that is, if the inner and outer glazing need not be the same length. If you

are using non-tempered glass for part or all of the south glazing, and are prepared to cut it, you can use a 2 x 4 instead of a 2 x 6 lintel at the top of the south wall, or simply use a double top-wall plate. This alteration will allow more room at the corners for the blanket. The false ceiling joists can also be raised somewhat to result in decreased shading. At the bottom, the inner glazing can be installed on a 2 x 2 to result in easier installation of the tube for the operator cord.

General Notes

1. Using the curtain for summer shading will shorten its life.
2. A false ceiling will reduce the amount of room available for an endwall high vent. You will have to modify your design accordingly.

We have given detailed instructions for the assembly of one particular inter-glazing system, which is suitable for one particular greenhouse configuration. Other greenhouse designs will require variations and modifications. Following is a brief look at some other systems. The description of the "Millet greenhouse" in the SURVEY section contains a detailed explanation of some other operator mechanisms.

Bottom-storing Inter-glazing Insulation

Bottom-storing inter-glazing insulation is necessary in situations where a restriction on the height of the greenhouse roof makes it undesirable or impossible to use a false

ceiling for storage. It is also applicable in a greenhouse requiring roof vents. While the insulation can be rolled up under the plant bench, this practice restricts the construction of deep soil beds (see "Millet greenhouse"). It is recommended instead that the storage box be built outside the greenhouse. This plan is much easier with slab on grade construction, but can be used with other types of foundations as well. If there is unrestricted passage of the blankets into the box, they will fold on their own and can be pulled up, either individually, or all at once, with the cords wrapping around a pipe. The box should be at least 750mm (30 in) high and it is preferable that the blankets fall towards the middle of the box instead of along the north edge. (If the blanket can lean against the wall, it may just stand there instead of folding.) The north wall of the box in this case is the south wall of the deep soil bed and should be constructed accordingly. This wall also acts as the vapour barrier and the defense line against infiltration. It may be necessary to weight the curtain if it is too light and stiff to fall on its own.

Bottom-storing can also be accomplished by rolling the insulation. This system will work in a situation where there is roof glazing and the insulation will not fall freely. For more details on a rolling mechanism system, see the "Millet greenhouse" in the SURVEY section.

Top, Rolled Storage

If the greenhouse has roof glazing or is two stories high, it is usually impossible to use the top-storage system we have detailed. In such a case, the insulation can be rolled in a box located at the top corner of the greenhouse. This is merely a variation of the rolled bottom-storage system just described. The insulation is pulled down by winding the cords around a pipe above the plant beds. As the insulation comes down, the single rear cord is wound around the large plywood pulley in the box. Pulling on this cord then pulls up the insulation. The weight of the blankets becomes significant when they get this long. It may be necessary to pull the cord with a simple hand winch, or to split the system and operate the two halves separately. Note that the greenhouse side of the insulation storage box is the vapour barrier defense line.

Blankets for Inter-glazing Insulation

Here are some options for the blankets used in the inter-glazing insulation system:
1. spun fibreglass metal building insulation sewn into a sleeping-bag-like tube of woven polyethylene
2. "Dacron" sewn into a tube of woven polyethylene
3. commercially available concrete curing blankets (used for keeping newly poured concrete warm in freezing weather while it cures) — these blankets can be custom-ordered and generally consist of "Fortrel" sewn into a tube of woven

polyethylene. The blankets are available in two densities of "Fortrel" with insulating values of RSI-0.58 (R-3.3) and RSI-0.88 (R-5).

Where available, the curing blankets are surprisingly cheap. They can be custom-made to fit your glazing width for well under a dollar per square foot ($10/m²). Check in the yellow pages under "Tarpaulins", or "Concrete Accessories".

Making your own blanket To make your own inter-glazing blanket, start with a piece of lightweight woven polyethylene material (available from tent, awning, or tarpaulin manufacturerers), sew it into the shape of a bag which is the width and height of your glazed areas, and fill it with fibreglass, Dacron, or a similar spun insulating material.

It is a good practice to start by making a sample blanket about a foot long in order to determine the exact dimensions, the placement of seams, and to get a feeling for what you are doing before you tackle the complete blankets.

Blanket Fabrication Procedure
1. Use lightweight, p-grade woven polyethylene material. This is not the type used for making truck tarpaulins; it is lighter than that. Cut a piece of the woven polyethylene which is about 150mm (6 in) longer than the south wall glazing height and which is about 75mm (3 in) wider than twice the glazing width:
If necessary, you can join pieces of woven

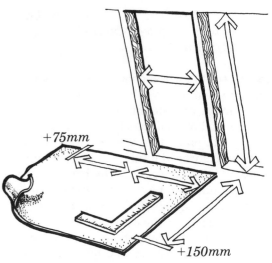

Fig. 250 Outer cover for inter-glazing insulation blanket 75mm more than twice width of window and 150mm more than length

polyethylene to make a larger piece, but make sure that the seams will be turned inward when the blanket is finished.

You will make the job much easier if you carefully measure and cut the woven polyethylene so that the sides are parallel. This will allow you to use the cut edges as a guide for subsequent seams rather than having to measure across wider distances.

2. Fold the woven polyethylene sheet in half lengthwise and join the long edges by sewing a seam parallel to, and about 25mm (1-in) in, from the edge. Use the heaviest thread possible.

3. Turn the tube inside out. Spread the tube out flat and arrange the seam so that

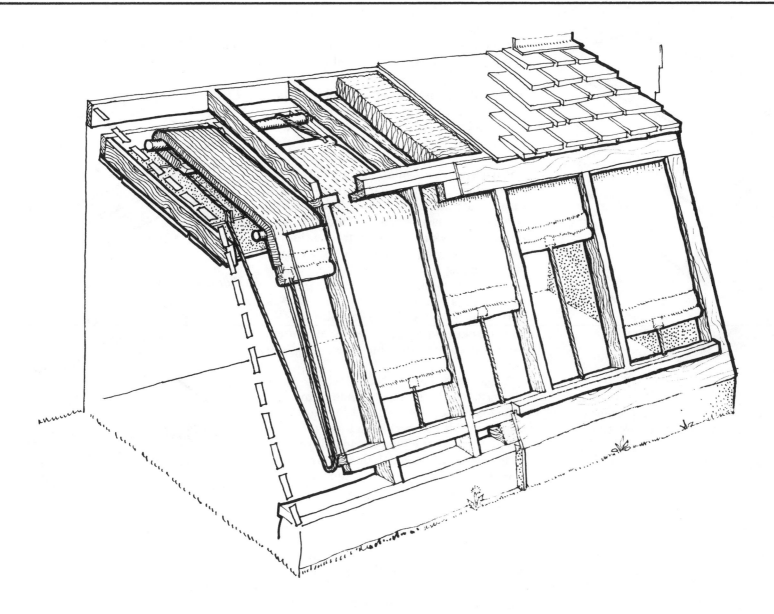

Fig. 251 Inter-glazing insulation installed and operating plus typical roof and ceiling structure

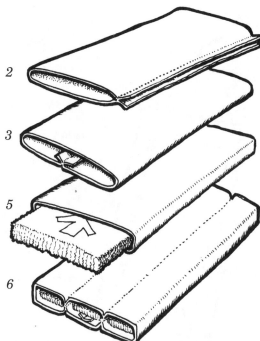

Fig. 252 Construction of an insulating
blanket

it is in the centre of one of the sides and
not at either edge. The flattened tube
should be about 25mm (1 in) wider than
the glazing material.

4. Fibreglass metal building insulation
comes in 3 ft and 4 ft widths (914mm and
1219mm). If you are using fibreglass
insulation for the blanket, cut it so it is
about 38mm (1¹/₂ in) narrower than the
flattened bag. Use 64mm (2¹/₂ in) thick
insulation. Dacron comes in widths of up to
1.83m (6 ft). You can sew two pieces of
Dacron together for use inside a blanket by
butting the ends and lightly stitching by
hand. If you are using Dacron filling for

the blanket, cut it so it is 25 to 50mm (1 in
to 2 in) wider than the flattened bag.

5. Stuff the insulating material into the
bag, taking care that the seam in the
woven polyethylene is at the centre, and
not at either edge.

6. To keep the insulation from moving
around inside the bag and to improve the
way the blanket travels over the rollers,
sew two more seams the length of the bag.
Locate these seams as far in from either
side as the sewing machine will reach. If
you are using fibreglass insulation, you
will have to do this latter stitching by
hand, unless you have access to a heavy-
duty sewing machine. You can also take
your blankets to a tarp or tent maker and
have it sewn at reasonable rates.

7. Cut strips out of 11mm (¹/₂ in)
plywood, which are about 25mm (1 in)
wide and which are 75mm (3 in) shorter
than the width of the blanket. On the
leading edge of the blanket, install the
strips, as shown, about 150mm (6 in) in
from the edge. The bolts and the strips also
serve to fasten the pull cord and a piece of
flannel. The flannel not only finishes and
seals off the end of the blanket, but wipes
the glass clean each time the curtain is
operated. Once the strips and cord are
bolted in place, sew another patch of
flannel over the cord so that the leading
edge will track properly when rounding
corners. At the other end of the blanket,
install another set of strips, bolts, and cord
about 25mm to 50mm (1 in to 2 in) from

the edge. No flannel is needed at this end.

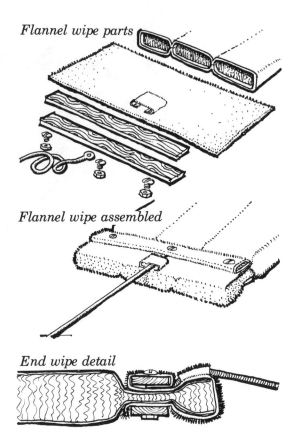

Flannel wipe parts

Flannel wipe assembled

End wipe detail

Fig. 253

We recommend the construction of a deep soil bed against the south wall of the greenhouse. In the Sundance Greenhouse, the soil bed extends above the concrete foundation wall to the height of the opaque portion of the south wall and endwall framing. It is essential that the soil bed be constructed with rot-resistant materials or materials which can be replaced when they begin to rot. More importantly, it is essential that the framing be well protected from rot.

South wall and Endwall

The configuration of the south wall and endwalls of the soil bed in the Sundance Greenhouse, which provides this protection against rot is shown in figure 254. The 14mm (or ½ in) plywood against the framing members should be protected using one of the following methods:

1. Seal all sides of the plywood with a plastic or urethane-type varnish.
2. Treat the plywood with copper napthenate.
3. Paint all sides of the plywood with marine-grade enamel.
4. Treat the plywood with the following mixture:

> 30g (1 oz) paraffin
> 250ml (1½ c) boiled linseed oil
> Enough turpentine or paint thinner to make 4 l (1 gal)

We recommend the copper napthenate treatment, but whichever you choose, it is important that the plywood be protected.

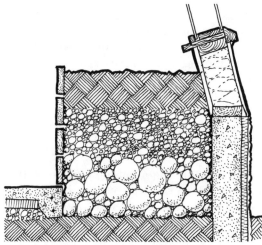

Fig. 254 Typical soil bed construction (against a rot-proofed opaque portion of south wall)

This plywood should be nailed into the framing with galvanized nails, and isolated from the soil using 6 mil polyethylene, which should in turn be protected from tearing by another piece of plywood. This second piece of plywood should be only tacked in place or held in place by the soil itself so that it is easy to replace since, as it is exposed to the damp soil, it can be expected to rot. To extend its life, you may want to paint or varnish this second piece of plywood as well.

North Wall of the Soil Bed

The north wall of the soil bed must also be protected from rot using a similar procedure. If you adopt our basic recommendation and do not extend the concrete floor beneath the soil bed, but connect the greenhouse

soil directly to the earth, build a 2 x 4 frame and cover it with plywood or 25mm nominal (1 in) lumber, protected from rot using one of the four methods described above. Cover this lumber with 6 mil polyethylene on the soil side and protect the polyethylene at the top with a replaceable piece of lumber tacked, or held in place by the soil.

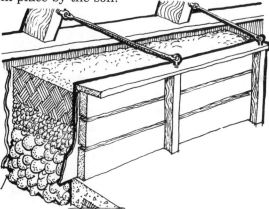

Fig. 255 Standard soilbed (lined with poly) with tension brace to window mullion

Fig. 256 An alternative soil bed — flagstones, soil in wire liner, and retaining board

This wall should then be bolted to the floor on cedar spacers . The spacers will help to keep the bottom plate dry and will aid in drainage. The top of the wall should be tied to the south wall of the greenhouse at its midpoint to prevent the soil from pushing it out.

If you have to build your soil bed on top of a complete concrete pad, the plywood or 25mm (1 in) boards covering the 2 x 4 north wall soil bed should extend only part way down to the floor . When the wall is bolted into place, fill up the bottom portion of the bed with rocks to allow proper soil drainage. Chicken wire along the top and north side of the rock pile will serve to prevent the rocks from falling out into the greenhouse. Put a layer of gravel on the rocks to prevent the soil on top of the rocks from trickling down in between the spaces.

Soil Bed Alternatives

1. The greenhouse foundation wall could be extended into a 600mm to 900mm (24 in to 36 in) high kneewall by building higher forms and pouring a concrete wall or by laying a concrete block wall on top of it. This design would provide a rot-proof south wall and endwalls for the soil bed, but would require changes in details of the south wall, the stud length, etc.

2. The north wall of the soil bed could be constructed of poured concrete, concrete blocks, or bricks. Some form of concrete represents the most durable type of soil

bed and is probably the best option if your uncle is in the concrete business.

The instructions in the foundation section for forming end pouring a grade beam contain all the information you need for building the north wall of poured concrete. It is also possible to pour the soil bed wall at the same time as you pour the grade beam and/or foundation wall.

If you are building a masonry north wall soil bed on top of a concrete floor which covers the entire greenhouse, you must allow for drainage. A number of pieces of pipes or tin cans (with both ends cut off)

whose length is equal to the thickness of the wall will provide the necessary space for water run-off. Place them in the bottom of the forms at floor level before pouring the concrete for the soil bed wall. The bottom portion of this soil bed should also consist of rocks with a chicken wire or gravel covering beneath the soil.

3. The Ecology House greenhouse uses fibreglassed soil beds (see SURVEY). We are not certain about the applicability of this construction in areas where the greenhouse is likely to freeze during the winter.

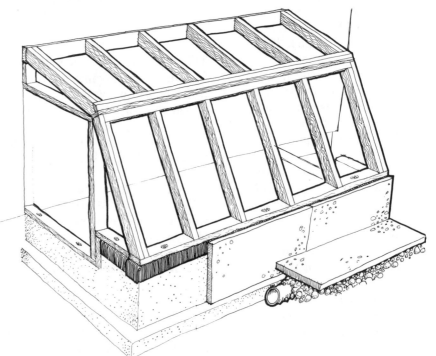

Fig. 257 Alternative foundation wall which provides south wall and end wall of soil bed

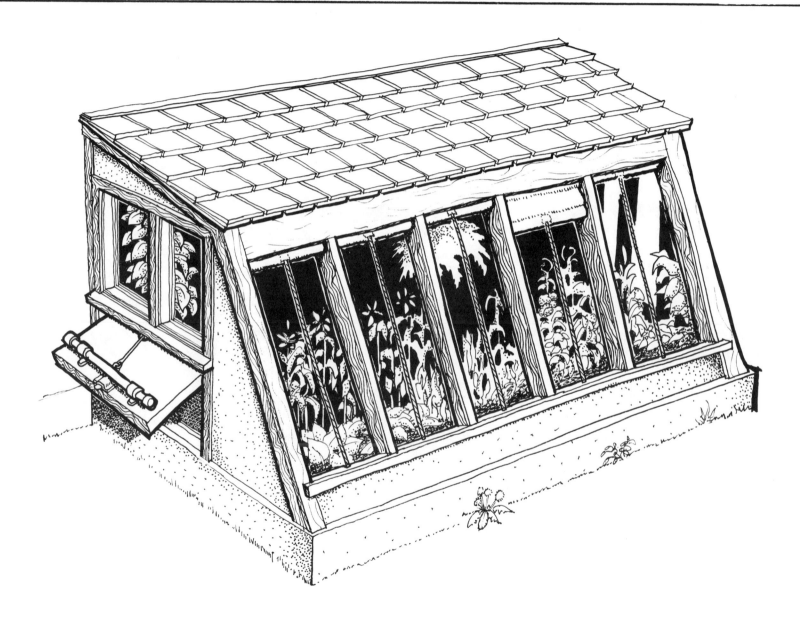

Fig. 258 Completed attached greenhouse with vents deployed and crop in production

MANAGEMENT

Greenhouse Management

Greenhouses are usually used to grow food, so that is the use we will assume when thinking about management. Exactly what you can grow in your greenhouse and how long each year you can raise crops in it depends upon your local climate, the latitude, and whether you are using the greenhouse simply as a season extender, or are attempting year-round production.

In northerly latitudes the limiting factor is often light. There may not be enough hours during the winter months to grow or maintain very many crops. In the lower latitudes of Canada and in the northern United States, leafy green vegetables may survive through the winter and provide enough of a harvest for winter salads. However, even plants with low light tolerances may do poorly or die during the dead of winter at higher latitudes (52-60°N).

The greenhouse is an ecosystem in miniature. The same principles apply to it as to the world outside the greenhouse. In fact, the greenhouse really isn't separate from the rest of the world. It can be thought of as a filter for excluding undesirable conditions (harsh winds, snow and hail, pests) while letting in desirable conditions (sunlight, fresh air). It is this interface between the greenhouse environment and the outdoors that the greenhouse gardener learns to manage. We will use the term *biological management* to mean those techniques which should be employed when treating the greenhouse as an ecosystem.

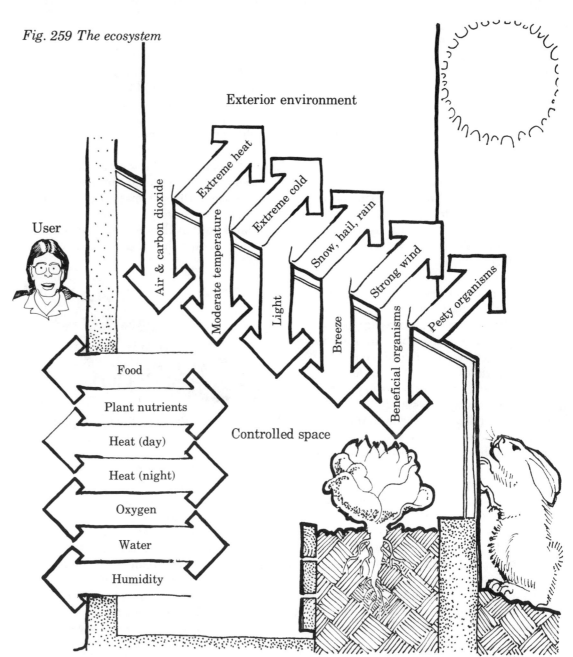

Fig. 259 The ecosystem

Exterior environment

User

Air & carbon dioxide

Extreme heat

Extreme cold

Moderate temperature

Snow, hail, rain

Light

Strong wind

Breeze

Beneficial organisms

Pesty organisms

Food

Plant nutrients

Heat (day)

Heat (night)

Oxygen

Water

Humidity

Controlled space

Management techniques which have a sweeping effect, such as fumigation, sterilization of the soil, and the use of broad-spectrum pesticides, have a long-lasting effect and will continue to create havoc in the greenhouse for a lengthy period after application as well as creating an unsafe environment for the gardener. There are certain insecticides which are derived from flowers and other natural sources which have a much shorter life span and which may, in certain, carefully controlled situations, be used in the greenhouse. These aids we will call *botanical insecticides*.

Learning to manage the home greenhouse is not difficult, especially if you are familiar with gardening. There are just a few more things to think about in order to provide a good growing environment indoors than there are for one outdoors. A gardener manages the soil nutrients, soil moisture, and controls pests, the greenhouse horticulturist adds to these priorities the management of air temperature, humidity, and available light.

Prevention is important. Do not give problems a chance to start. Take swift action when you see a problem beginning. You will get better with experience and learn what to plant, when to plant it, and how much to plant. You will learn how long into the winter your greenhouse can produce a crop. You will know where to look for insects, and be able to tell which is a pest and which is beneficial.

Maximizing Space

Layout   In a food producing greenhouse all space is valuable and the proper use of the available area will result in greater production. You should give careful thought to the succession of crops to make sure that no space in the greenhouse is long left empty. Climbing plants should be trellised upwards to make the most efficient use of the soil space. Be careful that short plants are planted in front of tall plants so that they are not shaded (except for plants that prefer shade, of course).

Fig. 260 Short plants at front, tall plants at rear

The layout of the greenhouse must take each of these factors into account and must allow for walkways, soil benches, and other containers. Tool storage and a workbench can take up a lot of space in a small greenhouse and are best placed elsewhere. In the case of an attached greenhouse you may be able to use the basement or fit out a special planting and storage room in the house itself. With a freestanding greenhouse an insulated vestibule can be attached to the structure to act as a

storage area and work room and to provide as well an air-lock entrance into the greenhouse.

Concrete provides an easily maintained and permanent greenhouse floor, but remember that it is an energy intensive product and quite expensive. Wooden walkways are attractive and allow spilled water to run between the slats instead of creating a soggy pathway. Dirt paths in a greenhouse generally make a mess. Gravel is inexpensive and works well, and should be used over an earth base even if you are going to build a wooden walkway on top of it. Walkways should be wide enough to allow you room to work and move. 550mm (21 in) is usually the minimum width for a walkway.

Wood is the cheapest and most readily available material with which to construct permanent soil benches. These benches are usually best located along the south wall of the greenhouse, and farther back and parallel to it if space permits. If you have not provided for heat storage beneath the beds (a good idea in cold climates) you can use this space for pot and flat storage or as a location for an earthworm bin.

As with other benches, soil beds should never be wider than your reach; 900mm (36 in) is a good, comfortable width for most people. If the bench is arranged so that you can work on either side of it, the width can double to almost two metres. Some gardeners find that they can make better use of space by increasing the width

Fig. 261 Easy reach across planting beds

of the soil bench along the south wall, particularly in the case of an attached greenhouse. In this case, make certain that you provide some way to reach to the front of the bed without lying on the plants. A narrow board running lengthwise down the middle of the soil bed can be used to lean on.

Fig. 262 Using a leaning board to reach wide beds

Soil benches can be sunk into the floor of the greenhouse so that they are at ground level, but are generally more convenient and easier to maintain if they are waist-high. It is helpful to decide what level of

beds you wish to use before you begin to build the greenhouse so you can design the shape of the south wall accordingly; a greenhouse with waist-high soil beds along the south wall is going to require a waist-high opaque wall along that side or, alternatively, the beds can be dug into the earth to waist level.

To hold flats, pots, and other containers, smaller benches of various types are useful. Design them to fit into the spaces you have in your greenhouse. The tops should be built so that there are regularly spaced openings to permit drainage. Welded mesh supported by cross-pieces is the most durable construction, but the cheapest bench top is made of 1 x 4s or 2 x 4s spaced 10mm apart. Stepped benches along the north wall make efficient use of space, expose all the plants to sunlight, and allow easy access to the plants for watering. In addition to the convenience, plants on benches are up out of the cold air near the floor of the greenhouse.

Tiered Intensive Beds One way to make the most use of space in the greenhouse is to install tiered soil beds. Such a bed occupies a floor area of only about 600mm x 1200mm, yet can provide a growing area of three or four times that because of the four or five 450mm x 1200mm tiers it contains. They are becoming available commercially, or you can easily construct your own from a standard-size sheet of plywood or aspenite.

The top of each level is flat, but the bottom of the bed is angled to allow the sun to reach the back of each bed. This design also allows as much soil space for roots as possible. Because of the angle (about 45°) there is direct light to all soil surfaces during the winter months.

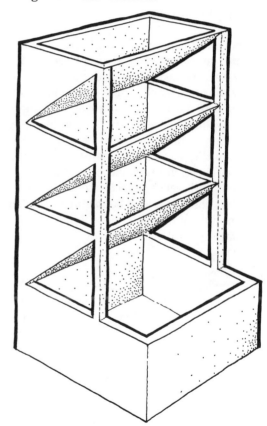

Fig. 263 Linda's planter-tiered intensive beds

Getting the Goods

Tools In general, the same hand tools used in the outdoor garden will be useful in the greenhouse: a trowel for mixing soils and transplanting, a small hand-held rake for gently working the soil surface or mixing in nutrients.

A watering can with a nozzle which passes a fine, gentle spray is always needed. A long-necked model will help you to water those hard-to-reach places at the base of the plants without leaving water droplets on the plant leaves. In periods of low humidity, a hand-held mister can be used to keep the plant leaves moist and clean. A bottle for window cleaner or a similar product will serve. Rigid extensions for garden hoses can also be useful in reaching the middle of a bench or for watering hanging pots.

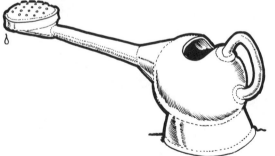

Fig. 264 Watering can with fine nozzle

A fine paintbrush or a feather should be kept handy to be used when pollinating certain flowers. A thermometer is important and should be moved as needed. A good magnifying glass will make it easier to identify insects and to determine if plant damage was caused by disease or by a pest.

You will need brushes and buckets to clean tools and planting containers. Mild soap is sometimes used to wash fungus off plant leaves. Strips of cloth or yarn can be used for tying up plants, and heavy string can be tied together in a trellising web. Don't forget labels and stakes.

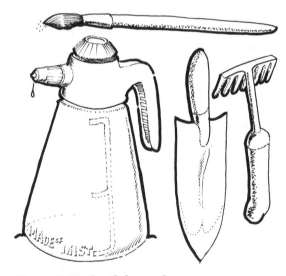

Fig. 265 Tools of the trade

Containers Besides the permanent soil beds, plants are grown in a number of other containers in the greenhouse. Seeds are usually started in large, shallow boxes called flats. Plastic flats are available which are easy to keep clean, long-lasting, and inexpensive. Wooden flats are simple to make, but you should use relatively thin lumber (10mm to 15mm) to lessen the weight since they can be awkwardly heavy when filled with soil. Make certain that you leave slight spaces between the bottom boards to allow for drainage.

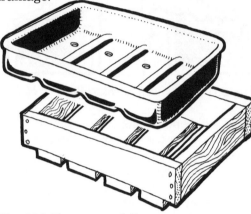

Fig. 266 Two sorts of flats

Seeds can also be started in small, pressed-peat pots. This method is convenient in that no transplanting is required — the pots themselves are planted into the bed and break down to become part of the surrounding soil. Shallow cans, cartons, and cups make fine seedling containers as long as you remember to put drainage holes in them.

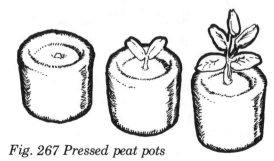

Fig. 267 Pressed peat pots

If you plant some of your crops in pots, remember that you have to provide drainage and allow air to get to the soil, and that the roots need sufficient room. If you use too small a pot the plant may become pot-bound and unhealthy.

Fig. 268 A variety of clay pots

The standard container is the unglazed, red clay pot. They are ubiquitous and come in a large number of sizes. The clay is porous and allows air to pass in, and water to pass out. This permeability means these pots will dry out quickly. If you are using water with a high mineral content, excess salts will filter through the sides of the pot and form a crust on the outside. Under humid conditions, a moss or mould may

Fig. 269 The trouble with clay pots

form. In either case, keep the pots cleaned off so that they remain porous. Clay pots are heavy and breakable.

Plastic pots are cheaper than clay pots and much lighter. Because they are less heavy, plastic pots are often more suitable for hanging plants and for placing on fragile benches. They are easy to keep clean too, but after several seasons they become brittle and can break. Another desirable feature of plastic pots is that they are not porous. They dry out much more slowly than clay pots, and plants therefore require less frequent watering. Make sure that plastic pots have sufficient drainage holes.

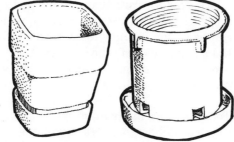

Fig. 270 A wide variety of plastic pots

Records Keeping records is strongly recommended because it will take several seasons to become familiar with the greenhouse, its microclimates, what grows best, and when to plant. Even after you are experienced in your greenhouse, it is very easy to forget things unless they are written down. A minimum-maximum thermometer for recording air temperatures and soil temperatures will enable you to maintain a regular record of temperature in the greenhouse.

A written record of varieties, planting dates, and yields, with space for added comments, is also strongly recommended to help weed out unproductive varieties and make the most efficient use of space. Recording yields in terms of number of servings rather than in grams or ounces may be the most useful. A clipboard hanging in the kitchen can contain information on what was picked in the greenhouse that day and how many people it served. Tomatoes and cucumbers are more easily counted for your records. Knowing that five kilograms of tomatoes were harvested is not as helpful as knowing that one plant produced thirty medium-sized tomatoes over the season.

Recording the dates of the appearance of insect pests or plant diseases can help you to develop a proper biological control program and to understand the cycles in the greenhouse more clearly. You should know when seedlings were transplanted, and when produce was harvested. Label your beds and containers as you plant seeds or transplant so you can tell at a glance what plant is there, what variety it is, and when it was planted.

The Greenhouse Environment

Treating the greenhouse as an ecosystem means realizing that all of its components are interrelated. Everything in it — the atmosphere, the soil, the water, the plants, the structure itself, the gardener — has to be considered as part of the whole. You cannot affect one factor without affecting others.

Even though all factors are interrelated, for purposes of discussion we might divide the greenhouse environment into *light* — how much the plants need and how they can get it; *atmosphere* — temperature, carbon dioxide, humidity, and ventilation; *soil* — mixes, amendments, fertility, and compost; and *water* — when to water, how much to water, and water quality.

Light

In a greenhouse, even with the best glazing systems, light levels are not as good as they are outdoors. There are structural members in the way; there are one, two, or three layers of glazing; condensation forms on the glazing. In the winter months, light levels can make the difference between being able to grow and not being able to grow certain crops. Anything which maximizes the light and minimizes condensation and shading will improve production potential.

Fig. 271 Light

All plants require light to power photosynthesis, but light requirements differ among various plants. If you are used to growing only house-plants you will soon discover that there is quite a difference between the amount of light required by them and the amount required by vegetables. House-plants may require several hundred foot-candles of light while tomatoes, for instance, require several thousand to produce fertile flowers and fruit. Plant varieties that do best in a greenhouse have been selected to tolerate lower light levels.

Direct sunlight is more important to plants which produce fruit than to leafy green crops such as lettuce and spinach, which can be grown in the winter in the diffuse light found towards the back of the greenhouse, and in the shaded areas which receive reflected light.

Tomatoes and many other fruiting crops (like cucumbers, peppers, eggplants, and squash) as well as root crops need bright, strong sunlight for several hours a day to allow the blossoms to set, form, and be pollinated. In the fall, as the days become shorter, it becomes increasingly difficult to get tomatoes to set. In a home greenhouse it is usually worth keeping the tomato plants long after it would be commercially viable because you can take the time to care for the plants, and to shake them every sunny day to make sure they are pollinated.

A simple, hand-held light meter can be used in various parts of the greenhouse to give an indication of the light levels and where the best spots are for the light-loving vegetables. (For comparison purposes you can use the light meter in a 35mm camera by focussing it on a square of white cardboard in various areas of the greenhouse.) The light levels in the home greenhouse are not as critical as in most commercial greenhouses.

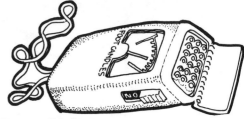

Fig. 272 Light meter

Atmosphere

The factors of the greenhouse environment that we have collected together under the heading of atmosphere — the air temperature, carbon dioxide, and relative humidity — are connected and collectively

Fig. 273 Atmosphere "weaving and swirling among the stems and leaves"

controlled by the common thread of ventilation. Ventilation brings in cool air and allows excess heat to escape to an attached dwelling or to the outside. The fresh air contains the carbon dioxide vital to plant growth.

Air Temperature   Most plants grow best between 13°C and 30°C. Some, such as cucumbers and tomatoes, become unproductive and susceptible to disease at temperatures outside this range. Others, such as lettuce and chard, can tolerate lower temperatures but growth becomes very slow. The ideal temperature range for plants is small compared to the extremes in temperature that are possible inside a glazed space. For example, when the sun shines, even in the winter, temperatures in a closed, unheated greenhouse can quickly soar to 40°C or higher. At night in the winter, if the greenhouse has no moderating influences such as thermal mass, movable insulation, or additional heat from the home, the temperature will drop rapidly to below the freezing point. Very few plants tolerate such extreme fluctuations. To maintain healthy, vigorous growth, they must have moderate temperatures and only moderate temperature changes.

Temperature is an area in which solar greenhouse design can conflict with greenhouse horticulture. It would be ideal, from one standpoint, to trap as much heat as possible during sunny periods for use in the home, and to close off the greenhouse from the home when more heat is being lost through the glazing than is being gained. This practice is fine if you are interested in storing heat, but not if you are interested in growing plants. Temperature fluctuations can be as wide as 25°C or 35°C in one day-night cycle — a circumstance incompatible with growing plants. Managing the environment for plants limits the efficiency of a home greenhouse as a solar collector. (This general statement applies to most greenhouses built today. The development of cheap, high-capacity heat storage systems for home greenhouses would improve considerably the thermal efficiency of the food producing greenhouse.)

Temperature Control   In a greenhouse, most of the heat loss occurs through the glazing at night. Double glazings can help to reduce this loss. Additionally, particularly in cold climates, movable insulation is necessary to prevent night-time temperatures which are too low.

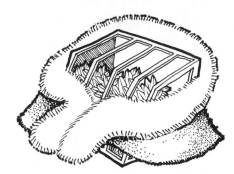

Fig. 274 Temperature control

Temperature Fluctuations

Unlike the artificially lighted and heated commercial greenhouses of recent years, a solar greenhouse does not maintain an even, steady temperature and relative humidity around the clock. Even using thermal mass and movable insulation, a solar greenhouse is going to be warmer when the sun is shining and cooler when it is not. Temperature swings of 8°C to 10°C are common. However, this instability is acceptable, since most plants grow better when there is a certain amount of fluctuation. Even in a perfectly controlled tomato greenhouse, for instance, the thermostat is lowered to about 15°C at night and raised to 20°C to 22°C during the day. A lettuce crop will produce better quality heads if the temperature is kept at 12°C to 13°C at night and no higher than 19°C during the day.

High Temperatures

Tomato flowers become sterile in air temperatures over 30°C. At such temperatures it is too hot for them to reproduce or to grow. The plants will run to foliage and there will be an increase in pest problems as the plants become more succulent. In fact, temperatures in this high range can sterilize forming blossoms for up to a week, or cause changes in the physiology of the blossoms so that even those still developing cannot be pollinated.

Thermal storage, in the form of masonry or water, is used in a greenhouse to moderate the temperature fluctuations. This mass absorbs heat during the day, helping to moderate overheating, then releases heat at night as the greenhouse temperature drops. It is usually used most effectively in conjunction with movable night-time insulation.

Judicious management of ventilation in the greenhouse is one of the most important ways the grower has of controlling temperatures. When the sun shines in the winter, a well-constructed greenhouse can overheat if ventilation is inadequate. Using natural convection or a small fan to direct hot air into the home is an excellent solution. If the excess heat can't be transferred to the home, it must be vented outside to keep maximum temperatures below 30°C.

Fig. 275 Ventilation

In the summer, when outdoor temperatures are high during the day, ventilation must be designed to move sufficient air. Some overheating can be preventing by shading compounds painted onto the outer glazing

surface, but this solution is not a good one when growing vegetables and fruit. Shade (not surprisingly) means the absence of light and many of the hot season vegetables need as much light as possible. It is also an error to assume that because the greenhouse is in shade, the air is cool. Heat builds up, even in a well-shaded place, if the air is stagnant. Adequate ventilation, without fans and control systems, can be provided by convection if the high and low vents in the greenhouse are large enough and are well-placed.

Fig. 276 shows how to use greenhouse vents to control temperatures. The size of the openings determines the rate of air flow through the greenhouse and with practice you will learn how far to open the vents to achieve the desired temperature.

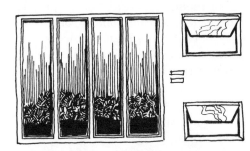

Fig. 276 Vent area should be 1/6th of glazing area

Carbon Dioxide In addition to cooling, ventilation causes air movement, which is important in the greenhouse environment. Carbon dioxide (CO_2) is an important nutrient in the air that plants use during photosynthesis. The lack of it can restrict

growth as surely as can cold temperatures or lack of soil nutrients. In a home greenhouse, carbon dioxide comes from people, from fresh air, from the soil (soil animals release it in the process of digesting organic matter) and from plants at night.

Fig. 277 Air

In a small greenhouse, enough CO_2 is usually present to insure adequate growth — the key is to make it available to the plants. When a plant needs carbon dioxide it takes it from the relatively thin layer of air which immediately surrounds the leaves. This area is called the *boundary layer*. One of the important reasons for

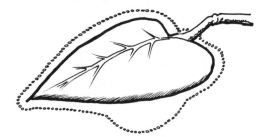

Fig. 278 Boundary layer

ventilation and air movement in the greenhouse is to keep the boundary layer broken up in order to give the plant access to fresh air and, hence, fresh sources of carbon dioxide. In a perfectly still environment, such as you can find only in an enclosed space, the plants rapidly use up the carbon dioxide in the boundary layer. In commercial greenhouses, large fans move air past the leaves, but on a small scale this effort isn't necessary since ventilation, air circulation to the house, and disturbances caused by the owner going in and out are sufficient to keep the boundary layer from becoming a problem.

Since plants benefit from concentrations of carbon dioxide greater than that normally found in the atmosphere, some greenhouse owners try to increase the amount of carbon dioxide in the greenhouse air by burning methyl alcohol in a small lamp or by evaporating dry ice. However, we feel that proper ventilation is the key to adequate levels of carbon dioxide. During the periods when temperatures and light levels are low, so will be the rate of photosynthesis (see p. 35) and, hence, carbon dioxide requirements. So, it is unlikely that it will be necessary to dump valuable, heated greenhouse air during the winter in order to provide fresh air and carbon dioxide to the plants. In any case, in an attached greenhouse there is probably sufficient fresh air due to infiltration into the home, where carbon dioxide is also produced by the oxygen-breathing occupants.

Relative Humidity Relative humidity is the actual amount of moisture in the air compared to the total amount possible at a given temperature. It is expressed as a percentage of the total amount. In a

Daytime Management of Greenhouse Vents

In an existing greenhouse, where the height and temperature differences between the upper and lower vents are established, the rate of air flow and the rate of cooling are determined by the amount the vents are opened.

Winter — Sunny Day

♦ Warm air rises and is either used in the home or vented outdoors.
♦ Cold air that comes in the top vent has a chance to warm up as it falls to plant level.
♦ Lower vents are not opened to prevent freezing air from flowing across plants.

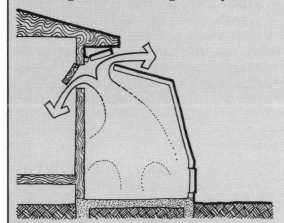

Fig. 279 Winter: sunny day

Spring and Fall
♦ Warm air rises and is used in the home or vented outdoors.

♦ Lower vents are opened as much as needed to provide cool (though not cold) air.

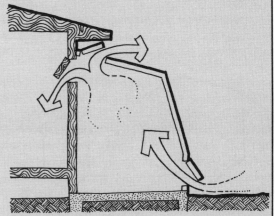

Fig. 280 Spring/fall

Summer
♦ Warm air rises and is vented to the outdoors.
♦ Top and bottom vents are opened wide.
♦ Ideally, the rate of air flow is enough to prevent overheating.

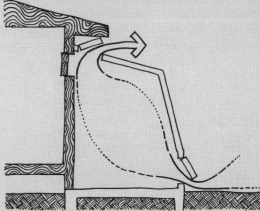

Fig. 281 Summer

greenhouse, the ideal relative humidity is around 60%. In practice, it fluctuates throughout the day with the temperature. (Warm air can contain more moisture than can cold air, so if the amount of moisture remains constant as the temperature rises, the relative humidity decreases.)

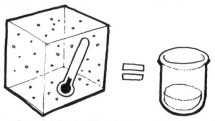

Fig. 282 Cold air holds less moisture than...

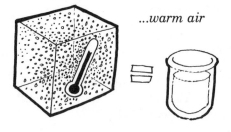

...warm air

Excessively high humidity inside the greenhouse causes a number of problems. When the relative humidity rises over 80%, spores of pathogenic fungi germinate and diseases develop. Condensation also becomes a serious problem as more and more moisture is held in the air. When warm, moisture-laden air contacts a cool surface, the water condenses. On the glazing, the tiny droplets of water scatter and reflect the incoming light, reducing the amount reaching the plant by as much as 50%. Condensation on wood surfaces also contributes to decay.

Excess moisture is most easily controlled by proper ventilation. Dry air from the home, circulating in the greenhouse, acts like a sponge, picking up water from glazing and leaf surfaces.

If the air in the home is too dry in the winter, extra humidity from an attached greenhouse will be a welcome addition. If a higher humidity in the house is not desirable, any excess greenhouse moisture must be vented directly to the outside.

High relative humidity is mainly a problem in humid regions, especially in the spring and fall. Inland areas, such as the prairies, usually experience uncomfortably low relative humidities. Air that is too dry stresses plants, causes soil to dry out too quickly, and encourages pests such as spider mites. The humidity can be raised by periodically watering walkways or spraying a fine mist into the air. Avoid wetting the plants on bright sunny days as the magnification of sunlight through the drops of water can cause leaf burning.

Soil

It is important to obtain the best soil possible. Greenhouse soils are worked harder than garden soils because they are usually used year-round, rather than for four to six months in the summer; the indoor soil does not receive the benefits of the freezing and thawing action which improves soil texture and helps correct the results of over-cultivation; there is not time for nutrients to weather out of the

soil and be made available for use by the plants, as happens in the garden; excessive concentrations of calcium mistakenly applied are not leached out by heavy rains or winter snows. Since greenhouse soil is worked harder than garden soil, fertility problems which might take years to appear in the garden may appear in the greenhouse in just a few months.

Fig. 283 Soil

Greenhouse soils, therefore, require a high proportion of amendments to improve their texture. The amendments will increase water retention and provide drainage, ensuring a good supply of oxygen, water, and nutrients to the roots. The soil should also contain a healthy, diverse population of micro-organisms, which assist plants in taking up nutrients and in combating diseases.

Loam   Good topsoil is the major ingredient of a soil mix. Ideally, it should be loam soil from a fertile garden or from a field under hay or pasture.

Soils are composed of three sizes of particles: sand, silt, and clay. The proportion of these particles determines the *texture* of the soil and, in turn, such physical properties as potential fertility,

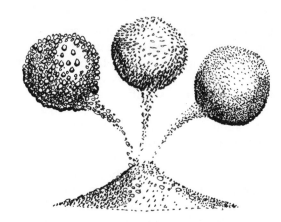

Fig. 284 Loam is composed of sand, silt and clay

water-holding capacity, drainage, and aeration. The properties of sand (fast drainage, few nutrients) predominate in a sandy soil, while the properties of clay (high water-holding ability, high nutrient potential) predominate in clay soils. Loam soil is one in which the properties of all three particle sizes are about equal. This combination is most desirable because the good drainage and aeration of sand is combined with the nutrient-releasing capacity of the finest soil particles. Various amendments are added to greenhouse soil mixes to give sandy or clay soils the desirable properties of loam. These amendments usually have little or no fertilizer value, yet are important in providing the necessary conditions for the plant roots. Peat moss, sand, vermiculite, and perlite are the most common amendments.

Sand Clean, coarse builder's sand can be added to clay soils to improve drainage and aeration.

Peat Moss Horticultural-grade peat moss will improve any soil because it improves both the water-holding capacity and the nutrient-holding capacity of sandy soil, while also improving drainage and aeration of clay soils. The beneficial effects of adding organic matter will be discussed shortly.

Vermiculite Vermiculite, which is expanded mica particles, increases the ability of soil to hold plant nutrients and aids in the aeration of a clay soil. Also, a large portion of vermiculite in a soil mix makes it lighter in weight, which is useful in pots or hanging planters.

Perlite Perlite is a gritty volcanic ash which is expanded by heat and used as a lightweight aggregate in concrete and plaster. Its soil conditioning properties are similar to those of vermiculite.

Soil Structure The *structure* of the soil is the degree to which the particles in the soil stick together. In pure sand, each grain is separate. In pure clay, the soil is one big lump. In a loam soil with good structure, moist soil will break apart into pea-sized, crumbly lumps made up of many individual particles stuck together. This structure is ideal for plant roots — they can penetrate it easily while air can enter, water can drain away, and carbon dioxide (a waste product) can pass into the atmosphere away from the root zone.

Do Not Sterilize or Pasteurize the Soil

Most greenhouse publications recommend sterilizing or pasteurizing soil to avoid importing soil-borne pests and diseases into the greenhouse. Sterilizing means heating up the soil to kill all organisms; pasteurization is heating the soil to a temperature that kills harmful organisms but supposedly does not harm the beneficial ones.

The effects of these techniques, however, are too broad, and the view that only harmful organisms are killed is too narrow. The soil ecosystem is very complex and in a healthy, living soil there are beneficial organisms which will keep the diseases in check. Heating the soil to kill pathogens will seriously disrupt this system and will result in the destruction of many organisms necessary for plant growth. Pasteurization, for instance, kills organisms that make nitrogen available to plants and break down organic matter. Sterilization is like a neutron bomb — it destroys the soil life, leaving only the structure.

Damping-off is a seedling disease often cited as a reason for using pasteurized soil. However, the organisms that cause this disease are everywhere and even pasteurized soil may be soon reinfected. Since these organisms reproduce one hundred times faster in wet, cool soil than in warm, light soil, the control of damping-off does not have as much to do with whether the soil was pasteurized, as it does with physical conditions.

Careful management of the greenhouse soil is needed to maintain its structure. Over-cultivation, the pounding of water, and walking or standing on soil beds all contribute to the destruction of the soil structure. Outdoors, the freezing/thawing cycle and crop rotations with hay and pasture aid in remedying the effects of cultivation and compaction in farm and garden soils, but none of these forces operate in the home greenhouse. Therefore, try to minimize cultivation simply by turning greenhouse soil beds over with a fork or trowel to incorporate annual additions of amendments and fertilizer. Never stand or lean directly on the soil, always spread your weight by standing on a wide board. Avoid watering the soil with a pounding stream of water directly from a hose. Instead, use hose fittings called 'water breakers' (available from garden supply catalogues). These attachments break the stream of water into a gentle rain. Watering can also be done using a seep hose at the base of the plants. When using a garden hose, do not use a nozzle or a strong spray; merely break the flow of

Fig. 285 Hose fitting called a water breaker

water coming from the hose by running the water down a board so that it spreads out and gently soaks the soil along its length.

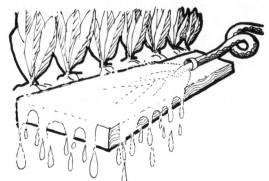

Fig. 286 Dribbling water down a board

Organic Matter Organic matter is a vital constituent of any soil. It modifies physical properties of the soil by increasing water-holding capacity in sandy soils and by decreasing the stickiness and improving the aeration and drainage of clay soils. Organic matter also greatly increases the ability of the soil to provide nutrients for plants, especially nitrogen, phosphorus, and sulphur. The breakdown of organic matter in soil produces humic acids which combine with the minerals in the soil to provide nutrients in a form useable by the plants.

Manure, compost, and leaf mould are sources of organic matter that contain plant nutrients. The levels of the various nutrients vary widely, however, depending on the origin and handling of these materials.

Compost Compost is an ideal soil amendment. It supplies the major plant nutrients — nitrogen and phosphorus — as well as organic matter, necessary soil bacteria, and micro-nutrients. The proportion of compost used in the soil mix will depend on the fertility and texture of the topsoil and the quality of the compost.

There are as many ways to produce compost as there are gardeners. Ingredients can be any locally available organic materials such as hay, grass clippings, leaves, manure, kitchen garbage, seaweed, garden wastes, etc. These elements are stacked together, moistened, and turned periodically until the mass has broken down into dark, crumbly compost. The most important points to remember when making compost are that it must be evenly moist in order to decompose, that smaller particles decompose faster (which is why shredding the ingredients will speed the process), and that some source of

Nutrient Composition of Fresh Manure			
	Total Nutrient Content Kg Per Metric Ton(ne)		
Animal	Nitrogen (N)	Phosphorus (P₂O₅)	Potassium (K₂O)
Cow	5.6	2.3	6.0
Steer	7.0	2.3	5.5
Sheep	14.0	4.8	12.0
Swine	5.0	3.3	4.5
Horse	6.9	9.0	7.5
Chicken	15.6	9.0	4.5

Source: Plant Industry Division, Alberta Department of Agriculture

nitrogen is needed to facilitate the breakdown of coarse materials such as straw or leaves.

Compost made only from grass clippings and kitchen garbage will take longer to break down than compost made with a lot of manure. In the composting process, organic matter, which contains much carbon, uses nitrogen to break down. A large amount of nitrogen is used in making compost and it comes from the air, urine, manure, blood meal, or other materials in the mix. Materials like straw or grass clippings, which have a lot of carbon compared to the amount of nitrogen, take longer to break down unless nitrogen is available from other sources in the compost pile. Nitrogen added to the pile, from whatever source, will help it to decompose faster.

Once compost is made, it should be protected from heavy rainfall to prevent nutrients from being washed away.

Fig. 287 Compost

Compost which has been further digested by worms gives good results in soil mixes. Wooden boxes filled with worms and compost can be covered with a sheet of burlap and kept in the greenhouse (beneath the soil benches, if there is room) throughout the cold months. The resulting humus is an ideal fertilizer when dug into the beds in the spring and fall. A good substitute for compost is well-rotted manure. Dried and bagged manure can be purchased from

garden centres if there is no other source nearby.

Soil Acidity A soil test tells you the pH of the soil. This measure of acidity in the soil is very important because soils that are too acidic release elements, such as aluminum, in amounts toxic to plants. A pH of 7 is neutral and most vegetables require a pH of 6.6 to 6.8. (Agricultural lime is usually added to acidic soils to raise the pH into

Soil Tests

Soil tests are an inexpensive source of information on the type of soil you have and of recommendations regarding the addition of nutrients. Check with the local department of agriculture, the nearest agricultural college, or your county extension office.

To take a soil test, either borrow a probe from your department of agriculture or collect samples with a trowel. The probe is a T-shaped, hollow tube which is inserted into the ground to a depth of about 150mm to remove a core sample. Take samples from the most average-looking area and avoid things such as pieces of sod or uncomposted manure which would affect test results. If there is sod on top of the soil, remove it first and take the samples from the soil underneath it. After collecting soil from twenty different spots, mix it up carefully and thoroughly in a bucket and put about half a kilogram of soil in a plastic bag and send it in for testing.

The results will list the organic matter content, the pH, and the amount of various nutrients such as nitrogen, phosphorus, and potassium. These figures may be expressed in parts per million (ppm), but there will probably also be a scale to help you to interpret the results (low, medium, high, etc.). A good garden soil should be rated medium or high and should have a pH of about 6.6.

If you subsequently wish to test your greenhouse soil, be certain to request the normal test done for the outdoor garden. Some labs do a special greenhouse soil test (which checks for soluble nutrients) for the commercial greenhouse operators who provide fertilizers through their irrigation system. Nitrogen in the soil of a biologically managed greenhouse will be held in the organic matter contained in the soil and is not readily soluble, hence it will not show up in such tests.

this range.) At this level of slight acidity, the most nutrients are available to the plants while the least amounts of toxic elements are released. Some soils, especially in western regions, have a pH higher than 7. These soils require amendments such as sulphur to lower the pH and, therefore, make nutrients more available.

Do not undertake pH adjustments until you have received soil test results. These results will give recommendations for the addition of agricultural lime or various nutrients. Liming recommendations should be followed carefully. If too much lime is added, creating an alkaline soil, it can be very difficult to correct.

The usual recommendation in Atlantic Canada, for instance, (where soils are acidic) is to add about 900 kg (2,000 lbs) of lime per acre. This quantity may sound like a lot, but when translated to a greenhouse scale, it represents only about 0.2kg

Organic Fertilizer Composition

Mineral nutrient values of some organic fertilizers which may be used to supplement the nutrients in compost:

Fertilizer	Percentage Composition		
	Nitrogen	Phosphorus	Potassium
Bone meal (raw)	2-6	15-27	0
Blood meal	12	1.5	0.57
Fish meal (dry)	10	4	0
Wood ashes	0	1-2	3-7

per square metre (about 4.5 lbs/100 sq ft). A very light dusting of the soil is all that is required.

Other Additives There are other organic soil additives which can be used to correct nutrient deficiencies. For example, bone meal supplies phosphorus, wood ashes supply potassium, and blood and fish meals supply nitrogen. Seaweed is an excellent addition to the soil mix. It contributes a variety of micro-nutrients and beneficial plant hormones. It can be dug in raw after collecting it from the beach after a storm, or purchased as a dried powder. Its benefits warrant purchasing it for the small area of soil in a greenhouse, even if you live far from the coast.

Soil Mixes Which amendments to use and what quantity of each will be required for a greenhouse soil mix will be determined by the type of soil you start with. Since it is not usually as fertile as garden soil, the use of field soil in a soil mix will require a higher portion of compost.

A good soil texture can be attained by adding peat moss, vermiculite, or sand, depending on whether you start with sand or clay topsoil. At right is a chart of suggested soil mixes. If you are able to locate only very poor soil for your soil mix, then change the proportions to five parts soil to the various amendments.

After the soil is mixed, and while it is damp, take some in your hands and squeeze it as hard as you can. When you

open your hand a lump of soil should remain which crumbles easily at your touch. If not, your soil mix requires further amendments.

Routine Soil Management Once or twice a year, usually in the summer months when heavier watering compacts the soil, the soil should be cultivated lightly with a trowel or fork to break up the surface. At this time, compost, well-rotted manure, or other amendments can be worked in. In the case of a perennial or long-lived annual (such as a tomato plant), compost should be dug in carefully around the root zone every three to four months. If the soil seems to be crusted and packed down, additions of peat moss or leaf mould are called for to increase the organic matter content. The

Suggested Soil Mixes

Here are some suggested soil mixes. The quality of the topsoil used must be considered when choosing a mix.

	Sandy Topsoil	Clay Topsoil
Garden Soil	7 parts topsoil 2 parts peat or vermiculite 1 part compost	7 parts topsoil 3 parts vermiculite or sand 1 part compost
Field Soil	6 parts topsoil 2 parts peat or vermiculite 1 part compost	6 parts topsoil 3 parts vermiculite or sand 1 part compost

addition of coarse sand or vermiculite is advisable if green algae, a symptom of waterlogged soil, can be seen growing on the surface. A mulch will protect the soil and plant roots from drying out during the heat of summer.

You may need to add soil to the bench periodically to maintain the level. It is possible to add too much organic matter. Use a light hand.

Soil Beds There are many different methods of constructing greenhouse soil benches, but several general principles must be followed for the best results.

Soil benches along the south wall of a greenhouse should be built so that the top of the soil is level with the bottom edge of the glazing. The low winter sun casts very long shadows over a surprisingly large area and shaded soil is cold and un-productive.

The soil should be as deep as possible. Shallow soil beds dry out quickly and require frequent watering, which leaches out soil nutrients. Further, soil in shallow beds allows changes in temperatures more rapidly than deep soil. Plant tops are able to withstand fluctuating temperatures much better than the roots. Increasing the thermal mass of the soil beds can minimize the effects of the unavoidable changes in air temperature in a solar heated green-house by slowing down the rate of temperature fluctuation in the root zone. In deeper soil, more nutrients are available

to the roots, allowing closer spacing of plants.

Ideally, soil beds should be built directly on the earth to provide proper, natural drainage. If you build the beds on concrete or another impermeable material, you must allow for drainage by providing as much gravel and stone under the soil as possible — at least 300mm between the impervious surface and the soil.

The Sundance Greenhouse is designed so that, with proper protection, the south wall and endwalls will form three sides of a deep soil bed. Wooden edging boards across the front will form the fourth side. If you have to build the soil bed on top of a concrete floor you will have to provide for drainage. A satisfactory configuration of such a soil bed is begun by laying down stone or rocks on which to build the beds. Wire mesh on top of the rocks will keep the soil from washing down through the rocks, although 100mm of gravel makes a satisfactory substitute for the mesh. Edging boards placed across the front will hold the soil, which is in contact with the rocks or gravel, in place. Soil should never be less than 300mm deep and 500mm to 600mm is preferable.

If you did not pour concrete beneath the soil bed, simply place edging boards across the front to a comfortable working level and fill the entire bin with soil. If you use rigid insulation on the bottom, be sure to leave gaps to allow drainage.

Because wood used to build soil benches is constantly exposed to damp, humid conditions and organisms in the soil, it is susceptible to rot. However, when building the benches, avoid wood preservatives which will come into contact with the soil. They are toxic to plants and will inhibit plant growth. It is better to use inexpensive scrap wood, which may need to be replaced every five years, than to try using a preservative such as pentachlorophenal or creosote inside a greenhouse. Cedar and redwood are very attractive and resistant to decay. However, they are expensive, and even though lower grades can often be obtained at a lower cost, remember that they are increasingly scarce resources. Hemlock, if available, is also resistant to decay.

Containers of water, gravel, or any other material with a high heat capacity can also be used under benches to lessen temperature fluctuations. If you are planting in pots, planters, or tubs, use the biggest ones possible and try to put them in areas where the temperature is most stable. You can discover these places in your greenhouse by checking with thermometers.

Water

How much and how often to water depends on the temperature in the greenhouse, the type of soil mix, whether there is a mulch, and the depth of the container or growing bed. Greenhouse soil, like garden soil, should be watered thoroughly and infrequently, rather than lightly watered daily. When the soil beds are thoroughly soaked they will start drying out from the top down, which forces the plant root to reach farther into the soil, where the environment is best for them.

Fig. 288 Water

The time to water is when the soil is dry on top and only slightly damp about 25mm deep. Push your finger into the soil to test, but avoid damaging plant roots. (When seeds are coming up, of course, you will have to keep the top layer of soil damp at all times.) This "rule of finger" applies to deep soil beds only. You will have to water pots and shallow beds more frequently.

Overwatering is as harmful as underwatering, because roots will die and rot in soggy, airless soil.

Avoid watering on cloudy, rainy, or snowy days. On these days plants need little water. The humidity is likely to be high and watering will only increase it. Because moulds grow more readily on wet leaves, water early in the morning so that any leaves that get wet will have a chance to dry off by evening.

Large greenhouses sometimes use a trickle irrigation system. This arrangement consists of permeable tubes, running along the surface of the soil beneath the plant leaves, distributing water slowly and evenly. This method of watering can be convenient in the winter, since the soil dries out slowly and the system may have to be turned on for only a short period every other week. However, the soils in some greenhouses may dry out so quickly during the summer that there will be a narrow band of wet soil along the tubing while the rest of the bed is very dry. Mulching over the seep hose remedies this problem.

At any time, mulch is a means of maintaining even soil temperature. If you have to leave your greenhouse unattended for a period, soak the beds well and put on mulch.

The routine of watering can become tedious in the summer, so make the process as convenient as possible. Provide easy access to the beds and a step-stool for checking and watering upper levels and hanging pots.

Water quality is important. Chlorinated city water should be allowed to stand in an open container for a day or two before being used, to enable the chlorine gas to escape. Drawing irrigation water into a holding tank is a good idea in any case, because it has an opportunity to warm up to room temperature before it is used. For seedlings, room-temperature water is necessary and it is desirable, though not essential, to use room-temperature water for the rest of the greenhouse.

A holding tank can be as simple as a metal or plastic garbage can which is filled up and allowed to warm to greenhouse temperature. A 50-gallon drum may be used to warm the irrigation water. If you are able to collect and store rainwater in a tank at head-level in the greenhouse, you can water your plants directly from that, benefiting from the force gravity.

Planning Planting

There are a number of factors to take into account when deciding what to plant in the greenhouse. The major determinant will be the greenhouse environment and the crops which will thrive in those conditions.

The temperature range and the amount of light available are two of these factors. Generally, the leafy green vegetables are the most productive of the crops to be found in the winter greenhouse since it is the leaves which are harvested, and they will continue to grow, albeit slowly, under conditions of low light and cool temperatures. While greenhouses in the northernmost latitudes and in the coldest climates may not be able to support these crops during the entire winter, they will certainly produce into December.

Plants which set fruit, such as tomatoes and melons, require more light and heat to be productive, although the plants themselves will often survive temperature extremes which make their flowers infertile. Some vegetables — such as radishes and onions — are particularly sensitive to the day length. This reaction to the length of light and dark periods is called photoperiodism. Radishes will not produce good roots in the short days of winter.

Personal taste must be another consideration. Space inside of a home greenhouse is limited and valuable, so be sure to grow what you and your family like to eat. Kale is a prolific, cold-hardy plant which will grow well in the greenhouse; if no one in your family likes kale, however, you will be wasting space, time, and energy if you plant it. You would do better to consider other hardy plants such as chard, lettuce, celery, broccoli, or spinach.

The size, success, and succession of your outdoor garden will also determine which varieties are grown inside. If you use the greenhouse to start seedlings for the outdoor garden, you must plan for this use of space. It makes little sense to grow carrots or radishes or other crops which take up a great deal of room in the greenhouse when they can easily be grown in the outdoor garden. When planning the fall and winter greenhouse garden, take into consideration the vegetables you will have harvested from the outdoor garden. Carrots are again a good example — there is no need to plant carrots in the greenhouse if you have a crop of carrots stored in the root cellar. If the greenhouse is the only garden space available to you, however, such things as carrots, zucchini, and leeks can certainly be grown in it.

To maximize the use of space in the greenhouse, try to plant crops that provide a continuous yield, such as many of the leafy vegetables, rather than those which are harvested only once. Vegetables such as the chinese cabbages, leaf lettuce, turnip greens, spinach, cress, endive, cornsalad, and even celery will continue to grow as you harvest the outer or lower leaves. If you start some of these plants in

Fig. 289 Kale

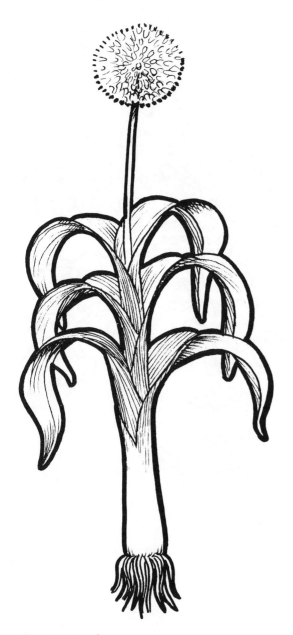

Fig. 290 Leek

late August, they will be quite large by November. Since these mature plants can survive in the cold and the light of winter, they can keep you supplied with salad and leafy greens into the winter months. The highest yields are obtained by picking every leaf as soon as it is big enough to eat.

There are several factors which make the use of permanent, deep soil beds in the greenhouse desirable, particularly for cold-climate greenhouses. In the summer, however, you may want to add pots and hanging planters to make use of all the space in the greenhouse. Many vegetables and herbs will do well in pots and shallow beds, which are easily moved in and out of sunlight and warm areas as summer progresses into fall.

To maximize use of the greenhouse, harvesting and planting should go on throughout most of the year so that there is never a wasted space. There is never an abrupt transition from the heat-loving crops of the summer greenhouse garden to the cool, leafy plants of the winter greenhouse, but rather a gradual change as you harvest one crop and replace it with another. Proper planning can also mean inter-cropping. Shorter plants, which soon will be harvested, can be placed between tall plants which mature later.

Seeding

In a greenhouse, seeds may be sown either directly into permanent beds, or into seed flats for future transplanting. There are advantages to both methods and although it is usual in a greenhouse to start the plants in flats, direct seeding is preferable for some varieties.

Seeding in Flats In greenhouses, maximum production is achieved by starting most seeds in flats or other small containers. It is easier to provide the extra heat and light necessary for germination to a small area, then to transplant the plants into the soil beds once they are well started. Transplanting can be done immediately after another crop is removed, thus shortening the time a plant occupies a soil bed, and permitting intensive use of the valuable space under glass.

There is no need to pasteurize the seedling soil to prevent damping-off. Damping-off is a seedling disease caused by several kinds of soil fungi. Affected seedlings die, sometimes even before they emerge from the soil. The stems of these seedlings shrivel and collapse at the soil line. When the soil is cool and wet, the fungi reproduce quickly and an entire flat can suddenly succumb to damping-off as the fungus rapidly spreads from plant to plant. The key to prevention is to provide the optimum soil conditions for seedling growth, for these are also conditions that inhibit the growth of damping-off fungi. Soil mixes made with compost also give good results, probably because beneficial soil fungi in the mix act to suppress the damping-off fungi. Warm temperatures along with good light, fresh air, and a friable, compost-rich soil mix are the best insurance against damping-off. Avoid overwatering the flats at all times.

The seedling soil mix should be fairly moist but not soggy, and should be lightly pressed into the flat to a depth of about 50mm. It should be slightly below the top of the flat so that water will not run off.

Germination

The time needed for germination depends upon the amount of water and oxygen available and, particularly, the soil temperature. The germination time for most common greenhouse crops will vary between three and fourteen days, depending on these conditions. A constant, minimum soil temperature is important not only for germination, but also to prevent damping-off disease.

Here is an indication of what vegetables require a warm soil for germination as well as those which will germinate in somewhat cooler soil:

Warm Soil (over 21°C)
Tomatoes
Peppers
Melons

Cool Soil (over 12°C to 13°C)
Cabbage
Lettuce
Onions

Sow the seeds in rows, or broadcast them over the surface of the soil and sprinkle a layer of vermiculite (twice the thickness of the seed) to cover them. If extra seed is available and not too expensive, sow more than will be required so that selection of the best seedlings can be made. Seeds such as petunia or angelica, which require light to germinate, should be covered by a very thin layer of fine vermiculite. Check the seed packages for specific information.

Thoroughly water the flats from the top with a gentle spray of room-temperature water, disturbing the seeds as little as possible. Watering the flat from the bottom by soaking it until the surface is moist is usually not advisable in humid regions because it leaves the soil waterlogged, without any air spaces, and seeds need oxygen to germinate. Also, wet soil is usually colder, which encourages damping-off. (However, in dry regions, this practice may be acceptable as flats tend to dry out quickly.)

When the surface of the soil becomes dry, water it gently from the top again. In the summer months, care should be taken that the flats are not placed in such a hot location that they dry out in less than a day. If the temperature is very high, seeds should be germinated in a cool corner or under a temporary shade of newspaper.

Since seeds require not only moisture and oxygen, but also sufficiently warm temperatures to germinate, keep the flats at a minimum constant temperature.

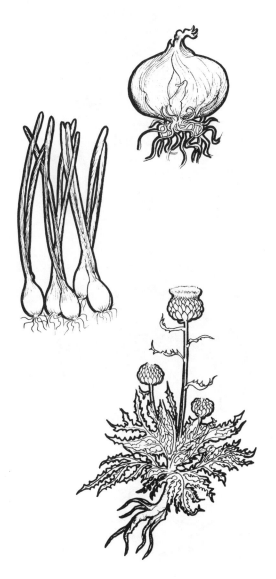

Fig. 291 Onions

Fig. 292 Eggplant

Fig. 293 White cabbage

Moving flats to a warm spot in the house at night will avoid temperatures that are too low.

Seedlings Healthy seedlings are stocky and dark green. Pale, spindly, and weak seedlings more readily fall prey to stem rot, diseases, and insect infestations. Poor quality seedlings can result from excessively high temperatures, overcrowding in the flat, or low light levels. This last factor is indicated by seedlings leaning toward the light source.

Once the seeds have germinated, they should be exposed to full sunlight for as long as possible each day. The healthiest seedlings are grown at daytime temperatures of 18°C to 21°C and night-time temperatures of about 16°C.

Watering with manure tea is a cheap way to give seedlings a boost if they are short of nutrients. Put a scoop of manure in a large bucket, add water, and let it sit for several days. Drain off the murky brown tea and dilute it to a pale amber colour before watering the seedlings.

Fish emulsion and seaweed extract are both good for seedlings although fish emulsion is high in nitrogen and too much of it may result in rapid, spindly growth. Seaweed extract is a good source of many nutrients and is an excellent all-round fertilizer for seedlings.

Transplanting

Most species are ready to be transplanted after they have their first set of true leaves. Do not be fooled by the first leaves which poke up through the soil. These are called seed leaves and usually are recognizably different from subsequent leaves. If space is a problem, seedlings may be left in the flats for a longer period once they have been thinned. To thin, gently pluck out the surplus seedlings, disturbing the soil as little as possible.

Do not transplant the seedlings to the soil beds in the greenhouse until the soil has warmed up. Seedlings that can be set out when the soil is less than 13°C include lettuce, chinese cabbage, broccoli, and other members of the cabbage family. Tomatoes and eggplants should never be set out until the soil remains above 13°C. At low soil temperatures they will not thrive and cannot, for instance, utilize the phosphorus in the soil.

Transplanting Techniques With a small tool such as a sharp stick, carefully dislodge the seedling and lift it out of the flat, retaining as much soil around the roots as possible. The seedling should be supported by a leaf or by its roots, rather than its stem. It is very easy to break or twist the stem and, even if the seedling is not killed, the injured tissue may allow the entry of disease organisms.

Seedlings should be set a little deeper in the new soil than they were in the flat.

Celery is an exception to this rule — if the heart of the celery is buried it will become susceptible to rot. Pack soil gently around the roots and water thoroughly with room-temperature water. At this stage, an application of a 1% seaweed extract solution, weak manure tea, or diluted fish emulsion speeds recovery from the transplant shock. Newly transplanted seedlings should be shielded from direct sunlight for a few days, to allow the roots to establish themselves. It is best to transplant on cloudy days, in any case, since the plant's rate of transpiration is greater on hot, sunny days.

Transplanting into Secondary

Flats The seedlings may be transplanted to slightly larger and deeper flats at a very young stage. This practice allows the seedlings to grow larger than the space in the original seed flat would permit, yet it preserves the valuable space in the greenhouse growing beds for more mature plants which need the full depth of the bed. More labour is involved in this method, but it is a useful technique to maximize the limited space in the greenhouse, with the plants occupying the smallest area necessary for good growth until they are permanently planted.

Choose the healthiest, sturdiest seedlings for transplanting. The spacing in the secondary flat depends on the species, with 25mm spacing used for lettuce, and wider spacing of 50mm used for tomatoes and peppers. Transplanting into individual pots, 80mm to 100mm in diameter, is ideal at this stage for tomatoes and peppers, because it eliminates further transplant shock when the plants are finally set out into beds.

Transplanting into Growing

Beds Seedlings can be set directly into growing beds from the seed flat if the space is available. This system requires less labour and exposes the seedlings to transplant shock only once. The spacing varies according to species. Follow the same transplanting technique.

Direct Seeding

Plants seeded directly into the greenhouse bed will occupy the valuable space longer, while producing the same yields, than seedlings already well started elsewhere, although direct seeding requires less labour and plants do not suffer any setbacks due to transplanting. Some plants, such as radishes, carrots, lettuce, dill, and chervil are not normally transplanted and it is necessary to seed them directly into deep soil beds.

For direct seeding, the soil must be warm enough for germination (18°C to 24°C) and light levels must be adequate. Because of these requirements, direct seeding is often not possible between November and March. In most home greenhouses the soil temperatures and light levels are too low throughout this period, particularly in northern regions. If plants have been well started, however, it is possible for them to continue to grow and yield well into the winter months.

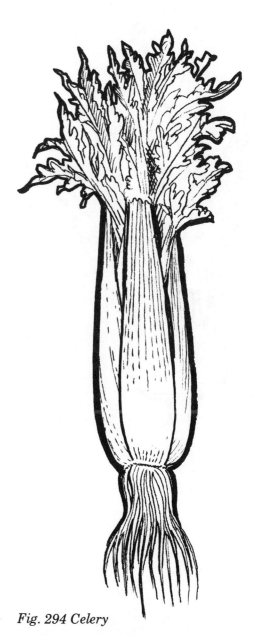

Fig. 294 Celery

Fig. 295 Kohlrabi

Bed Layout

Greenhouse owners use a variety of planting techniques and configurations. If, as is usually the case, your soil beds run lengthwise east to west, planting rows north-south across the beds will make it easy to weed, thin, and dig in extra compost at the sides of the rows. Some crops, like cress, are best seeded in little patches by broadcasting the seed.

The relative heights of the varieties you will plant should always be kept in mind: the shortest ones should go closest to the front glazing, with the taller ones behind them. Planting narrow blocks of each variety across the bench from north to south minimizes shading.

In deep soil, a mixture of species can be set quite close together if their roots occupy different soil zones. For example, a strip of lettuce, then one of radishes, then one of chinese cabbage makes better use of the whole soil than a solid planting of lettuce with roots all reaching to the same depth. Shallow-rooted vegetables, such as cress or leaf lettuce, will grow close to deep-rooted plants such as tomatoes after they have grown tall and their bottom leaves have been removed. Most crops should be placed so that the above-ground portions of the fully grown plants will not quite touch one another. Large vines, such as grapevines, are better set to the side or in a rear corner of the greenhouse where their vines can be trellised along the side or back wall, out of the way of the other plants.

Succession

You will be using greenhouse space to the fullest if you try to fill every empty space within 24 hours. However, this ability requires planning, a knowledge of the plants' life cycles, and experience. Seeds must be started in flats three to eight weeks before they will be needed for transplanting to the soil beds. The exact amount of time needed will depend on the variety and the season. Seeds take longer to germinate during the cool months and seedlings grow fastest in the late spring. Because chinese cabbage (Michihili) is one crop which does well in most seasons and in most regions, it may be useful to have a small flat of these seedlings ready throughout the greenhouse season, so that there is always something to transplant into open spaces in the soil benches.

Greenhouse Season Just as there are seasons outdoors, so there are seasons inside the greenhouse. As with the outdoor seasons, there are no distinct boundaries between the greenhouse seasons but, rather, slow, almost unnoticeable changes. The climate inside a greenhouse varies from region to region — particularly with cloud cover and most particularly in the winter. In all greenhouses, plants will take longer to grow during the cold months.

The planting schedule provides a useful guide to greenhouse management in northern regions. It is intended for a greenhouse which can maintain above-freezing temperatures throughout the winter. Once you have used your greenhouse for a season, you will know how to adapt the schedule to accommodate your particular greenhouse environment as well as your tastes and requirements.

A Sample Succession

Starting in the fall, a selection of green leaf lettuce, head lettuce, chinese cabbage, mustard, turnip greens, etc. is seeded into small flats. As the greenhouse harvest progresses and space becomes available in the benches, the young greens are set out 100mm to 200mm apart. When they grow enough to become crowded, every second plant is pulled and used in salads. The remaining plants then have time to fill out before the cool, dark season of mid-winter, when growth is very slow.

Several tomato vines seeded in June and set out in August for a late crop are left in the benches. Although they will not grow or set new fruit, the green tomatoes on them will continue to ripen slowly and provide fresh tomatoes into the winter. As the fall greens are set out, compost or other necessary soil amendments (as indicated by a soil test) are worked into the top several inches of soil. A few clear areas of bench are sown directly with chervil, some radishes, onions or scallions, and a row of dill.

Winter   In late January, peppers, tomatoes, and eggplants are seeded in small flats. These flats are kept on a bench equipped with bottom heat, and are covered against the cold. In most areas, if these seeds are planted this early, artificial lighting will be required. The resultant seedlings are transplanted to 100mm pots after several weeks and are ready to be set into the beds in late March or when the greenhouse is sufficiently light and warm. (The minimum soil temperature for tomatoes is 13°C.) Melons and cucumbers are started in individual pots in early March, and are held in a warm place well into April, when they are set out. In February, a patch of radishes is seeded directly into the beds, and more lettuce seedlings are started so that the spring crop can replace the worn out winter plants. In year-round greenhouses, the greens are usually grown to a schedule which permits three crops per year, with the exception of chard and spinach, which occupy a space in the bench for up to one year before needing replacement. Greens are seeded in the fall for winter harvest, again in February for a spring harvest, and once more in the summer for a fall harvest. Lettuce is generally unproductive in the heat of the summer greenhouse, although the cos and romaine varieties of lettuce do better than head lettuce.

Spring   In the spring, when winter plants are pulled, the soil is again very lightly cultivated. Peat and a little compost are worked in, as required. Soil is added once a year as the bench soil compacts or works down.

Summer   As summer progresses, the hot season crops grow and take over the benches, along with a few rows of chard,

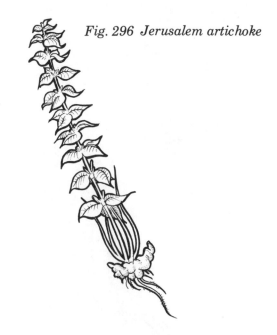

Fig. 296 *Jerusalem artichoke*

Fig. 297 *Spinach*

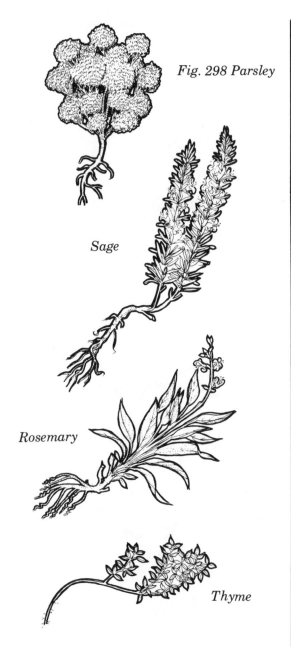

Fig. 298 Parsley

Sage

Rosemary

Thyme

Pruning and Trellising of Tomatoes

Pruning   Tomato plants should be pruned so that they grow with two leaders. This method increases yields by at least one third, and may be effected by using the following pruning techniques:

As the plants grow, all the suckers in the axils of the leaves should be carefully snapped off, except for the one strong sucker that develops below the first blossom cluster . Allow this sucker to become the second top. Suckers should not be pinched or cut off, as infected plant juices might be spread from plant to plant. Hold the sucker firmly, and snap it downward so that it breaks cleanly.

Trellising   To trellis, tie the twine in a loose knot at the base of the plant, wind it gently around the main stem and tie it very securely to a strong, overhead trellis string, two metres above the bed. When the second top grows sufficiently, string it up to the trellis also. Every week, gently train the tops around the supporting strings as the plants grow.

Low temperatures and poor light levels mean that crops will take longer to mature and, in fact, that certain crops cannot be grown. For a specific crop, summer temperatures 10°C cooler than the ideal growing temperature can increase the time to maturity by 50%. When light levels are low (at high latitudes and during the winter) a 10°C temperature difference is even more severe because it can cause the maturation time to more than double.

chives, parsley, and several varieties of flowers and herbs.

Fall   In the fall, the cycle continues as the greens are re-seeded; the cucumbers, eggplants, and peppers are harvested; a few tomatoes are left to ripen slowly into the winter.

Trellising and Training

The closely spaced plants in the greenhouse require regular training and trellising to make the most efficient use of space. Tomato vines quickly grow into an inaccessible tangle if not controlled. Pruning tomatoes to double leaders provides a 33% to 50% greater yield than a single plant, taking up the same space. Train the vines around a string tied to the base of the plant and secured to an overhead hook on a rafter.

The string must be very strong. A full-grown tomato plant with fruit can weigh up to 11kg (25 lbs). Sturdy nylon fishnet twine is recommended (not baling twine which is treated with rat repellent and should not be used on food producing plants).

Once a week, gently wrap the top of the plant around the string and pull off any suckers and yellowing lower leaves. This system works well for tomatoes as well as other vines, but any kind of trellis system that is easy to maintain and doesn't block light to other plants is suitable. Plants such as dill or broccoli, which can grow to large sizes in the home greenhouse, may need to be staked to prevent them from falling over on other plants in the crowded benches. Strips of cotton, looped around the stem and tied securely to stakes, are recommended to support heavy plants. (String will cut into the stems.)

Pollination

The flowers of cucumbers, tomatoes, peppers, eggplants, beans, and peaches must be fertilized before they produce. If the pollen does not reach the ovary, then no fruit forms and the blossoms eventually fall off.

Plants such as tomatoes, peppers, eggplants and beans are wind-pollinated. The flowers contain both male and female parts and the movement of the wind is sufficient to shake the pollen inside the flower onto the tip of the stigma and effect pollination. In the relatively still environment of a greenhouse, the plants require assistance to insure that fertilization has occurred. Gently shaking the plants accomplishes the same thing as the wind. Shaking the plants three or four times a week is sufficient to insure a good crop when temperatures and light levels are optimum, but it should be done daily in periods of unsettled or cloudy weather to pollinate as many flowers as possible. The plants should be shaken around midday because the pollen is shed only after several hours of bright sun.

Crops such as melon, squash, and many cucumbers have separate male and female flowers and pollen must be transferred from the male to the female blossom. Bees do an excellent job of this outdoors, but the greenhouse grower may find a fine bristle paintbrush useful. The flowers with the yellow, powdery pollen are male, and the flowers with the miniature fruit showing as a green bulge behind them are female. If you do not have a paintbrush handy, you can also pick a male flower (of which there usually seems to be an abundance), peel back the petals and tap the pollen directly from the stamens onto the stigma.

An exception to this rule is the European or English cucumber (the long, smooth greenhouse varieties) which must not be pollinated or the fruit will be ruined. These varieties produce mostly female flowers, but the vines should be checked daily and any male flowers should be picked off in case a roving insect does the pollinating. A fertilized flower produces a misshapen, gourd-like cucumber.

Aside from the case of the English cucumber, a female flower which has not been fertilized will grow into a rudimentary fruit before it withers and falls off, which may mislead you into thinking that the fruit had been fertilized and fell off for other reasons.

Extremes of temperature and unfavourable light can prevent some flowers from setting fruit. The pollen in tomato flowers becomes sterile at temperatures below 13°C and,

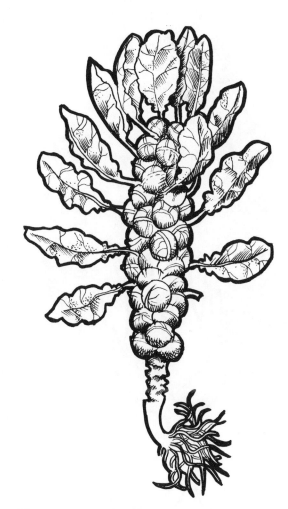

Fig. 299 Brussels sprouts

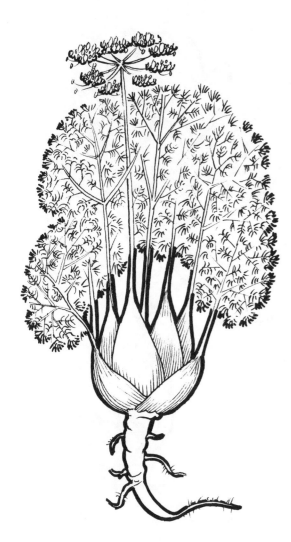

Fig. 300 Fennel

late in the year, when light levels are poor, days are short, and temperatures are cool, fertilization becomes less and less likely. If tomatoes develop strange distortions but are otherwise healthy, pollination has been inadequate. This occurrence is known as 'catfacing.' High temperatures will sterilize flowers as well, a fact that should be remembered when managing the summer temperatures inside a greenhouse.

Transplanting into the Greenhouse

Generally, it is better to start young plants specifically for the greenhouse than to dig well-grown plants from the garden. If you must dig plants up, the tops should be cut back by at least a third to compensate for severed roots. Careful transplanting of parsley, lettuce or other small greens usually succeeds, although tomatoes and peppers loaded with fruit usually do not survive.

Some herbs can be transplanted successfully if they are cut back. Very large plants can be managed by slicing down around one side of the root ball. A week or two later, slice down around the other half of the plant. Spreading roots are severed in this way but the plant has time to grow feeder roots within a smaller area before transplanting. Put the plant into the largest manageable container with a fertile soil mix and cut back the tops as much as possible (this amount won't be much for a tomato or pepper plant in full fruit). Keep the plant in the shade, out of the wind, for 3 or 4 days and mist it regularly to help it

recover from the shock of transplanting before introducing it to the different environment of the greenhouse. If the plant is placed directly into the bench, provide shade for a week and mist the tops daily. If you plant ahead in the spring, you can set plants out in large fibre pots, plunged in the garden soil for the summer. The pots can be taken up in the fall, and will experience little shock when moved into the greenhouse because their roots have been confined throughout the summer. Scrutinize plants carefully before they are brought in, because transferring plants from outside is one of the most common ways to introduce pests and diseases to the greenhouse.

Vegetable Varieties

The types of vegetables you grow and the varieties you choose will be determined by your eating habits and the amount of space available. There are certain varieties, however, which are specifically bred for growing in greenhouses or cold frames and are the best place to start when selecting varieties. Check for the word 'forcing' in the name of the seed variety, as this usually means that it was developed for culture under glass. For example, 'Scarlet Globe Forcing' radishes are a greenhouse-selected strain of Scarlet Globe and will probably grow best.

The existence of greenhouse varieties of seeds does not mean that vegetables sold for outdoor gardens will not grow in the greenhouse and, in fact, some produce extremely well. But, in general, a variety adapted to cool greenhouse culture will produce better in a greenhouse than one that has been selected for a summer garden. Several kinds of European tomatoes, radishes, lettuce, and spinach produce vigorous greenhouse crops. Though they are not generally available in North America, some are sold through Sutton Seeds in England, which has a mail-order service to Canada and the United States. A few varieties of Dutch greenhouse lettuce are sold by Stokes Seeds as well and are recommended for greenhouse use.

Seed catalogues will give days to maturity for the various crops. These figures are not intended to be exact, and should be used only for comparison between varieties in the same catalogue. The Greenhouse Variety Recommendation chart (p. 162) lists some varieties that we have found to perform particularly well in the greenhouse.

Fruit

In many regions, perennial fruits can be grown in the home greenhouse, providing wonderful treats for the gardener who has the patience to await the results. Grapevines grow very well under most greenhouse conditions and are easily trellised out of the way. The vine can be rigidly controlled for fruit production in a small area, or allowed to grow more luxuriantly on a trellis wherever shading is desired in the summer. It can provide a beautiful living screen between the house and the

greenhouse. When choosing a variety, look for good quality table grapes, preferably those with resistance to powdery mildew; grape fungus diseases are more of a problem under glass than on outdoor vines. Grapes lose their leaves in the fall and become dormant over the winter.

Peach trees (such as the Garden Sun variety) can be grown in large tubs and will produce fruit after a couple of years. Fruit quality and size can be improved with proper thinning of the blossoms. For tubbed fruit trees, the soil should be rich and very well drained. Great care should be taken to insure a steady supply of water from fruit set to harvest. Red spider mites may prove to be a problem as peaches are quite susceptible to this pest.

Figs can be grown in a large planter or pot. The roots must be well confined or they will spread rapidly, resulting in an immense, vigorous tree with very little fruit. Confine the tree in a concrete planter or clay tub, 700mm to 1000mm square (2ft to 3ft square), which has a good layer of gravel in the bottom, and keep it well pruned.

Select self-fruiting varieties of figs, such as Everbearing or Celeste. As with grapes and peaches, figs will lose their leaves in the winter. Figs are quite sturdy and trouble-free in the greenhouse.

Other exotic fruits can also be grown in greenhouses in many parts of North America. Guava trees and dwarf citrus

Fig. 301 Beans

trees such as lemon and orange are available from suppliers. You may be able to save seeds from particularly appealing oranges, tangerines, or miniature apricots and, with care and patience, raise them in your greenhouse.

If you live at 56°N latitude, and it gets to be 40° below in the winter, and you don't use any back-up heating in the greenhouse, and on Christmas Day you didn't see the sun because you slept a little too long — well then, in these conditions, you're not going to be growing Guava trees in your greenhouse. Slip into another sweater and dream on.

Greenhouse Variety Recommendations

The varieties listed in the following chart perform well in greenhouses. Since the seed catalogues can change from year to year, you may not be able to find a particular variety listed below. Others have been standards for many years. There are useful varieties not listed in this chart as well as many other types of vegetables appropriate for the greenhouse. (See "Planting Schedule")

Crop	Variety	Comments	Typical Source
Tomatoes	Vendor	Excellent yields, especially in the fall. Best grown as two crops per season because plants aren't strong enough to carry more than 5 or 6 fruit trusses.	Stokes
	Jumbo	Excellent yields, huge beefsteak tomatoes. Vigorous plants with thick foliage.	Stokes
	Tuckcross 533 Forcing	Similar to Jumbo	Stokes, Wm. Dam
	Michigan, Ohio Forcing	Similar to Jumbo, but needs high light levels to produce well.	Stokes
	Tuckqueen	Will set fruit under cooler, lower light levels than others. Susceptible to early blight.	Stokes
	Sweet 100	Huge, sprawling plants yield enormous number of very sweet cherry tomatoes. Good in hanging planters.	Stokes
	Tiny Tim	Cherry tomatoes on compact plants. Excellent in hanging baskets, planters.	
Loose Head Lettuce	Dandie		Suttons (U.K.)
	Ostinata	Excellent flavour and yield in the fall. Most suitable for spring crop.	Stokes
	Deci-Minor	Suitable for fall and winter crop.	Stokes
	Winter Density	Romaine-type head; performed well in cold frames in early spring; very popular in salads. Worth a try in the greenhouse.	Suttons, Butcher (U.K.)

Crop	Variety	Comments	Typical Source
Cutting Lettuce	Avon	Sow thickly in beds and cut back completely instead of just the outer leaves. Crisp leaves grow back quickly and give exceptional yield per area.	
Chards	Fordhook	Broad white-stemmed chard; Slow in winter, excellent crop rest of year.	
	Rhubarb	Slow in winter, not quite the yield of above but a favourite in flavour and appearance.	Wm. Dam
	Perpetual Spinach (Leaf Beet)	English variety similar to chard but has fine stems and smoother leaves. Excellent growth early spring through fall. Some people prefer the flavour to that of chard.	Suttons, Butcher
Turnip Greens	Namenia	Smooth, serrated leaf; a favorite winter salad green, always mild and tender. For maximum yields, cut entire plant back to 1″ above soil level. Plants regrow, and yield continuously for 6 months.	Wm. Dam
Mustard	Green Wave	Good in cool weather for quick short crop. Gets hot and tough if left too long.	Wm. Dam
Spinach	Giant Winter	Far and away the best yields in fall and winter so far. Large, tender leaves.	Wm. Dam, Dominion
	New Zealand	Thrives in hot weather, fine in cool conditions. Has a high oxalic acid content and should only be eaten cooked. Self sows madly. (Restores anyone's confidence in their gardening ability).	Dominion, Stokes
Misc. Greens	Sorrel	Thrives year round in greenhouse from annual replanting. A treat in salads.	
	Rocket (Brassica eruca)	Hot, peanutty flavour; great in salads. Sow at frequent short intervals.	
	Parsley	All varieties tried have done well.	Wm. Dam
	Collards, Kale	Both are cold hardy, insect and disease resistant, vigourous.	

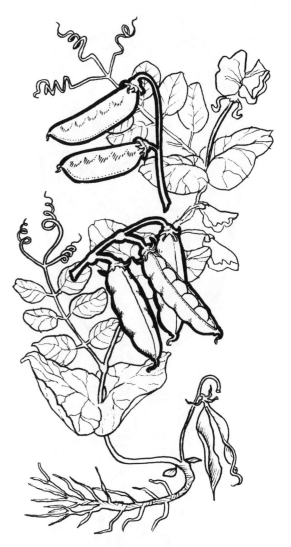

Fig. 302 Peas: pod and sweet

Fig. 303 Chinese cabbage

Crop	Variety	Comments	Typical Source
Celery	Florimart, Tendercrisp	Both grow slowly but tolerate continuous picking of outer stalks quite well.	Stokes
	Leaf Celery	Tender, light green foliage with narrow stalks; for flavouring in soups and salads.	Wm. Dam
Broccoli	Cleopatra F₁	Takes up space but yields continuously all winter after main head is cut.	Stokes, McFayden
Radishes	Scarlet Globe Forcing	Bred for greenhouse culture. Worth planting even in mid-winter. Very quick crop in the spring; produces mild radishes of high quality.	Stokes
Cucumbers	Sweet Slice	Superior yield of dark green, smooth cucumbers, vines resist insect pests.	Stokes, Wm. Dam
Chinese Cabbage	Michihili (also Chihili, Michili)	One of the best for continuous harvest.	Stokes, Wm. Dam
	Snow Mountain W R Crusader Pe Tsai	Excellent growth under cool conditions characteristic of most chinese greens.	Wm. Dam
Herbs	Rosemary	Thrives in the cool, moist greenhouse over winter.	
	Sage, Thyme, Oregano	Dig from the summer garden and over winter indoors in the brightest, warmest location.	
	Basil, Sweet Marjoram	Need very warm conditions, neither do well in the winter at the Ark. Fine spring to fall.	
	Chives, Mint, Lemon Balm	Dig from outdoor garden after a cold snap has frozen foliage. Cut back old tops and they will grow vigorously indoors.	
	Dill, Chervil	Sow seed directly in benches regularly over the year for fresh herbs.	

Crop	Variety	Comments
Flowers	Geraniums	Indestructible old standbys. When leggy, cut back tops and retire to a cool, dim location until new growth starts. Report and bring out again. Lovely in hanging baskets.
	Petunias	Virtually perennial in the greenhouse. Produces lavish masses of blossoms. Reseed every spring, buy young plants or cut down the old ones and let them grow again. Fine in hanging planters and pots.
	Primula	Thrives in cool, moist conditions of winter greenhouse.
	Hyacinths, Narcissus,	Pot up in the fall and leave in cool area for 2 months. Bring into greenhouse a few pots at a time for beautiful scent and blooms from January onward.

Planting Schedule

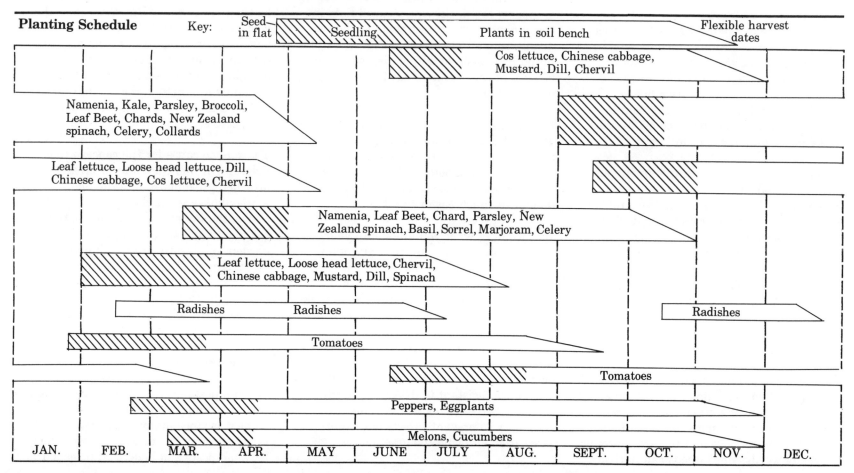

Key: Seed in flat — Seedling — Plants in soil bench — Flexible harvest dates

Cos lettuce, Chinese cabbage, Mustard, Dill, Chervil

Namenia, Kale, Parsley, Broccoli, Leaf Beet, Chards, New Zealand spinach, Celery, Collards

Leaf lettuce, Loose head lettuce, Dill, Chinese cabbage, Cos lettuce, Chervil

Namenia, Leaf Beet, Chard, Parsley, New Zealand spinach, Basil, Sorrel, Marjoram, Celery

Leaf lettuce, Loose head lettuce, Chervil, Chinese cabbage, Mustard, Dill, Spinach

Radishes   Radishes   Radishes

Tomatoes

Tomatoes

Peppers, Eggplants

Melons, Cucumbers

JAN.   FEB.   MAR.   APR.   MAY   JUNE   JULY   AUG.   SEPT.   OCT.   NOV.   DEC.

Death and Destruction

Although insects and, especially, diseases, are infrequently a problem in the home greenhouse, a fair amount of space is devoted to them here because they worry so many people. The two main problems that arise in the home greenhouse are nitrogen deficiency, which is fairly easily solved, and aphid infestation.

Prevention

The first line of defense against diseases and pests is prevention, which means keeping things clean and not giving the fungi and the insects a chance to get started. Anything in the greenhouse furnishing an ideal site for infection to begin must obviously be removed in order to keep the greenhouse sanitary.

After vegetables grown in the greenhouse are harvested, the plants should be removed so that vegetable matter grown in the greenhouse never returns to it. Plant matter from the greenhouse is more likely to contain some fungus spores; therefore, if it is used for composting, it should be composted outdoors and the resulting compost used in the outdoor garden. This method will make certain that fungus disease spores are not recycled in the greenhouse.

Do not leave plants which are no longer fruiting, which have gone to seed, or which are diseased, in the greenhouse. Remove dead leaves and damaged or fallen fruit. Keep the greenhouse and the areas around it free of weeds, since weeds can harbour

pests. Any plant which is heavily infested with a pest should probably be taken out of the greenhouse, even if you feel there are controls available. A heavily infested plant is worth neither the trouble involved in saving it nor the risk it poses to other plants.

Scrub your pots, flats, and garden tools with a stiff brush and water before reusing or storing them. Leaving wooden flats in the summer sun exposes them to the disinfecting effects of ultraviolet radiation. If you have been handling diseased plants, be sure to wash your hands before working on other plants.

Frequent inspections and watchfulness are also part of prevention. Inspect your plants regularly, checking stems and leaves on both the top and bottom. If you catch a problem before serious damage has been done, it is much easier to solve.

Be careful of what you allow into your greenhouse. Be particularly wary of any plants you introduce. Inspect them carefully and, if possible, keep them in an isolated area for a couple of weeks to make sure that no problems develop. You will eliminate the possibility of introducing diseases or pests on imported plants if you start all of your greenhouse plants from seed. Choose varieties which are hardy and which are resistant to diseases and insect damage. Screened doors and vents are necessary to prevent insects and other pests from entering the greenhouse.

Insects

Several factors lead to some insect pest problems in the greenhouse. A greenhouse provides a moderate environment year round, and this protected environment is as favorable to the growth and reproduction of insects as it is to plants. Pests also become trapped inside and are forced to feed on plants that normally would not be their first choice. But remember, the vast majority of insects are either beneficial or non-pests. Insects play an extremely important role in the web of life on this planet. It is only within the system set up by a human gardener that an insect can be considered a pest. It is a matter of perspective.

There is no cause for the concern that insects will find their way from an attached greenhouse into the home. Even if a greenhouse is completely open to the house, the insects will not choose to leave the plants and sunlight of the indoor garden to migrate into the dim and, to them, barren interior of the human home.

Although insects are inevitable to some degree in the greenhouse, if the plants are healthy the pestiferous insects can be managed using safe and acceptable techniques.

When a pest appears in the greenhouse, the first thing to do is to find out exactly what it is since many of the controls are fairly specific. Be certain to distinguish between pests and beneficial insects. Don't automatically assume that the insect you find on a damaged leaf caused the damage — it may be preying on the pests that had been there before it.

Controls

The best defense against insect pests is to grow healthy plants. Aphids, for example, thrive on the soft, succulent growth which results from too much nitrogen in the soil or from a combination of low light levels and high temperatures. Aphid control can sometimes be effected by such simple methods as increasing the ventilation in order to lower the greenhouse temperature, since high temperatures create stressed, weakened, and unproductive plants on which aphids will readily proliferate.

Some methods of control can be called *mechanical controls*. They include vacuuming the insects from the leaves, letting the greenhouse freeze for a period during the winter (extremely low temperatures are fatal to many greenhouse pests), and collecting insects by hand and squashing them. (For this latter operation, the non-squeamish are advised to use thumb and forefinger. We have previously recommended bricks or hammers to particularly vengeful greenhouse owners, but quickly discovered that these implements could have a rather unfortunate effect on nearby plants.)

Cultural controls presuppose a knowledge of the life cycles of both the plants and the pests. In the greenhouse this method involves selecting varieties of crops which are resistant to disease and pests; planting trap crops, which are more attractive to the insects than other crops and which are used to draw insects away from the important vegetables; maintaining an environment in the greenhouse which is favorable to crops and beneficial insects and unfavorable to pests; planning your planting and harvesting to avoid periods of major pest infestations.

Prevention

The best way to approach the problems of diseases and pest infestation is to try to prevent the problem before it occurs.

1. Keep the greenhouse clean. Pull weeds and remove dead leaves and fallen fruit.
2. Disinfect all used pots, flats and planting containers by washing them with a stiff brush and water, and drying them in bright sunlight.
3. Remove old and diseased plants. The most common cause of pest and disease problems are plants which are left too long and infected plants introduced into the greenhouse (see#4). Any plant which is past its usefulness, which has gone to seed, or which is already heavily infested should be removed from the greenhouse.
4. Do not bring plants into the greenhouse which are already diseased or infested. This safeguard may seem obvious, but it was in just this manner that the whitefly pest was spread from greenhouse to greenhouse throughout North America. Whenever possible, it is always better to start your own plants from seeds.
5. Handle the plants as little as possible to avoid damaging the waxy, protective layer. Never handle wet plants since diseases are easily transferred under moist conditions.
6. Wash your hands if you have been working with diseased plants.
7. Do not smoke in the greenhouse. Tobacco mosaic virus is deadly to tomatoes, peppers, and petunias and can be spread by smokers. If you do smoke, wash your hands and rinse them with milk before working in the greenhouse.
8. Regularly inspect your plants so that you may be able to, literally, nip a problem in the bud.
9. Plant only disease-resistant varieties.
10. Healthy plants are themselves the best prevention. Well-balanced soils, proper watering and sufficient ventilation will help to minimize the stress on your plants and will allow them to more readily resist disease and pests.

Many types of *biological controls* have been used effectively over the years, making use of beneficial insect predators and parasites to control the insect pests. Learning to manage pest populations through establishing a system of natural checks and balances will ultimately prove the best solution. An exciting potential for control with beneficial insects is offered by the use of indigenous insects, which can be collected outdoors and released in the greenhouse to control some of the common greenhouse pests.

Botanical Insecticides

The majority of currently available pesticide sprays and dusts cannot be used safely in an attached greenhouse, whether it is completely open to the living area or joined by only a doorway. When pesticides are used in the greenhouse, even if they are applied carefully and according to instructions, they will infiltrate into the house, exposing the occupants to the risk of contaminated food, air, and water. Even the organically-derived pesticides, such as rotenone, are highly toxic at the time of application and should be used only as a last resort.

These organic insecticides may be effective, but because they also harm beneficial insects they are not a good, long-term solution. They have other drawbacks as well. Thorough application is tedious and they must be used regularly to be effective.

Another problem resulting from pesticide use is that the insects which do survive obviously are more resistant to the lethal chemical than the ones that were killed. When these surviving insects breed, they engender a pesticide-resistant population, requiring the application of ever higher doses or more potent pesticides. This problem is currently worrying many entomologists, and perhaps one good result of it is that recently, more time and money have been devoted to researching biological control methods.

Rotenone Rotenone is commonly used in organic gardens, but it should be treated as a deadly poison. It is an insecticide derived from any of several tropical plants. Rotenone should never be used anywhere fish are being raised. It has a short effective life and breaks down into harmless, inert compounds, especially in the presence of heat and light; applying it on a sunny day will decrease its life span.

Problems with Inorganic Pesticides

1. These pesticides leave a poisonous residue on the fruits and vegetables on which they are used.
2. Because they are poisons, they are hazardous to wildlife, and to the people applying the pesticide.
3. Inorganic or synthetic pesticides have a very long lifetime unlike rotenone, for instance, which quickly breaks down into inert compounds when exposed to the sun. Since inorganic pesticides cannot simply disappear after being introduced in the environment, they must end up somewhere. Consequently, their use has resulted in the pollution of streams, lakes and ground water. Many such substances are extremely toxic to fish and other marine life.
4. Because of the persistence of inorganic pesticides, they tend to build up higher in the food chain. Hence, there are concentrated amounts of many such chemicals in the higher mammals, including man.
5. The continued use of these pesticides results in the development of immunity among the insect population which survives. Thus, larger doses of stronger pesticides become necessary.
6. There is a possibility of the occurrence of a damaging infestation of a secondary pest which had previously been held in check by natural enemies now destroyed by the pesticide.
7. There may, following the application of a pesticide, occur a damaging infestation of a primary pest coming in from untreated areas, now being unchecked by their natural enemies.
8. Points number 6 and 7 result in repeated, increased applications of the pesticide causing greater pollution and increasing the amount of poisons in the food system.
9. Inorganic pesticides are made from our increasingly scarce fossil fuel reserves.

Rotenone is effective against only sucking and chewing insects because it must be ingested to affect their system.

Rotenone is a nerve poison and can also affect humans. Be very careful when using the powder and wear a mask. It is, in fact, wise to use the wettable powder form, which is mixed into a spray and cannot dust up into the face of the person doing the spraying.

Pyrethrum Pyrethrum was originally made from the pyrethrum flower, a type of chrysanthemum, the head of which was ground to a powder. Only synthetic pyrethrum is now commonly available. It is an irritant to those who suffer from hay fever. Although it is safer than most other pesticides, remember that it is a poison nonetheless and must be handled with care.

Diatamaceous Earth A botanical pesticide which is safe to humans and animals but deadly to insects is diatamaceous earth. It is usually referred to as DE and is used in industry as a filter material.

Diatamaceous earth is a fine silica dust mined from deposits of the shells of diatoms, one-celled plants that lived in the earth's oceans millions of years ago. Though it looks like a soft powder, under a microscope DE can be seen to consist of very small particles with sharp edges. When an insect crosses or touches these particles, the waxy surface of the

exoskeleton is worn off and the insect slowly dehydrates through the scratches. The same effect occurs if the insect ingests DE. In this case, the sharp particles wear through the insect from the inside out. DE is a contact insecticide and is extremely effective, but it kills beneficial insects as well as pests and you must be conscious of the insects' life cycles and not apply DE indiscriminately. It is therefore of limited use in a biological control program, though it may be used, with extreme care, for localized problems.

Insecticidal Soaps: These soaps are a relatively new pest control product. How the fatty acids in them act on insects is not clearly understood, but they affect the nervous system, disrupt respiration, and interfere with the metabolism of some groups of insects. White flies, aphids, and other pests are affected, while honeybees, beetles, and parasitic wasps are not.

Pests and Controls

As we have mentioned, insect damage is usually not a major problem in the home greenhouse. There are, however, a few pests you are likely to discover, of which the most serious are aphids, white flies, thrips, spider mites, and slugs.

Beneficial Insects Botanical insecticides are fine if you are not using biological controls. But while they may seem a quick, attractive solution, botanical insecticides should be used only in emergencies in a biologically managed greenhouse. Proper

greenhouse management involves the use of biological controls, using beneficial insects. To use them, it is important to understand the life cycles of these insects.

Most insects undergo complete metamorphosis; they pass through four stages of development in their lifetime: egg, larva, pupa, and adult. The first stage, the egg, hatches into a young insect (called a larva) differing markedly in appearance from the adult. Larvae are usually soft-bodied and wingless (such as caterpillars, grubs, and maggots). They grow larger as they feed, shedding their skins several times. When they reach their last stage of development as larvae, the larval skin hardens into a case (called pupa) which protects the insect while it changes into the adult form. At the end of pupation, the adult emerges from the pupal case and flies away to mate and lay eggs, and so completes the cycle.

Aphids There are 80-90 varieties of aphids (family *Aphididae*) and they are the most common pests in the home greenhouse. They are a small (2mm to 5mm), soft-bodied insect whose shape is characteristic. The aphids usually found in greenhouses, such as the green peach aphid *(Myzus perslcae)* are pale green, yellow, or pink, but outdoors the colours of the many species range from bronze and white to dark brown and black. Many different species occur in North America, and there are winged and wingless forms as well. Though generally pear-shaped, they may vary from an elongated oval to

Success with Beneficial Insects

Bringing insects into your greenhouse to control other insects may seem a bit puzzling at first. But this technique of biological control is effective, exciting, and easier than you may think. It can provide long-term control of insect pests, and armed with a little knowledge of the life cycles and needs of those insects under your care, you will find that keeping track of them and watching their results will be as exciting as harvesting your first tomato or watching a flower bud open. Providing the proper conditions and care for your team is important, but not difficult if you keep in mind the following points:

1. **Screen the vents.** Screening all doors and vents in the greenhouse keeps beneficial insects inside. The benefits of unscreened vents (better air circulation, free entry of wild, beneficial insects, cheapness) in a home greenhouse are greatly outweighed by problems with pests coming in. Mice (and rats) can enter through the lower vents, and moths, attracted to lights inside, enter through upper vents. These moths lay eggs that hatch into destructive caterpillars.

2. **Use no insecticides.** Most garden insecticides (including the organic insecticides such as rotenone, pyrethrum and diatamaceous earth) will kill beneficial insects as well as pests. If absolutely necessary, individual plants or small areas of the greenhouse may be treated with a botanical insecticide, using extreme care. It is best, when possible, to remove infested potted plants from the greenhouse entirely and treat them outdoors. General spraying or fumigation is not only unnecessary to control pests, but is fatal to your biological control program.

3. **Feed your insects.** It is only the immature stage (the larva) of most beneficial insects that feeds on the pests. Most adults require pollen or nectar to survive and reproduce, so an essential component of a biological control program is the provision of flowers for the adult insect. These plants can be grown among the vegetables or in pots or planters placed around the greenhouse. Plants with small flowers are most suitable because the insects themselves are small — they cannot feed from large flowers. Dill is ideal for this purpose because it grows quickly from seed and is attractive to many insects. Perennials such as lemon balm, pennyroyal, and sweet clover are excellent, as are the weeds Queen Anne's Lace and Wild Parsnip. Also, many of the vegetables (such as parsley, broccoli, and celery) grown in a home greenhouse are excellent sources of pollen and nectar if allowed to run to seed after they are past their prime as food crops. As few as two or three plants of dill or parsley in flower are adequate in a small greenhouse.

4. **Provide water.** Most beneficial insects need water. In humid areas, it is provided plentifully by condensation on the glazing or droplets on leaves. In dry regions, however, a source of water that will not trap and drown tiny insects should be provided. A roll of cloth plugging the top of a bottle of water will act as a wick and stay wet enough to allow insects to drink safely.

5. **Protect your insects.** Care must be taken not to destroy the pupae of the beneficial insects while they are resting. Lady beetles usually pupate on the sides of pots, flats or benches and can be easily injured when pots are moved. This precaution also applies to lady beetle egg clusters, which are usually laid in the same locations. Syrphid flies pupate in or on the top layer of the soil, predatory midges pupate about an inch below the soil surface. Soil fumigation or pasteurization kills pupae of both these insects. Their presence is another reason for minimizing cultivation of the soil.

Your beneficial insects must be protected from other insects and spiders which could prey on them. For example, introducing preying mantes would not be wise because they would eat the large beneficial insects before working on the smaller pests (such as aphids). Spider webs near the glazing trap hundreds of predatory gall midges, and many midges die at night from flying into lights left burning in the greenhouse.

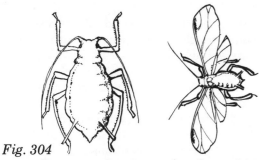

Fig. 304

Green peach aphid   Another aphid

almost round. A distinguishing characteristic on most aphids is a pair of tubes, called cornicles, resembling tiny exhuast pipes that protrude from their abdomens. Other characteristic features are that aphids move more slowly than do most other insects, even when disturbed, and they do not hop to escape (as will the similar leaf hoppers). They are usually found feeding on the growing tips or the undersides of lower leaves.

Aphids are attracted by succulent plants with fat, sappy stems. It is thought that aphids are nature's way of removing the sugars from plants which have been growing so quickly (often from an overabundance of nitrogen in the soil) that their stems contain excessive sugar. The insects have a tiny stylus which they insert into the leaf and with which they suck the juices. The sugar from the plant is almost immediately excreted by the aphid in the form of honeydew. The insects need to pass vast quantities of plant sap through their systems in order to obtain the proteins they require, and enormous amounts of honeydew can be produced by

these small creatures. In fact, ants "raise" (that is, live in a symbiotic relationship with aphids) in order to collect the honeydew. There is some thought that this continuous excretion of sugar onto the ground is beneficial to the plants.

Aphids thrive in a protected environment with a fairly even temperature range and high relative humidity — which means that the greenhouse provides a perfect environment for about six months of the year. The bright sunlight, high heat and humidity of summer, and the cool of winter create a less suitable environment for the aphids, although even in these unfavorable periods, aphid colonies may still survive on the lowest leaves in the back of the greenhouse and in hydroponics systems, which have proven particularly susceptible to aphids.

Because they can inject a toxic fluid when they pierce the plant, large numbers of aphids on a plant cause leaf distortions and withering. Sometimes you will see distorted leaves along with new, undistorted leaves on the same plant. This phenomenon is due to an aphid attack in the early stages of plant growth, from which the plant recovered. An aphid colony will typically cause a shrivelling, puckering injury to plant leaves.

Sucking the juices is usually not enough to cause significant or irreversible damage. The aphid honeydew which falls on the leaves promotes a grey, fuzzy mould. This fungi is not pathogenic; it does not grow

into the leaf but on the honeydew. However, the leaf beneath this mould begins to suffer from a lack of light. The mould and honeydew can be washed off using mild soap and water at room temperature. Wash the leaves in the evening or on a cloudy day so sunlight hitting the water droplets will not burn them.

This fungi is usually the worst damage to result from aphids, although serious damage can be inflicted by viral and bacterial diseases they transmit with their sucking mouth parts.

Even at fairly low levels of infestation, aphids are a nuisance on salad greens because washing them off is tedious work. Other plants, like tomatoes, tolerate a higher level of infestation.

Because their bodies are so fragile, aphids are among the easiest of insects to kill. Outdoors, even a hard-driven drop of rain will flatten them. A good stiff stream of water directed onto an infested plant will knock off and kill a great many. Their power lies in their amazing reproductive rates. Through much of the summer season they reproduce rapidly, without mating, giving live birth to more aphids day after day. Females can give birth to live offspring that already have aphids developing inside them. In the fall, the last generations mate and lay eggs, in which form the colony survives over the winter. A population which may appear to have been brought under control in a pesticide spraying program will rebound rapidly if a few individuals survive. The key to aphid control, whatever the method chosen, is continuous vigilance — either by regular dusting or spraying, or by using beneficial insects which are always on patrol for aphids.

Control of Aphids Rotenone and pyrethrum are effective against aphids and insecticidal soaps are also claimed to work.

Biological Controls Lacewings *(Chrysopa carnea)* are voracious predators and aphids comprise only part of their diet. They also consume white flies, insect eggs, thrips, and mites. It is the larvae which are predatory and a single lacewing larva can consume more than 400 aphids in its lifetime.

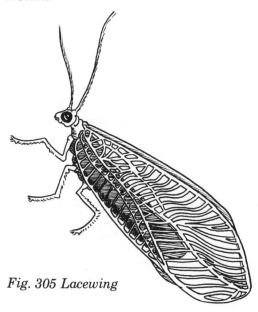

Fig. 305 Lacewing

If they can be purchased when needed, lady beetles are very good biological control insects in warm, bright conditions. If the greenhouse vents are screened, the beetles will provide good control because they cannot migrate when the aphid population begins to decline, as they would if they were outdoors. At some point in the late spring or summer, however, lady beetles usually die out (probably from starvation) and a new batch must be released in the fall or the next spring when aphid populations build up.

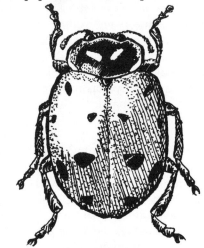

Fig. 306 Ladybird beetle Hippoclamia convergens

Lady beetles come in various colours of orange and yellow with any number of black spots. The lady beetle available from suppliers is *Hippodamia convergens*. The reason they are reasonably cheap is that they are collected in piles when they begin to hibernate. (They are called *convergens* because they converge to hibernate in the

winter.) Laboratory-raised insects are usually much more expensive, eat too many aphids, and die out quickly. The various species of lady beetles prey on specific pests — *convergens* eat mainly aphids and each requires more than 5000 aphids during its life cycle (which explains why they cannot survive in the face of dwindling aphid populations).

Lady beetles are kept in cold storage until they are shipped. Some companies advertise them as "crawl cleaned" which means that they have been warmed up and made to walk to make certain no dead beetles are shipped. It is the adult lady beetles which are shipped. When ordering them, specify clearly when they will be needed and that they are for greenhouse use. Greenhouse aphid populations usually begin to reach serious proportions in late winter or early spring, but a supplier will be concerned about shipping an order in March if he thinks the beetles are for an outdoor garden in Beaver Breath, Manitoba.

When beetles arrive, they should be kept cool until evening, then gently placed around the base of the plants in the greenhouse. They will slowly revive and for a few days you will see them everywhere as they eat and build up their body reserves. When using lady beetles to control aphids on tomatoes, the beetles should be released about three weeks after the tomato plants have been set out in beds. At this time, the plants are still small enough not to shade each other, which is important because lady beetles prefer warm, bright conditions.

Releasing lady beetles into the greenhouse in the fall is often quite advantageous. Since suppliers do not have them available at that time, maximum use of one large spring shipment of lady bugs can be obtained by releasing half when they arrive and keeping the rest in the refrigerator until early October (as long as they are chilled they remain in a state of suspended animation). These autumn-released lady beetles will briefly feed on aphids, then hibernate in cracks, crannies, and even light sockets. They become active again when the greenhouse warms up in late winter and will be able to control aphids before they become a serious problem in the spring garden.

A few days after they settle in and mate, bright yellow oval eggs will be noticeable in odd places. The clusters of 20 to 25 eggs, about 4mm across and 2mm high, will be found in bright, warm spots in the greenhouse and on the sides of benches and the edges of pots. They are quite easy to identify so if you think you have lady bug eggs, you probably do. Later, the dark alligator-like larvae will be seen feeding on aphids. The pupae usually hang on the sides of pots and the stems of plants. At all times, care should be taken to avoid damaging eggs, larvae, and pupae when moving pots or working at the benches.

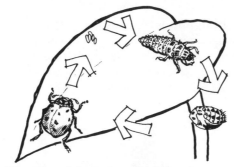

Fig. 307 A lady beetle's lifecycle

Indigenous Predators of Aphids The drawbacks to the use of lady beetles (and some other commercially available aphid predators) are that they must be purchased and they must be replaced each year. The future of biological control in the home greenhouse lies in the use of wild insects. Aphids have a host of natural enemies in the insect kingdom and are food for many kinds of beetles, wasps, gall midges, and flies. Patient observation of aphid colonies on wild plants outdoors will turn up many different aphid predators and parasites, some of which will be useful in the home greenhouse.

Foremost among these other aphid controls is *Aphidoletes aphidimyza*, a predatory gall midge which lives naturally over the entire northern half of the globe. The tiny, bright orange larvae of this insect, 2mm to 3mm long, first immobilizes aphids by seizing a leg joint and injecting a paralysing toxin. Then, they suck out the body fluids, leaving the aphid's outer skeleton still attached to the leaf. A few larvae feeding in an aphid colony will destroy it in a couple of days. They feed on aphids for 1 to

2 weeks (depending on the temperature) and eat from seven to twenty aphids per day, although they may kill more than they eat if aphids are numerous. The larvae feed on at least 61 kinds of aphids.

When mature, the larvae spring from the leaf and burrow 30mm into the soil to pupate. The last generation of the fall of *Aphidoletes* larvae spends the winter in the soil and emerges in the spring. In a greenhouse, because the days are short, *Aphidoletes* will spend December through February in this hibernation in the soil.

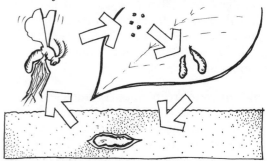

Fig. 308 Life cycle of Aphidoletes aphidimyza
(from Biological Control of Greenhouse Aphids by Gilkeson and Klein, pub. by Ark Project, Institute of Man and Resources)

In warm temperatures, the adults hatch in two weeks and fly away to mate and lay eggs in other aphid colonies. The adults do not feed on aphids and require nectar for food in order to live more than a few days. They are active only at night, and during the day they rest on the undersides of leaves. The eggs which the females lay are barely visible, orange specks. Through a magnifying glass they appear as smooth transparent orange cylinders with rounded ends. They hatch after two or three days into the bright orange larvae. The characteristic colour of the maggot, which ranges from pale orange to brilliant vermillion (depending on the kind of aphids they feed on) makes it easy to spot in a wild colony of aphids. They can be readily located in old orchards, where young succulent tips support an aphid population.

Like lady bugs, *Aphidoletes* require so many aphids to satisfy their appetites and thereby sustain the colony, that it is difficult to store them for commercial greenhouse use. It is unlikely that these predators will be available from commercial sources.

Once in your greenhouse *Aphidoletes* will settle immediately. The adult females lay from 30 to 100 eggs which hatch in three to four days so the population will readily increase. Being an indigenous insect, they will not be affected by the cool spells in the greenhouse.

These tiny orange maggots may look like they are eating the leaves of your plants, but they are, in fact, eating only aphids. The *Aphidoletes* larva is very susceptible to insecticide. Any treatment of the soil would also kill them. While it may not be necessary, it would be wise to minimize cultivation when you know they are present in the soil. (You should minimize the cultivation of the greenhouse soil in any case so as not to destroy soil structure.)

Other Indigenous Predators   There are also parasitic wasps native to the United States and most of Canada (such as the *Chalcid* and *Braconid* wasps) which prey on aphids. These minute members of the

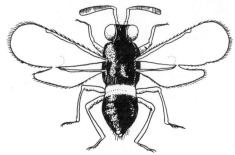

Fig. 309 Chalcid Aphelinus mali

wasp family are about the same size as aphids (2mm to 4mm range) and parasitize them by inserting an egg into the aphid. After the egg hatches, the wasp larva kills the aphid gradually from the inside and uses the aphid's outer skin as its own pupae case. Aphids parasitized by chalcid

Fig. 310 Female braconid wasp parasitizing an aphid and branconid wasp emerging from an aphid mummy (from Gilkeson and Klein)

wasps are often black and shiny, preserved in the original form, with antennae drawn back and legs solidly positioned on the leaf. The larva of the braconid wasp spins its cocoon inside the aphid's dead skin, giving the aphid mummy a characteristic bronzed or pearly appearance. After five to six days the tiny wasp emerges. Examining an aphid mummy closely with a magnifying glass will reveal, if the wasp has emerged, a little hole neatly cut through the back of the mummy. If you find these mummies without holes, you can collect them and introduce them into your greenhouse. Because the parasitic wasp larva feeds on only one aphid, they are effective at very low densities of aphids. Since each species of these wasps is also specific as to the type of aphid it parasitizes, they may not affect the aphids in your greenhouse. It requires careful observation in the wild along with identification of the aphids in your greenhouse to discover the appropriate parasitic wasps.

In Europe, these wasps are used fairly successfully in large greenhouses as a biological control because the wasp can survive even if the aphid density is very low, which is not the case with lady bugs. Sometimes, the wasps have been introduced accidentally into the greenhouse and have proven very effective against aphids.

Syrphid flies or hover flies are stripped or spotted insects which can be confused with honey bees or yellow-jacket wasps. The adults feed on nectar and pollen and have a characteristic way of hovering over flowers (very similar to the hover of a hummingbird) which makes them easy to distinguish from bees and wasps. They do not sting.

Fig. 311 Adult syrphid fly

The female lays single white eggs close to a developing aphid colony. Visible as minute (1mm) oval sausages, the eggs hatch within two or three days, depending upon the temperature.

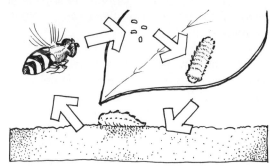

Fig. 312 Life cycle of the syrphid fly from Gilkeson and Klein

The larva is grey, beige, or light green in colour and varies in length from 1mm to 13mm depending upon the stage of development. It is easily identified by the pulsating internal organs visible beneath its partially transparent skin. The larva seizes aphids with its mouth parts, sucks the contents, and discards the aphid skin. In the month it takes for the larva to mature, it can consume hundreds of aphids. The brown, tear-shaped pupa are usually found on the soil surface, though they may also remain on the plant. Hover flies are indigenous to most parts of the continent and can sometimes be captured near garden flowers by using an insect net.

Several native species of lady beetles which prey on aphids, spider mites, and other soft-bodied insects can be released in the home greenhouse to good effect. Do not confuse the pestiferous stripped potato beetle with the normally spotted lady beetle.

Collecting Indigenous Predators The first step in locating predators is to find an active colony of aphids. The best time to search is during warm and humid weather, when aphids thrive. Since there are over 4,500 species of aphids, the range of plants which act as hosts is very wide.

Search in areas that are least likely to have been sprayed with pesticides such as waste land, vacant lots, country roadsides, and/or any area with weeds and flowers in bloom. The largest number of predators are to be found on plants growing in uncultivated areas.

Look for signs that plants have been damaged by aphids, such as curled or deformed leaves. Gently uncurl these leaves and examine the undersides for aphids at work. Don't be discouraged if you do not locate an aphid colony immediately. It takes time to adjust your eyes to the small scale of the insect world.

When you find a colony of wild aphids, examine the entire plant carefully and try to determine if eggs or larvae of predators are present. A hand magnifying glass (from 6 to 10 power) is very helpful.

The larvae, pupa, and adult stages of lady beetles are easily recognized. You can either take the whole leaf home or gently lift the larvae and adults with a fine paintbrush into a collecting container. Pupa cases are firmly attached, and the section of the stalk or leaf they are on should be removed with the pupa. If the collecting container (which can be any box or jar) is made of a transparent material, it should be shaded from the sun as overheating will quickly kill the insects.

Look for the bright orange *Aphidoletes* larvae which show up well against the light,colourful aphids. Using the magnifying glass, check for eggs on the leaf and for very small larvae that may be attached to the undersides of aphids. They are almost impossible to see with the naked eye.

Syrphid fly larvae are frequently found feeding on aphids in the sheltered, curled portions of leaves. The mature larvae are easier to spot than the predatory midge larvae because they are considerably larger, but you must look closely to find the tiny, young larvae. With their pale, mottled green or beige colour, they blend into the background.

If possible, take the entire leaves with aphid colonies and predatory larvae home in the collecting container. Doing so lessens the risk of injuring soft larvae in transit.

Incubation of Aphid Colonies Occasionally a large number of beneficial insect larvae can be collected in the field, but incubating colonies of aphids is another technique for accumulating larvae, especially when very few larvae are initially visible. Aphid-infested plant material can be taken home and held at room temperature for several days and will often reveal a surprising number of aphid predators that were either too small to be seen or were hidden under aphids.

To incubate a colony, place a portion of the infested plant with aphids on it, such as the tip of the branch with three or four leaves, in a plastic bag. Blow into the bag to fill it with air, and tie it closed. Place the bag in the direct sun for two or three days, making certain that the bag is filled with air so that the moist sides won't collapse onto the plant material. After a few days, tiny larvae that were hidden among the aphids will have grown and migrated to the sides of the bag where they will be visible.

Transferring Larvae to the Greenhouse Once you have located beneficial insects or larvae, whether in the field or after incubating a bagged plant sample, they must be moved to the greenhouse. Use the moistened tip of a very fine paintbrush to lift the larvae gently from the leaf or sides of the bag and place them among aphids in the greenhouse. It is important to place them in a shady spot initially because they can die in the sun before they recover from the shock of being handled. Lady beetles and other pupal cases can be transferred directly into the greenhouse.

How Many to Collect The number of predators you find will depend on the season, the environmental conditions, and your patience. The more predators you release into the greenhouse, the sooner the aphids will be controlled. Introducing a mixture of different aphid predators has its advantages, but there should be enough of at least one species to maximize its chances of reproducing and becoming established.

Because there are numerous species of sphyrid flies and lady beetles, it is difficult to tell whether all the larvae you are able to collect are from the same species. However, if a large number of larvae are collected at one time from a small area, you can usually assume that they are of the same species. Look for large colonies of syrphid larvae or native lady beetle larvae and, if you can find such a concentration, collect 50 or 60 larvae, which should be an

effective number in a small greenhouse.

Although there are several species of all the beneficial insects described, there is only one common species of *Aphidoletes*. Of all indigenous, beneficial insects, it is the most numerous. They are particularly good candidates for collection from the wild because a few individuals reproduce quickly in the warm greenhouse environment. Concentrate on collecting at least 50 of these larvae for a small greenhouse.

The first predators you release may not control the aphids, but their offspring should have an impact. For example, if you collect 50 *Aphidoletes* larvae and introduce them into your greenhouse, in as little as 14 days the eggs of the next generation will start to hatch into voracious larvae — as many as 40 to 50 per original adult — which means that this second generation of *Aphidoletes* may contain from 1500 to 2000 individual larvae.

Where aphid populations are low, the second generation may control the aphids adequately. If aphid populations are high (numerous aphids on every plant or greater than 5% of the plant surface affected) then many more larvae or several generations will be necessary to control the aphids.

The best chance of establishing aphid control when confronted with a high population is to first spray the greenhouse with a non-residual insecticide such as the insecticidal soaps or wettable powder rotenone in water. After the insecticide kills as many aphids as possible, wait two or three days and spray the plants with water to wash the leaves. Then introduce the aphid predators you have collected. This method reduces the number of aphids and prevents plants from being damaged further during the time needed for the predators to reproduce.

Your goal is to establish a year-round population of beneficial insects, and you can continue to add predators to the greenhouse whenever you find the need. As you become familiar with the beneficial insects and their various immature forms, you should be able to determine which insects are most effective in your greenhouse.

Whiteflies   Whiteflies (*Trialeurodes vaporariorum*) are another greenhouse pest, attacking tomatoes, cucumbers, and melons. Some greenhouses never have them and some seem to acquire them almost immediately. You likely will not have trouble with whiteflies in the home greenhouse, but whiteflies and aphids are the major pests in commercial greenhouses. If you are not growing the types of plants they prefer, whiteflies will attack lettuce or other greenhouse crops.

The chances of seeing just one whitefly are pretty small. By the time you notice them there will be a large number on the underside of a leaf. The adults are minute (1mm to 2mm), snow-white flies which rest on the underside of the upper leaves of plants and lay their eggs there. They fly up in a cloud of white when the leaf is disturbed.

The eggs and the various larval stages of the whitefly are difficult to distinguish with the naked eye. The larvae — small, greenish-white, almost translucent scales on the underside of leaves — travel very little. The pearly "pupa" (which is actually the fourth larval stage) is about the size of a tiny aphid, but it does not grow or move. If you look closely, you will see that it does not have the colour of the aphid.

The adults themselves do not directly cause damage. It is the larvae which suck plant sap and secrete honeydew, weakening the plant and causing the same problems with sooty mould growth that occur from an aphid infection. Whiteflies do not survive outdoors over the winter in Canada and the colder parts of the United States, and are spread when plants are transferred from one greenhouse to another. Reducing whiteflies to a small number is often better than completely eliminating them because the remaining small colony can then support your parasitic insects.

Control of Whiteflies   As with aphids, the botanical insecticides effective against whiteflies include rotenone and pyrethrum. Some greenhouse owners have reported good control of whiteflies by regularly vacuuming the insects from the upper leaves. This method is probably quite satisfactory on a small scale.

Yellow sticky traps are effective against whiteflies. The traps are easily constructed out of a square of wood, painted bright yellow. Pieces of plywood 200mm square are convenient, but any size will work. The yellow trap board is spread with a sticky coating and suspended by a string or wire in the vicinity of the tops of the infested plants. The best sticky substance is Tanglefoot, which is sold in garden centres and seed catalogues for banding fruit trees. It is extremely sticky and it is recommended that simple wire guard be used to protect hands, sleeves and hair from contact with the Tanglefoot. The whiteflies are attracted to the yellow surface and flutter fatally into it whenever they are disturbed. The traps are most effective in cool weather and if the plants are regularly shaken to dislodge the flies. The trapped whitefly bodies deteriorate and seem to melt away in the Tanglefoot without impairing its stickiness; the traps need to be replenished about once a month. This trapping method can be used in conjunction with the parasitic wasp, *Encarsia formosa,* a biological control for whitefly, because *Encarsia* are not particularly attracted to the colour yellow. The traps can be used to reduce a high population level before the introduction of *Encarsia,* which take a few weeks or a month to establish a controlled balance in the greenhouse.

Encarsia Formosa is a type of tiny parasitic wasp (0.6mm) which kills whitefly larvae much the way other parasitic wasps kill aphids. The female wasp (and all but about .15% of *Encarsia* are female, who reproduce without mating) pushes an egg into the larva, which hatches and gradually destroys its host just about the time that the fly larva is ready to pupate. The wasp larva uses the body of the whitefly larva for a pupa case, turning it black, and in fact, *Encarsia formosa* is sold and shipped that way — in the larval skin.

Encarsia is not hardy and is not indigenous to North America, surviving only where temperatures do not go below 13°C. You have to purchase them to establish them in your greenhouse.

This insect was very commonly used before the 1950's. It was the only control available for whiteflies in the greenhouse and the outdoor garden at that time. When DDT and other pesticides were introduced the *Encarsia* wasps were destroyed along with the whiteflies. The use of *Encarsia* for whitefly control is merely one of going back to a tried and proven system in a controlled environment. Since the 1920's, large-scale rearing of *Encarsia* has taken place in Canada, and Canada is still a major source of these predators.

The *Encarsia* become more effective the warmer the temperatures are in the greenhouse, until at 21°C, they multiply faster than the whitefly. In the small greenhouse during the warmest part of the year they often eradicate the entire whitefly colony, then starve to death themselves. In some situations the whitefly

may not reoccur, but if they do, *Encarsia* must be re-introduced. *Encarsia* usually are sold in lots of 500, which is adequate for a small greenhouse.

Encarsia pupae are usually shipped attached to leaves. Lay these gently at the base of your plants and allow the pupae to hatch out. Be sure to open the package in the greenhouse because some adults will have already hatched and will fly out immediately. Introduce them in your greenhouse as soon as you see a whitefly. If you consistently have a problem at a particular time of year, order some to arrive at that time each year.

When *Encarsia* are being used in your greenhouse, inspect your plants occasionally and count the larvae on a few of the leaves. If over half of the larvae in the plant leaves are black (*Encarsia*-parasitized) and less than half are white (unparasitized), that indicates a good, stable relation. In spring, as it becomes warmer, the whiteflies will increase more rapidly for a period so that the black *Encarsia* larvae might decrease to 30% of the total. But it will soon rise to as much as 90% in the heat of summer.

Encarsia are advantageous for greenhouse use because they are mobile and search actively for prey; easy to distribute by moving the parasitized pupa on leaves; and easily kept track of by the simple count mentioned above.

In a home greenhouse, the work of the *Encarsia* is concentrated. They are very active in a small area and almost always completely destroy the flies in the summer, which is unfortunate since the *Encarsia* population cannot then be sustained and you have to purchase more the next year. But do not buy *Encarsia* until you have a whitefly problem again. Larger greenhouses attempt to maintain a balance in order to continue the *Encarsia* population, but it is virtually impossible to do so in the small area of a home greenhouse because the *Encarsia* are too efficient.

Thrips Thrips have straw-coloured, long bodies and move very swiftly so that it is difficult to see them on the leaves. They suck juices from beneath the leaves and can disrupt the photosynthetic process. They pupate in the soil, going through numerous stages before becoming an adult. Thrips thrive in warm temperatures.

The majority of vegetables grown in the greenhouse are not affected by thrips, but they will attack onions, peppers, eggplants, cucumbers, and spinach. They cause characteristic patches of damaged tissue on the leaves, or produce a silvery, rippled effect on onion tops which results from the collapse of tissues as the thrips pierce the cell walls of the plant.

Control of Thrips While in Europe a predatory mite is now being used to control thrips in a few commercial greenhouses, it is unlikely that you will have serious problems with this pest, and spot application of diatamaceous earth, applied sparingly and only when necessary, will effect a control. Apply the diatamaceous earth to the underside of the leaf and in a ring around the base of the plant to control the thrips when they are developing in the soil.

Spider Mites   Mites are not insects, but belong to the same biological class to which spiders and ticks belong. The presence of these tiny arachnids can be detected by shaking a bit of flour onto the underside of a leaf. If spider mites are present, there will appear a characteristic matted webbing of tiny fibres, made visible by the flour. This webbing can spread, in the case of serious infestations, until it virtually engulfs the plant, and chokes it. Spider mites also suck on the leaves and you may see silver or brown spots appear until, eventually, the leaves pucker and turn brown. Mites are very hard to see with the naked eye, the adults growing to a size of only 0.5mm.

The two-spotted spider mite *(Tetranychus urticae)* usually causes problems on cucumber and melon vines, occasionally on house-plants, and nearly always on indoor peaches. They thrive in hot, dry conditions and regular misting or otherwise increasing the humidity is a good control.

Some of the botanical insecticides such as rotenone, pyrethrum and diatamaceous earth are effective against spider mites. These mites join thrips, aphids, and whiteflies on the menu of the voracious lacewing. In the case of a one-plant problem, such as an infested house-plant, simply use a light salad oil to wipe the leaves.

Predatory mites (such as *Phytoseiulus persimilis*) are available from suppliers and are usually very successful against spider mites because they reproduce faster than the pest. If only a few plants in the greenhouse are affected, a shipment of 100-500 mite predators should be adequate.

Slugs   Slugs are a problem for which satisfactory controls are lacking. Popular wisdom notwithstanding, neither beer baits, yeast baits (a lid-full of beer or yeast set in the greenhouse to attract slugs) or diatamaceous earth have been effective in controlling slugs in greenhouses. Plants with a central stem, such as peppers and tomatoes, can be protected from serious injury by a thick ring of wood ashes sprinkled on the soil around the base of the plant (but not too close to the stem). Pieces of board, plastic lids or saucers left on the soil surface are attractive to slugs and a regular inspection each morning yields a good catch. In most situations, this method is the most effective (if the most distasteful) method of control.

Toads eat slugs and make beneficial greenhouse pets if you can catch any.

Feeding Your Predators   Your greenhouse might profitably contain an island of plants which provide pollen and nectar for some of your control insects.

Nectar is essential to lacewings, for instance, and will help to double their reproductive rate and to increase their life span. The hover-fly also must have nectar. You might, therefore, plant begonias or another flowering plant to which you have seen bees attracted (a sure sign of nectar). The ideal plants are dill or parsley that has gone to seed. The tiny flowers of the parsley have such short nectaries that the smallest wasp can reach them. Herbs such as mint and lemon balm are excellent sources of nectar in the flowering stage. Although most areas classify it as a noxious weed, Queen Anne's Lace is one of the most attractive plants for this purpose. Keep a few flowering plants to meet the needs of the various insects.

Beneficial insects require water as well and in a small greenhouse water should be available to them. Avoid deep pools of water in which many insects would drown.

Diseases

On the whole, the plants in a biologically managed home greenhouse are surprisingly free from disease. Plants which are grown in well-balanced soil containing sufficient organic matter and nutrients, and which have their water and other environmental requirements met, will be generally healthy. A good mixture of plant species also will present little opportunity for epidemic diseases to spread.

"Better safe than sorry" is an adage that should be kept in mind while working in the greenhouse. Avoid damaging plants; if leaves or stems are accidentally broken, remove them, before the damaged tissue can become infected. The best defence against fungus disease is good ventilation and the practice of retaining only healthy plants in the greenhouse. It is common sense to remove broken stems or suspicious-looking plants as soon as they are noticed, and to keep old and dying leaves picked off and thrown out. It is best to burn plant material that is diseased or infested with pests. Other plant waste should be disposed of outside the greenhouse, preferably in the centre of an actively heating compost pile. Sanitation is the best means of preventing disease. Using a disinfectant on benches, tools and the greenhouse interior is usually not necessary. However, the glazing should be washed every year to keep light level high, and the rest of the greenhouse should be washed with water whenever it gets dirty. Obviously, pots and tools that come in contact with diseased plants should be disinfected before being used again (use rubbing alcohol or diluted bleach).

One highly infectious disease that can spread to tomatoes, peppers, and others of their family is *tobacco mosaic* virus. It can be transmitted by people who smoke cigarettes, because the virus remains alive through the tobacco curing process. Commercial growers of tomatoes and peppers are careful not to employ smokers, because the risk of infection is too great.

Some varieties of tomatoes are bred for resistance to *tobacco mosaic,* and should be grown by smokers or anyone who has had trouble with this disease in the greenhouse. The virus is deactivated by milk and smokers should rinse their hands in milk before handling susceptible plants. If there are a number of valuable plants involved this precaution is only prudent.

SURVEY

Barrhead Greenhouse

This greenhouse was built during the winter of 1980-81 and was used from the spring of its completion to produce tomatoes, green peppers, and eggplant into the early winter. The greenhouse experiences relatively low light levels resulting from a limited amount of vertical, south-facing glazing and the absence of any roof glazing. Yet it produced tomatoes almost until Christmas. A benefit of the limited glazing has been the absence of summer overheating problems.

The house itself is entirely wood heated and there is no auxiliary heat supplied to the greenhouse other than what comes through from the house. Although the greenhouse froze in early winter, the owners feel that the growing season could have been extended further if the infiltration of cold air into the greenhouse had been reduced.

Heat Storage   Heat is stored in a masonry wall which is common to the house. There is also a duct connection to the rest of the house consisting of hollow concrete blocks laid under the basement floor. (The greenhouse is attached at the basement level).

Movable Insulation   A south wall, interior movable insulation system which stores against the ceiling when not in use was devised for this greenhouse. It consists of a bifold shutter, constructed of 2 in (50mm) expanded polystyrene (white styrofoam) with a wooden frame. It is operated by a pulley system with a crank on the north wall. During the day, the shutter folds up so that it stores flat against the ceiling above head level. At night it is lowered into place and pushed tightly against the glazing. Removable push-in shutters are used for the endwall glazing.

The system has been quite effective in reducing heat loss. A drawback, however, is that it

(Photographs supplied by Peter Amerongen)
Designers: Bryan and Cathy Caverhill
Location: Barrhead, Alberta
Latitude: 54°N
Design temperature: −36°C
Degree days: 5800 C°
Size: 2.44m x 7.32 m (8ft x 24 ft)
Cost: $1150 (CDN)
Year of construction: 1980
Glazing material: Recycled double glass

Comments: This attached greenhouse with vertical glazing has performed well in spite of low light levels. It features an interior movable insulation system which is made of rigid white styrofoam and which stores up against the ceiling during the day. The greenhouse is used from early spring until early winter.

restricts the use of the soil in the front of the growing bed since the shutter swings close as it is raised or lowered. There can be no tall plants in the first 600mm (24 in) of the bed for the same reason. However, this is not serious since it makes sense not to have tall plants at the front as they would shade plants at the rear.

Another drawback, common to interior movable insulation systems, is that condensation forms on the glass every morning as soon as the shutters are removed.

Fig. 315 Greenhouse interior with shutter lowered in place

Fig. 314 Shutter operator

Fig. 316 Operating the shutters. So easy that even...

Photograph by Michael Kerfoot
Designer: Michael Kerfoot, Sunergy Systems Ltd.
Location: Blackfalds, Alberta
Latitude: 52°N
Design temperature: -34°C
Degree days: 5500 C°
House size: 195m²
Greenhouse size: 15.0² x 2 storeys
Year of construction: 1980/81
Glazing material: Double glass

Comments: Blackfalds greenhouse uses superinsulation construction techniques, double stud walls with 50mm of rigid insulation on the exterior and 2 x 2 interior strapping. Verticle south wall glazing is used on a triangular greenhouse. Excess greenhouse heat is delivered primarily to a gravel bed below the den floor and, secondarily, to large soil beds in the greenhouse. Auxiliary heat is provided by a woodstove; there is no conventional fossil fuel heating system. The owners are commercial greenhouse operators.

Blackfalds Greenhouse

Michael Kerfoot designed a two-storey, triangular greenhouse (the sides of which are 5.5m x 5.5m x 7.3m) as the major physical and psychological focus of this greenhome. The house is built to superinsulation standards and includes such features as concrete slab on gravel for thermal storage, a destratification duct to deliver heat from the ceiling of the upper level to the lower floor level, an earth-to-air preheated ventilation system, and "pocket" insulating shutters for north facing windows.

Michael's numerous greenhouses are designed for the Canadian Prairies — most particularly for the geographical region of the southern half of Alberta. When designing a greenhouse he takes into account not only such things as heat management and construction techniques, but also many human elements — including the important and often neglected need for a connection with and an awareness of the outdoor environment and cycles.

The Blackfalds greenhouse demonstrates many of the criteria he applies when designing a residential greenhouse:

1. **Integration** The greenhouse should be an active extension or, better, integration of the living area. As such, it is able to do double duty as a dining room, recreational room, retreat, or space for a domestic solar water heater, since no antifreeze or heat exchange are then required. This arrangement also provides for a strong visual and thermal connection between the home and the greenhouse, which is important for aesthetic reasons, for better lighting, and so the house itself can act as part of the direct gain/thermal storage system.

Michael uses such a greenhouse as a strong and obvious transitional zone between the natural outdoor environment and the interior living space. This concept suggests to him the use of natural finishing materials — wood, stone, brick, ceramic tile — rather than highly finished and highly refined materials. The natural materials will also have lower maintenance requirements. This emphasis on transition encourages a natural flow between the two areas — the indoors and the outdoors — while respecting the sanctity of each.

2. **Plant Growth** A greenhouse should also be designed for plant growth. It should allow for large planting areas (the Blackfalds greenhouse features a 0.91m (3 ft) soil bed), use easily maintained materials, provide a floor drain, a water tap, and so on. An active plant growing area provides humidity to the house air, improved food quality, and savings on grocery bills. In addition, it offers the opportunity to take direct responsibility for an important part of our lives.

3. **Vertical Glazing** Michael usually elects to use vertical glazing in his greenhouse for a number of reasons:
- It is cheaper and easier to install.
- Any overhead glazing incorporating glass must employ tempered glass, a very expensive product.
- Some people are concerned about the safety of *any* overhead glass.
- Vertical glazing is easier to keep clean.
- Angled glazing is more difficult to fit with the interior insulating curtains which Michael uses.

In southern Alberta, a high proportion of winter solar gain is from direct and reflected sunlight (assuming a clean snow reflector). There is very little contribution from diffuse radiation so that vertical glazing is an ideal choice for the winter months. The more a greenhouse is to be used for plant production, the more Michael increases the glazing height relative to the depth of the greenhouse, thereby allowing more light to reach the back of the greenhouse during the summer months.

4. **Glazing Materials** The normal criteria Michael applies to glazing materials include ability to resist harsh weather, longevity, impact resistance, transmissibility, availability, cost, and ease of installation. While most of these criteria agree with those set forth elsewhere in this book, Michael places more emphasis on the transmission characteristics than we have. His preference for glazing is the use of water white glass on the inside and outside, with three layers of polyester film sandwiched in between. Often, visual clarity is not wanted, such as in upper glazings where Michael may use a transluscent plastic glazing material to reduce uncomfortable glare. Also, in most urban situations a significant amount of diffusing glazing is desired for reasons of privacy. Even so, the durability, clarity, availability, and low expansion coefficient of glass make it the dominant glazing of his designs.

5. **Heat Storage** Michael integrates as much thermal mass directly into the greenhouse area as is feasible. Such mass may include concrete slab floors, fibreglass water tubes, drums of water below the planters, decorative brick work, and deep soil beds. Because the greenhouse areas and the adjoining living area are visually and partially thermally connected, the house itself will contribute to thermal storage.

Even with these thermal flywheels in place, Michael finds that a large greenhouse on a sunny day will still produce excess heat — in fact, about one-quarter to one-third of its total gain. Rather than venting this heat to the outdoors, he utilizes sub-floor storage systems within the house itself. This most typically consists of an insulated rock bed below a slab floor in one of the common rooms of the house — dining room, living room or family room. The air is delivered from the peak of the greenhouse by a thermostatically-controlled fan. There is usually also a manually-controlled damper at the peak of the interior direct gain zone.

The fans Michael uses are typically in the order of only one-quarter horsepower since he carefully minimizes the pressure drops through the ducts and the gravel beds. The length of the air path through the beds determines the size of rock needed in them. The rocks are usually 30mm to 50mm in diameter but are sometimes much larger for particularly long gravel beds. The size of available rocks will often influence the design of the storage layout.

The delivery of heat from the storage occurs by means of simple radiation. The large floor slab area with its increased mean temperature makes for a comfortable heating system, Michael says. It does, however, depend upon a good conducting floor. In the Blackfalds residence, carpeting on the den floor may reduce heat delivery from the storage.

Michael also thinks that there is useful latent heat associated with transpiration and perhaps even internal plant processes. Particularly with large plantings this possibility is of considerable importance to overall heat storage. He expects that this is an area which will be attracting more study and appreciation.

6. **Heat Control** Michael's approach in this area differs from that of many other designers. He points out that traditional commercial greenhouses require very high ventilation rates mainly to control excess heat, but finds that this is only infrequently required in an integrated greenhouse. A large expanse of vertical south wall glazing, he says, does not necessarily lead to overheating in the houses he designs. Even during the hottest days of August his greenhouses remain pleasant, a circumstance ascribed to many things: high quality construction, high levels of insulation, appropriate landscaping, thermal storage elements, good venting design, etc.

With the wide azimuth angles and high altitude of the summer sun, considerably less radiation will enter a properly designed greenhouse than in the winter. In fact, Michael finds that the September/October period is normally the only time significant venting is necessary. Operable windows strategically located to encourage natural cross-drafts, and chimney venting meet the needs effectively. In two-storey greenhouses, he provides a couple of large operable windows at floor level and a couple of others as high as operational ease from a balcony will allow. This system, contrary to other opinions, appears adequate.

Michael agrees that air movement is important for plant growth, but finds that the use of a fan moving typically 28 to 56 cubic metres per minute through the storage system along with occasional use of external vents, provides adequate air movement. Further, he feels that the carbon dioxide levels in an integrated greenhouse are probably more favourable than outdoors.

In the related areas of shading, Michael notes that roof overhangs designed to shade the greenhouse from the late August sun will also block the late April sun, when the heat from the sun is needed in the greenhouse. He doesn't feel that the trouble and expense of changeable or adjustable overhangs is necessary. Some well-placed windows and the occasional partial lowering of a reflective insulating curtain are all that is necessary.

Michael advocates the use of movable insulation in cold climate greenhouses and usually uses the "sunseal" insulating curtain system fabricated by Sunergy. It is a vertical roll-up curtain of two reflective layers, which achieves an insulating value of about R51-0.88 (R-S).

The Greenhouse Garden

To achieve a strong thermal performance, the greenhouse should be allowed to fluctuate quite widely in temperature between the daytime solar collection and the night-time thermal buffering. During the former period, Michael designs the greenhouse to operate at as high a temperature as possible to collect heat for thermal storage. At night, whenever possible, a low temperature should be maintained to reduce the temperature difference between the interior and exterior and, thus, reduce the heat loss.

To allow for this dynamic fluctuation in temperature, the greenhouse activities must be planned accordingly. Specifically, the plants grown must be appropriate for the conditions of the season. In winter, for instance, plants must be chosen which survive in cool, low light conditions — such as salad greens and herbs. Michael dissuades greenhouse owners from attempting to grow tropical plants in a prairie greenhouse because the costs in terms of thermal performance are great. He encourages growers to give more attention to those plants that can survive the rigors of a Canadian winter in a greenhouse. Tropical plants, he suggests, should be moved into the inner enclave of the house itself during the winter months. (In fact, however, the Blackfalds greenhouse — as many others — contains large tropical plantings.)

Photographs by Jim Wylie

Designer: Jim Wylie
Location: Detroit Lakes, Minnesota
Latitude: 47°N
Design Temperature: -35°C
Degree Days: 5400 C°
Size: 3.05m x 7.32m (10 ft x 24 ft)
Cost: $4000 (US)
Year of construction: 1981
Glazing material: Double FRP

Comments: The Detroit Lakes greenhouse is one of a series of freestanding greenhouses employing commercial vegetable production techniques. No glazing insulation is used but conservation features include an insulated north wall, endwalls and perimeter; airlock entry; and an infrared heating system which makes use of a water ceiling and insulating flap. The performance of the system has been above calculated expectations. Expected economic returns are $1200-$1500 (US) per year.

The energy conservation and crop production effects Jim Wylie assumed when designing the Detroit Lakes greenhouse:

Design Factor	Effect on Energy Savings	Effect on Crop Production
Double glazing	+30%	−20%
Insulated north wall	50%	−15%
Sloping north wall	None	+20%
Overhead reflective shutter	+40-60%	−5%
Reducing temperatures 5.5°C	+26	+5-8%
Earth sheltering	+25-50%	−25% (est.)
Radiant heating	+15-40%	None
Soil heating	+15-60%	+10%
Perimeter insulation	+10%	None
White, reflective surfaces	None	+5-10%

Detroit Lakes Greenhouse

Over the past few years, more than a dozen energy conserving solar greenhouses have been constructed in northwestern Minnesota. The centre of this activity is at Detroit Lakes, where Jim Wylie teaches a solar greenhouse design and greenhouse production course at the Area Vocational Technical Institute. The design of these greenhouses results from some years of researching the data available from institutions and individuals across the continent. Numerous design features were adapted for use in the cold climate of northern Minnesota, and were selected to optimize the growing conditions. The greenhouse most indicative of these features is the one built in late 1981 on the campus of the Institute.

1. **Earth Sheltering** In order to benefit from the buffering action of the earth and to allow as much of the greenhouse as possible to be in contact with a material much warmer than the Minnesota winter air, the greenhouse is of a semi-pit design, sunk to a depth of about 1.2m.

2. **Double Glazing** The south wall is sloped to an angle of about 40° and is double glazed with fiberglass reinforced polyester (FRP).

3. **Sloping Reflective North Wall** To provide the best growing conditions in January and February, an angle of 60° from the horizontal was chosen to reflect winter sunlight onto the plant canopy, where it is most needed. For this reason the north wall also has a reflective surface.

4. **Insulated Walls** Because it was determined that the amount of possible light gain was more than offset by the possible energy savings, the north wall as well as the east and west walls are insulated and sealed.

5. **Airlock Entry** Since the floor and growing beds of this greenhouse are below ground level, it was particularly important that an airlock

entry be provided, to prevent cold air from flooding into the greenhouse the moment a door directly to the outside was opened.

6. **Perimeter Insulation** Rather than insulating along the foundation and beneath the floor, rigid insulation is buried horizontally just below ground level to form a 600mm wide skirt around the greenhouse. Insulation then runs vertically from that point to a depth level with the greenhouse floor. This plan helps the greenhouse take better advantage of the heat from the earth and, it is thought, to use the surrounding soil as added thermal storage.

7. **Buried Air Intake** Buffered air tubes are provided to temper the incoming ventilation air. Plastic drain field pipes are laid around the exterior perimeter at the base of the greenhouse (buried 1.2m). An entry pipe rises just above ground level outside the north side of the greenhouse, and the exit pipe is inside the greenhouse at floor level. Before winter ventilation air is introduced into the greenhouse, it is warmed by the soil and by heat escaping from the greenhouse perimeter. Hot summer air is cooled by the soil on its way into the greenhouse. It was initially estimated that at −29°C the air coming into the greenhouse would be warmed to about −7°C, but in actual use at this outside temperature, the ventilation air comes in at +8°C.

8. **Solar Chimney** Another part of the cooling and ventilation system is a solar chimney rising from the peak of the greenhouse. This chimney is diamond-shaped with one corner pointing south. The southeast and southwest faces are glazed, while the other two are painted black. A heat-responsive vent opener is located at the top, and a barometric damper is used to nullify wind and to insure that the vent responds only to excess heat from solar radiation. The movement of solar heated air up and out through the chimney creates a vacuum in the greenhouse so that fresh air is drawn in through the buried air tubes.

Fig. 319 Vo-Tech Institute Greenhouse

9. **Hinged Reflective Shield** Near the peak of the roof is installed a two-piece reflective shield. During the day, it is raised to reflect sunlight down into the greenhouse. At night the shield, which is made from a rigid insulation, is lowered to a horizontal position to help minimize heat loss.

10. **Water Ceiling** Above head level, and running the depth and length of the greenhouse, is a transparent water ceiling which holds 50mm of water. This feature, and the pivoted reflective insulating shield above it, were adapted from work done by Reed Maes in Ann Arbor, Michigan. During the day, when the shield is raised, the water is heated by sunlight passing through it. At night, when the shields are lowered, the water is able to radiate heat to the plants.

11. **Root Zone Heating** Another feature of the greenhouse heating system is a series of hot water pipes buried in the soil of the growing beds. The pipes are connected to the water ceiling so that sun-warmed water can be run through the beds. The water pipes are also connected to a propane-fired boiler for back-up heating.

These greenhouses were designed with an energy equilibrium in mind which takes into account the temperature inside, the temperature outside, and infrared radiation. The emphasis in the heating system is on infrared radiation, which is used to heat the plants directly without raising the surrounding air to a high temperature. This scheme allows for lower greenhouse air temperatures and means that the difference between the inside and outside temperatures will be less, resulting in much lower heat losses. Fuel savings of over 60% are expected. The sources of night-time infrared radiation in the greenhouse are the water ceiling, the soil, and the walls of the structure. The soil provides about 25% of the radiant heat.

Air temperatures in the greenhouse are maintained at about 7°C to 10°C for tomatoes and as low as 4.5°C for lettuce, which should result in an increase in production of about 10% due to lower pest and disease problems, which almost always occur at high temperatures. However, the colder temperatures also result in a 2% decrease in marketable produce, so that a net increase of about 8% can be expected. These figures have been confirmed by work in Ontario and by John White at Penn State.

Management

Jim Wylie employs a complex crop management plan which uses high production commercial techniques modified to a biological approach. He expects to be able to produce, annually, 32.2kg of vegetables per square metre. A recent comparison of this management system with a nearby greenhouse using a commercial hydroponics system, showed Wylie's system very slightly ahead in production. Currently, an 18.6m² (200 ft²) greenhouse supplies about 27kg of tomatoes per week and each plant in a spring cropping system yields from 5.5 to 7.7kg overall.

Results and Future Plans

In northwestern Minnesota, there is insufficient solar radiation from December 15 to January 30 to produce satisfactory plant growth or provide the heat needed by the greenhouses. Even so, at the end of December, on bright sunny days, daytime greenhouse air temperatures have reached 38°C and water ceiling temperatures have been 35°C. These extremes, however, occurred without ventilation and are exceptions more than rules.

Fig. 320 Daryl Jorud greenhouse at Battle Lake, Minnesota which uses a wind generator to supply current to an electric hot water heater for soil heating.

The greenhouses require supplementary heat only from December 10 to about January 30. In the worst cases, propane consumption is only between 225 *l* and 375 *l* per season and is significantly lower for the latest greenhouses, which have incorporated the thermal storage

system and the perimeter insulation as described above.

Currently, these greenhouses require a fair amount of upkeep and attention to maintain high levels of energy conservation and productive capacity. The biological management system is, however, being improved each year and Jim Wylie expects to lower the amount of labour involved significantly and to be able to predict productive potential according to the management techniques employed more accurately.

Fig. 321 A cold frame in northern Minnesota — a low
until the first week in December.

He is now working on a design for an attached greenhouse which will employ many of the same conservation features and production concepts. Jim states that an average attached solar greenhouse owner will spend from 15 to 30 minutes each day caring for and harvesting the crops. The actual work, if done by an experienced labourer, he says, could be accomplished within 6.5 minutes.

Research is being done to employ different soil heating zones to grow a diversity of crops. Jim hopes to improve yields 5 to 7 times over normal solar greenhouse production by using the commercial techniques which have been successful in his freestanding greenhouse.

Ecology House Greenhouse

This attached solar greenhouse incorporates 13.38m² (144ft²) of south-facing double glass glazing pitched at an angle of 55°. Interior walls are insulated to RSI-3.52 (R-20), the roof to RSI-4.93 (R-28), and the exterior door to RSI-2.46 (R-14).

The greenhouse, part of a demonstration project in downtown Toronto, was designed and constructed acknowledging several liabilities. Because of zoning and lot line restrictions, the greenhouse had to be attached to the west wall of the house, so that the north wall is exposed. Secondly, a twenty-storey building located to the southeast of Ecology House shades the greenhouse until 10:10 am in the dead of winter, limiting solar access by as much as 18%.

Construction The greenhouse was constructed as part of a workshop involving fifteen people over the course of two weekends. Many of the design decisions were made with the understanding that the greenhouse would be built predominantly by unskilled labour.

The foundation wall was constructed of a novel type of dry-stacking block with a fairly high insulating value. The 250mm (10 in) blocks were stacked above a footing located below the frost line to a height 760mm (30 in) above ground level. Once stacked, the polystyrene-filled concrete block was covered on both sides with a fibreglass reinforced stucco which provided the required tensile strength. The lightweight nature of the blocks and the dry stacking method make this an attractive option for the builder seeking simplicity.

Because the greenhouse extends off of the west wall of the house, both south and north walls of the greenhouse needed to be framed. The south wall glazing assembly was designed to house eight 864mm x 1930mm (34 in x 76 in) sealed, double glazed units of tempered glass in two

Photographs by Judith Klein

Designer: Ecology House
Location: Toronto, Ontario
Latitude: 43°N
Design Temperature: −19°C
Degree Days: 3793 C°
Size: 13.38m² (144ft²)
Cost: $2700 (CDN)
Year of construction: 1979
Glazing material: Double tempered glass — sealed units

Comments: This attached greenhouse is part of the Ecology House demonstration of conservation techniques applicable to existing urban housing. The greenhouse was designed and built by volunteers and workshop participants. It extends from the west wall of Ecology House, which required that an insulated north wall be built. Two large deep soil beds are used in the greenhouse.

levels of four units each. This construction resulted in a large area of glass and a high roof peak. The 2 x 6 cedar was mounted on the sill plate and nailed to a ridge pole extending out from the house.

The north wall and the roof section of the greenhouse were fabricated from 2 x 8 studs, nailed together at the roof line with plywood gussets. These sections were individually assembled, mounted on the sill plate, and nailed into the ridge poles on 24 in (610mm) centres.

The west wall of the greenhouse was framed with 2 x 6s and incorporated openings for two triangular pieces of glass and an exterior door.

The eight thermopane units of glass were installed over the 2 x 6 glazing rafters and laid onto a bed of glazing tape. At the mid-section of the glazing, cedar mullions were installed to provide a base for the glazing tape and a backing for the clamping bars. At the horizontal joint of the glazing, silicon caulking was used to provide an air and water seal, then galvanized steel clamping bars were overlaid.

The vertical clamping bars were made of 1 x 2 cedar and were laid on to a second bed of glazing tape to prevent water penetration. The bars were screwed to the 2 x 6 rafters using 3 in (75mm) stainless steel round head screws.

Heat Storage   On the north wall, two hundred 4 l (1 gal) recycled and antifreeze containers were painted black (later changed to blue), filled with water and stacked up against the wall in the direct sunlight. The flooring of the greenhouse consisted of recycled bricks laid over a 100mm (4 in) bed of screened sand. Finally, the growing beds were constructed to hold a minimum of 600mm (24 in) of soil and, in the case of the southwall growing bed, 1200mm (48 in). This combined thermal mass works effectively in controlling temperature fluctuations within the greenhouse.

Ventilation   Ventilation is provided through a large (1.67m; 18 ft²) insulated vent located at the peak of the north-facing roof. The vent is manually operated and when the exterior door is opened, effectively cools the structure, even during the hot summer months.

A door through the west wall of the house allows excess heat from the greenhouse to be vented into the kitchen, primarily during the spring and fall. Ducting was installed as part of a hybrid storage system but has not been employed.

Growing areas   The 1200mm (48 in) deep soil bed runs along the south wall of the greenhouse. This bed, made of fibreglass, provides 3.34m² (36 ft²) of growing area and is tied to the greywater system of the house. The greywater (recycled bathwater and dishwater from the house) passes through a primary filter in the house basement and is then pumped through small PVC pipes laid into the soil bed

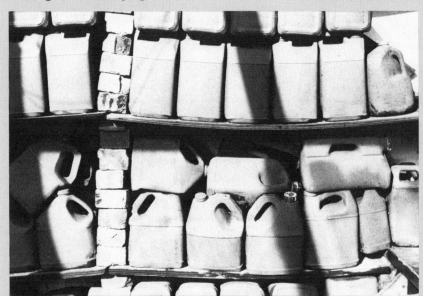

Fig. 324 Heat storage: antifreeze of a different sort

Fig. 325 Vent on north-facing roof

at a depth of 150mm (6 in). The water flowing through these pipes provides irrigation to the bed then flows through the soil to drain at the base of the bed.

A second growing bed of 3.25m² (35 ft²) is located in the centre of the greenhouse. This bed was constructed of plywood lined with 6 mil polyethylene and filled with 600mm (24 in) of rich topsoil and organic compost.

Performance   Several movable insulation options (both interior and exterior) have been tried without great success, and the Ecology House staff feels that lack of shutters is the major flaw in the design of the greenhouse.

However, even without a movable insulation system, the structure is able to maintain plants through the winter. Plants which are seeded in late October provide small yields throughout the darker months and survive for harvesting in early March, even though temperatures fall to nearly freezing levels at night during long, cloudy periods.

Insect pests are controlled successfully through the use of biological controls. Lady beetles and parasitic wasps form the main line of defense against aphids and whiteflies, but are sometimes supplemented with insecticidal soaps.

Fig. 326 Watering the centre growing bed

Photograph by Stephen Marshall
Designer/Builder: Sun Shelters Ltd.
Location: Keswick, Ontario
Latitude: 44°N
Design temperature: -25 C
Degree days: 4300 C°
Size: 23 m²
Year of construction: 1982
Glazing material: Double-glazed, tempered glass

Keswick Greenhouse

This 23 m² (250 sq. ft.) attached greenhouse was built by a Toronto firm specializing in the construction of solar greenhouses and sun spaces. This structure represents a balance between the use of a structure as a greenhouse and as a sun space.

The structure is built onto the back of a house with perfect southerly orientation and totally clear solar access. The 12.1 m² (130 sq. ft.) of south-facing glass is tilted at an angle of 55°

from the horizon, using double glazed, tempered patio door units. Walls and ceiling of the structure are framed with 38 x 140 mm (2 x 6) lumber and insulated with RSI 3.52 (R20) fibreglass batt insulation. The ceiling is cross strapped above the insulation to provide a ventilation cavity. Foundation walls are insulated to the footings with RSI 2.64 (R15) extruded polystyrene.

The greenhouse has been tied to the house to match the existing roof line and siding of the building. Access from the house to the structure is provided by two sliding glass doors which were already in place to allow access to a patio area.

Construction The foundation wall of the structure was laid onto a 400 mm (16 inch) concrete footing. The 200 mm (8 inch) concrete blocks were extended from below the frost line to 760mm (30 inches) above the finished grade and were then covered with 2 layers of 38 mm (1¹/₂ inch) extruded polystyrene held into place by the backfill below grade and by the sill plate detail at the top of the foundation wall. The insulation was covered with a protective layer of pressure treated plywood which was nailed to the sill plate. This exterior insulation allows the foundation wall mass to provide some heat storage capacity to the greenhouse.

Framing the glazing wall was performed in a single unit on the ground in front of the structure. 38 x 140 (2 x 6) clear cedar was used for the glazing rafters with top and base plates of 38 x 190 mm (2 x 8) clear cedar. The glazing wall was positioned in place before the individual roof rafters were installed from the house rafters to the top of the wall.

The end walls of the structure were framed to incorporate a small triangular window and an operable casement window on the east and another triangular window and a sliding glass door on the west. Additional ventilation was incorporated into the roof of the structure by the use of three operable skylight units (Velux windows).

For the main glazing, six 864 x 1930 mm (34 x 76 inch) patio door units and two 533 x 1930 mm (21 x 76 inch) custom tempered units were installed onto glazing tape on the glazing rafters. A 19 x 140 mm piece (1 x 6) was installed along the base of the glazing wall to act as the glazing stop. The flashing was extended 6 mm under the glass to provide a water-tight seal. Flashing was also installed along the peak of the glazing wall to prevent any water leakage. The glazing units were held in place with 19 x 38 mm (1 x 2 inch) cedar clamping bars. A thin layer of glazing tape was installed on the underside of the clamping bars to provide a weatherproof seal for the glazing.

Heat storage in the structure is provided in three phases. The growing bed extending across 4.8 mm (16 feet) of the south wall is 100 mm (4 in.) poured concrete with an exposed aggregate. The bed holds 4 cubic metres (144 ft^3) of soil to provide a tempering element for the crop roots. The floor of the greenhouse is laid over a 150 mm (6 inch) bed of crushed stone. The 50 mm (2 inch) flagstone floor is not bedded in mortar. The north wall of the structure is covered with containers of water holding approximately 680 l (150 gallons) of water.

The structure is divided into two distinct areas. The growing area includes the south wall, deep soil bed and other movable planting beds, encompassing approximately 70% of the interior floor space. A small sitting area is incorporated into the west end of the structure where the floor has been elevated by 200 m (8 inches). This area houses a cedar slat bench on the south wall for seeding flats or for house plants.

Ventilation Ventilation is provided at the peak of the structure through 3.1 m^2 (10 ft^2) operable skylights. Cross ventilation is provided through the casement window and sliding glass door on the east and west wall respectively. Heat circulation to the house is accomplished through the two sliding doors in the house wall.

Performance In its initial winter, the structure maintained an adequate temperature for the plants without the need for back-up heat. Humidity levels were sometimes excessively high resulting in condensation on the glazing in the morning. This was attributed to the high humidity levels in the house itself which was causing damage to sills within the living room of the house. Installation of an air-to-air heat exchanger was recommended as a solution to the problem.

Overheating was not a major concern during the summer because of adequate ventilation and the relatively large amounts of thermal mass. During a hot spell in the summer, the owners found the greenhouse cooler than the outside by circulating house air into the structure.

Food production was, as expected, slowed during the peak winter months due to a lack of adequate light; however, good yields of vegetables were obtained until November.

King Greenhouse

This small attached greenhouse has excellent southern exposure and is tied to the house on both its west and south walls. The 7.90m² (85 ft²) of south-facing glass is titled at an angle of 50° and employs sealed, double glazed, tempered glass. The structure's unglazed sections are insulated to RSI-3.52 (R-20) and the building is tightly sealed with a carefully installed air-vapour barrier.

The greenhouse has been aesthetically tied to the main structure by closely matching the roof slope and roofing material, and by siding the greenhouse with the same type and colour siding as was used for the house. Access from the house to the greenhouse is provided by a newly installed sliding glass door.

Construction The greenhouse was constructed over a water cistern which provides a concrete floor for most of the structure. The foundation wall was constructed with two 150mm (6 in) concrete block layers sandwiching 51mm (2 in) of rigid, extruded polystyrene. This design provides some thermal mass to the interior of the structure as well as a low-maintenance interior wall. The foundation wall extends from below the frost line to 600mm (24 in) above grade. A 2 x 12 cedar sill plate was installed over the foundation cap.

The glazing members and the roof rafters were pre-assembled as single units, using plywood gussets. These assembled units were installed onto the sill plate, then nailed into the roof rafters of the house. This framing system allowed the rafter/glazing units to be prefabricated away from the site.

The east wall of the greenhouse was framed with 2 x 6s, allowing for a triangle of glazing and an exterior door.

Five 864mm x 1930mm (34 in x 76 in) thermopane units were laid onto a strip of

Photograph by Stephen Marshall
Designer: Brian Marshall
Location: King Township, Ontario
Latitude: 44°N
Design Temperature: −25°C
Degree Days: 4167 C°
Size: 11.1m²
Year of Construction: 1980/81
Glazing Material: Double tempered glass — sealed units

Comments: This greenhouse shares two walls with the house and is aesthetically connected to the house by the roof slope and the use of the same siding and shingling. A 3400*l* (750 gal) cistern located beneath the floor of the greenhouse is available for use as thermal storage.

glazing tape on top of the 2 x 6 cedar glazing members. The units were held in place with 1 x 2 cedar clamping bars which were screwed to the rafters. Flashing was installed over the peak of the glazing assembly. The bottom of the glazing assembly was also flashed and equipped with a drip edge. The bottom glazing stop was made from a 1 x 6 cedar board, and the glass was set onto neoprene glazing blocks with the spaces filled with "Mono" caulking before the bottom clamping bar was installed.

More than 2.4m³ (85 ft³) of masonry heat storage is provided by a concrete floor, the foundation wall, and waterproof gypsum board used on the north wall. Additional water heat storage may be added by using the 3400 l cistern or by adding water storage containers in the greenhouse, provision for which has been made.

Ventilation A skylight vent was installed in the roof to provide additional sunlight and a high exit vent. Further ventilation is provided by the exterior door on the east wall and by an opaque, triangular-shaped vent on the west wall of the greenhouse where it protrudes beyond the main building. This small vent is sealed by an insulated plug which is removed during the warmer months.

Air exchange with the house is carried out via a window on the common endwall (west wall of the greenhouse) and the sliding glass door on the north wall.

Growing Area A 1.86m² (20 ft²) deep soil bed was installed on the south wall of the greenhouse and filled with topsoil. Additional growing area is provided by 2.79m² (30 ft²) of cedar slatted benches, which are used primarily for flats for seedlings which are to be transplanted to the outdoor garden. Plants are hung from the ceiling throughout the rest of the greenhouse.

Insufficient screening of the outside openings (door and vents) led to serious problems with insects during the start-up period. Screening and biological controls have remedied this problem.

Performance Excessive build-up of heat, even during cold, bright winter days, reflects the need for increased thermal mass. A tie-in to the large volume of water located below the structure should help to alleviate this problem, but will require costly materials such as heat exchangers, pump and controls.

Better planning of the interior floor area would have resulted in increased space for plant and vegetable production.

Pottageville Greenhouse

This 18.58m² (200ft²) greenhouse located north of Toronto was constructed as part of a greenhouse workshop, with the majority of the work being performed by a group of fifteen untrained participants. The structure includes more than 11.61m² (125ft²) of south-facing glass at an angle of 50°, and more than 1.49m² (16ft²) of double glazed roof venting. The building is very well insulated throughout, although a movable insulating system for the glazing has not been installed. The greenhouse serves a dual purpose as a growing area for vegetables and as a small sunroom during the winter.

Construction   The foundation of the structure is a cement block wall extending from below the frost line to 600mm (24 in) above grade. The entire foundation wall was insulated with 100mm (4 in) of rigid extruded polystyrene. The initial design called for backfilling the foundation wall to include an earth berm extending up the front wall, but the owners eventually decided to remove the berm and retain the original ground level. This decision seems wise in light of the large amounts of regional snowfall which would have rapidly built up snowbanks against the glazing. A major mistake was made during the installation and excavation of the footing for the greenhouse. Because an adequate survey of the site was not made, the backhoe dug into the septic system line, resulting in a large amount of unneeded, and not entirely pleasant, work. The greenhouse was framed using western cedar for all exposed interior measures and with construction-grade spruce in the endwalls and roof. A short kneewall was built above the foundation to allow for the installation of low vents, supplementing the vents at the peak of the greenhouse.

The entire glazing assembly was pre-fabricated on the site, and lifted into place onto the short kneewall and temporarily braced in place. Because of the odd, wing-shaped roof line of the

Photographs by Stephen Marshall

Designer: Ecology House
Location: Pottageville, Ontario
Latitude: 44°N
Design temperature: −27°C
Degree days: 4250 C°
Size: 18.58m² (200ft²)
Cost: $3000.00
Year of construction: 1981
Glazing material: Double glass

Comments: The design and construction of this greenhouse presented a challenge because of the curved roof of the house. Each rafter was individually cut and fitted. Two double glazed skylights provide ventilation. The greenhouse was built at a workshop by volunteers with little experience in construction.

existing house, each of the roof rafters had to be individually measured and cut to fit between the glazing header and the fascia of the existing house. This roof line also results in a variation in the pitch of the greenhouse roof from one end of the structure to the other.

Most of the greenhouse glass is oriented almost due south. Small triangular pieces of glass were installed into the east and west end of the greenhouse. The doors installed at each end of the building also included small glass panels at eye level. The south-facing glazing is sealed, double glazed, tempered glass. The skylight vents installed on the roof of the greenhouse are glazed with double-wall rigid acrylic.

The greenhouse is well insulated throughout. The foundation wall, endwalls, and roof are insulated to RSI-3.52 (R-20). An air-tight vapour barrier was carefully installed.

Heat Storage   The majority of the thermal mass of this greenhouse is provided by the concrete block wall of the existing house and by the brick flooring material installed throughout the greenhouse. The soil bed which comprises the bulk of the vegetable production for the greenhouse is loaded with almost 1.2m (4 ft) of soil, adding to the heat storing capacity of the greenhouse. Additional thermal mass, using small plastic containers, is planned for the future.

Growing Area   A deep soil bed of approximately 2.80m² (30ft²) is used for year-round vegetable production. This bed is supplemented by more than 5.5m² (60ft²) of slatted cedar benches which are used for seeding trays in the spring and for pots and planters throughout the year. The greenhouse provides greens through the winter months although yields in the dead of winter are limited by the shortened day length. As in many attached greenhouses, aphids and whiteflies appear at certain times of the year, reportedly from the interior of the house where they feed on house-plants. The owners have been satisfied with the crop yields from the structure. The growing area comprises approximately 2/3 of the interior space of the greenhouse with the remainder used as a living and sitting room.

Performance   During the winter, the greenhouse performs satisfactorily as a food producer and is well used as a sitting area. The desire of the homeowners to keep the greenhouse at a temperature above 7°C (because of the house-plants located in the structure) led to the purchase of a small space heater which is used during the colder periods of the winter. Some of the inefficiencies of the structure result from the construction techniques — specifically the fact that a totally air-tight seal on the skylight vents was not obtained. Overheating during the spring and fall can occur if the vents are not manually opened in the morning. This problem could also be alleviated by the addition of more thermal mass.

The greenhouse is capable of providing large amounts of heat to the main house through the sliding glass door which links the two structures. No specific records or results were available regarding these energy flows.

Fig. 330 The sunspace during winter

Millet Greenhouse

This greenhouse is attached to a low-energy house employing double-wall construction techniques and other conservation features. It was built for two energetic and talented gardeners. Maximizing light levels for optimum growing conditions was the primary greenhouse design consideration. To accomplish this goal and to make the greenhouse as energy efficient as possible, it was designed with roof glazing to accommodate inter-glazing insulation, patterned on the University of Saskatchewan solar greenhouse.

Heat exchange There is a thermostatically controlled fan which blows excess heat into the house during the winter and, by operating a damper, to the outdoors during the summer. The heat supply in the winter is effective and welcome. However, there is an overheating problem during the summer. The 100 CFM fan and the size of the vents are not quite adequate to move enough air to keep the temperature at satisfactory levels and, consequently, some shading is required during the hot months. Besides being too small, the vents are covered with louvres which reduce their effective area substantially.

Fig. 332 Detail of fan/damper assembly near greenhouse ceiling. One duct leads to house, the other to the outdoors. A sliding damper in the lower compartment lets the operator direct the air.

(Photos supplied by Peter Amerongen)
Designers: Peter Amerongen and Bryan Caverhill
Location: Millet, Alberta
Latitude: 53°N
Design temperature: −34°C
Degree days: 5600 C°
Size: 3.05m x 6.10m (10 ft x 20 ft)
Cost: $4500 (CDN)
Year of construction: 1980
Glazing material: Double tempered glass

Comments: An attached greenhouse designed to maximize light levels, the Millet greenhouse is constructed using the rib technique for roof glazing outlined in the CONSTRUCTION section. The inner and outer glazings are spaced about 125mm (5 in) apart to accommodate inter-glazing insulation in both the south wall and the roof.

Four 200 *l* (50 gal) drums in the back of the greenhouse hold water for thermal storage.

Movable Insulation This inter-glazing insulation system was a prototype attached greenhouse and valuable lessons were learned in its development and construction.

The blankets are stored under the south wall plant bench and are raised by winding cords around 1 in (25mm) pipe mounted near the ceiling at the back of the greenhouse. The pipe turns in bushings consisting of 1¹/₂ in (38mm) lengths of 1¹/₄ in (32mm) ABS electrical conduit, held in place with pipe clamps. The bushings are lubricated with paraffin wax. The 1 in pipe is pinned inside a section of 1¹/₂ in pipe to which a used 10-speed bicycle rear sprocket has been welded. This sprocket is driven by a similar sprocket fastened to a small boat winch. The chain is tensioned by hinging the boat winch on the plywood box as shown,

which enables the easy disengaging of the chain from the lower sprocket so the top pipe can revolve freely when the blanket is being pulled down.

It was assumed in the original design that the blankets would simply fall down and fold under the plant bench, much as they do in the University of Saskatchewan greenhouse. However, it didn't happen that way. The main problem was that the foundation wall obstructed a free fall into the storage compartment.

The blankets were finally induced to fall ("most of the time," the builders tell us) by installing rollers, adding weights to the blankets at strategic points, and unrolling the crank mechanism to provide slack in the cords. Since the storage compartment had to be sealed from the rest of the greenhouse, the curtain could not be manually pulled down when it snagged by simply reaching into the compartment.

The solution finally arrived at was to abandon the hope of the blankets falling by themselves, and to pull down the blankets by rolling them around a piece of 2 in (50mm) ABS drain pipe. This pipe turns inside of 1¹/₂ lengths of 3 in (75mm) ABS drain pipe clamped to 2 x 4 supports with pieces of plumbing strap. These bushings are also lubricated with paraffin.

The pipe has a plywood pulley pinned to it. The pulley is composed of two ¹/₂ in (11mm) plywood discs about 430mm (17 in) in diameter ("the bigger the better," we are instructed) with ¹/₄ in (6mm) plywood discs about 480mm (19 in) in diameter screwed on either side. A 150mm (6 in) long pin through the 2 in pipe fits into a slot cut in one of the 430mm discs. This pin was installed with three of the discs already on the pipe, and the last 480mm disc was screwed to the others, finishing the pulley and holding the whole assembly in place.

Fig. 333 Interior of greenhouse showing blankets partially raised, wind-up pipe and cords, hinged bottom sprocket, and fan/damper box.

Fig. 334 Reconstructed south wall bench and insulation storage compartment.

As the blankets are pulled up, the pulley winds a rope which is laying loose on the greenhouse floor. (The rope enters the storage compartment through a copper tube.) The blankets are later pulled down and rolled up by pulling on this rope.

Several important lessons were learned from this system:

1. It is essential to minimize friction. The blanket should be sized to just touch the sides of the glazing space. Rollers should be installed wherever the curtain must make a bend. The ropes should slide through bushings made of copper tubing with flared ends where they enter the glazing space. The pipe bushings must be carefully aligned and lubricated. The sides of the glazing cavity where the blanket enters should be smooth and free of snags to allow the blanket to funnel in smoothly. The blanket material should be as slippery as possible; the woven polyethylene is better than the vinyl. (If the glass has any moisture on it the vinyl tends to stick to it.)

2. It is important that the back wall be free of obstacles and that the pipe supports and drive do not interfere with the windings of the ropes. If a set of ropes begins to double up before the rest because of an adjacent obstruction, then its blanket will travel faster because of the diameter difference. Also, in this greenhouse, the fan/damper assembly had been installed before the insulation system so that the pipe later had to be run through it.

3. Storing the insulation under the plant bench eliminates the possibility of a deep soil bed.

Fig. 335 *Wind-up pipe and top sprocket.*

Fig. 336 *Insulation storage compartment with blankets wound down.*

Fig. 337 Type C greenhouse

Photographs by Don Schwartz

Designers: The Appropriate Technology Solar Crew, District IX Human Resource Development Council.
Location: Bozeman, Montana
Latitude: 46°N
Design temperature: −32°C
Degree days: 4650 C°
House size: single-wide mobile homes of standard lengths
Greenhouse sizes: Type A - 27.9m² (10ft x 30ft)
Type B - 18.6m² (10ft x 20ft)
Cost: Type A: $600
Type B: $500
Year of construction: 1980/81
Glazing material: Outer glazing — "Flexiguard" (polyester/acrylic film)
Inner glazing — UV treated polyethylene

Comments: Three types of low cost greenhouses were designed to provide heat and food to mobile homes which had first undergone a retrofit including superinsulation and complete weatherproofing. The payback period on the greenhouses was less than 3 years. The payback period for the total retrofit, including the greenhouse, was about 1.8 years.

Mobile Home Greenhouses

The mention of "mobile homes" sends shudders up the spines of greenhouse designers and energy conservationists. Mobile homes are notoriously poorly insulated and poorly sealed. Many people who live in mobile homes do so because they cannot afford anything else, and these are the very people who are going to be hit the hardest by increasing heating bills.

In 1980 and 1981 the Human Resource Development Council in Bozeman, Montana made a first attempt at finding solutions to this problem. A retrofit program for mobile homes was established which included re-insulation; skirting, sealing, and weatherstripping; and the construction of an attached greenhouse. The project was designed to demonstrate the use of conservation features and solar heating to replace the traditional fossil fuels. The greenhouse was intended to enable low income mobile home dwellers to lower their space heating costs while providing an extended growing season for vegetable production. Throughout the period of the project, three designs were developed.

Type A

(See photograph p. 204) This type was the original greenhouse designed for mobile homes whose long side faced south. It measures about three metres deep by nine metres long (10 ft x 30 ft) and is constructed of 2 x 6s. Endwalls were opaque and insulated to R11, the roof to R19. 3M "Flexiguard" (which is UV treated) was stapled on as an outer glazing and held in place by lath strips. 4 mil polyethylene was used as inner glazing.

In an attempt to provide thermal mass, about 4000kg of washed gravel was used as the greenhouse floor. Water storage was also provided through the use of ten or more 50 gallon drums, painted black, and placed inside the greenhouse in direct sunlight.

Total cost for a Type A greenhouse was about $600 or $21.50/m² ($2.00/ft²). Seven of these greenhouses were constructed in 1980 and all of them appeared to work well. Four of them functioned throughout the following winter and the owners reported 40% to 50% fuel bill reductions. Although the greenhouses did not have insulating curtains, none froze. At −34°C temperatures of +4°C were reported in the greenhouses.

A problem with this design was ventilation. The screened vents in the endwalls were not large enough to prevent overheating. Future modifications were intended to include the installation of a small exhaust fan or a solar chimney.

Projected Heat Savings	Annual Energy Consumption	
	(kWh)	% of original
Existing, pre-retrofit mobile home	53,325	100
Insulated mobile home with no floor insulation	26,077	49
Insulated mobile home with floor insulation	18,544	35
Addition of greenhouse to above	10,840	20

The projected heat savings (above) show that the annual fuel consumption in a mobile home which has undergone a total insulation and weatherproofing retrofit drops from 53,325 kWh to 18,544 kWh. Addition of the greenhouse lowers this amount by another 8,000 kWh. At 1980 energy costs, annual savings for the greenhouse alone were about $230/year for a payback period of less than three years.

Fig. 338 Exterior of Type A greenhouse

Fig. 339 Interior of Type A greenhouse

Type B

This unit is smaller and cheaper than Type A. It measures about 3m x 6m (10 ft x 20 ft) and was built with prefabricated panels. This shed-type structure could be easily constructed in three to four days. Because of its smaller size in relation to the vent size, it avoided the overheating problem experienced in Type A.

An interesting aspect of this design was that it could be used as the collector surface for a solar hot water heating system, installed near the peak. The greenhouse itself cost about $500; with the solar water heater, the total cost was about $750.

Type C

The last of the three designs was developed for mobile homes with a south-facing endwall. It utilizes prefabricated arches, easily built with a jig. Rigid plastic glazing was used, rather than the roll-type plastics used in Types A and B. Because Type C is attached to the endwall of the mobile home, it does not provide heat to the entire length of the home as the other designs do. However, excellent heat is provided to the living room and kitchen. The cost was about $550.

Fig. 340 Type B greenhouse

Payback Analysis

Pre-retrofit Mobile Home (4.27 x 16.76 m)
annual energy consumption	53,325 kWh	
annual cost @ 3.0¢/kWh	$1,600	
average monthly cost @ 3.0¢/kWh	$ 133	

Post-Retrofit Mobile Home
annual energy consumption	10,840 kWh	
annual cost @ 3.0¢/kWh	$ 325	
average monthly cost @ 3.0¢/kWh	$ 27	

Annual savings following retrofit: $1,275

Payback period on $2,300 material cost 1.8 years
for complete retrofit

Postscript

Appropriate if anything ever was, and conserving energy and resources, the mobile home greenhouse project was made possible by a grant from the U.S. Department of Energy and used labour from the U.S. Department of Labour, which was only sensible since the project produced both energy and jobs.

The new U.S. federal administration which came into office at the beginning of 1981 had other priorities so that projects such as these were given neither sufficient encouragement nor funding.

The Newfoundland Greenhome

The Newfoundland Greenhome was designed as a low-energy, passive solar home to meet the cool and cloudy conditions prevalent in Newfoundland. Priority was given to superinsulation, with secondary consideration to solar gain and the least to thermal mass. This decision, as John Evans says, turned out to be a wise one for a climate which experiences long periods of overcast weather during the heating season.

It was felt that in a cold, foggy climate, a highly insulated living space was necessary to minimize heat loss. To this end, the superinsulation features of the Saskatchewan Conservation House were duplicated. Double-wall construction was used and the walls were insulated to R40 and ceilings to R60. Care was taken to effect a continuous vapour barrier and an air-to-air heat exchanger was installed to provide fresh air to the living area. Other conservation features included the use of an insulated, preserved wood foundation; the elimination of windows on the north side of the house; the use of earth berms on the north, east and west; and air-lock entries on all doors.

On the other hand, even on overcast days there was a potential for a significant amount of solar gain if large areas of glazing could be provided. This object was accomplished by designing a large solar greenhouse attached to, but thermally separate from, the living area. In a unique feature, 90% of the house windows are located in a corrugated south wall which also acts as the north wall of the greenhouse. The staggered orientation of these windows not only makes an interesting bay window effect, but also allows sunshine to enter the house all day long, as the sun changes position in the sky.

Initially, the house was composed of two distinct zones: the superinsulated living area, which utilized direct solar radiation through the windows and skylights, and a surrounding

Photographs by John Evans

Designers: John Evans, Robert E. Mellin
Location: St. John's, Newfoundland
Latitude: 47°N
Design temperature: −15°C
Degree days: 4877 C°
Size of house: 220m²
Size of greenhouse: 50m²
Year of construction: 1980
Glazing material: 3mm acrylic

Comments: This greenhome consists of a superinsulated living area with a large greenhouse covering the entire south wall of the house. The greenhouse encloses a large garden and also serves to buffer the south-facing house windows. No gardening is done during the winter months.

Fig. 342 *Interior of greenhouse showing staggered windows*

envelope of spaces which utilized indirect solar radiation. This envelope consisted of the greenhouse, a solar attic which was connected to the greenhouse by operable vents, and a thermal storage bin beneath the floor of the living room. Air heated in the greenhouse would rise through the vents into the attic where a fan-driven vent and duct system would force it down through the rock storage and back to the greenhouse at a rate of 1500 cubic feet per minute.

The rock storage bin (which had a 50 cubic metre volume) was insulated on the sides and the bottom, but was not insulated from the living room floor directly above it.

The original intent was that heat from the storage would rise convectively, and passively warm the family room floor. Additional heat to the living area was to be provided by direct solar radiation and from two air-tight woodstoves — one on each floor.

Summer cooling was to be provided to the greenhouse by opening low vents along the south wall as well as the east and west doors. The vents to the attic were also opened during these periods where the excess heat was expected to escape through two large gable openings.

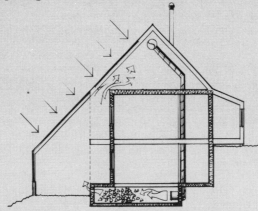

Fig. 343 *The way the system was intended to function*

During the first year of use, however, it became apparent that there were problems with this original design and, therefore, changes were made to correct the errors.

It was found that the indirect solar gain system (the heat envelope) failed to add to the heating of the house. Nevertheless, due to the conservation methods employed, the house functioned very satisfactorily. No auxiliary heating was required for the living area up to December 1 and after March 31. During the winter months only about two thirds of a cord of low quality balsam firewood was burned in the wood stoves. On sunny winter days the stoves are used for about four hours a day; on cloudy winter days, a maximum of eight hours per day.

The indirect gain "envelope" was abandoned after the first winter of operation for a couple of reasons. On bright sunny days in December, January, and February the temperature in the solar attic seldom rose above 25°C. As a result, the thermostat had to be set down to 22°C in order for the fan/storage system to operate. On a day of full sun, the fan operated only a maximum of three hours per day. Because of the low temperature of the solar heated air and the short periods of fan operation, the rock storage never rose above 15°C — well below the room temperature of most houses.

Since the house is in a climate which features long periods of overcast weather during the winter, there were often periods of up to several weeks in which no heat was added to the rock storage. The temperature of the rock storage, during these periods, would drop to as low as 8°C. Under these conditions, since the store was not insulated from the family room, the rock storage tended to withdraw heat from the house rather than add to it.

A more serious negative effect of the indirect solar heating system was that it caused extensive frost accumulation in the attic. Moisture in the humid air which was circulating up from the greenhouse apparently condensed and accumulated on the cold, inside surface of the north slope of the roof. Because of its orientation, this slope received no sunshine during the four winter months.

Often during sunny winter days, the temperature inside the attic would rise to above freezing so that the accumulated frost would begin to melt. This water then streamed down into the north wall of the house. These problems were solved by abandoning the indirect solar gain system. The fan was disconnected and the openings between the greenhouse and the attic were closed off with insulated panels which could be removed during the summer. The crushed rock was removed from the storage bin and the living room floor was insulated to RSI-7.04 (R-40).

The modified winter arrangement now consists of three separate spaces: the living space, the greenhouse, and the solar attic. The superinsulated living space has continually performed satisfactorily and was relatively unaffected by the changes.

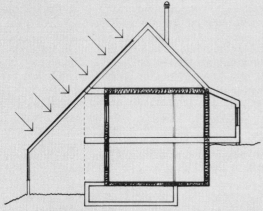

Fig. 345 The current system

The greenhouse no longer supplies heat to the living space but it continues in the more important role of protecting the multi-windowed south wall from the wind.

Another modification to the living space system was the removal of the air-to-air heat exchanger. Although it was installed due to the concern about air quality and excess moisture in a tightly sealed house, these two problems failed to develop. Relative humidity was consistently between 50% and 58% and the air quality was high. John concludes that sufficient ventilation is induced by the three chimneys, although some energy, in the form of heated air, is inevitably lost.

The Greenhouse

Under the modified arrangements described, the greenhouse of the Newfoundland Greenhome serves more as a space for plant growth than as a solar collector. Because the greenhouse area was to be occupied, the tall, 45° slope of the south face was glazed with 3mm acrylic for reasons of safety.

The glazing of the greenhouse presented few problems because it was decided that a few leaks or cracks were tolerable. Each vertical section is composed of two overlapping 2.5m x .55m sheets of acrylic. It is installed in a concave fashion so that rain will run off down the centre of the acrylic and away from the supporting redwood rafters.

Angled aluminum caps were screwed into the rafters and serve to grip the edges of neighbouring sheets of acrylic and maintain the concave format.

Ventilation   Initially the greenhouse was ventilated during the summer by opening low vents along the south wall as well as the east and west doors. Top ventilation was carried out through the attic and out the two large openings in the gables. This system proved to be inadequate and led to overheating in the second floor living area.

Now that the attic is shut off from the greenhouse, top venting is effected by opening a door at the west end of the greenhouse at the second level and through a newly installed window in the top east end of the greenhouse. So far these changes have resulted in adequate cross ventilation and comfortable temperatures.

Moisture   The moisture problems associated with circulating the greenhouse air through the attic, fan, and rock storage were solved when the described modifications were made. The greenhouse is now separate from both the attic and the living space.

The moist greenhouse air does not cause problems either in or on the house. The reasons are obvious when it is remembered that water vapour always condenses on the coldest surface. In this case the glazing is always the coolest surface.

This phenomenon is most clearly seen in the early morning after a cold winter night. As much as 6mm of frost may have accumulated on the inner surface of the glazing. This amounts to a considerable volume of water when spread over 110m² of acrylic. By 9:45 a.m. most of this frost has melted off. The water runs down the glazing and collects in the gutters and hence it is channelled back to the greenhouse soil. This little cycle repeats itself every night but the house wall stays completely dry because it is a much warmer surface.

The Garden   The greenhouse is unheated and relies entirely on the sun for warmth. John has divided the year essentially into four quarters from the point of view of growing strategy.

From December through February both John Evans and his greenhouse rest. There are no plants growing during this time. Fall-harvested vegetables like carrots, beets, potatoes, turnips, leeks, and chicory are buried in 300mm deep trenches during the winter. The moist greenhouse soil keeps the vegetables in excellent condition and they remain available in the unfrozen soil throughout the winter. The crowns of the chicory roots are placed upright and covered by 150mm of soil, which is in turn covered by 300mm of leaves. In February and March the soil starts to warm and the chicory sprouts up through the 15cm of soil. They are harvested at this time — the sprouts make a marvelous winter salad. The sprouts are sold in the stores under the name of "French Endive."

Spring season extends from early March through May. At the beginning of March, carrots, beets, radishes, lettuce, and cauliflower are seeded directly in the greenhouse soil.

Harvest extends from early April through mid-June. Onion seeds are started in flats in the house and transplanted into the greenhouse around mid-April, and the harvesting of small green onions starts in early June.

The summer season starts in early June with the planting of sweet corn and the transplanting of tomatoes, peppers, and cucumbers. These plants start producing in early August and finish in late September or at the time of the first hard frost.

The fall season begins in early September with the transplanting into the greenhouse of mature plants of Swiss chard and broccoli from the outside garden. These vegetables often continue to produce right through until Christmas time.

University of Saskatchewan Solar Greenhouse

This greenhouse was developed and tested by the Department of Mechanical Engineering at the University of Saskatchewan as part of a program to investigate features applicable to an energy conserving greenhouse. A large structure was built to duplicate the conditions of a commercial greenhouse and to more readily assess the commercial viability of the features incorporated into the design.

The greenhouse is built on a treated wood, post foundation and consists of tubular steel arch ribs and wood framed endwalls. The south endwall is double glazed with fibreglass reinforced plastic (FRP) and the inner glazing of the arch is also FRP. The outer glazing on the arch portion consists of a large polyethylene sheet, UV-treated, which is supported by inflating the space between the glazings by means of a fan.

The inflated polyethylene outer glazing has some benefits and drawbacks that are not immediately apparent. A major drawback is that it must be replaced every three years. However, since it costs only about $100 (in 1981 Canadian dollars) for this size greenhouse, it is acceptable economically.

Another drawback is that polyethylene is virtually impossible to repair. The simplest way to repair rips, it was found, is to use duct tape. It will hold for a relatively long period, but will eventually come off after weathering.

The fan allows the polyethylene layer to be inflated so that it is either extremely hard and stiff or so that it can flap a little. This flexibility eliminates the problems of wind damage and snow buildup. In high winds, the polyethylene is completely inflated, presenting a smooth hard surface. If snow is falling, it is allowed to become more flexible so that the snow is shaken off.

Photographs by Greg Schoenau

Designers: G. W. Schoenau, G. H. Green, R. W. Besant, E. A. Arinze
Location: Saskatoon, Saskatchewan
Latitude: 52°N
Design Temperature: −35°C
Degree days: 6077 C°
Size: 12.8m x 8.1m
Cost: $11,310 (CDN)
Year of construction: 1980
Glazing materials: FRP and polyethylene

Comments: The University of Saskatchewan solar greenhouse is a commercial size greenhouse built for research purposes. Conservation features included an insulated north wall and kneewalls, an air-lock entry, perimeter insulation, and a night shuttering system in which movable insulation is located in the space between the glazings.

Because it was designed as a commercial tomato production greenhouse, the structure was oriented with its long direction along a north-south line to reduce the shading effects from tall tomato plants. Research has indicated that a 10% reduction in light results in a 10% decrease in tomato productivity.

Greenhouse Construction Costs	
Basic structure	4090
Heating and ventilating system	2610
Hydroponics system	750
Cost of Nonconserving Greenhouse	$7450
Automated arch shutter system	1400
Added insulation	380
Cost of Conserving Greenhouse	$9230
Heat exchanger	710
Active thermal storage system	1370
Cost of U.S.S.G.	$11,310

There are six energy conserving features in the University of Saskatchewan Solar Greenhouse (USSG). Some do not add to the cost of construction, while others require a significant initial outlay of money.

1. Insulated Reflective North Wall

Particularly in the case of this north-south oriented quonset greenhouse, very little sunlight comes through the north wall, yet it can account for a considerable portion of the heat loss. This wall was consequently insulated to RSI-3.52 (R20) and a reflective surface applied to the inner wall to reflect light back onto the plants. The east and west kneewalls were also insulated to RSI-3.52 (R20).

2. Air-lock Entry

A small (2.4m x 2.4m) porch was built on the north side to act as an air-lock entry to reduce air infiltration through the door. The porch also serves as a storage area. The walls and ceiling of this porch were insulated with fiberglass batts to RSI-3.52 (R20).

3. Air-to-Air Heat Exchanger

Because of the nature of this greenhouse and the care taken to reduce infiltration at such points as the north entry, the University of Saskatchewan Greenhouse experiences only about $1/2$ air change per hour. This rate caused concern that moisture levels would be too high and CO_2 levels too low for optimum plant production. Therefore, a controlled ventilation system was installed to vent humid stale air and admit fresh air to increase the CO_2 level. To avoid merely dumping warm greenhouse air and bringing in cold outside air, a heat recovery system was designed using an air-to-air heat exchanger. This device, also developed at the University of Saskatchewan, is an insulated plywood box containing stretched polyethylene sheets placed to created 55 thin (12.7mm), parallel air spaces. A fan blows fresh outside air through every other space in one direction, and stale greenhouse air through the alternate spaces in the other direction. By this means, the warm greenhouse air gives up some of its heat to the incoming outside air.

Due to the high moisture levels in the greenhouse and the coolness of the outside air, continuous use of such a heat exchanger will result in frost and ice buildup, eventually plugging it up. To try to avoid this problem, a single glazed, double pass solar collector was installed on top of the heat exchanger to raise the temperature of the incoming outside air by 20°C to 30°C on sunny days.

4. Perimeter Insulation

In an energy conserving greenhouse, the heat loss from the perimeter of the greenhouse can be substantial. To reduce heat loss by conduction through the ground, insulation was placed around the perimeter of the greenhouse. Layers of flat polystyrene were buried just below ground level with a slight slope to permit drainage of moisture away from the greenhouse. 102mm (4 in) of the rigid insulation was used and it extends the width of one sheet (1.22m) out from the edge of the wall.

5. Thermal Storage

Initially, an insulated rock storage bed was located beneath the greenhouse floor to store any excess heat during the heating season and to help prevent overheating in the summer. During early experiments, air was continually circulated through the rock storage bed in one direction.

Later, a water thermal storage system was developed to replace the rock storage bed. It was thought that the cost of a water system would be somewhat less and that it would offer better protection from freezing for the plants. The otherwise wasted space beneath the five plant benches was used for this scheme and the water was stored in both polyethylene bags and plastic pails. The sides of each bench were closed in and air was fan-forced into one end of the bench and out the other.

Finally, the sides of the benches were removed and black pails filled with water were used under the plants as plant trays. No air was actively circulated through these passive thermal energy storage pails.

6. Insulating Night Shutters

This addition was the most innovative part of the experimental system and, it turns out, the most cost effective. It was known that shutters make a substantial contribution to energy savings, but there was numerous problems with the existing schemes. Exterior shutters were rejected because of the exposure to weather. Shutters or curtains inside the greenhouse were too often expensive and cumbersome to implement. Condensation on the glazing due to air leakage around interior curtains would be a very difficult problem in the cold, northerly climate of Saskatoon.

To avoid all of these problems the U.S.S.G. shutters were designed to operate between the glazings. The arch shutter consisted of curtains made of fibreglass roll insulation (one curtain for each side) which is drawn up in the inflated space between the FRP and the polyethylene glazing layers.

The shutter material is commercially available metal-building insulation. It is spun fibreglass bonded to a layer of white vinyl. Aluminum-backed fibreglass was tried but it was found that, due to the constant bending, the aluminum soon ripped. 89mm (3.5 in.) insulation was used with a value of RSI-2.11 (R12). It is available in rolls 1.22m wide and up to 30m long.

The arch shutter consists of two separate shutters, each 6.1m wide and 12.2m in length. The shutters were made by taping together the individual strips of insulation along the joints (every 1.22m). A header board was attached to the end of the shutters and ropes attached to the board to pull the shutters up over the arch of the quonset greenhouse. A steel pipe mounted along the middle axis of the greenhouse above the FRP and below the polyethylene cover provided a means of winding up the rope to pull the shutters over the arch. Originally, a hand crank was used; later a small motor was installed.

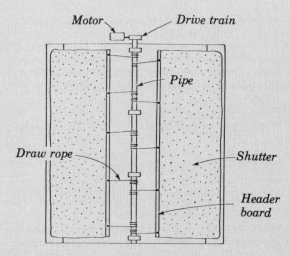

Fig. 347 Top view

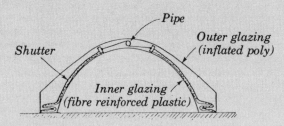

Fig. 348 Elevation

This fibreglass shutter system was a serendipitous discovery. Initially, it was thought some sort of roll would have to be used at the bottom to roll up the insulation as the curtain was lowered. Not only was this method unreliable and complicated, but it was found to be unnecessary when it was discovered that the insulation would naturally zigzag itself into a nice pile as the curtain was lowered. A subsequent experiment indicates that the individual strips of insulation need not even be taped together to form a continuous curtain. It was found that when a curtain consisting of unattached strips of insulation reached the peak of the arch, all the strips nicely came together to form a continuous piece.

Fig. 349 End view with curtain piled at bottom

The south wall, which was constructed of 2 x 6 lumber and which consequently had a 140mm air space between the two layers of FRP, was fitted with a similar movable insulation system. In this case, the fibreglass rolls were pulled straight up in this hollow space. This system, it was found, was not very effective since the 89mm thick insulation hung loosely in the 140mm hollow space and allowed convection currents to establish which carried heat away from the greenhouse. During cold nights this heat loss resulted in condensation on the inside surface. In order for this system to be effective, the insulation must seat against the inner glazing. The arch ridge is a perfect shape for this use. In the case of a flat, vertical, glazed wall, it would have to be sloped slightly toward the inside, to allow the insulation to lay against the inner glazing when the curtain is in use.

Results

The performance of the USSG was compared to the performance of three similar nearby greenhouses which did not incorporate the energy conserving features. As you are probably expecting, almost all of the energy conserving features turned out to be worth while even for a commercial greenhouse which must carefully weigh initial costs against output and operating costs.

Figure 350 shows the performance of the USSG with and without shutters in the spring (March-April) and Figure 351 shows the performance during winter (December-January). With the shutters in place there was a substantial reduction in the energy used for heating the greenhouse in both tests. In fact, the shutter system, combined with the reduced infiltration and the perimeter and north wall insulation, decreased the heating needs by 60%.

The thermal storage system was somewhat less effective. The March-April chart shows us that with the shutters closed, no backup heat was needed at night when the outside temperatures were up to 10°C lower than inside temperatures. On sunny spring and fall days, when the greenhouse would otherwise overheat, we can conclude that the thermal storage system will help to prevent overheating and contribute to reduced energy consumption at night.

In the winter months, however, the thermal storage provided no contribution to night-time energy consumption. Considering costs versus energy saved, it was felt that the fan-driven

thermal storage system had too long a payback period to be economically viable for a commercial greenhouse. Researchers speculated that a strictly passive storage system, consisting of black pails full of water placed beneath benches to receive as much direct sunlight as possible, would be 75% as effective as the active system they were using and would have a much lower initial cost and hence, a more attractive payback period.

A benefit of the thermal storage system as tested was that in the event of a power failure

during the heating season, the greater mass lessened the chance of frost damage. The many gallons of water had stored enough energy to radiate heat to prevent the plants from freezing while the gas furnace was not running.

A surprising result was the discovery that the air-to-air heat exchanger was unnecessary during most of the year as there was enough natural air infiltration to provide CO_2 and control moisture. Even with the lowered rates of infiltration, carbon dioxide levels were satisfactory and excess moisture was never a problem.

Crop Performance While the conservation features proved to make economic sense when comparing initial costs to long term energy savings, the most important function of a commercial greenhouse is to produce a satisfactory crop. Tomatoes were grown under close to identical conditions in four greenhouses.

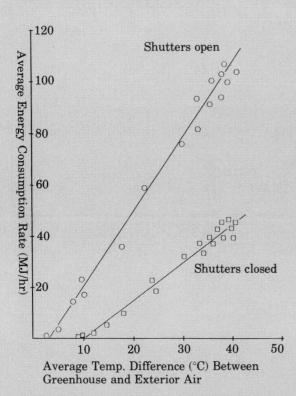

Fig. 350 Effect of shutters on night time energy consumption (March-April)

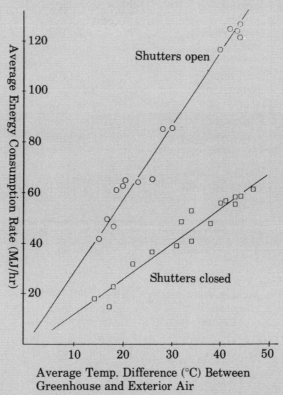

Fig. 351 Effect of shutters on night time energy consumption (Dec.-Jan.)

Comparison of Greenhouse Tomato Production			
Greenhouse	Market-able (kg)	Un-market-able (kg)	Total (kg)
USSG - Double Glazing - Thermal Storage	744	71	815
House A - Single Glazing - No Thermal Storage	907	116	1023
House B - Double Glazing - No Thermal Storage	739	168	907
House C - Double Glazing - No Thermal Storage	575	234	809

All of the greenhouses were constructed with metal arches similar to the University of Saskatchewan Solar Greenhouse. The USSG was double glazed with FRP and polyethylene. All of the others were glazed with polyethylene over the arches. House A had single glazing, Houses B and C were double glazed inflated structures.

The results show that the USSG performed well compared with the other commercial greenhouses. It is interesting to note that House A had the highest productivity, which was probably due to the fact that the single layer of polyethylene has a higher solar transmittance (92%) than either the double-polyethylene structure (83%) or the FRP-polyethylene glazing of the solar greenhouse (77%). While House A was the most productive greenhouse, the energy consumption of this single glazed structure was on the order of six times that of a double glazed solar greenhouse with night shutters.

Comparing the USSG to House C, we see that they produced about the same total quantity of tomatoes, but that House C produced considerably more unmarketable produce. Most of these were misshapen, which is usually caused by thermal stressing of the plants. Due to the increased thermal mass and the greater tightness of the USSG, the plants therein enjoyed a more uniform and stable environment.

Finally, the crops harvested in late May and early June were approximately twice as large as those in December. This again suggests that lighting levels and length of day are the most important factors.

Payback Period for Energy Conservation Features of USSG

The costs shown are in 1980 Canadian dollars. Energy costs are assumed to be: natural gas — $1.94/GJ; Propane — $6.25/GJ; electricity — $9.05/GJ. The payback period assumes that one of these three fuels is used to provide supplemental heating.

An annual increase of 5% in the cost of fuel was assumed. Since the escalation is now greater than that, and energy costs are increasing faster than capital costs, actual payback periods will be less than shown.

Conservation Feature	Added Cost	Annual Energy Savings (gigajoules)	Payback Period - Years		
			Natural Gas	Propane	Electricity
North Wall & Side Wall Insulation	$ 130	60.2	0.8	0.3	0.3
Arch Shutter System	$1400	151.0	2.9	0.9	0.9
Heat Exchanger	$ 710	37.2	6.1	2.1	2.0
Active Thermal Storage System	$1400	19.5	24.7	6.9	6.8
Passive Thermal Storage System	N/A	N/A	3.8*	1.1*	1.1*

*Estimate

West Vancouver Greenhouse

This freestanding solar greenhouse has a reflector/insulating shutter mounted above the south-facing glazings. This reflector acts as an insulating shutter in winter to keep the heat in at night. During the day it reflects additional heat and light from the low winter sun into the greenhouse. In the summer the reflector can be lowered during the day to shade the greenhouse.

Fig. 353 *Greenhouse with shutter raised*

The greenhouse is 2.6m high. It has a concrete foundation and earth floor. The south side is double glazed with tempered glass, the lower glazing set at a 60° angle and the roof glazing set at 25°. The north and endwalls are insulated to RSI-3.5 (R-20) to reduce heat loss.

Thermal storage is provided by two sets of water-filled metal storage cylinders, normally used as air conditioning ducts. Each is 250mm in diameter, with the front set of ten cylinders being 0.7m high and the rear set of fourteen

Photographs courtesy of Solar Applications and Research
Designer: Solar Applications and Research
Builder: Northwest Design
Location: West Vancouver, British Columbia
Latitude: 49°
Design temperature: −7°C
Degree days: 3007
Size: 3.2m x 4.8m
Cost: $400 (CDN) — including labour and design
Year of construction: 1978
Glazing material: Tempered glass.

Comments: This greenhouse in the cloudy Vancouver climate, employs roof glazing and an exterior, reflective roof flap. It is operated year-round and uses water-filled air conditioning ducts for heat storage.

being 1.7m high. In all, 1560kg of water is provided to store excess solar energy on clear days — about 84 *l* of water per square meter of south-facing glazing. The storage cylinders are painted a rust red colour.

The greenhouse has been in operation since the summer of 1978. During the winter, in the months of January, February and March, it sustained an average daily indoor temperature of about 16°C, even though the outside temperature dropped well below freezing. Electric heat was used for only about four hours on each of two days for the whole winter, for a total cost of about 25¢ in electric backup.

A variety of indoor and outdoor plants have done well in this greenhouse. Particularly successful have been flowering maples and citrus fruits such as dwarf lemons and oranges. Numerous flowers and a variety of vegetable and seedlings have been grown.

Fig. 354 *North wall at greenhouse showing thermal storage*

and tied in place. Eight 200 l drums are used for heat storage. If the insulating shutters are operated regularly, the greenhouse does not freeze in the winter. With the vents open in the summer, temperatures in the greenhouse are not more than 3 C° above the outside temperature. Excess heat is vented into the living room via a kitchen/basement window heat loop and the greenhouse provides 10% of the home heating needs during the winter months.

Fig. 356 *Greenhouse interior in February. Kitchen windows are open to allow excess greenhouse heat into house. Note roof glazing to allow sunlight to pass through kitchen windows. Water is stored in the black drums against the north wall.*

Photographs by Joe Crachiola

Builders: Mike and Irmgard Gelletly
Location: Ypsilanti, Michigan
Latitude: 42°N
Design temperature: −19°C
Degree days: 3478 C°
Size: 14.6m²
Cost: $400.00 (US)
Year of construction: 1977
Glazing material: recycled storm windows, FRP

Comments: This is an inexpensive greenhouse making use of recycled materials (including the glazing and the fibreglass insulation). One half of the cost of the greenhouse is due to the excavation and concrete foundation. The endwalls and the roof are opaque and insulated except for the portion of the roof above the kitchen windows where a recycled storm window is used as a glazed vent. All glazed areas are covered with styrofoam insulation at night: the roof with a sliding panel on the inside of the greenhouse, and the south wall with panels laid on the outside of the glazing

APPENDIX

GLOSSARY

Air-lock The space created to reduce the amount of heat lost each time an exterior door is opened. An additional door is installed so that only one door is open at a time, reducing the direct flow of exterior air to the house.

Air-To-Air Heat Exchanger A means of extracting much of the heat from stale air that is exhausted from a building. While the stale air is removed from a building, fresh air is drawn in. Concurrently, the heat is transferred from the exhausted air to the incoming air.

Butt Joints Any joint made by fastening two members together without overlapping.

Convection The transfer of heat energy by the motion of fluids which are carrying the heat; fluids can be either liquids or gases.

Clamping Bars Bars that rest on top of glass to hold it to rafter.

Cripples "Half-Studs" used to support window and door frames.

Conduction The movement of heat through a material by molecular agitation.

Degree Days A measurement of the total number of degrees occurring each day below a set temperature. Also shown as DD.

Design Temperature The lowest temperature to be expected during the heating season; the time at which the heat loss from a building is at its maximum rate.

Earth Berm A mound of earth strategically designed and placed to deflect winds away from a building.

Expansion Joint A joint in a concrete or masonry structure designed to permit expansion without damage to the structure.

Fascia Board A finished piece of wood around the face of eaves and roof projections.

Flange A projecting edge, rib or rim.

Glazing A covering of transparent or translucent material which allows light to enter a structure. While permitting solar gain to a space, glazing also slows the flow of heat to the exterior. Commonly used materials include glass, plastics and fibreglass. Simply stated a greater number of layers of any material employed will result in reduced heat loss.

Grade The ground surface around the foundation.

Greenhouse Hall of Fame An institution devoted to the commemoration of rarities of greenhouse technology such as Krazy Glue construction, beer bottle heat storage and, of course, the ever famous greenhouse camper car trailer.

Gusset A plywood (in most cases) support used to strengthen two joining members.

Header A wood member at right angles to a series of joists or rafters where the joist or rafters terminate.

Infiltration The uncontrolled movement of air into a structure through cracks and holes in the shell of a building.

Insecticidal Soap Soap applied as a spray, the soap's fatty acids have damaging effects on some detrimental insects such as whiteflies and aphids.

Insolation Short for *in*coming *sol*ar radi*ation*.

Inter-glazing Insulation Insulation placed in between two layers of glazing.

Jamb The side post or lining of a doorway; window or opening.

Joist One of a series of horizontal wood members (usually 2 x n) used to support a floor, ceiling or roof.

Kneewall A short wall used to close off space that has inadequate head room.

Ledger Plate A strip of lumber fastened along the bottom of the side of a beam on which joists rest.

Mullions A bar installed vertically in frame between doors or windows.

Mortise Hole in a framework designed to receive the tenon of a board or plank to form a joint.

Photosynthesis The process powered by light which involves plants using carbon dioxide and water to produce some simple plant sugars.

Pest Controls *Biological pest controls* involve the use of beneficial insect predators and parasites to kill or control the insect pests. *Cultural pest control* involves the use of music and the visual arts to eradicate harmful insects. Aphids have been found to be particularly susceptible to the music of nineteenth century Russian composers and to the visual art of Andy Warhol, the Group of Seven and Toller Cranston. Cultural controls also presuppose a knowledge of the life cycle of both the plants and pests. *Mechanical pest controls* involve such steps as vacuuming the insects into oblivion, letting the greenhouse freeze during the winter, and squashing them by sheer manual force.

Reflective Shield Panels with a reflective face angled to reflect light into the greenhouse. It can also be used as exterior insulation.

Root Zone Heating Heating at root level usually making use of warm water passing through pipes.

Racking Lateral shifting of a structural section due to a horizontal pressure due to such factors as wind and bulldozers.

Rabbet A groove cut in the surface along the edge of a board, plank, or other timber. The recess in a door frame to receive the door.

Strip Footing A concrete slab poured on undisturbed soil around the perimeter of a foundation, used to support poured concrete or concrete block walls.

Slab On Grade A concrete floor poured at ground level for houses or buildings without a basement.

Soffit The underside of building element such as roof overhang.

Screeding Levelling concrete by pulling a board across forms set up for this purpose.

Stratification Natural convections resulting in the accumulation of the hottest material at the top of a container or house.

Thermal Mass The amount of heat storage capacity available in a given material or assembly. Thermal mass will absorb excess heat generated during the day and store it until the ambient temperature drops; most commonly water, concrete or rocks.

Toe Nailing Nailing at an angle to the first member (such as a stud) to ensure penetration into a second member.

Vapour Barrier Material used to retard the passage of water vapour or moisture.

Weatherization The process of preparing a building to deal with the weather's fluctuations in the most efficient manner.

Active thermal storage systems

We've occasionally referred to the use of a separate heat storage area using fans and ducts for large attached greenhouses. Some of our survey examples also employ an active thermal storage system, as this is called. Greg Allen, a solar designer and consultant with Allan-Drerup-White in Toronto, contributes the following introduction to such systems.

If a greenhouse is optimized for plant growth (i.e. most of the solar radiation is received by plants) most of the solar energy is converted to heat and convects off the plants to heat up the air. In this case the heat transfer to passive storage elements is limited to natural convection and some radiant heat transfer — which may be insufficient to prevent overheating. This will result in the need for ventilation and the consequent loss of solar heating potential. It is possible with forced convection to store and retrieve excess solar gain, thereby improving the controllability and solar utility of a greenhouse.

Many such systems have been used successfully. In attached greenhouses, the greenhouse may perform a similar function to a solar collector in an active solar heating system. If there is sufficient thermal mass in the house, warm air may be circulated directly throughout the house from the greenhouse or a convectional storage system may be incorporated.

The greenhouse may be treated as a separate thermal activity with its own thermal storage and circulation system whether it is attached or separate from a building. Many configurations for delivering heat to and from storage are possible.

Storage media may be rocks, water, masonry or latent heat storage materials. Rocks have the advantage of being inert, inexpensive and having a built-in heat transfer capability which will allow thermal stratification to occur — an advantage that is illustrated by a reverse-flow system to input and extract heat. Water storage is considerably more compact and may also be inexpensive but requires a heat transfer mechanism such as small containers to create a large surface/volume ratio, or a finned tube air-to-water heat exchanger. Masonry such as a concrete floor can serve as part of the structure as well as for heat storage by running a grid of small ducts through it. Latent heat storage in the form of specially formulated mineral salts is attractive because of its compactness and is commercially available in stackable form to provide the necessary convective heat transfer surface area (e.g. Saskatchewan minerals, Thermol 81) but they are more costly.

It is necessary to size the storage and air handling equipment to control temperature swing in the greenhouse. Typically, about 6800 kJ/day per square meter of south facing glazing area should be stored and the air handling should carry 1700 to 2300 kJ/hr. per square meter of glazing. For an 11°C temperature difference between supply and return, this translates to 75 to 110 CFM/m² of glazing.

For attached greenhouses, the simplest and generally most cost-effective active heat management technique is simply to run a blower when temperatures in the greenhouse rise above a thermostat set-point to take air from the peak of the greenhouse and distribute it to the house. In the case of forced air heating in the house, this may be accomplished by dumping air next to or into a return air duct and running the furnace fan. A low grill with a back draft damper is required to close the loop to the house. Unless there is a large amount of solar gain, including windows in the house (in excess of 10% of floor area,) the thermal mass of the house should be sufficient to prevent excessive temperature swings.

As has been mentioned, the greenhouse can be considered a collector in an active solar heating configuration with the various modes being operated with blowers and dampers. In retrofits, greenhouses in tandem with collectors have been used and the storage located below the greenhouse. These systems tend to be expensive and complex but at least your "collector" is good for more than heat. Attention must be paid to minimizing night loss and providing some heat to the greenhouse as required, though at a greater tolerance than the house.

A very attractive system is to duct air through masonry walls and floor. We have used galvanized downspouts, on 200mm (8″) centres buried in concrete and manifolded at two ends to carry the air flow. (Caution: they float in concrete so must be anchored down and tied to re-mesh.) Heat transfer back to the greenhouse is via the slab.

Rock storage systems are quite effective in controlling temperature swing. The warm air introduced at one end gives up its heat readily and will return to the greenhouse at cool temperatures until the storage is practically full (i.e. all the rocks are up to the higher temperature.) Reversing flow direction for returning heat is advantageous as the warm temperatures are made available immediately. It is possible to have a unidirectional flow whereby air is continuously circulated through the rocks and the time it takes the input heat to pass through the rocks is 12 hrs. — tricky to size however. For reversing flow through the rocks, we suggest a reversing damper. If the rock storage is below the greenhouse, special care must be taken to avoid water accumulating in the rocks (waterproofing and a drain).

In place of rocks, containerized water or mineral salt trays may be used but surface area is critical so that their effectiveness and ability to stratify heat is reduced. For water, beer-bottle size would work nicely and 50-gal. drums are useless. Various latent heat products are advertised in a variety of sources but they should change state at low temperatures (19°-24°C; 67-75°F) in order to limit temperature swing.

Summer ventilation is a critical element of greenhouse mechanics and can often make use of the same blower used for storage. Air changes and humidity control may also be integrated or at least interact with the mechanicals for thermal storage.

The ideas we have here sketched are inadequate for the layman to design his/her own system. Some engineering and knowledge of construction and mechanical system technology is necessary to do a competent job, so you are urged to seek assistance and thoroughly understand the calculations involved and the construction details.

Automatic Vent Opener

You may be able to find these in the greenhouse supply catalogues and at specialty Energy or Greenhouse stores. Here are the major manufacturers.

Bayliss Autovents Ltd., *Compton Street, Ashbourne, Derbyshire, England DE6 1DA*

Bramen Company, Inc. *(Importers of British "Thermofor"), Box 70, Salem, Massachusetts 01970*

Dalen Products Inc. *(Solarvents), 201 Sherlake Drive, Knoxville, Tennessee 37922*

Heat Motors Inc., *635 W. Grandview Avenue, Sierra Madre, California 91024*

Glass

Glass manufacturers or major glass distributors will frequently have batches of glass which are slightly imperfect, the wrong size, or simply not selling. It is not unusual to find tempered glass (for instance, non-standard-sized patio door glass) which a glass distributor is anxious to unload. This is a great source for very reasonably priced glass.

But remember that any truly good deal has to benefit both parties. You want glass at a low price, that's easy enough. The glass distributor wants to get rid of a large batch of glass, quickly, with no fuss. Do not expect to drive up to a glass distributor and buy eight or ten sheets of glass for next to nothing. Most often there will be dozens of uniformly sized sheets of glass

that the distributor wants to move. Get together with your friends and neighbors or place an ad in the newspaper to try to contact people who may want to split a large batch of glass with you. Once you've organized your buying group, then contact the glass distributors. Don't be picky about glass size, either. At the prices we have in mind you can afford to take whatever is available and adjust your greenhouse size accordingly. We've shown you elsewhere how you can glue two pieces of glass end-to-end to "stretch" them.

To locate potential glass sources, look in the yellow pages under "Glass Manufacturers" or look for the retailers with the biggest ads. Remember that, since these are "dogs" a local glass shop is not likely to have them. You will have to look for them at glass manufacturers or their distributing divisions.

Manufactured double glazings. Sealed, double-glazed units can be custom ordered in any size from any glass shop. But we think you'll find that the cost of these units is prohibitive. They also eliminate the possibility of using our interglazing insulation system in the greenhouse.

Greenhouse and Horizontal Supplies

Many of the things you need for the greenhouse can be found at places like hardware stores and garden supply centres. However, some equipment, such as trickle irrigation systems, may be harder to locate. Here is a list of only a few of the

many specialty greenhouse supply companies. Some of them claim to sell only to the commercial greenhouse industry, so tell them you're going to be selling your tomatoes.

Charley's Greenhouse Supply, *12815 N.E. 124th Street, Kirkland, Washington 98033*

Westcan Horticultural Specialists Ltd., *1900 - 11 Street S.E., Calgary, Alberta T2G 3G2*

Domestic Grower's Supply, *Box 809, Cave Junction, Oregon 97523*

Golden West Seeds, *1108 - 6 Street S.E., Calgary, Alberta T2G 2Y2*

Equipment Consultants and Sales, *2241 Dunwin Drive, Erin Mills, Mississauga, Ontario L5L 1A3*

Harry Sharpe and Son Limited, *7028 MacPherson Avenue, Burnaby, B.C. V5J 4N4*

Heat Storage Containers

We have recommended flat red or blue metal containers which provide a large amount of surface area. Metal 5-gal buckets are one option and can be easily stacked (use recycled buckets.) But remember that water, especially with calcium chloride, will corrode the buckets, so we recommend a polyethylene liner. Another option is to use tall, metal cylinders of about 26 gauge metal, such as air conditioning ducts. A Canadian manufacturer of these ducts is *SPIR-L-OK Industries Canada Limited, 1320 Vulcan Way, Richmond, B.C. V6V 1J2,* but such spiral pipe should be available from any sheet metal shop, which should also be able to custom make metal cylinders to your specifications, if you desire.

A convenient type of liner to use for the metal cylinders or buckets are polyethylene tubes usually sold to the food packaging industry. Look in the yellow pages under Plastic Products for a company that sells this type of plastic tubing.

Insulation

The insulation we recommend for filling the roof and wall cavities is fibreglass batt insulation. For insulating opaque vents and doors we recommend the use of extruded polystyrene (blue styrofoam) rigid insulation. To insulate beneath the floor and around the perimeter of the greenhouse use expanded polystyrene (white styrofoam) rigid insulation. This has a lower insulating value per unit thickness than the blue styrofoam, but it costs significantly less. To increase the RSI value in these underground areas simply increase the thickness of the white styrofoam insulation.

For the movable interglazing shutter look for metal building insulation. This is spun fiberglass with a vinyl backing and usually comes in 4 ft (1.22cm) widths, so you will have to cut it to fit between the south wall studs. Whether you use the $1^1/_2$ in (38mm) or $2^1/_2$ in (64mm) thickness will depend on the spacing of the south wall glazing and how much money you want to spend.

Remember that any fiberglass glazing has to be protected from the moist greenhouse air by a vapour barrier. The glazing acts as a vapour barrier for the south wall shutter and 6-mil polyethylene should be used as a vapour barrier in opaque walls and roofs.

Pest Controls

Many seed and greenhouse supply companies sell botanical insecticides such as diatamaceous earth and rotenone. (They also sell a lot of inorganic pesticides which you don't want to use in your greenhouse under any circumstances.)

Beneficial insects are available from specialty suppliers in the United States and Canada. While not exhaustive, here is a list of some North American sources:

Applied Bionomics Ltd., *8801 East Saanich Road, Sidney, B.C. V8L 1H3* *Encarsia formosa*, predatory mites, lacewings and other beneficial insects.

Better Yield Insects, *13310 Riverside Dr., E., Tecumseh, Ontario N8N 1B2* *Encarsia*, predatory mites, *Aphidoletes*, sticky traps.

William Dam Seeds, *West Flamboro, Ontario L0R 2K0* Rotenone dust, wettable rotenone, diatamaceous earth, insecticidal soap, Tanglefoot.

Eaton Valley Agricultural Service, *Box 25, Sawyerville, Quebec J0B 2A0* Insecticidal soap, Rotenone, diatamaceous earth, etc.

Fossil Flower, *463 Woodbine Ave., Toronto, Ontario M4E 2H5* Diatamaceous earth formulas and insectidal soap (sold through numerous outlets.) Also lady beetles, and trichogramma wasps.

Rincon-Vitova Insectaries Inc., *Box 95, Oak View, California 93022* Lacewings, lady beetles, trichogramma, predatory mites, *Encarsia*.

Safer Agro-Chem Ltd., *5271 Old West Saanich Road, RR 3, Victoria, B.C. V8X 3X1* Insecticidal soaps.

Plans

Plans for other greenhouses and greenhouse components can be obtained from the following:

Drawing Room Graphic Services Ltd. *Box 86627, North Vancouver, British Columbia V7L 4L2.* The seven greenhouse plans they have available are introduced in their book, *Solpan 3: Solar Greenhouses for Canada* ($4.50). They also sell a complete set of working drawings of the Sundance Greenhouse.

Solar Applications & Research Ltd., *3683 West 4th Avenue, Vancouver, British Columbia V6R 1P2.* Plans for attached greenhouse with exterior hinged reflective flap over roof glazing. $25.00.

Rodale Plans Department, *33 East Minor Street, Emmaus, Pennsylvania 18049* or **Rodale Plans c/o Rodale Press,** *125 Bermondsey Road, Toronto M4A 1X3 1G1.* Plans for a solar gardening shed (in which is included a greenhouse,) a solar growing frame, and insulating window shades.

Vegetable Crops Department Cornell University, *Ithaca, New York 14853*. A manual for building a plastic greenhouse. $2.00.

Solar Survival, *Cherry Hill Road, Harrisville, New Hampshire 03450*. Plans for a solar growing frame. $11.00.

Plastic Glazing Materials

Some of the greenhouse supply companies sell such glazing materials as fiberglass reinforced polyester (FRP) and polyethylene. If you shop for plastic glazing materials at local hardware stores or lumber yards make very certain that what you are buying includes an ultraviolet (UV) inhibitor and is intended for greenhouse or solar energy applications. FRP and polyethlyene without this protection will have a short life. Here are some manufacturers and major suppliers of plastic glazing materials. There are dealers for most of these products in most areas, look in the yellow pages under "Plastic Products".

Graham Products Limited, *Box 2000, Inglewood, Ontario L0N 1K0* "Excelite "FRP", "Exelac" UV-coating, accessories, fiberglass insulation.

Chemplast Inc., *150 Dey Road, Wayne, New Jersey 07470* "Llumar" polyester film, "Teflon" FEP film.

Filon Division Vistron Corporation, *12333 South Van Ness Ave., Hawthorne, California 90250*. Three types of FRP,

including one which is Tedlar-clad.

E.I. DuPont De Nemours & Co., *Films Division, Wilmington, Delaware 19898* "Tedlar" PVF film, "Mylar" polyester film; manufacturer of "Teflon" film distributed by Chemplast.

CY/RO Industries, *859 Berdan Avenue, Wayne, New Jersey 07470* "Acrylite SDP" also called "Exolite" double skinned acrylic and "Cyrolon SDP" double skinned polycarbonate rigid glazing material.

Chemacryl Plastics Limited, *360 Carlingview Drive, Rexdale, Ontario M9W 5X9* Canadian distributor of "Acrylite SDP" and "Cryolon SDP."

Kalwall Corporation, *88 Pine Street, Manchester, New Hampshire 03013* "Sun-Lite" FRP glazing manufacturer.

Solar Components Corporation, *Box 237, Manchester, New Hampshire 03105* Retail arm of Kalwall supplying "Sun-Lite" to U.S. market only. Also "Teflon".

Rohm and Haas Company, *Independence Mall West, Philadelphia, Pennsylvania 19105* "Plexiglass" acrylic sheets; "Tuffak-Twinwal" double skinned polycarbonate.

General Electric Company. *Appliance Division, Louisville, Kentucky 40225* "Lexan" polycarbonate sheets and film.

Seeds

Most seed companies list varieties in their catalogues which are suitable for a greenhouse garden. Some varieties are specially selected for growing under glass — look for the word "forcing" in the

variety name. There are dozens of good seed companies in the United States and Canada and we can't list them all here. If you've been gardening long you will already have your favourites. The selected list below is not meant to indicate our preferences, although we do particularly like William Dam who offers only untreated seeds and a good selection of European seeds and Chinese cabbage. We list the two British companies because they are sources for hard-to-find cool season crops (especially Suttons).

Abundant Life Seed Foundation, *Box 772, Port Townsend, Washington 98368*

Alberta Nurseries & Seeds Ltd., *Box 20, Bowden, Alberta T0M 0K0*

W. Atlee Burpee Co., *300 Park Avenue, Warminster, Pennsylvania 18974*

Thomas Butcher Ltd., *60 Wickham Road, Shirley, Croydon CR9 8AG, Surrey, England*

William Dam Seeds Limited, *West Flamboro, Ontario L0R 2K0*

Dominion Seed House *Georgetown, Ontario L7G 4A2*

J.L. Hudson, Seedsman, *Box 1058, Redwood City, California 94064*

McFayden Seeds, *Box 1800, Brandon, Manitoba R7A 6N4*

W. H. Perron & Co. Ltd., *Box 408, Ville de Laval, Quebec H7S 2A6*

Geo. W. Park Seed Co. Inc., *Box 31, Greenwood, South Carolina 29646*

Stokes Seeds Ltd., *Box 10, St. Catharines, Ontario L2R 6R6 3070 Stokes Building, Buffalo, New York 14240*

Sutton Seeds Ltd., *Hele Road, Torquay, Devon TQ2 7QJ, England*

T & T Seeds Ltd., *Box 1710, Winnipeg, Manitoba R3C 3P6*
Thompson & Morgan, *Box 100, Farmingdale, New Jersey 07727*
Vesey's Seeds Ltd., *York, Prince Edward Island C0A 1P0*
(We haven't listed Johnny's Selected Seeds only because they told us that they want to concentrate their growth (no pun intended) in the New England region.)

Further Reading

Windowsill Ecology: *Controlling Indoor Plant Pests with Beneficial Insects. William H. Jordan. Rodale Press, 229 pages.*
We hesitate to recommend an out of print book (this title was not listed in the 1982 Rodale Press catalogue) but we think this book is worth looking for. It suffered from perhaps having the second worst title Rodale Press has ever chosen (the worst was the Rodale paperback version of this same book: *What's Eating Your House Plants?*) This is one of the best popular books we've seen explaining the use of beneficial insects in the home — or greenhouse.

Fish Farming in Your Solar Greenhouse. *William Head and Jon Splane. Amity Foundation, Box 11048, Eugene, Oregon, 43 pages. $5.00 (U.S.)*
A report on work done in Oregon and elsewhere on raising fish in a solar greenhouse.

Carpentry in Building Construction.
John L. Feirer and Gilbert R. Hutchings.

Charles A. Bennett Company, 1120 pages.
Consult this or another standard carpentry text for further carpentry details and techniques.

The Super Insulated Retrofit Book.
Brian Marshall and Robert Argue. Renewable Energy in Canada, 208 pages.
Subtitled *"A Home Owner's Guide to Energy-Efficient Renovation,"* this book can help you to evaluate an existing house and to determine what are the best conservation features to add to it.

The Well-Tempered House. *Robert Argue. Renewable Energy in Canada, 222 pages.*
An introduction to superinsulation and energy conservation features for new housing. The book has an emphasis on passive solar heating and presents the work of 12 well-known solar architects, designers and builders.

Plant Physiology. *F. Salisbury and C. Ross. Wadsworth Publishing Company.*
If you want to learn almost everything about the chemistry of plants, what they are and how they grow, this is the standard text.

Air-Vapour Barriers. *D. Eyre and D. Jennings. Saskatchewan Research Council, 105 pages.*
An excellent book detailing air-vapour barrier practices.

Canadian Wood-frame House Construction. *Canada Mortgage and Housing Corporation (CMHC), 261 pages.*
A good little book on standard Canadian construction techniques. Details, snow loads, lumber sizes, spans, etc. Only $1.00 (in Canada).

Periodicals

Renewable Energy News (formerly *Canadian Renewable Energy News*), *Box 4869, Station E, Ottawa, Ontario K1S 5J1, or Box 32226, Washington, D.C. 20007. $28.00/year.*

Organic Gardening, *Rodale Press, Emmaus, Pennsylvania 18049. $11.00/year (U.S.)*

New Shelter, *Rodale Press, Emmaus, Pennsylvania 18049. $10.00/year (U.S.)*

Rain, *2270 N.W. Irving, Portland, Oregon 97210. $15.00/year (U.S.) add $2.80/year (U.S.) for delivery to Canada.*

Harrowsmith Magazine, *Camden East, Ont. K0K 1J0*

Fine Homebuilding, *The Taunton Press, 52 Church Hill Rd., Box 355, Newtown, CT. 06470. $14.00/year U.S. add $3.00/year (U.S.) in Canada.*

Watershed Magazine, Bag 5000, Fairview, Alberta T0H 1L0. $12.00/year (Cdn.) Editorial style remarkably similar to this book.

Bibliography

Books

Alward, Ron and Shapiro, Andy, 1980. **Low Cost Passive Solar Greenhouses:** A Design and Construction Guide. Butte, Montana: National Center for Appropriate Technology.

Anderson, Bruce and Riordan, Michael, 1976. **The Solar Home Book.** Harrisville: Chesire Books.

Argue, Robert, 1980. **The Well-Tempered House.** Toronto: Renewable Energy in Canada.

Bryten, Roger; Cooper, Ken; Mattock, Chris; Lyster, Terry, 1980. **The Solar Water Heater Book.** Toronto: Renewable Energy in Canada.

Carr, Anna, 1979. **Rodale's Color Handbook of Garden Insects.** Emmaus: Rodale Press Inc.

Clegg, Peter and Watkins, Derry, 1978. **The Complete Greenhouse Book.** Charlotte, VT: Garden Way Publishing.

van Dresser, Peter, 1977. **Homegrown Sundwellings.** Sante Fe: The Lightning Tree.

Feirer, John, L. **Carpentry in Building Construction.** Peoria: Charles A. Bennett Co.

Fisher, Rick and Yanda, Bill, 1980. **The Food and Heat Producing Solar Greenhouse.** 2/e. Santa Fe: John Muir Publications.

Gilkeson, Linda and Klein, Miriam, 1981. **A Guide to the Biological Control of Greenhouse Aphids.** Charlottetown: The Ark Project of the Institute of Man and Resources.

Halliday, David and Resnick, Robert, 1967. **Physics.** New York: John Wiley and Sons Inc.

Johnson, Willis; Laubengayer, Richard; Delanney, Louis; and Cole, Thomas, 1966. **Biology.** 3/e. New York: Holt Rinehart and Winston.

Jordan, William H. 1977. **Windowsill Ecology.** Emmaus: Rodale Press Inc.

Kadulski, Richard; Lyster, Eswyn and Lyster, Terry. **Solplan 3: Solar Greenhouses for Canada.** Vancouver: The Drawing Room Graphic Services Limited.

Kadulski. Richard and Lyster, Terry, 1980. **Solplan Almanac.** Vancouver: The Drawing Room Graphic Services Limited.

Klein, Miriam, 1980. **Horticultural Management of Solar Greenhouses in the Northeast.** The Memphremagog Group.

Langdon, William K. 1980. **Movable Insulation.** Emmaus: Rodale Press Inc.

McCullagh, James C., ed., 1978. **The Solar Greenhouse Book.** Emmaus: Rodale Press Inc.

Marshall, Brian and Argue, Robert, 1981. **The Super Insulated Retrofit Book.** Toronto: Renewable Energy in Canada.

Matthews, Diane; Flower, Robert; Ganser, Stephen; Weinsteiger, Eileen, 1981. **Design Elements in Solar Grow Frames and Horticultural Adaptations for their Winter Use.** Emmaus: Rodale Press Inc.

Mazria, Edward, 1979. **The Passive Solar Energy Book.** Emmaus: Rodale Press Inc.

Odum, Eugene, 1971. **Fundamentals of Ecology.** 3/e. W.B. Saunders Co.

Salisbury, F. and Ross, C., 1978. **Plant Physiology.** Wadsworth Publishing Company.

Seymour, John, 1979. **The Self-Sufficient Gardener.** Garden City: Doubleday and Co.

Shorlety, George and Williams, Dudley. 1965. **Elements of Physics.** Englewood Cliffs: Prentice-Hall Inc.

Swan, Lester A. 1964. **Beneficial Insects.** New York: Harper and Row.

Yorke, B.V. and Kendall, G.R. 1972. **Daily Bright Sunshine 1941-1970.** Downsview: Atmospheric Environment Service.

White, John W. and Aldrich, Robert A. 1980. **Greenhouse Energy Conservation.** Pennsylvania State University.

Articles

ARKDEX GH/1, 1980. *"Preparation and Management of Greenhouse Soils."* Souris: The Ark Project of the Institute of Man and Resources.

ARKDEX GH/2, 1980. *"Seeding and Planting Techniques for Use in Greenhouses."* Souris: The Ark Project of the Institute of Man and Resources.

ARKDEX GH/3, 1980. *"Commercial Tomato Production in a Solar Heated Greenhouse, Using Biological Pest Controls."* Souris: The Ark Project of the Institute of Man and Resources.

ARKDEX GH/4, 1980. *"Aphid Control."* Souris: The Ark Project of the Institute of Man and Resources.

Bond, T.E., Godbey, L.C. and Zornig, H.F. 1979. *"Transmission of Solar and Long-Wavelength Energy by Materials Used as Covers for Solar Collectors and Greenhouses."* Transactions of the A.S.A.E.

Canada-Department of Transport — Meteorological Branch, 1968. *Climatic Normals, Volume 5: Sunshine, Cloud, Pressure and Thunderstorms.* Toronto.

Evans, John, 1981. *"Performance of the Newfoundland Greenhome; Success and Failures after One Year of Habitation."*

Evans, John W. and Mellin, Robert E. *"The Newfoundland Greenhouse Energy Efficient Design for a Cold Foggy Climate."* Proceedings of the 5th National Passive Solar Conference pp 1257-1262.

Fulford, Bruce, 1981. *"Revolution Breeding in the Compost Pile: Composting in Solar Greenhouses for More Profitable Small-Scale Local Agriculture."* Brooks, Maine: Compost Energy Center.

Kane, Mark, Nov. 1981. *"Sun-Powered Ventilation For Plants Under Glass"* Organic Gardening Vol. 28, No. 11, pp. 62-67.

Kane, Mark, Jan. 1982. *"Caution: Treated Wood."* Organic Gardening Vol. 29, No. 1, pp 106-112.

Klein, Miriam, 1979. *"Biological Management of Passive Solar Greenhouses: an annotated bibliography and resource list."* National Center for Appropriate Technology Pub. No. B008.

Maes, Reed E. 1978. *"A Large Scale Northern Climate Solar Garden."* Ann Arbor: Environmental Research Institute of Michigan.

Maes, R; McKenney, Henry; and Riseng, Catherine, 1979. *"The Design, Experimental Results and Socio-Economical Impact of a Northern Climate Commercial Greenhouse."* Ann Arbor: Environmental Research Institute of Michigan.

Maes, R; Riseng, C; Thomas, G; and Mandeville, M; 1980. *"Demonstration of an Advanced Solar Garden with a Water Ceiling."* Ann Arbor: Environmental Research Institute of Michigan.

Roller, Warren L. 1977. *"Energy and the Food Chain."* Proceedings of a Conference on Solar Energy for Heating Greenhouses and Greenhouse Residential Combination. Ohio Agriculture Research and Development Center.

Schoenau, G.J; Green. G.H; Besant, R.W; Arinze, E.A; *"A Night Shutter System for Greenhouses in Cold Climates."* College of Engineering, University of Saskatchewan.

Solar Applications and Research Ltd., *"Solar Greenhouse Siting and Operations Guide."* Vancouver, Canada.

Wylie, Jim. 1982. *"Attached Solar Greenhouses for Food and Fuel."* Detroit Lakes, MN: Area Vocational — Technical Institute

Greenhouse Heat Loss Worksheet   Calculations

Using this worksheet to determine the heat loss of your proposed greenhouse can give you an idea of how long the greenhouse can extend the growing season (or how much auxiliary heat you will need to keep it running year round). The heat loss is directly related to the area of the building surface exposed to the exterior, the difference between inside and outside temperatures, and the insulating value of the materials used in the construction. As a formula it would read:

$$Q = \frac{A \times dT}{R}$$

where:

Q = heat loss
A = surface area
dT = temperature difference
R = total insulating value.

In order to calculate the maximum possible heat loss it is necessary to know the difference between the coldest outdoor temperature likely to occur (the design temperature, see p. 256-7), and the lowest acceptable temperature for the types of plants you intend to grow. For the variety of plants commonly grown in a greenhouse 7°C is an acceptable low, although tomatoes will not do well at such low temperatures unlike leafy greens which can withstand even colder temperatures. Use 7°C for these calculations unless you will be growing only tomatoes or tropical plants. The design temperatures for selected cities can be found on p. 256-7. If your location is not listed your local weather or agricultural office should be able to supply this information.

Design Temperature		Design Temp. Difference	
_____°C	– 7°C =	[1]_____	°C

As your greenhouse is built of many materials in various configurations, all exterior wall components must be measured separately. The net area of each element in square metres should be used. While you should be as accurate as possible, remember that you are not measuring laboratory specimens. If you are within 20-30mm in each dimension, you will be close enough. (20mm in 3m is not significant.)

Calculations

East Wall Area	Area of Openings (glazings, doors, vents)	Net East Wall Area
_____ −	_____ =	(i) _____ m²

West Wall Area	Area of Openings	Net West Wall Area
_____ −	_____ =	(ii) _____ m²

South Wall Area	Area of Openings	Net South Wall Area
_____ −	_____ =	(iii) _____ m²

Net Exterior Wall Area = (i) + (ii) + (iii) = [2] _____ m²

Roof Area	Area of Openings	Net Roof Area
_____ −	_____ =	[3] _____ m²

Total Glazing Area of East and West Walls	[4]	m²
Total Area of Roof Glazing (if any)	+ [5]	m²
Total South Wall Glazing Area	+ [6]	m²

Total Glazing Area	[7]	m²
Length of Greenhouse Perimeter at Ground Level (south, east, and west sides)	[8]	m²

The volume of the greenhouse must be calculated because much heat is lost through ventilation. A reasonably close and acceptable figure can be obtained if you calculate the overall floor area, and multiply it by the average floor-to-ceiling height.

Total Greenhouse Volume   [9] _____ m²

Different building materials resist heat flow at different rates. The resistance to heat flow is expressed in terms of RSI values; the higher the number, the more resistant the material is. Representative values are given for common building materials on p. 246. The total thermal resistance of a wall or roof is the sum of the thermal resistances (the RSI values) of the individual components that make up that roof or wall.

Sample Calculation: Wall

	RSI
Outside air film	0.03
Bevel siding	0.14
8mm plywood sheathing	0.07
Fibreglass insulation (3½ in)	2.11
Gypsum board (13mm)	0.08
Inside air film	0.12
Total RSI-value	2.55

Calculations

To calculate the total heat loss of the greenhouse (excluding glazing):

Wall Area [2]		Total RSI		Wall Heat Loss
_____	÷	_____	=	[10] _____

Roof Area		Total RSI		Roof Heat Loss
_____	÷	_____	=	[11] _____

Door Area		Total RSI (If door is mostly glazed assume overall RSI of 0.32		Door Heat Loss
_____	÷	_____	=	[12] _____

Vent Area		Total RSI		Vent Heat Loss
_____	÷	_____	=	[13] _____

Heat is also lost through the foundation. Most heat is lost through the area near the finished grade line with a diminishing heat loss rate the deeper one goes. To calculate foundation heat losses can be tedious, but a reasonably close approximation can be obtained by assuming that the heat loss is proportional to the length of the exposed edge (perimeter of the building) at a rate of 0.86 W/m°C/hour. This assumes that the foundation is insulated along the perimeter with 50mm of rigid insulation in one of the ways we have recommended in CONSTRUCTION.

Greenhouse Perimeter		Foundation Heat Loss
[8] _____	x 0.86 W/m°C =	_____

Heat is also lost because of ventilation and infiltration. If you have followed the CONSTRUCTION details carefully, a well constructed winter greenhouse will probably average about two air changes per hour (this figure must be much higher in hot weather to avoid overheating).

Calculations

Greenhouse Volume		Air Changes		Air Change Heat Loss
[9] _____	x	___2___	x 0.33 =	[15] _____

The total heat loss of your greenhouse (less the glazing) per °C is the sum of the heat losses of the various elements as calculated above.

Total Greenhouse
Heat Loss
(Less Glazing)

[10] + [11] + [12] + [13] + [14] + [15]	=	[16]	W/°C

The greatest portion of the heat loss in a greenhouse takes place through the glazing. To help minimize this, we have recommended the use of movable insulation. To calculate heat loss we will have to determine the RSI value of the glazing with and without the movable insulation in place as well as the number of hours per day that it actually is in place. For glazed areas using double glass (as we recommend) assume an RSI value of 0.31 *without* movable insulation.

Heat Loss of Total Glazing
Area *Without* Movable Insulation

Total Glazing Area		RSI	
[7] _____	÷	0.31 =	[17] _____ W/°C

Next we need to calculate the glazing heat loss *with* movable insulation in place. Because the RSI value of the south wall shutter might be different from that of the east or west wall shutters, we must calculate them separately. To determine total RSI add 0.31 to the RSI value of the shutter.

Heat Loss of Endwall Glazing
with Movable Insulation

Total East and West Glazing Area		Total RSI	
[4] _____	÷	_____ =	[18] _____

Total South Wall
Glazing Area   Total RSI   Heat Loss of South Wall
                                         Glazing *with* Movable Insulation   Calculations

[5] _____ ÷ _____ = [19] _____

Total Roof Glazing Area   Total RSI   Heat Loss of Roof Glazing
                                                    with Movable Insulation

[6] _____ − _____ = [20] _____

                                         Total Glazing Heat Loss
                                         with Movable Insulation

_____ [18] + [19] + [20] _____ = [21] _____ W/°C

We now want to determine the total greenhouse heat loss when the movable insulation is *not* in place and the total heat loss when it *is* in place.

                                         Total Greenhouse Heat Loss
                                         without Movable Insulation

__[16]__ + __[17]__   x 3.6 kJ/w-hr   = [22] _____ kJ/°C/hr

                                         Total Greenhouse Heat Loss
                                         with Movable Insulation

__[16]__ + __[21]__   x 3.6 kJ/w-hr   = [23] _____ kJ/°C/hr

Heat Loss without   Temperature   Peak Heat Loss *without*
Movable Insulation   Difference   Movable Insulation

_____ [22] _____   x   _____ [1] _____   = [24] _____ kJ/°C/hr

Heat Loss with   Temperature   Peak Heat Loss *with*
Movable Insulation   Difference   Movable Insulation

_____ [23] _____   +   _____ [1] _____   = [25] _____ kJ/hr

To determine the number of hours that the movable insulation will be in place we need to know the average number of daylight hours and the average number of dark hours per day in each month. See p. 251 for possible hours of sunshine by latitude.

	JAN	FEB	MAR	APR	MAY	JUN	JUL	AUG	SEPT	OCT	NOV	DEC	Calculations
[27] Hours of Possible Sunshine per Day (Table)													
[27] Hours of Possible Darkness per Day (24 hrs - [27])													
[27] Daily Heat Loss without Movable Insulation ([27] x [22])													
[30] Daily Heat Loss with Movable Insulation ([28] x [23])													
[31] Total Daily Heat Loss in kJ/degree day ([29] + [30])													
[27] Plant Degree Day per Month (Table)													
[27] Average Monthly Heat Loss ([31] x [32])													

Solar Contribution Worksheet   Calculations

This part of the worksheet will help you with an estimate of how much solar heat you can expect in any given month for any geographical region. Comparing that to the greenhouse heat loss will help you get a feeling for the length of the growing season (or for the amount and period you will need to supply supplemental heat).

The location of the greenhouse must be known in order to estimate the solar contribution. Pages 254-5 list latitudes of selected cities. If the south facing glazing of the greenhouse is in two planes, then each section must be calculated separately.

South Facing Glazing
[34] South Wall Glazing Angle_____
[34A] Roof Glazing Angle _____
[6] South Wall Glazing Area_____
[5] Roof Glazing Area _____

Daily total solar energy (page 251) is the maximum possible amount of energy that can fall on your greenhouse glazing each day of the month. The figures are listed by latitude and by glazing angle. Choose the one which most closely approximates your situation.

                    JAN FEB MAR APR MAY JUN JUL AUG SEPT OCT NOV DEC

Daily Total
[35] Solar Energy
(Table   )

Now we want to determine the average amount of sunshine falling on the south face per hour. The average number of hours per month of actual sunshine given in weather data does not tell you at what time of day (for any particular day) that the sun was shining. The amount of heat collectable on a partly sunny day with sunshine in the early morning is going to be much less than on a day with sunshine around midday. Our method uses an hourly heat value averaged over the maximum possible hours of sunshine.

                    JAN FEB MAR APR MAY JUN JUL AUG SEPT OCT NOV DEC

Hourly Average
[36] Solar Energy
([35] ÷ [27])

The hourly average sunshine is the amount of energy reaching the glazing. However, not all of this energy is transmitted by the glazing material. To determine how much energy actually gets through, we will need to know the transmission properties of the glazing material. Page 244 lists fractional transmission factors of common single-layer glazings as well as the most common double-glazing combinations.

Calculations

[37] Light Transmission Factor of Glazing _____

Maximum heat collectable per square metre of window area, per hour, is the portion of solar energy falling on the glazing that passes through as useful heat.

	JAN	FEB	MAR	APR	MAY	JUN	JUL	AUG	SEPT	OCT	NOV	DEC
[38] Maximum Heat Collectable per m² of Glazing per hour ([36] x [37])												
[27] Hours of Actual Sunshine per Month (Table)												

The total heat collectable is the amount of solar energy available in a month. However, we must take into account the amount of shading from surrounding sources. From the silhouetted sunpath chart for your latitude (p. 240-3) note the amount of shading on your collecting surfaces, and determine the portion of the sun chart not in shadow.

	JAN	FEB	MAR	APR	MAY	JUN	JUL	AUG	SEPT	OCT	NOV	DEC
[40] Total Heat Collectable per Month ([38]x[39]x[6])												
[41] Portion of Unshaded Sunshine (from Unsilhouetted Sunpath Chart)												
[42] Total Solar Heat Collectable per Month ([40] x [41])												

If you have roof glazing on your greenhouse, go back now to [34A], determine the total solar heat collectable per month by the roof glazing, and add this figure to [41] to give you the total of both glazing surfaces.

If the sun provides more heat than is required, then the excess heat is not useful for heating the greenhouse. A portion of this excess heat will go into thermal storage. Whatever cannot be so absorbed must be vented to the outdoors or, if needed, into the house. The net heat gain does not take into account heat exchange with the house.

Calculations

JAN FEB MAR APR MAY JUN JUL AUG SEPT OCT NOV DEC

[43] Net Heat Gain
      per Month
      ([42] − [43])

If the net heat gain is a positive figure you will have excess heat in the greenhouse as a monthly average. Some of that heat may be useable in the house, the rest will have to be vented outdoors. If the net heat gain figure is negative, the greenhouse will require more heat to stay above 7°C than solar energy can provide. However, with an attached greenhouse often that extra heat can come from the house, particularly if you have supplied heat to the house from the greenhouse during other periods.

Using a Sunpath Chart

The sunpath charts included in this section consist of a series of approximately parallel lines indicating the path of the sun across the sky throughout the year. The vertical scale of the chart shows the altitude of the sun at a specific time. The altitude is how high the sun is above the horizon and is measured in degrees. The horizontal scale indicates the solar azimuth (the number of degrees the sun is from due south).

You may understand how a sunpath chart is determined and used if you imagine yourself standing on the site of your proposed greenhouse for an entire year and somehow etching the path of the sun, on the 21st of each month, on the sky. If you could then split the sky from a point directly above you down to the northern horizon, peel it open and flatten it out, you'd more or less have a sunpath chart.

During the year that you were standing there plotting your sunpath chart you would have noticed that nearby objects, such as trees, hills or buildings, blocked the sun from your view at certain times of the day in certain periods of the year. When building a greenhouse it is important to know how often it will be shaded by such obstructions to solar energy. A sunpath chart can tell you exactly that — without requiring you to stand outside all that time.

To look more closely at a sunpath chart,

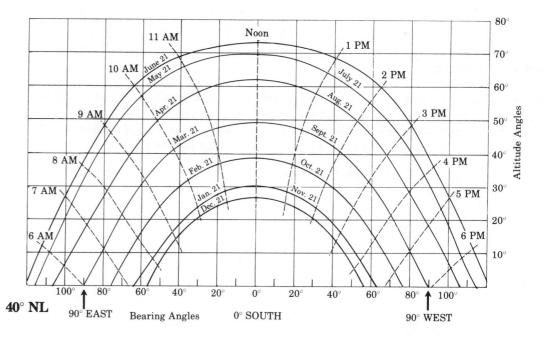

and for examples on how to use the one which is the closest to your area, let's use the example of the sunpath chart for Pittsburgh at 40° north latitude.

The sunpath chart has seven curved lines, forming seven arches. Each line indicates the sunpath on the 21st of a specific month or months. The names of the months of the year the various lines represent are written above the arches. The reason that February and October, March and September, etc. use the same arches is that their sunpaths are almost identical.

The broken lines indicate the time of day the sun is at that position (remember that this is solar time, not necessarily local time.)

Example: Let's say we want to find the solar azimuth and solar altitude at 10:00 in the morning on September 21 in Pittsburgh. (Note: reproduction of miniature sunpath chart with example lines.)

First, locate the 10:00 line for this month and follow it down until it crosses the September 21 curve. Reading horizontally, right or left, from this point, you can determine that the altitude is *(slightly more than)* 40°. Reading vertically from the point of intersection, on the other hand, indicates that the azimuth is about 43° East of south.

Using the sunpath chart. Finding the solar position at any given time is interesting, but the true value of the sunpath chart is in determining how much nearby objects will shade your greenhouse. This requires that you know which way is true south and that you have a protractor, compass, clinometer or transit. The less accurate equipment will yield less accurate results, but useful results nonetheless.

Stand on your greenhouse site with your equipment, facing due south. What you will do is note the direction and height of all obstructions and then plot them on the sunpath chart for your latitude. Instead of measuring the height of the objects in meters or feet, you will determine the angle from the horizon to the tops of the trees or buildings. This is called the altitude (get the connection?) and you can determine it be siting along your protractor or using one of the more sophisticated devices we mentioned.

The direction of the object is called the azimuth and is measured in degrees from due south. If you use a compass for this, be sure to correct for the difference between magnetic north and true north. For most objects you will be worrying about, the azimuth will be a range of degrees to account for its width. A nearby building, for instance, might block the area between 30° and 55° west of south.

Plot the heights (altitude — in degrees) and the directions and widths (azimuth — in degrees) of the nearby obstructions onto your sunpath chart and sketch in the shape of these objects. This will give you a

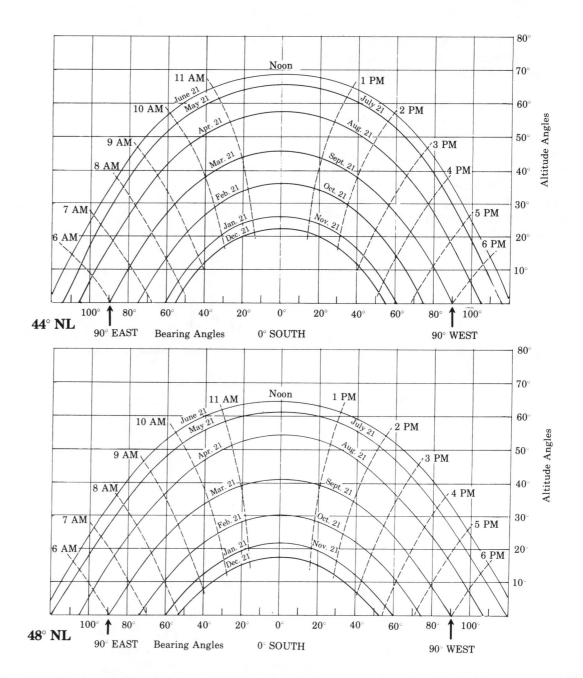

useful visual tool which will indicate the impact of these objects in shadowing the greenhouse throughout the year.

Shading factor. The figure transposed on the sunpath charts indicates the fraction of the total daily sunshine which falls on the greenhouse surface in that hour. By noting the extent to which each of these boxes is covered by silhouettes on your sunpath chart, and by adding these fractions to get a total, you can determine how much of the possible daily sunshine actually falls on your greenhouse.

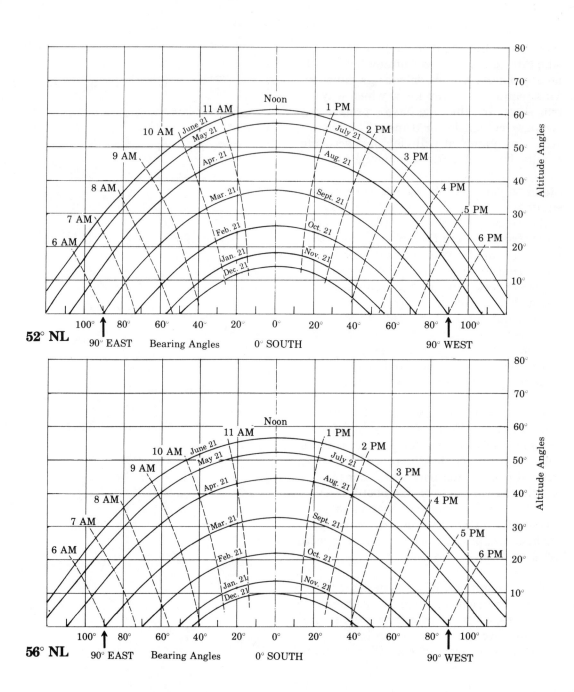

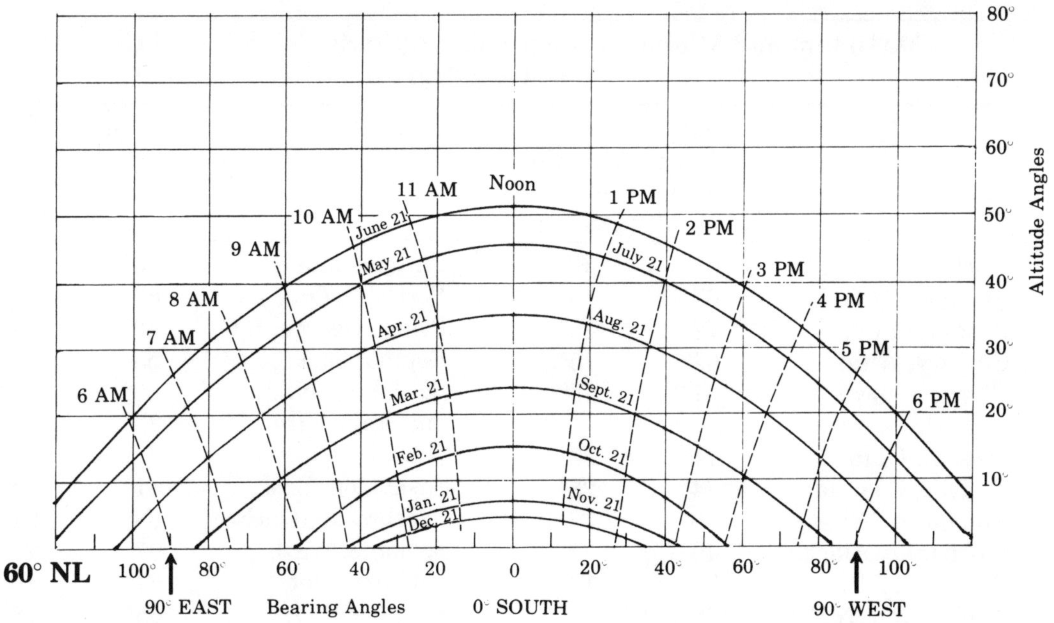

Total Possible Sunshine on 15th of Each Month (in hrs)

	Latitude					
Month	40°	44°	48°	52°	56°	60°
Jan	9.7	9.3	8.8	8.2	7.6	6.7
Feb	10.7	10.5	10.3	10.0	9.6	9.2
Mar	11.9	11.9	11.9	11.8	11.8	11.7
Apr	13.3	13.5	13.6	13.9	14.2	14.6
May	14.4	14.9	15.2	15.7	16.3	17.1
Jun	15.0	15.5	16.0	16.8	17.6	18.8
Jul	14.8	15.2	15.7	16.3	16.9	18.1
Aug	13.8	14.0	14.3	14.7	15.1	15.7
Sep	12.5	12.5	12.6	12.7	12.8	12.9
Oct	11.2	11.1	10.9	10.7	10.5	10.2
Nov	10.0	9.6	9.3	8.8	8.2	7.6
Dec	9.4	8.8	8.4	7.7	7.0	5.9

Maximum and Minimum Noon Solar Altitude For Selected Cities
(to nearest degree)

City	Solar Altitude, Noon June 21	Solar Altitude, Noon Dec. 21	City	Solar Altitude, Noon June 21	Solar Altitude, Noon Dec. 21
Anchorage, Alaska	53°	6°	Philadelphia, Pa.	74°	27°
Bismark, N.D.	67°	20°	Portland, Ore.	68°	22°
Boston, Mass.	72°	25°	Prince George, B.C.	59°	13°
Calgary, Alta.	62°	15°	Regina, Sask.	63°	16°
Charlottetown, P.E.I.	67°	20°	St. John's, Nfld.	66°	18°
Dayton, Ohio	74°	28°	Salt Lake City, Utah	73°	26°
Denver, Colorado	74°	28°	Saskatoon, Sask.	61°	14°
Edmonton, Alta.	60°	13°	Sherbrooke, Quebec	68°	21°
Fairbanks, Alaska	49°	3°	Spokane, Wash.	67°	20°
Fairview, Alta.	57°	10°	Sudbury, Ont.	67°	20°
Fredericton, N.B.	68°	21°	Thunder Bay, Ont.	65°	18°
Great Falls, Mon.	67°	20°	Toronto, Ont.	70°	23°
Halifax, N.S.	68°	22°	Vancouver, B.C.	64°	17°
Hull, Quebec	68°	21°	Whitehorse, Yukon	53°	6°
Minneapolis, Minn.	69°	22°	Winnipeg, Man.	64°	17°
Omaha, Nebraska	72°	25°	Yellowknife, N.W.T.	50°	3°
Oslo, Norway	53°	7°			

Transmission Factors of Glazing Materials
Single Glazings

Material	Light Transmission
Glass	0.89
Fiberglass .635mm	0.87
Acrylic	0.92
Polycarbonate	0.86
Polyethylene film	0.92
Tedlar film	0.93
Polyester film	0.88
Teflon film	0.96
Acrylite-SDP (Double-Wall)	0.83

Double Glazing Combinations

For an approximation of a double glazing combination not included in the chart, multiply the transmission factors, e.g. double acrylic: $0.92 \times 0.92 = 0.85$

Outer Material ╱Inner Material	Light Transmission
Glass/Glass	0.80
Glass/Polyethylene	0.80
Glass/Tedlar	0.83
Glass/Polyester Film	0.78
Fiberglass/Fiberglass	0.73
Fiberglass/Polyethylene	0.76
Fiberglass/Tedlar	0.80
Fiberglass/Polyester Film	0.76
Polyethylene/Polyethylene	0.83
Polycarbonate/Polyethylene	0.77
Polycarbonate/Tedlar	0.80
Polycarbonate/Polyester	0.77
Tedlar/Tedlar	0.88

Temperature Conversion Chart

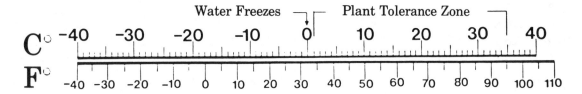

GLAZING MATERIALS

	Material and Typical brand names	Overall Trans-mission %	Long Wave Absorp-tion %	Remaining Trans-mission After 10 years %	Remaining Strength After 10 years %	Life years
GLASS	GLASS	89	97	100	100	Ind
	Recycled or Imperfect Glass	89	97	100	100	Ind
	Tempered Glass	89	97	100	100	Ind
RIGID PLASTICS	FIBREGLASS (FRP) .635mm (25 mil) - flat Kalwall, Filon	87	88	95	N/A	20
	ACRYLIC Plexiglass	92*	N/A	N/A	N/A	20
	Double-wall Acrylite-SDP (Exolite)	83*	N/A	N/A	N/A	20
	POLYCARBONATE 1.59mm (1/16 in) Lexan	86	94	90	65	20
ROLL PLASTICS	POLYETHYLENE UV-treated .102mm (4 mil) Monsato 602	92	20	0	0	2
	POLYVINYL FLUORIDE 0.076mm (3 mil) Tedlar	93	57	95	70	10-20
	POLYESTER .127mm (5 mil) Mylar Llumar	88	68	90	74	8-20
	Teflon FEP	96*	N/A	95**	70**	25**

Notes:
— Figures for transmission represent total transmission for a single layer of glazing at an angle of incidence of 0°.
— Transmission figure for double-wall acrylic already takes into account both layers and need not be corrected for double glazing.
— Transmission and absorption figures from T.E. Bond, *et al*, 1978, except for:
  *from other sources
  **should only be considered estimates, as should the figures for life of all plastic glazing materials.
— Ind = Indefinite

THERMAL RESISTANCE VALUES

Material	RSI-Value Typical or given thickness	Per 10 mm thickness
Exterior Siding		
Metal siding	0.11	
Bevel siding (wood)	0.14	
Wood shingles (single course)	0.14	
Asbestos (cement shingle)	0.03	
Stucco		0.014
Plywood (8 mm)	0.07	
Plywood (11 mm)	0.10	
Plywood (14 mm)	0.13	
Plywood (19 mm)	0.18	
Masonry		
Common brick		0.014
Face brick		0.007
8 in (203 mm) hollow concrete block	0.18	
w/core filled with insulation	0.34	
Finish Materials		
1/2 in (13 mm) gypsum board	0.08	
Plywood panelling (8 mm)	0.07	
Plaster (13 mm)	0.05	
Wood (softwood)		0.086
Air film		
Outside air film	0.03	
Inside air film	0.12	

Material	RSI-Value Typical or given thickness	Per 10 mm thickness
Insulation		
Air space (25 mm or greater)	0.17	
Fiberglass batts: R8 (2 1/2 in)	1.41	
R12 (3 1/2 in)	2.11	
R20 (5 1/2 in)	3.52	
R28 (7 1/4 in)	4.93	
Expanded polystyrene: 1 in	0.68	
1 1/2 in	1.03	
2 in	1.37	
3 in	2.05	
Extruded polystyrene: 1 in	0.81	
1 1/2 in	1.22	
2 in	1.63	
3 in	2.44	
Roofing		
Asphalt shingles	0.08	
Built up roofing	0.06	
Wood shingles	0.16	
Wood deck (per 25 mm)	1.25	
Inside air film	0.10	
Outside air film	0.03	
Doors		
Solid core wood: 25 mm (1 in)	0.27	
32 mm (1 1/4 in)	0.32	
38 mm (1 1/2 in)	0.36	

Annual Degree Days (U.S.)

Degree days below 18.3°C — in C° (not for use in our worksheet — see pages 256-7.)

Anchorage, Alaska	6062
Fairbanks, Alaska	7969
Juneau, Alaska	5004
Denver, Colorado	3058
Hartford, Connecticut	3528
Boise, Idaho	3241
Pocatello, Idaho	3924
Chicago, Illinois	3404
Springfield, Illinois	3088
Fort Wayne, Indiana	3449
Indianapolis, Indiana	3098
Des Moines, Iowa	3728
Sioux City, Iowa	3863
Portland, Maine	4166
Bangor, Maine	4417
Boston, Massachusetts	3123
Detroit, Michigan	3566
Grand Rapids, Michigan	3778
Sault Ste. Marie, Michigan	5107
Duluth, Minnesota	5420
Minneapolis, Minnesota	4533
Billings, Montana	4036
Havre, Montana	4826
North Platte, Nebraska	3746
Concord, New Hampshire	4089
Atlantic City, New Jersey	2748
Albany, New York	3827
Buffalo, New York	3848
Bismark, North Dakota	5024
Fargo, North Dakota	5151
Cleveland, Ohio	3419
Columbus, Ohio	3723
Portland, Oregon	2662
Philadelphia, Pennsylvania	2702
Pittsburgh, Pennsylvania	3294
Providence, Rhode Island	3317
Huron, South Dakota	4475
Rapid City, South Dakota	4069
Seattle, Washington	2881
Spokane, Washington	3797
Green Bay, Wisconsin	4499
Madison, Wisconsin	4294
Cheyenne, Wyoming	4031
Sheridan, Wyoming	4822

Annual Degree Days (Canada)

Kamloops, B.C.	3756
Prince George, B.C.	5388
Vancouver, B.C.	3007
Victoria, B.C.	3076
Calgary, Alberta	5345
Edmonton, Alberta	5589
Grande Prairie, Alberta	6144
Medicine Hat, Alberta	4674
Prince Alberta, Saskatchewan	6562
Regina, Saskatchewan	5920
Saskatoon, Saskatchewan	6077
Swift Current, Saskatchewan	5482
Yellowknife, NWT	8593
Whitehorse, Yukon	6879
Brandon, Manitoba	6037
Churchill, Manitoba	9213
The Pas, Manitoba	6852
Winnipeg, Manitoba	5889
North Bay, Ontario	5318
Ottawa, Ontario	4673
Sault Ste Marie, Ontario	5090
Toronto, Ontario	3793
Thunder Bay, Ontario	5746
Windsor, Ontario	3590
Chicoutimi, Quebec	6097
Montreal, Quebec	4297
Quebec City, Quebec	5080
Rimouski, Quebec	5228
Sherbrooke, Quebec	5242
Edmunston, New Brunswick	5177
Fredericton, New Brunswick	4699
St. John, New Brunswick	4709
Halifax, Nova Scotia	4123
Nappan, Nova Scotia	4586
Sydney, Nova Scotia	4459
Charlottetown, P.E.I.	4623
Corner Brook, Newfoundland	4877
St. John's, Newfoundland	4804

Spans for Various Depths of Lintels made from Nominal 89mm thick Lumber or Two Thicknesses of Nominal 38mm Lumber installed on edge

Location of Lintels	Supported Loads Including Dead Loads and Ceiling	Depth of Lintels, mm	Maximum Allowable Spans, mm
Interior walls	Limited attic storage	89	1220
		140	1830
		184	2440
		235	3050
		286	3810
	Full attic storage or roof load or limited attic storage plus 1 floor	89	610
		140	910
		184	1220
		235	1520
		286	1830
	Full attic storage plus 1 floor or roof load plus 1 floor or limited attic storage plus 2 or 3 floors	89	—
		140	760
		184	910
		235	1220
		286	1520
	Full attic storage plus 2 or 3 floors or roof load plus 2 or 3 floors	89	—
		140	610
		184	910
		235	1100
		286	1220
	Roof with or without attic storage	89	1120
		140	1680
		184	2230
		235	2750
		286	3350
		89	330

Location of Lintels	Supported Loads Including Dead Loads and Ceiling	Depth of Lintels, mm	Maximum Allowable Spans, mm
Exterior walls	Roof with or without attic storage plus 1 floor	140	1230
		184	1840
		235	2230
		286	2520
	Roof with or without attic storage plus 2 or 3 floors	89	330
		140	1120
		184	1680
		235	1840
		286	2230

From *Canadian Wood-Frame Construction,* Central Mortgage and Housing Corp. (Canada), 1981

Calcium Chloride

% Solution by Weight	Freezing Point Depression in °C
5	2.3°
10	5.8°
15	11°
20	18°
30	41°

For 1000 l storage:

1000 l water = 1000 kg water

30% solution = 300 kg calcium chloride
+ 700 kg water

300 kg ≃ 8 bags ≃ $196.00 (CDN)

Cost (1982) 40 kg Bag : $24.50 (CDN)

Methanol (Methyl Alcohol)

% Solution		Freezing Point Depression in °C
By Weight	By Volume	
5	6.1	3°
10	12.1	7°
15	17.9	10°
20	23.6	15°
30	34.6	26°
40	45.1	38°

For 1000 l storage

45.1% = 451 l methanol
+ 549 l water

451 l methanol ≃ $374.00 (CDN)

Bulk Cost (1982) in 205 l drums: $0.83/$l$ (CDN)

Ethylene Glycol (Engine Antifreeze)

% Solution		Freezing Point Depression in °C
By Weight	By Volume	
5	4.5	1.5°
10	9.0	3.4°
20	18.1	8°
40	37.1	20°
50	46.9	37°

For 1000 l storage

46.9% = 469 l ethylene glycol
+ 531 l water

469 l ethylene glycol ≃ $882.00 (CDN)

Bulk Cost (1982) in 205 l drums:$1.88/$l$ (CDN)

Heat Storage Capacity of Selected Materials

For easy comparison, the materials are listed in relationship to the heat capacity of water (which is assigned a value of 100.0). To obtain actual heat capacity in (kilogram) calorie/m³ °C, multiply the figure by 10.

Material	Heat Storage Capacity
Water	100.0
Cast iron	86.5
Stone (quarried)	30.4
Concrete (w/stones)	50.8
Brick:	
Building Brick	39.4
Adobe	22.3
Fireclay brick	35.6
Wood	33.4
Gypsum	32.4
Cement	30.8

Nails

Penny weight	Length (in)	Length (mm)
4d	1¹/₂	38
6d	2	51
8d	2¹/₂	64
10d	3	76
12d	3¹/₄	83
16d	3¹/₂	89
20d	4	102
30d	4¹/₂	114

Lumber Sizes

Name	Actual Metric Size (mm)	Actual Imperial Size (in)
1 x 2	19 x 38	³/₄ x 1¹/₂
1 x 3	19 x 64	³/₄ x 2¹/₂
1 x 4	19 x 89	³/₄ x 3¹/₂
1 x 6	19 x 140	³/₄ x 5¹/₂
1 x 8	19 x 184	³/₄ x 7¹/₄
2 x 2	38 x 38	1¹/₂ x 1¹/₂
2 x 4	38 x 89	1¹/₂ x 3¹/₂
2 x 6	38 x 140	1¹/₂ x 5¹/₂
2 x 8	38 x 184	1¹/₂ x 7¹/₄
2 x 10	38 x 235	1¹/₂ x 9¹/₄

Plywood Sizes

Metric Standard (mm)	Closest Imperial Equivalent (in)
6	¹/₄
8	⁵/₁₆
11	⁷/₁₆
14	⁹/₁₆
19	³/₄
24	¹⁵/₁₆

Insulating Value of Common Insulation

Fibreglass Batts

Standard Thickness	RSI	R
2¹/₂ in. (64 mm)	1.41	8
3¹/₂ in. (89 mm)	2.11	12
5¹/₂ in. (140 mm)	3.52	20
7¹/₄ in. (184 mm)	4.93	28

White Rigid Styrofoam (Expanded Polystyrene)

Standard Thickness	RSI	R
1 in. (25 mm)	.68	3.89
1¹/₂ in. (38 mm)	1.03	5.83
2 in. (51 mm)	1.37	7.78
3 in. (76 mm)	2.05	11.67

Blue Rigid Styrofoam (Extruded Polystyrene)

1 in. (25 mm)	.81	4.62
1¹/₂ in. (38 mm)	1.22	6.93
2 in. (51 mm)	1.63	9.24
3 in. (76 mm)	2.44	13.86

Conversion Tables

Multiply	by	To Obtain
feet	0.03048	metres
inches	25.4	millimetres
square feet	0.0929	square metres
gallon (Imp.)	4.55	litres
gallon (U.S.)	3.79	litres
litre	0.001	cubic metres
cubic feet	0.0283	cubic metres
pounds	0.4535	kilogram
lb/cubic foot	16.03	kg/cubic metre
Btu	1054.35	Joules
Btu	0.0002929	Kilowatt-hours
Btu/hr	0.293	Watt
Btu/ft²	.0113	MJ/m²
(R) hr ft²°F/Btu	0.176	(RSI) m²°C/W

Multiply	by	To Obtain
metres	3.2808	feet
millimetres	0.0393	inches
square metres	10.76	square feet
litre	0.2197	gallon (Imp)
litre	0.2638	gallon (U.S.)
cubic metres	1,000	litres
cubic metres	35.33	cubic feet
kilogram	2.204	pounds
kg/cubic metre	0.623	lb/cubic foot
Joules	.0009485	Btu
Kilowatt-hours	3,414.4	Btu
Watt	3.412	Btu/hr
MJ/m²	88.05	Btu/ft²
(RSI) m²°C/W	5.679	(R) hr ft²°F/Btu

Daily Total Solar Energy in kJ/m² (Clear Day)

40°N	Possible hours of sunshine	Glazing Slope Angle			
		60°	75°	90°	15°
Jan.	9.7	20,463	20,213	18,590	13,188
Feb.	10.7	22,699	21,439	18,670	17,478
Mar.	11.9	22,687	19,952	15,741	21,519
Apr.	13.3	20,293	16,127	10,929	24,288
May	14.4	18,170	13,256	7,990	25,831
June	15.0	17,206	12,110	7,059	26,251
July	14.8	17,818	12,961	7,820	25,559
Aug.	13.8	19,646	15,549	10,509	23,822
Sept.	12.5	21,666	19,067	15,061	20,679
Oct.	11.2	21,802	20,542	17,841	17,024
Nov.	10.0	20,066	17,793	18,182	13,052
Dec.	9.4	18,885	18,919	17,694	11,338

44°N	Possible hours of sunshine	Glazing Slope Angle			
		60°	75°	90°	15°
Jan.	9.3	18,681	18,726	17,512	11,168
Feb.	10.5	21,836	20,974	18,670	15,811
Mar.	11.9	22,744	20,451	16,672	20,384
Apr.	13.5	21,042	17,228	12,280	23,812
May	14.9	19,305	14,629	9,352	25,866
June	15.5	18,488	13,562	8,342	26,513
July	15.2	18,942	14,311	9,136	25,628
Aug.	14.0	20,361	16,604	11,792	23,381
Sept.	12.5	21,666	19,475	15,889	19,567
Oct.	11.1	20,951	20,066	17,818	15,391
Nov.	9.6	18,295	18,318	17,115	11,044
Dec.	8.8	16,525	16,774	15,923	9,205

48°N	Possible hours of sunshine	Glazing Slope Angle			
		60°	75°	90°	15°
Jan.	8.8	16,377	16,649	15,810	9,057
Feb.	10.3	20,747	20,259	18,386	14,040
Mar.	11.9	22,585	20,724	17,387	19,113
Apr.	13.6	21,609	18,182	13,528	23,188
May	15.2	20,336	15,934	10,759	25,776
June	16.0	19,657	14,947	9,715	26,627
July	15.7	19,963	15,594	10,509	25,571
Aug.	14.3	20,917	17,523	12,904	22,791
Sept.	12.6	21,450	19,668	16,502	18,307
Oct.	10.9	19,861	19,339	17,501	13,654
Nov.	9.3	16,037	16,275	15,435	8,955
Dec.	8.4	14,028	14,448	13,914	7,139

52°N	Possible hours of sunshine	Glazing Slope Angle			
		60°	75°	90°	15°
Jan.	8.2	13,789	14,211	13,710	6,958
Feb.	10.0	19,407	19,260	17,807	12,179
Mar.	11.8	22,211	20,769	17,875	17,683
Apr.	13.9	22,018	18,976	14,652	22,405
May	15.7	21,223	17,126	12,132	25,537
June	16.8	20,690	16,241	11,100	26,593
July	16.3	20,849	16,774	11,837	25,367
Aug.	14.7	21,291	18,272	14,050	22,053
Sept.	12.7	21,008	19,623	16,888	16,900
Oct.	10.7	18,511	18,318	16,888	11,827
Nov.	8.8	13,472	13,869	13,358	6,878
Dec.	7.7	11,054	11,565	11,304	5,040

56°N	Possible hours of sunshine	Glazing Slope Angle			
		60°	75°	90°	15°
Jan.	7.6	10,816	11,327	11,077	4,866
Feb.	9.6	17,660	17,807	16,763	10,102
Mar.	11.8	21,575	20,542	18,091	16,106
Apr.	14.2	22,233	19,570	15,628	21,463
May	16.3	21,950	18,193	13,404	25,140
June	17.6	21,620	17,455	12,473	26,468
July	16.9	21,586	17,818	13,097	25,015
Aug.	15.1	21,496	18,851	14,981	21,168
Sept.	12.8	20,315	19,317	17,013	15,357
Oct.	10.5	16,763	16,854	15,821	9,886
Nov.	8.2	10,543	11,032	10,782	4,824
Dec.	7.0	7,286	7,718	7,649	2,963

60°N	Possible hours of sunshine	Glazing Slope Angle		
		60°	75°	90°
Jan.	6.7	7,381	7,778	7,654
Feb.	9.2	17,045	17,294	16,182
Mar.	11.7	22,451	21,417	19,055
Apr.	14.6	24,233	21,405	17,283
May	17.1	24,483	20,344	15,069
June	18.8	24,324	19,691	14,058
July	18.1	24,086	19,940	14,683
Aug.	15.7	23,427	20,577	16,545
Sept.	12.9	20,997	19,992	17,749
Oct.	10.2	15,455	15,574	14,683
Nov.	7.6	7,222	7,602	7,472
Dec.	5.9	3,974	4,252	4,235

HEATING DEGREE DAYS — below 18°C (64°) for Selected Canadian Cities

City	Jan.	Feb.	Mar.	Apr.	May	June	July	Aug.	Sept.	Oct.	Nov.	Dec.
Brandon, Manitoba	1125	947	818	442	239	86	24	44	189	374	690	989
Churchill, Manitoba	1414	1262	1187	871	630	359	194	204	366	590	902	1234
The Pas, Manitoba	1247	1027	891	528	292	115	34	70	238	437	780	1087
Winnipeg, Manitoba	1122	941	796	434	225	66	14	30	164	333	662	966
North Bay, Ontario	956	823	725	444	248	87	37	62	176	343	564	853
Ottawa, Ontario	898	783	659	370	181	45	10	27	121	287	491	791
Sault Ste Marie, Ontario	869	764	666	418	265	97	44	49	157	310	524	761
Toronto, Ontario	715	637	569	359	209	58	11	20	87	235	421	635
Thunder Bay, Ontario	986	847	732	469	305	139	49	68	190	358	596	865
Windsor, Ontario	691	606	520	295	141	29	3	8	64	204	411	618
Chicoutimi, Quebec	1014	865	720	453	265	89	29	52	167	348	553	880
Montreal, Quebec	859	747	632	376	178	44	9	25	112	277	480	758
Quebec City, Quebec	898	788	679	430	221	68	18	41	147	321	525	804
Edmunston, New Brunswick	949	808	714	456	248	98	29	59	175	351	553	845
Fredericton, New Brunswick	846	749	640	419	235	88	20	37	141	311	486	755
St. John, New Brunswick	756	670	598	413	264	134	49	46	126	277	432	661
Halifax, Nova Scotia	679	622	573	410	263	122	27	23	101	244	394	598
Nappan, Nova Scotia	776	708	634	440	269	116	30	46	140	296	447	684
Sydney, Nova Scotia	696	664	633	475	320	158	41	41	130	283	413	605
Charlottetown, P.E.I.	761	701	644	452	273	113	20	29	116	275	429	659
Cornerbrook, Newfoundland	716	686	647	482	342	182	60	70	173	337	453	630
St. John's, Newfoundland	674	629	634	507	387	229	98	91	184	337	435	599
Kamloops, B.C.	748	545	451	268	129	41	12	19	103	297	493	646
Prince George, B.C.	932	681	613	411	269	156	99	127	248	411	626	804
Vancouver, B.C.	480	379	379	277	180	92	39	42	115	248	363	438
Victoria, B.C.	464	375	383	288	198	114	64	66	125	252	360	427
Calgary, Alberta	888	706	686	440	273	159	69	103	225	381	605	772
Edmonton, Alberta	1066	854	790	454	258	142	75	112	249	429	707	951
Grande Prairie, Alberta	1095	861	790	469	249	133	75	107	236	431	731	968
Medicine Hat, Alberta	934	739	659	361	189	79	17	34	157	324	588	793
Prince Albert, Saskatchewan	1204	987	883	489	265	119	45	74	234	436	753	1073
Regina, Saskatchewan	1102	914	831	447	241	105	33	52	209	410	711	959
Saskatoon, Saskatchewan	1122	929	821	440	225	94	28	52	190	383	699	982
Swift Current, Saskatchewan	989	811	738	426	239	110	35	53	193	366	643	858
Yellowknife, N.W.T.	1445	1235	1138	777	435	178	76	126	333	596	967	1287
Whitehorse, Yukon	1155	884	790	528	332	171	119	173	306	530	812	1066

HEATING DEGREE DAYS — below 18.3°C (65°) for Selected U.S. Cities

City	Heating Degree Days by Month in °C											
	Jan.	Feb.	Mar.	Apr.	May	June	July	Aug.	Sept.	Oct.	Nov.	Dec.
Anchorage, Alaska	898	717	693	477	306	156	104	139	264	502	714	878
Fairbanks, Alaska	1307	1032	938	584	287	99	64	151	326	668	1019	1281
Juneau, Alaska	697	558	552	417	296	179	142	167	246	382	524	632
Denver, Colorado	535	447	439	255	105	15	0	0	39	183	372	491
Harford, Connecticut	674	577	488	271	108	0	0	0	41	196	377	616
Boise, Idaho	602	441	394	249	122	79	0	0	53	388	402	549
Pocatello, Idaho	702	536	492	311	169	59	0	0	89	268	471	638
Chicago, Illinois	707	587	487	252	222	72	0	0	32	182	412	635
Springfield, Illinois	642	521	423	184	56	0	0	0	9	139	367	577
Fort Wayne, Indiana	666	564	473	244	102	0	0	0	32	184	395	609
Indianapolis, Indiana	621	516	418	197	71	0	0	0	17	150	371	569
Des Moines, Iowa	768	617	518	241	86	0	0	0	34	177	436	671
Sioux City, Iowa	792	629	530	246	87	1	0	0	45	177	461	697
Portland, Maine	732	637	554	354	194	41	0	13	93	256	422	659
Bangor, Maine	788	682	587	371	192	39	1	9	102	273	451	707
Boston, Massachusetts	599	521	446	256	103	0	0	0	24	149	312	533
Detroit, Michigan	663	575	492	264	114	0	0	0	27	172	381	592
Grand Rapids, Michigan	702	612	532	291	132	7	0	0	46	209	421	630
Sault Ste Marie, Michigan	857	757	688	429	258	93	36	52	144	306	519	756
Duluth, Minnesota	955	805	697	422	251	90	19	40	159	322	592	854
Minneapolis, Minnesota	892	737	614	314	133	18	0	0	78	244	526	781
Billings, Montana	724	567	540	322	167	55	0	0	105	253	471	640
Havre, Montana	907	719	646	339	160	63	0	4	129	299	566	788
North Platte, Nebraska	699	556	511	272	114	18	0	0	61	226	462	640
Concord, New Hampshire	747	642	546	329	157	14	0	7	83	253	432	674
Atlantic City, New Jersey	538	466	394	204	55	0	0	0	2	128	299	497
Albany, New York	732	628	527	284	123	4	0	0	57	217	406	656
Buffalo, New York	693	614	549	317	161	14	0	1	59	215	402	621
Bismark, North Dakota	961	783	669	349	171	50	0	2	122	296	584	833
Fargo, North Dakota	1000	827	685	361	168	36	0	1	112	292	589	878
Cleveland, Ohio	638	559	480	261	118	4	0	0	35	179	372	580
Columbus, Ohio	613	522	427	214	80	0	0	0	24	172	371	573
Portland, Oregon	446	328	314	222	129	53	9	13	48	175	311	401
Philadelphia, Pennsylvania	546	466	380	186	50	0	0	0	3	121	296	496
Pittsburgh, Pennsylvania	574	496	406	194	72	0	0	0	14	148	331	528
Providence, Rhode Island	613	536	466	277	126	2	0	0	34	177	344	559
Huron, South Dakota	887	715	602	302	134	22	0	0	76	250	526	771
Rapid City, South Dakota	724	592	564	322	159	57	0	0	88	246	476	646
Seattle, Washington	392	301	311	221	126	51	13	14	51	167	279	354
Spokane, Washington	664	492	456	297	164	62	0	8	91	278	474	602
Green Bay, Wisconsin	837	713	609	336	170	33	0	12	88	254	497	742
Cheyenne, Wyoming	643	542	557	354	201	69	0	0	107	277	474	599
Sheridan, Wyoming	740	591	568	339	191	76	0	0	118	278	509	663

Hours of Bright Sunshine by Month for Selected U.S. Cities

City	Latitude	Jan.	Feb.	Mar.	Apr.	May	June	July	Aug.	Sept.	Oct.	Nov.	Dec.
Anchorage, Alaska	61	78	114	210	254	268	288	255	184	128	96	68	49
Fairbanks, Alaska	64	54	120	224	302	319	334	274	164	122	85	71	36
Juneau, Alaska	58	71	102	171	200	230	251	193	161	123	67	60	51
Denver, Colorado	39	207	205	247	252	281	311	321	297	274	246	200	192
Hartford, Connecticut	41	141	166	206	223	267	285	299	268	220	193	137	136
Boise, Idaho	43	116	144	218	274	322	352	412	378	311	232	143	104
Pocatello, Idaho	43	111	143	211	255	300	338	380	347	296	230	145	108
Chicago, Illinois	41	126	142	199	221	274	300	333	299	247	216	136	118
Springfield, Illinois	39	127	149	193	224	282	304	346	312	266	225	152	122
Fort Wayne, Indiana	41	113	136	191	217	281	310	342	306	242	210	120	102
Indianapolis, Indiana	39	118	140	193	227	278	313	342	313	265	222	139	118
Des Moines, Iowa	41	155	170	203	236	276	303	346	299	263	227	156	136
Sioux City, Iowa	42	164	177	216	254	300	320	363	320	270	236	160	146
Portland, Maine	43	155	174	213	226	268	286	312	294	229	202	146	148
Boston, Massachusetts	42	148	168	212	222	263	283	300	280	232	207	152	148
Detroit, Michigan	42	90	128	180	212	263	295	321	284	226	189	98	89
Grand Rapids, Michigan	42	74	117	178	218	277	308	349	304	231	188	92	70
Sault Ste. Marie, Michigan	46	83	123	187	217	252	269	309	256	165	133	61	62
Duluth, Minnesota	46	125	163	221	235	268	282	328	277	203	166	100	107
Minneapolis, Minnesota	44	140	166	200	231	272	302	343	296	237	193	115	112
Billings, Montana	45	140	154	208	236	283	301	372	332	258	213	136	129
Havre, Montana	48	136	174	234	268	311	312	384	339	260	202	132	122
North Platte, Nebraska	41	181	179	221	246	282	310	343	304	264	242	184	169
Concord, New Hampshire	43	136	153	192	196	229	261	286	260	214	179	122	126
Atlantic City, New Jersey	39	151	173	210	233	273	287	298	271	239	218	177	153
Albany, New York	42	125	151	194	213	266	301	317	286	224	192	115	112
Buffalo, New York	43	110	125	180	212	274	319	338	297	239	183	97	84
Bismark, North Dakota	46	141	170	205	236	279	294	358	307	243	198	130	125
Fargo, North Dakota	46	132	170	210	232	283	288	343	293	222	187	112	114
Cleveland, Ohio	41	79	111	167	209	274	301	325	288	235	187	99	77
Columbus, Ohio	40	112	132	177	215	270	296	323	291	250	210	131	101
Portland, Oregon	45	77	97	142	203	246	249	329	275	218	134	87	65
Philadelphia, Pennsylvania	39	142	166	203	231	270	281	288	253	225	205	158	142
Pittsburgh, Pennsylvania	40	89	114	163	200	239	260	283	250	234	180	114	76
Providence, Rhode Island	41	145	168	211	221	271	285	292	267	226	207	153	143
Huron, South Dakota	44	153	177	213	250	295	321	367	320	260	212	142	134
Rapid City, South Dakota	44	164	182	222	245	278	300	348	317	266	228	164	144
Seattle, Washington	47	74	99	154	201	247	234	304	248	197	122	77	62
Spokane, Washington	47	78	120	197	262	308	309	397	350	264	177	86	57
Green Bay, Wisconsin	44	121	148	194	210	251	279	314	266	213	176	110	106
Madison, Wisconsin	43	126	147	196	214	258	285	336	288	230	198	116	108
Cheyenne, Wyoming	41	191	197	243	237	259	304	318	286	265	242	188	170
Sheridan, Wyoming	44	160	179	226	245	286	303	367	333	266	221	153	145

Hours of Bright Sunshine by Month for Selected Canadian Cities

City	Lati-tude	Jan.	Feb.	Mar.	Apr.	May	June	July	Aug.	Sept.	Oct.	Nov.	Dec.
Kamloops, B.C.	51°	55	92	157	197	247	243	320	284	207	134	66	44
Prince George, B.C.	54°	54	87	130	183	248	240	267	243	166	101	56	41
Vancouver, B.C.	49°	58	89	124	195	250	229	311	250	190	114	71	44
Victoria, B.C.	48°	70	97	156	210	275	277	337	298	208	141	81	66
Fort St. John, B.C.	56°	74	102	153	202	278	257	288	262	168	130	79	60
Calgary, Alta.	51°	101	117	146	188	240	234	318	275	186	159	111	91
Edmonton, Alta.	53°	86	119	163	221	258	251	315	269	186	157	100	78
Lethbridge, Alta.	49°	103	126	162	210	265	271	345	300	216	177	113	96
Prince Albert, Sask.	53°	94	116	171	209	253	256	306	263	171	147	80	72
Regina, Sask.	50°	98	118	152	215	266	249	334	286	197	170	96	85
Saskatoon, Sask.	52°	96	129	191	226	275	270	340	293	210	166	99	86
Brandon, Man.	50°	103	128	160	200	238	230	302	269	187	145	86	81
Winnipeg, Ont.	51°	101	133	167	207	244	248	310	270	181	153	82	81
Thunder Bay, Ont.	48°	96	126	156	183	205	206	251	226	134	94	50	70
London, Ont.	43°	61	90	129	167	234	242	278	253	175	153	76	64
Toronto, Ont.	44°	77	106	149	184	223	263	286	256	201	151	84	67
Windsor, Ont.	42°	78	98	125	165	217	232	257	246	190	167	89	72
Ottawa, Ont.	45°	92	116	151	185	228	250	274	249	177	137	78	73
Montreal, Que.	46°	79	102	145	167	203	222	244	223	170	126	69	61
Quebec, Que.	47°	82	104	142	161	191	200	221	206	155	119	67	66
Fredericton, N.B.	46°	103	118	141	160	201	203	234	218	166	140	85	91
Moncton, N.B.	46°	105	123	144	162	207	205	228	219	159	145	92	88
Charlottetown, P.E.I.	46°	89	111	140	156	212	221	244	236	177	134	78	59
Halifax, N.S.	45°	95	113	148	152	200	212	139	219	169	152	89	88
Sydney, N.S.	46°	69	97	122	139	182	208	258	218	173	144	73	62
St. John's Nfld.	48°	66	80	97	101	166	173	232	181	151	108	58	51
Whitehorse, Yukon	61°	42	81	160	230	267	271	250	225	134	96	48	21

PLANT DEGREE DAYS — Heating Degree Days below 12.8°C (55°F) for Selected Canadian Cities

City	Design Temperature in °C	Plant Degree Days by Month in °C											
		Jan.	Feb.	Mar.	Apr.	May	June	July	Aug.	Sept.	Oct.	Nov.	Dec.
Kamloops, B.C.	−23	588	439	288	106	21	2	0	0	13	129	325	455
Prince George, B.C.	−35	724	566	441	247	106	37	34	28	102	237	447	607
Vancouver, B.C.	− 7	307	236	194	107	37	6	0	0	10	79	192	255
Victoria, B.C.	− 5	262	204	175	91	29	7	3	3	14	58	158	214
Calgary, Alberta	−31	703	599	522	277	106	39	0	8	81	227	453	589
Edmonton, Alberta	−32	823	677	557	263	71	18	0	11	84	232	505	708
Prince Albert, Saskatchewan	−37	989	812	684	317	96	21	0	3	84	264	583	858
Regina, Saskatchewan	−33	909	770	636	278	89	21	0	2	67	237	537	768
Saskatoon, Saskatchewan	−34	920	786	632	278	76	14	0	0	70	232	545	799
Whitehorse, Yukon	−41	948	748	622	378	155	59	19	47	141	364	620	853
Brandon, Manitoba	−32	948	798	638	298	93	27	0	0	59	241	540	813
Winnipeg, Manitoba	−31	936	789	632	278	81	12	0	0	48	206	518	787
Ottawa, Ontario	−25	720	627	498	221	60	0	0	3	22	143	348	634
Toronto, Ontario	−17	553	509	417	192	53	0	0	0	10	111	273	481
Thunder Bay, Ontario	−30	813	698	584	310	126	19	0	3	58	208	457	705
Windsor, Ontario	−13	498	442	366	142	34	0	0	0	3	74	250	441
Montreal, Quebec	−23	688	601	471	207	55	0	0	0	6	116	313	591
Quebec City, Quebec	−25	743	654	538	278	91	2	0	0	28	175	377	660
Fredericton, New Brunswick	−23	674	599	469	242	78	3	2	0	14	149	332	591
Halifax, Nova Scotia	−15	489	452	389	231	86	7	0	0	3	78	216	416
Sydney, Nova Scotia	−15	519	503	457	290	136	31	0	0	19	111	249	436
Charlottetown, P.E.I.	−19	599	553	483	293	124	10	0	0	16	128	285	507
St. John's, Newfoundland	−14	519	483	477	338	213	78	12	11	42	180	285	436

PLANT DEGREE DAYS — Heating Degree Days below 12.8°C (55°F) for Selected U.S. Cities

City	Design Temperature in °C	Jan.	Feb.	Mar.	Apr.	May	June	July	Aug.	Sept.	Oct.	Nov.	Dec.
Anchorage, Alaska	−32	726	561	521	311	136	22	0	2	99	330	547	706
Fairbanks, Alaska	−47	1134	877	766	417	128	9	0	26	162	496	852	1108
Juneau, Alaska	−22	525	402	380	251	127	45	12	25	81	209	357	459
Denver, Colorado	−19	363	296	272	108	0	0	0	0	0	52	211	318
Hartford, Connecticut	−17	502	421	316	113	7	0	0	0	0	47	211	444
Boise, Idaho	−16	434	286	222	94	16	0	0	0	0	67	236	377
Pocatello, Idaho	−22	530	381	320	152	41	0	0	0	1	112	304	466
Chicago, Illinois	−20	535	432	319	100	19	0	0	0	0	57	246	463
Springfield, Illinois	−18	469	365	265	53	0	0	0	0	0	31	203	404
Fort Wayne, Indiana	−18	494	408	307	95	13	0	0	0	0	55	229	437
Indianapolis, Indiana	−18	449	360	258	62	0	0	0	0	0	33	206	397
Des Moines, Iowa	−22	596	461	354	96	5	0	0	0	0	57	269	499
Sioux City, Iowa	−23	619	474	367	102	7	0	0	0	0	60	294	524
Bangor, Maine	−22	616	527	414	204	56	0	0	0	0	106	284	535
Portland, Maine	−21	559	482	382	187	44	0	0	0	0	93	256	487
Boston, Massachusetts	−14	427	365	273	98	6	0	0	0	0	21	148	361
Detroit, Michigan	−16	491	419	324	112	18	0	0	0	0	47	214	419
Grand Rapids, Michigan	−17	530	457	359	133	28	0	0	0	0	70	254	458
Sault Ste. Marie, Michigan	−24	685	601	516	262	107	0	0	0	18	144	352	583
Duluth, Minnesota	−28	783	649	525	256	92	0	0	0	26	157	426	682
Minneapolis, Minnesota	−28	719	581	442	161	28	0	0	0	0	99	359	609
Billings, Montana	−23	561	412	372	164	41	0	0	0	15	102	307	468
Havre, Montana	−20	744	564	482	185	33	0	0	0	29	144	405	616
North Platte, Nebraska	−21	527	401	344	126	17	0	0	0	0	80	296	468
Concord, New Hampshire	−24	574	486	373	164	36	0	0	0	0	89	266	502
Atlantic City, New Jersey	−10	366	311	224	50	0	0	0	0	0	8	134	325
Albany, New York	−21	559	472	354	129	22	0	0	0	0	64	239	483
Buffalo, New York	−16	521	458	377	158	42	0	0	0	0	71	236	449
Bismark, North Dakota	−31	788	628	503	193	46	0	0	0	24	139	417	661
Fargo, North Dakota	−20	828	671	513	203	45	0	0	0	13	136	422	106
Cleveland, Ohio	−17	466	404	313	110	22	0	0	0	0	48	206	408
Columbus, Ohio	−17	441	367	262	73	1	0	0	0	0	44	204	401
Portland, Oregon	−6	281	174	144	67	12	0	0	0	0	34	147	228
Philadelphia, Pennsylvania	−12	373	311	216	51	0	0	0	0	0	12	132	323
Pittsburgh, Pennsylvania	−15	402	340	244	62	0	0	0	0	0	32	166	356
Providence, Rhode Island	−14	441	381	294	115	11	0	0	0	0	33	177	387
Huron, South Dakota	−27	714	559	437	152	28	0	0	0	0	101	359	599
Rapid City, South Dakota	−23	552	437	398	168	41	0	0	0	8	103	312	473
Seattle, Washington	−7	227	148	142	64	6	0	0	0	0	22	116	182
Spokane, Washington	−19	497	337	284	135	37	0	0	0	5	117	307	430
Green Bay, Wisconsin	−24	664	558	437	174	47	0	0	0	0	104	331	569
Madison, Wisconsin	−23	640	522	409	152	36	0	0	0	0	98	321	552
Cheyenne, Wyoming	−21	471	387	385	194	58	0	0	0	10	122	307	427
Sheridan, Wyoming	−24	568	435	396	179	56	0	0	0	22	124	338	491

Absorption 30
Air exchange 51
Altitude 27-28
Aphids 169-177
Azimuth 27-28

Barrhead greenhouse 183-184
Biological management 4, see management
Blackfalds greenhouse 185-189
Building codes 73

Carbon dioxide 35, 36, 142-143
Caulking 102-103, 116
Chard 157
Compost 146-147
Construction: 73-131
Cosmic importance 4
Costs 73
Cucumbers 157, 159

Degree days 44, 247
Design 17-69
Design temperature 44
Detroit Lakes greenhouse 188-190
Diatamaceous earth 169
Diseases 179-180
Doors 107-109

Ecology House greenhouse 191-193, 198
Ecosystem approach 1-2, 135
Energy in food production 7-9

Finishing 120-122
Flashing 98
Floors 68, 114, 117-119
Footings 77-78, 84-86
Foundation 77-87, 114; excavation 80;
    forms 80

Framing 88-106
Fruit 161-162

Germination 153
Glass: 225; cleaning 105; cutting 105
Glazing: 62, 68-70, 103-106, 244-245; angle
    30-31; 64-65; details 99-103; materials
    38-43
Glazing tape 116
Glossary 221-222
Greenhome 6
Greenhouse: attached 5; 21-22, 23-24;
    definition 5-6; freestanding 5, 19-21, 74;
    history 12-13; performance 61-63; plans
    226-227
Growing flats 138
Growing seasons 9-10, 156-158

Heat: 31-32; control 34; gain 24, 39, 56,
    (worksheet) 237-239; loss 24, 33,
    (worksheet) 231-236; management 46-47;
    storage 52-57, 62-63, 223-224, 225-226,
    249
Humidity 36, 143-144

Infiltration 47
Insects 166-168
Insecticides 168-169
Insulation: 37-38, 114-115, 226, 246, 250;
    types 38

Keswick greenhouse 194-195
King greenhouse 196-197

Latitude 27
Ledger plate 94
Lettuce 157

Light 28-31, 140; artificial 35-36; infrared
    29; ultraviolet 28
Loam 144

Metric system 4, 250
Millet greenhouse 200-202
Mobile Home greenhouse 203-205
Movable insulation 4, 56-60; exterior
    57-58; inter-glazing insulation 4, 59-60,
    123-128, 201-202; interior 58-59

Newfoundland greenhouse 206-209

Orientation 45-46

Parasitic wasp 177-178
Pests 166-180; prevention 166, 167, 226
Pesticides 168-169
Photosynthesis 34
Plants: requirements 19; varieties 162-165
Planting: 151-165; layout 154
Plastic glazing 103-104, 227
Pollination 159
Pottageville greenhouse 198-199
Predators 175-177
Preservatives 121-122
Pruning 158
Pyrethrum 169

Roof: 68, 88, 92-94, 98, 114; rafters 94-95
Rot 74-75
Rotenone 168-169

Seeding 152-154
Seeds 227-228
Shading 47-48
Shadow analysis 46
Site 44-46, 75, 244

Slugs 179
Smoking 180
Snow load 89
Soil 37, 144-146, 147-148
Soil beds 129-130, 136-137, 149
Solar Applications 69
Solar chimneys 51
Solar data
Solar greenhouse; definition 4;
Spider mites 179
Spinach 157
Sun 25-26
Sundance greenhouse 2-3, 10, 44, 149
Sunergy Systems Ltd. 185
Sun path charts 28, 44-46, 240-243
Sun Shelters Ltd. 194

Temperature: 36, 141; control 24, 141-142
Thrip 178
Tomatoes 157, 158
Tools 138
Transmission 29
Transplanting 154-155, 160
Trellising 158

University of Saskatchewan 8, 60, 210-214

Vapour barrier 47, 115-116
Ventilation 48-52, 143
Vents 109-112, 225

Walls: 68, 88, 114; end 96-97; north (house)
   112-113; south 76, 90-93, 97-98
Water, 146, 150
Weatherstripping 47
West Vancouver greenhouse 215-216
Whiteflies 177

Ypsilanti greenhouse 217

Afterword

Contributors

This book is the result of the work of many people. The major contributors were:

Joan Harrison of Saskatoon who provided the outline, the research and most of the writing for the DESIGN section.

Peter Amerongen, a low-energy carpenter (that is to say, his *houses* are low-energy, not Peter himself) and solar greenhouse builder from Edmonton. He *is* the CONSTRUCTION section and he made great contributions to the rest of the book.

Linda Gilkeson, former Greenhouse Horticulturist at the now defunct Ark Project in P.E.I. whose special interest is pest control using beneficial insects. Linda contributed most of the information used in the management section.

Terry Lyster, one-half of The Drawing Room Graphic Services Ltd. and co-author of their SOLPLAN series. Terry provided the illustrations and clear comment.

Ken Cooper is a part of the Vancouver design and consulting firm, Solar Applications and Research Ltd. Ken provided not only direction and advice, but also the performance examples of the Sundance greenhouse in Edmonton.

Other contributions came from:
* Jim Wylie
* Brian Marshall
* John Evans
* Michael Kerfoot
* Greg Allen

Special thanks in this area also go to:
* Gordon Howell
* George Green
* Greg Schoenau
* Tom Olson
* Reed Maes
* Bob Dumont

Credits

Much of the MANAGEMENT material was derived from Linda Gilkeson's work at the Prince Edward Island Ark. The Ark Project of the Institute of Man and Resources was funded through the Canada-P.E.I. Agreement on Renewable Energy Development. I am grateful to the Institute for permission to use the Ark Project material. Susan Mahoney of the Ark Project was co-author of some of the original material.

The Greenhouse Worksheet included in the appendices is adapted from the worksheet in **Solplan 3: Solar Greenhouses for Canada** and I am grateful to The Drawing Room for letting us use it.

Finally, I'd like to thank the National Center for Appropriate Technology (NCAT) for supplying us with a copy of their excellent book **Low Cost Passive Solar Greenhouses** and to credit the influence it had on us.

Acknowledgments

Thanks to all the following who contributed to this project in myriad ways:
* Mary Crunkilton (who kept me going)
* Joe Crachiola
* Richard Kadulski
* Mrs. and Mrs. Gerrard Amerongen
* Carolyn Lyster
* Brian Hirst
* Leslie Davis
* Bob Besant
* J. A. Kernahan
* Steve Bengtson
* Tyeve Arkham
* Paul Taterawicz
* John Hughes
* Nancy Goodman
* Don Schwartz
* C. d'Lagune-Noir
* Bill Lazar
* Marion Bierwirth
* Joe Hall
* Dale Seward
* Fairview College, especially:
  * Darlene Dobson
  * Sandy McKenna
  * Sherril Roy
* Audrey Harsh
* Peaceworks, especially:
  * Mel & May Lungle
  * Bob Cameron
  * Elizabeth Surridge
* Irene and Loretta Davis

Value Calculation of This Book

As with the rest of the subjects we have presented, I applied both traditional, tested techniques and the results of modern research in determining the actual value of the present work. Using the most precise methods of calculations available:

$I = W \times 10^3$

where

I = illustration or picture and

W = word

etc.

and since, in the case of this book

$I = 356$

we can determine that the book contains 356,000 word equivalents, which we will show as

$W_e = 3.56 \times 10^5$

To determine the total word equivalent (W_t), we must add to this the number of words in the text, which we will call W_p (for printed), so that

$W_t = W_e + W_p$

Since

$W_p = 0.95 \times 10^5$

we see that

$W_t = 4.51 \times 10^5$

Which means that, given a cover price of $14.95, in 1983 Canadian dollars

$W = \$3.31 \times 10^{-5}$

which is to say that each word costs only $0.00003.

What else can you buy at 33,333 to the dollar?

While this book would not have been possible without the contributions of all these people I must accept responsibility for its final shape and content. The blame for any errors or omissions must lie where such blame must always lie. With the Post Office.

Mark A. Craft
Deske-on-Flor
April 01 83

Printed by the workers of
Editions Marquis Ltée, Montmagny, Québec